Global Plastics Outlook

POLICY SCENARIOS TO 2060

OECD
BETTER POLICIES FOR BETTER LIVES

Please cite this publication as:
OECD (2022), *Global Plastics Outlook: Policy Scenarios to 2060*, OECD Publishing, Paris, https://doi.org/10.1787/aa1edf33-en.

ISBN 978-92-64-97364-0 (print)
ISBN 978-92-64-89881-3 (pdf)

Photo credits: Cover © design by Andrew Esson/baselinearts.co.uk based on images © JasminkaM, Liubovart/Shutterstock.com.

Corrigenda to publications may be found on line at: www.oecd.org/about/publishing/corrigenda.htm.

Preface

Plastic pollution is one of the great environmental challenges of the 21st century, causing wide-ranging damage to ecosystems and human health. This OECD report, *Global Plastics Outlook: Policy Scenarios to 2060,* provides global projections of the sectoral and regional drivers and consequences of plastics use for the coming decades.

An earlier related report, *Global Plastics Outlook: Economic Drivers, Environmental Impacts and Policy Options,* released in February 2022, provided the first comprehensive global assessment of trends in plastics use, waste generation and leakage to the environment. It also identified four policy levers – markets for recycled plastics, innovation, domestic policies and international co-operation – to curb the environmental impacts of plastics.

Shortly thereafter, the United Nations Environmental Assembly adopted the landmark resolution to convene an intergovernmental negotiation committee to develop an internationally binding instrument on plastic pollution. Less than a month later, on 31 March 2022, the Declaration of the OECD Environment Ministerial Meeting committed to develop comprehensive and coherent life-cycle approaches to tackle plastic pollution and promote co-operation internationally.

This growing global momentum to address plastic pollution also faces headwinds, with the world still reeling from an uneven economic recovery from the COVID-19 pandemic, and with significantly heightened geopolitical tensions in the context of the war in Ukraine.

In such a complex environment, how can governments chart the course of global action to deliver on the ambitions set at the United Nations Environmental Assembly and beyond?

The *Global Plastics Outlook: Policy Scenarios to 2060*, provides such a roadmap. Leveraging the OECD's unique expertise in global environment-economy modelling, this Outlook quantifies both the consequences of "business as usual" on the leakage of plastics to the environment, and the benefits of more ambitious global policy action. The analysis in the report shows that in the absence of strengthened policies, plastics use and waste would increase almost three-fold, while plastic leakage to the environment would double.

Two policy packages – *Regional Action* and *Global Ambition* - present a set of policy instruments at two levels of international action which can both help flatten the plastics curve while substantially curbing plastic leakage. The Outlook also finds that combining policy action to mitigate both climate change and plastics challenges can enable countries to achieve their climate objectives while making the plastics lifecycle more circular.

I hope the findings presented in this report will serve as a reference for policy makers to underpin discussions on the path to zero plastic pollution. The OECD stands ready to assist governments in the design, development and implementation of the ambitious policy action required to address this challenge with a coordinated global approach.

Mathias Cormann
Secretary-General, OECD

Foreword

The *Global Plastics Outlook: Policy Scenarios to 2060* provides policymakers with a long-term perspective on plastics, presenting a set of coherent projections on plastics use and waste as well as their environmental impacts. Through a series of policy packages, the Outlook demonstrates the environmental benefits and economic consequences of adopting more stringent policies.

This report follows the earlier related report, *Global Plastics Outlook: Economic Drivers, Environmental Impacts and Policy Options,* released in February 2022, which provided the first comprehensive global assessment of trends in plastics use, waste generation and leakage to the environment as well as policy levers to curb the environmental impacts of plastics.

This report is structured as shown below. Using state-of-the-art environment-economy modelling, the Outlook first uncovers the economic drivers that are projected to give rise to unprecedented volumes of plastics use, waste, and plastic-related environmental impacts until 2060. The Outlook then present policy scenarios with different levels of stringency, to understand their environmental and economic impacts by 2060: the *Regional Action* and the *Global Ambition* Scenario. Finally, the Outlook outlines interactions between plastics and climate mitigation policies.

Report roadmap

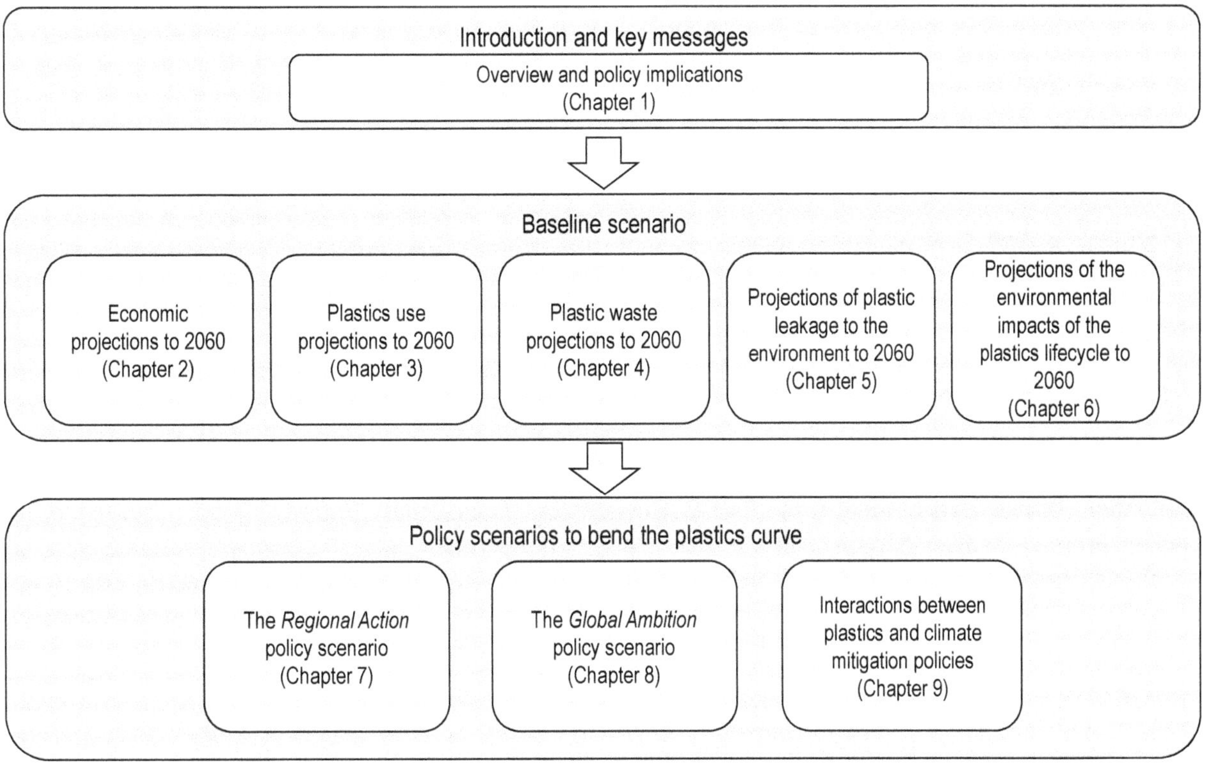

Acknowledgements

This report was conceptualised and directed by Shardul Agrawala, Head of Division of the Environment and Economy Integration Division (EEI) in the Environment Directorate of the OECD. Elisa Lanzi led the cross-cutting co-ordination of the report and the modelling team. The report was edited by Shardul Agrawala, Elisa Lanzi and Rob Dellink.

The authorship of the chapters is as follows: Shardul Agrawala and Norbert Monti (Chapter 1), Elisa Lanzi, Ruben Bibas and Daniel Ostalé Valriberas (Chapter 2); Ruben Bibas, Elisa Lanzi, Rob Dellink, Eleonora Mavroeidi and Daniel Ostalé Valriberas (Chapter 3); Eleonora Mavroeidi, Maarten Dubois, Rob Dellink, Ruben Bibas and Elisa Lanzi (Chapter 4); Ruben Bibas, Eleonora Mavroeidi, Maarten Dubois, Elena Buzzi and Daniel Ostalé Valriberas (Chapter 5); Maarten Dubois, Ruben Bibas and Jean Fouré (Chapter 6) ; Eleonora Mavroeidi, Rob Dellink, Elisa Lanzi, Maarten Dubois and Ruben Bibas (Chapter 7) ; Rob Dellink, Eleonora Mavroeidi, Elisa Lanzi, Ruben Bibas and Elena Buzzi (Chapter 8); Jean Fouré and Elisa Lanzi (Chapter 9) (all OECD Environment Directorate). Peter Börkey provided expert input and feedback throughout the preparation of the report.

The following external experts: Morten Ryberg, Teddy Serrano and Alexis Laurent (Technical University of Denmark), Costas A. Velis, Ed Cook and Josh Cottom (University of Leeds), Laurent Lebreton (The Ocean Cleanup) and Nikolaos Evangeliou (Norwegian Institute for Air Research) contributed with the modelling of global plastic leakage. The LifeCycle Analysis of plastics use and waste was provided by Gustavo Longaray Moraga, Jo Dewulf and Maíra Caetano de Andrade (Ghent University), while the analysis of bio-based plastics by Neus Escobar (IIASA) and Wolfgang Britz (University of Bonn). Roland Geyer (University of California, Santa Barbara) advised on the OECD modelling strategy and provided valuable feedback.

The report received insightful feedback from Alain de Serres (Acting Director of the OECD Environment Directorate) and Kumi Kitamori (Acting Deputy Director of the OECD Environment Directorate). The report also received expert feedback from Stephanie B. Borrelle (University of Toronto), Johan Eyckmans (KU Leuven), Costas A. Velis (University of Leeds) and the Ellen MacArthur Foundation. Earlier drafts benefited from discussions during the Technical Expert Workshop on Modelling Approaches for Plastics Use Projections, organised by the OECD on the 22 and 23 June 2020. Expert input and feedback were provided by Shunta Yamaguchi, Frithjof Laubinger, Damien Dussaux, Ioannis Tikoudis and research support by Grace Alexander, Laura Atarody and Linda Livingstone (all OECD Environment Directorate).

Illias Mousse Iye and Aziza Perrière (OECD Environment Directorate) provided administrative support. Elizabeth Del Bourgo, William Foster, Stéphanie Simonin-Edwards and Norbert Monti (OECD Environment Directorate), as well as Catherine Bremer (OECD Public Affairs and Communications Directorate) provided assistance with communication and outreach aspects of the report. Elena Buzzi, Norbert Monti, Grace Alexander, Daniel Ostalé Valriberas (OECD Environment Directorate), Andrew Esson (baselinearts), Nadieh Bremer (visualcinnamon) and Martiene Raven (independent graphic designer) assisted with the preparation and design of the Policy Highlights, the cover and figures throughout the report. The report received copy-editing support from Janine Treves (OECD Public Affairs and Communications Directorate), Fiona Hinchcliffe, Meral Gedik and Annette Hardcastle (independent editors).

The OECD Environment Policy Committee (EPOC) was responsible for the oversight of the development of the report. In addition, the Working Party on Resource Productivity and Waste (WPRPW) and the Working Party on Integrating Environmental and Economic Policies (WPIEEP) reviewed earlier drafts.

Table of contents

Preface 3

Foreword 5

Acknowledgements 6

Abbreviations and acronyms 14

Executive summary 17

1 Overview and policy highlights 21

1.1. Introduction 22
1.2. An overview of the modelling framework 22
1.3. Scenario analysis for plastics projections 23
1.4. Projections to 2060 in the Baseline scenario 24
1.5. Policy packages to eliminate plastic leakage 35
References 42
Notes 43

Part I Baseline scenario 45

2 Economic projections to 2060 47

2.1. The global population is projected to increase to 10 billion by 2060, with the strongest growth in Sub-Saharan Africa 48
2.2. The engines of economic growth will gradually shift from China to other emerging economies in Asia and Africa 49
2.3. Services will represent an increasing share of the global economy 56
2.1. Production processes will rely on more efficient technologies 59
References 60
Notes 60

3 Plastics use projections to 2060 61

3.1. Plastics use is projected to almost triple by 2060 62
3.2. The drivers of plastics use vary by region 72
3.3. COVID-19 affects plastics use in both the short and long run 78
References 80
Notes 81

4 Plastic waste projections to 2060 83
4.1. Plastic waste is projected to almost triple by 2060 84
4.2. Despite better waste management, mismanaged waste will still almost double to 2060 89
4.3. Plastic waste projections depend on key uncertainties surrounding waste management, trade and COVID recovery rates 98
References 107
Notes 108

5 Projections of plastic leakage to the environment to 2060 109
5.1. Plastic leakage the environment presents a wide range of environmental and human health hazards 111
5.2. Plastic leakage to the environment is projected to double by 2060 113
5.3. Plastic leakage into aquatic environments is projected to almost double by 2060 120
5.4. The projected increase in transport will lead to more airborne microplastics 127
References 129
Notes 130

6 Projections of the environmental impacts of the plastics lifecycle to 2060 133
6.1. Plastics use and waste contribute to climate change 134
6.2. The environmental impacts of the plastics lifecycle are wide and significant 142
References 147
Notes 148

Part II Policy scenarios to bend the plastics curve 149

7 The *Regional Action* policy scenario 151
7.1. The policy package in the *Regional Action* scenario is broad and regionally varied 153
7.2. The *Regional Action* policy package limits growth in plastics use and waste 157
7.3. The environmental benefits of policy action are clear, but plastic leakage to the environment continues 167
7.4. The macroeconomic impacts of the *Regional Action* scenario are small 172
References 178
Notes 179

8 The *Global Ambition* policy scenario 181
8.1. The policy package in the *Global Ambition* scenario assumes immediate global action 182
8.2. Plastics use and waste are largely decoupled from economic growth in the *Global Ambition* scenario 184
8.3. The environmental benefits of the *Global Ambition* scenario are substantial 191
8.4. The macroeconomic impact is limited, though highest for non-OECD countries 196
References 199
Notes 201

9 Interactions between plastics and climate mitigation policies 203
9.1. Climate mitigation policies complement policy action on plastics 204
9.2. The *Global Ambition* scenario contributes to climate change mitigation but only limitedly 206
9.3. The joint *Global Ambition and Climate Mitigation* scenario decreases plastics lifecycle greenhouse gas emissions 209
References 216
Notes 217

Annex A. Modelling framework 218

Annex B. Details on the Baseline, Regional Action, Global Ambition, and Climate Mitigation scenarios 275

Glossary 280

Tables

Table 1.1. The policies in the two main scenarios vary in their levels of ambition 37
Table 2.1. The more efficient production of manufacturing goods sees plastics inputs decline 59
Table 4.1. OECD countries will still use the most plastic waste per capita in 2060 89
Table 4.2. The share of recycling residues decreases in OECD countries but increases in non-OECD countries 94
Table 4.3. Comparison of projections with the existing literature 96
Table 6.1. Policy measures can boost the market share of biobased plastics, but environmental consequences vary 139
Table 7.1. Annualised benchmark costs for waste management solutions 175
Table 8.1. The reduction in plastic leakage to aquatic environments in the *Global Ambition* scenario is substantial across a range of model assumptions 194
Table 8.2. Estimates of clean-up costs vary widely 199
Table 9.1. Description of the *Climate Mitigation* scenario 205

Table A A.1. Sectoral aggregation of ENV-Linkages 221
Table A A.2. Regional aggregation of ENV-Linkages 222
Table A A.3. Data sources and methodologies 223
Table A A.4. Characteristics of waste plastics and their influence on sorting reprocessability 225
Table A A.5. Assumptions used to determine loss rates for plastic packaging waste that has been collected for recycling 227
Table A A.6. Average loss rates by plastic type and application for high income countries and low- middle income countries (MSW) 228
Table A A.7. Average loss rates by plastic type and application for high income countries and low- middle income countries (Non-MSW) 228
Table A A.8. Average loss rates by plastic type and OECD region for MSW and non-MSW combined 229
Table A A.9. Share of the secondary production technology 230
Table A A.10. The large range of polymers allows for a multitude of plastics applications 230
Table A A.11. Mapping of plastics use by application to economic sectors 231
Table A A.12. Data sources for plastic recycling rates in base year 233
Table A A.13. UN Comtrade plastic waste series mapping to polymers in ENV-Linkages 234
Table A A.14. Share of litter lost the environment considered based on income levels of the regions 235
Table A A.15. Tyre wear rates used 237
Table A A.16. Brake pads wear rates used 237
Table A A.17. Losses sources of microplastics dust and losses values for the year 2060 238
Table A A.18. Microplastics removal rate for different levels of wastewater treatment 240
Table A A.19. Validation of incineration data 243
Table A A.20. Data used to model the activities of the informal recycling sector 244
Table A A.21. Deliberate dumping into water 244
Table A A.22. Plastic waste transfer rate from terrestrial to aquatic environment 245
Table A A.23. Transfer coefficients used to distribute mismanaged plastic waste from MSW to four main components of the ENV-Linkages-SPOT plugin 245
Table A A.24. Transfer coefficients used to distribute mismanaged plastic waste from Non-MSW to four main components of the ENV-Linkages-SPOT plugin 246
Table A A.25. Transfer coefficients used to attribute mismanaged plastic waste from MSW excluding waste in dumpsites to components of the ENV-Linkages-SPOT plugin 247
Table A A.26. Transfer coefficients used to attribute mismanaged plastic waste from Non-MSW excluding waste in dumpsites to components of the ENV-Linkages-SPOT plugin 248

Table A A.27. Fraction of mismanaged plastic waste entering aquatic environment and fraction reaching the ocean environment 251
Table A A.28. Parameters for fate of plastic in aquatic environments by polymer type 253
Table A A.29. Uncertainty parameters for the analysis of biobased plastics penetration rates 260
Table A B.1. Details on the implementation of the circular plastics scenarios 276
Table A B.2. Carbon pricing in the *Baseline* and *Climate Mitigation* scenarios 277

Figures

Figure 1.1. The scenario analysis involves four steps 24
Figure 1.2. Without new policies, the plastics lifecycle will only be 14% circular in 2060 25
Figure 1.3. Plastics use will grow fastest in developing and emerging economies in Africa and Asia 27
Figure 1.4. The use of all polymers will significantly increase by 2060 28
Figure 1.5. Half of all plastic waste will continue to be landfilled in 2060 29
Figure 1.6. Macroplastic and microplastic leakage show different trajectories when income per capita increases 31
Figure 1.7. Leakage into aquatic environments is projected to double between 2019 and 2060 32
Figure 1.8. Without new policies, the environmental and health impacts of polymers will double in 2060 34
Figure 1.9. The policy packages target the entire plastics lifecycle 36
Figure 1.10. Policies targeting different steps of the plastics lifecycle all contribute to reducing plastic leakage to the environment 39
Figure 1.11. The costs of both regional and globally coordinated action are less than 1% of global GDP 41
Figure 2.1. The world population is projected to keep growing but at a slower pace 49
Figure 2.2. Living standards are projected to increase, especially in lower-income regions 50
Figure 2.3. Global GDP is projected to grow more slowly, driven by emerging economies 51
Figure 2.4. The regional distribution of GDP will change in the following decades 52
Figure 2.5. GDP projections are subject to uncertainty 53
Figure 2.6. A slower recovery from COVID-19 implies lower GDP levels in the long-run than in the *Baseline* scenario 54
Figure 2.7. The demand for services is projected to increase more than the economy-wide average 57
Figure 2.8. A slow recovery from COVID-19 is projected to dampen growth in the plastics and chemical sectors 58
Figure 3.1. Plastics use is projected to almost triple, mostly driven by economic growth 63
Figure 3.2. Plastics use will grow fastest in developing and emerging economies in Africa and Asia 64
Figure 3.3. Plastics use in the transport sector will grow the most by 2060 66
Figure 3.4. The use of all polymers will increase to 2060 67
Figure 3.5. Primary plastics will still make up the lion's share of production in 2060 68
Figure 3.6. Changes in fossil fuel prices have little impact on plastics production in the long run 70
Figure 3.7. Plastics use outpaces most other raw materials in the *Baseline* scenario 71
Figure 3.8. The drivers of plastics use vary by region 73
Figure 3.9. Population strongly drives plastics use in Sub-Saharan Africa 74
Figure 3.10. Regional income levels drive per-capita plastics use 75
Figure 3.11. Output growth is fast in some sectors that rely on plastics 77
Figure 3.12. Overall, the COVID-19 pandemic will reduce regional plastics use projections 79
Figure 3.13. A slow recovery from COVID-19 will maintain lower global plastics use levels 80
Figure 4.1. Plastic waste is projected to almost triple by 2060 85
Figure 4.2. The time lag between plastics use and waste varies by application 86
Figure 4.3. Plastic applications with long lifespans delay waste generation and build up stocks of plastics in the economy 87
Figure 4.4. Africa and Asia will see the biggest increase in plastic waste 88
Figure 4.5. Waste collected for recycling and litter flows are partly incinerated, landfilled and mismanaged 90
Figure 4.6. Waste management improves more substantially in non-OECD countries 91
Figure 4.7. Sanitary landfilling will remain the most widespread waste management approach 92
Figure 4.8. More plastic waste and better waste management drive the increase in recycled waste 93
Figure 4.9. The increase in mismanaged plastic waste is only partly offset by better waste management 95
Figure 4.10. Only 17% of global plastic waste is projected to be recycled by 2060 97
Figure 4.11. Mismanaged plastic waste remains a significant issue in most non-OECD regions 98
Figure 4.12. Current policies significantly slow down the growth of mismanaged plastic waste 99

Figure 4.13. Alternative waste trade scenarios have limited impact on global mismanaged plastic waste and available scrap, masking regional shifts 102
Figure 4.14. The effects of COVID-19 on plastics use and waste remain noticeable even in 2060 104
Figure 4.15. The impact of COVID-19 on plastic waste depends on the polymer and application 105
Figure 4.16. A slow recovery from COVID could lower global plastics use and waste by 4% in 2060 106
Figure 5.1. All estimates agree that global plastic leakage is growing, though magnitudes vary 113
Figure 5.2. Leaked macro- and microplastics will double, with regional differences 114
Figure 5.3. Plastic leakage comes from a wide range of sources 116
Figure 5.4. While plastic leakage per capita increases, leakage rates will decouple from GDP and plastics use levels 118
Figure 5.5. Macroplastic and microplastic leakage show different trajectories when income per capita increases 119
Figure 5.6. Global leakage to aquatic environments could at least double by 2060 120
Figure 5.7. By 2060 non-OECD countries will be the main source of plastic leakage into aquatic environments 122
Figure 5.8. Regional contributions to plastics leaking into aquatic environments shift over time 123
Figure 5.9. Only a small share of leaked plastics reaches the ocean via the coast 124
Figure 5.10. There are more leaked plastics stored in freshwater systems than in the ocean 125
Figure 5.11. The flow of macroplastics into rivers and lakes is substantially larger than outflows to the ocean 126
Figure 5.12. Deposition of airborne microplastics from tyre and brake abrasion will increase 128
Figure 6.1. Greenhouse gas emissions from fossil-based plastics are projected to more than double by 2060 135
Figure 6.2. Growing plastics use and waste drives the increase in plastics GHG emissions 136
Figure 6.3. High fossil fuel prices reduce the GHG emissions of plastics significantly 137
Figure 6.4. Changes in land use with higher penetration rates of biobased plastics 140
Figure 6.5. The *Efficiency* scenario leads to a decrease in GHG emissions 141
Figure 6.6. The plastics lifecycle is linked to a variety of environmental and human health pressures 143
Figure 6.7. With no new policies, the environmental and health impacts of seven common plastics polymers will be substantial in 2060 145
Figure 6.8. All environmental impacts included in the analysis more than double by 2060 146
Figure 7.1. A policy roadmap for more circular use of plastics 153
Figure 7.2. The policy package of the *Regional Action* scenario 155
Figure 7.3. The combined pillars of the *Regional Action* scenario bring plastics use, waste and mismanaged waste below *Baseline* projections 158
Figure 7.4. The combined effect of the policy package is smaller than the sum of the three pillars implemented individually 159
Figure 7.5. The more plastics-intensive non-OECD regions see the largest reductions in plastics use in the *Regional Action* scenario 160
Figure 7.6. Business services contribute most to plastics use reductions in the *Regional Action* scenario 161
Figure 7.7. Secondary plastics use grows faster than primary plastics in the *Regional Action* scenario 162
Figure 7.8. Changes in plastic waste largely follow changes in plastics use in the *Regional Action* scenario 163
Figure 7.9. The *Regional Action* scenario induces a significant shift from mismanaged to recycled waste 165
Figure 7.10. Mismanaged waste volumes are projected to fall most in non-OECD countries in the *Regional Action* scenario 166
Figure 7.11. All pillars contribute to reducing plastic leakage to the environment 167
Figure 7.12. The *Regional Action* scenario will lower plastic leakage per capita, and decouple leakage from GDP and plastics use 168
Figure 7.13. The *Regional Action* scenario reduces macro- and microplastic leakage in all regions 169
Figure 7.14. Non-OECD countries will see greatest reductions in plastic leakage into aquatic environments in the *Regional Action* scenario 170
Figure 7.15. The *Regional Action* scenario still leads to a tripling of accumulated plastic leakage stocks 171
Figure 7.16. The *Regional Action* policy package reduces plastics use much more than regional GDP 173
Figure 7.17. Plastics use reductions are driven by domestic policies, but GDP is also affected by policies implemented abroad 174
Figure 7.18. Significant additional waste treatment investment in the *Regional Action* scenario is needed to enhance recycling and close leakage pathways 177
Figure 8.1. Mismanaged waste is almost completely eliminated worldwide in the *Global Ambition* scenario 185
Figure 8.2. Regional reductions in plastics use to 2030 are substantial in the *Global Ambition* scenario 186
Figure 8.3. A few sectors make up the bulk of plastics use reductions in the *Global Ambition* scenario 187
Figure 8.4. Secondary plastics production can meet almost all demand growth in the *Global Ambition* scenario 188
Figure 8.5. In the *Global Ambition* scenario recycling rates triple while mismanaged waste is almost completely eliminated 189

Figure 8.6. Mismanaged waste gradually declines to almost zero in the *Global Ambition* scenario 190
Figure 8.7. All pillars combined reduce plastic leakage to the environment dramatically 191
Figure 8.8. Non-OECD countries account for the largest reductions in plastic leakage to 2060 in the *Global Ambition* scenario 192
Figure 8.9. The plastic leakage reductions in the *Global Ambition* scenario stem from different sources in OECD versus non-OECD countries 193
Figure 8.10. Plastic leakage to aquatic environments will be vastly reduced across all non-OECD regions in the *Global Ambition* scenario 195
Figure 8.11. Despite ambitious global action, stocks of plastics in aquatic environments still grow substantially 196
Figure 8.12. The additional costs of *Global Ambition* are concentrated in non-OECD countries 197
Figure 8.13. The effects on regional GDP of the *Global Ambition* scenario are strongest outside of OECD 198
Figure 9.1. The *Global Ambition* scenario is projected to halve plastics lifecycle GHG emissions, mainly by reducing volumes of plastics use 207
Figure 9.2. Restraining plastics demand contributes the most to emissions reductions 209
Figure 9.3. The *Climate Mitigation* scenario alone has limited impact on global plastics use 210
Figure 9.4. The *Climate Mitigation* scenario reduces primary plastics more than secondary plastics 211
Figure 9.5. The *Global Ambition and Climate Mitigation* scenario reduces plastics lifecycle GHG emissions to below 2019 levels 212
Figure 9.6. The policies in the *Climate Mitigation* scenario mainly reduce the GHG intensity of plastics production 213
Figure 9.7. The GDP and emissions effects of climate and plastics policies are greatest when they are combined 215

Figure A A.1. Methodological steps 219
Figure A A.2. Fate of microplastics in wastewaters 239
Figure A A.3. ENV-Linkages-SPOT plugin model structure 242
Figure A A.4. Probability of mismanaged and littered plastic waste emissions into aquatic environments 250
Figure A A.5. Mass balance budget model for plastic in global aquatic environments 252
Figure A A.6. Greenhouse gas emission factors for plastics lifecycle in ENV-Linkages 257
Figure A A.7. Considered stages of the LCA analysis for the seven polymer types 261
Figure A B.1. World-average electricity mix in the *Baseline* and *Climate Mitigation* scenarios 278

Boxes

Box 1.1. The effects of the COVID-19 pandemic on plastics use could linger for decades to come 26
Box 1.2. How does climate mitigation interact with policies to reduce plastics leakage? 40
Box 2.1. Uncertainties in projections need to be kept in mind 53
Box 2.2. What if the global economy recovers more slowly from the pandemic? 54
Box 2.3. The current war in Ukraine will affect economic growth at the global level 55
Box 2.4. How might a slow recovery from the COVID-19 pandemic affect sectoral trends, including plastics? 58
Box 3.1. Fossil fuel prices show little impact on plastics use in the long run 70
Box 3.2. Plastics grows more than most raw materials 71
Box 3.3. The increasing use of transport in developing economies affects plastics use 78
Box 3.4. How will the speed of recovery from the COVID-19 pandemic affect plastics use? 80
Box 4.1. Long-lived plastics will contribute to waste levels even after the end of the century 87
Box 4.2. The final treatment amounts of waste differ from the amounts collected 90
Box 4.3. A large share of waste collected for recycling is lost in the process 94
Box 4.4. The wider scope of the OECD projections explains differences with existing studies 96
Box 4.5. What if trade flows of plastic waste evolved differently? 100
Box 4.6. How would a slow recovery from COVID-19 affect plastics use and waste? 106
Box 5.1. How is plastic leakage quantified in the Global Plastics Outlook? 112
Box 6.1. Emissions from the plastics lifecycle are closely linked to fossil fuel prices 137
Box 7.1. How can the impacts of Extended Producer Responsibility schemes be modelled? 156
Box 7.2. The interactions between the three pillars in the policy package are significant 159
Box 7.3. Domestic effects and trade effects both matter for the macroeconomic costs of the *Regional* Action scenario 174
Box 8.1. The reductions in leakage to aquatic environments are large, regardless of uncertainties 194

Box A A.1. The ENV-Linkages model 220

Follow OECD Publications on:

http://twitter.com/OECD_Pubs

http://www.facebook.com/OECDPublications

http://www.linkedin.com/groups/OECD-Publications-4645871

http://www.youtube.com/oecdilibrary

OECD Alerts http://www.oecd.org/oecddirect/

This book has...

StatLinks

A service that delivers Excel® files from the printed page!

Look for the StatLink at the bottom of the tables or graphs in this book. To download the matching Excel® spreadsheet, just type the link into your Internet browser or click on the link from the digital version.

Abbreviations and acronyms

ABS	Acrylonitrile butadiene styrene
ASA	Acrylonitrile styrene acrylate
Bn	Billion
BWP(s)	Brake Wear Particle(s)
CO_2	Carbon dioxide
CO_2e	Carbon dioxide equivalent
DTU	Technical University of Denmark
ECHA	European Chemical Agency
EEA	European Environment Agency
EoL	End of life
EPA	(United States) Environmental Protection Agency
EPR	Extended producer responsibility
EU	European Union
EUR	Euro
FLEXPART	FLEXible PARTicle
GAINS	Greenhouse gas – air pollution Interactions and synergies
GDP	Gross domestic product
GHG	Greenhouse gas
Gt	Gigatonnes (billion tonnes)
Gt CO_2e	Gigatonnes of CO_2 equivalent
GTAP	Global Trade Analysis Project
HDPE	High-density polyethylene
kt	Kilotonnes
LCA	Life cycle analysis
LDPE	Low-density polyethylene
LLDPE	Linear low-density polyethylene
MSW	Municipal solid waste

Mt	Million tonnes
Mt CO_2e	Million tonnes of CO_2 equivalent
NOx	Nitrous oxide
ODA	Official development assistance
PBT	Polybutylene terephthalate
PC	Polycarbonate
PCB	Polychlorinated biphenyl
PET	Polyethylene terephthalate
PM	Particulate matter
$PM_{2.5}$	Fine particulate matter
PP	Polypropylene
PPE	Personal protective equipment
PPP	Purchasing power parity
PS	Polystyrene
PUR	Polyurethane
PVC	Polyvinyl chloride
SAN	Styrene acrylonitrile
SDG	Sustainable development goal
TWP(s)	Tyre wear particle(s)
UN	United Nations
UNEA	United Nations Environment Assembly
UNEP	United Nations Environment Programme
USD	United States Dollar
WEEE	Waste from electrical and electronic equipment
WtE	Waste to energy
WWTP	Waste water treatment plant

Executive summary

Plastic pollution is one of the great environmental challenges of the 21st century, causing wide-ranging damage to ecosystems and human health, while the fossil-fuel origins of most of the plastics produced have implications for climate change. Yet plastics have become an integral part of the global economy, being used in almost all economic sectors. The OECD's *Global Plastics Outlook: Policy Scenarios to 2060* first provides an overview of plastics use, waste and environmental impacts with current policies until 2060 and then compares two scenarios to understand the policies needed for, and economic implications of, drastically reducing the environmental impacts of plastics. An additional scenario, which has climate mitigation as its primary objective, examines the cross implications of policies aimed at climate mitigation and plastics leakage reduction.

A companion volume to the *Global Plastics Outlook: Economic Drivers, Environmental Impacts and Policy Options* released earlier, this report, together with its predecessor, provides a comprehensive roadmap for a more circular plastics lifecycle.

The business-as-usual outlook is unsustainable

The core of the analysis in the *Global Plastics Outlook: Policy Scenarios to 2060* is based on simulations using the OECD's multi-sectoral, multi-regional dynamic computable general equilibrium model, ENV-Linkages, extended to include 14 polymer categories and both primary and secondary (recycled) plastics production.

The modelling projections suggest that under current policies, by 2060:

- The use of plastics could almost triple globally, driven by economic and population growth. While OECD countries are projected to double their plastics use, the largest increases are expected in emerging economies in Sub-Saharan Africa and Asia.
- Plastic waste is also projected to almost triple by 2060, with half of all plastic waste still being landfilled and less than a fifth recycled.
- Primary plastics will continue to dominate the feedstock. While recycled (secondary) plastics are projected to grow more quickly than primary plastics, they will only make up 12% of all plastics in 2060.
- Plastic leakage to the environment is projected to double to 44 million tonnes (Mt) a year, while the build-up of plastics in aquatic environments will more than triple, exacerbating environmental and health impacts.
- Other environmental impacts through the plastics lifecycle are also projected to increase, mostly due to the plastics production phase. Greenhouse gas emissions from the plastics lifecycle will more than double, from 1.8 gigatonnes of carbon dioxide equivalent (Gt CO_2e) to 4.3 Gt CO_2e. A range of other plastics lifecycle impacts, including for instance ozone formation, acidification, and human toxicity are also projected to more than double.

Two policy scenarios can bend the plastics curve

Achieving a global goal of eliminating plastic pollution, as articulated by the United Nations Environment Assembly in its resumed fifth session, requires shared objectives and co-ordinated efforts at the international level. All countries will need to implement policies to curb plastics demand, increase product lifespans through repair and reuse, and improve waste management and recyclability. The *Global Plastics Outlook* models two policy packages, with different levels of stringency, to understand their environmental and economic impacts by 2060:

1. The *Regional Action* policy scenario models the impact of a policy package to improve the circularity of plastics use and diminish the environmental impacts of plastics. The package ensures that economic growth can continue, while reducing plastic leakage to the environment. It comprises a mix of fiscal and regulatory policies targeting all phases of the plastics lifecycle, but is more ambitious for OECD countries than for non-OECD countries.
2. The *Global Ambition* policy scenario explores a very stringent policy package that aims to reduce plastic leakage to near zero by 2060. The package includes the same instruments as the *Regional Action* policy scenario, but with more ambitious targets. Furthermore, it is implemented more rapidly and globally.

By 2060, the *Regional Action* policy package could decrease plastic waste by almost a fifth below the *Baseline* and more than halve plastic leakage to the environment, compared to the *Baseline* (where leakage grows over time). This is largely due to a tax on plastics use, which gradually increases to USD 750/tonne by 2060, and a tax on packaging that is one-third higher. These taxes restrain both the demand for and production of plastics. The global recycling rate would increase to 40%. Policies that boost demand for plastic scrap and increase the supply of recycled plastics see the market share of secondary plastics surge, from 12% to 29%. Meanwhile, mismanaged waste would decline by more than 60% from *Baseline* levels, falling below 2019 levels, largely through improved waste management systems in non-OECD countries. Despite its positive impacts, plastics use and waste would still more than double by 2060 from 2019 levels in the *Regional Action* scenario. Although plastics use and waste will be partially decoupled from economic growth, stocks of plastics in the environment continue to build up rapidly.

The *Global Ambition* package could reduce plastics use and waste by a third below the *Baseline* and almost completely eliminate plastic leakage to the environment by 2060. The reductions in use and waste would largely be achieved through a tax on plastics that increases to USD 750/tonne globally by 2030 and to USD 1500/tonne by 2060, and a tax on packaging that is one-third higher. Recycling would increase to almost 60%, becoming the most common waste management option. Meanwhile the market share of secondary plastics would surge to 41% by 2060, primarily due to important pull policies such as increased recycled content targets. Mismanaged waste would fall to near zero (6 Mt, down from 153 Mt in the *Baseline* scenario). Leakage to the environment is also substantially curbed, falling by 85% compared to the *Baseline*. Macroplastic leakage is almost completely eliminated, including to aquatic environments, though microplastic leakage is only reduced by 9% compared to *Baseline* projections. The *Global Ambition* package is projected to reduce emissions by 2.1 Gt CO2e, underlining the positive impact of circular policies on achieving climate goals.

What will it cost?

Both the *Regional Action* and *Global Ambition* policy packages can be implemented at relatively modest costs to GDP. Compared to the *Baseline*, global GDP would be only 0.3% lower in the *Regional Action* scenario, showing that this policy package can be achieved with relatively moderate economic costs. However, there are important regional differences, with the People's Republic of China slightly benefitting (less than 0.1%) but higher costs in other regions: 1.1% in Sub-Saharan Africa and 1.8% in non-OECD European Union countries. A significant part of the costs of the policy package concerns the cumulative additional investment required to achieve the *Regional Action* policy objectives; this amounts to USD 320 billion (bn) between 2020 and 2060. In OECD countries this investment is almost entirely in additional recycling (USD 160 bn), whereas non-OECD countries would need to invest USD 100 bn in recycling and USD 60 bn in improved waste collection to ensure adequate disposal.

The *Global Ambition* policy package is estimated to lower world GDP by only 0.8% compared to the Baseline; thus the economic cost of policy action is still limited at a global level. However, the bulk of the costs will be borne by non-OECD countries, as substantial investments in improved waste management must be made to achieve the ambitious policy target. The largest costs are projected for Sub-Saharan Africa, whose GDP would be reduced by 2.8% below the *Baseline.* This highlights the need for supportive policies and international financial support to ensure the situation for vulnerable households is not exacerbated.

1 Overview and policy highlights

This overview chapter outlines the methodology and key findings of the *Global Plastics Outlook: Policy Scenarios to 2060*. It presents projections of plastics use, waste and leakage in the absence of new policies, as well as with a set of ambitious policy packages to bend the plastics curve.

This second volume of the Global Plastics Outlook is a follow-up to the *Global Plastics Outlook: Economic Drivers, Environmental Impacts and Policy Options* released in February 2022 that quantified trends up to 2019 in plastics use, waste generation and leakage, as well as four policy levers – markets for recycled plastics, innovation, domestic policies and international co-operation – to curb the environmental impacts of plastics.

1.1. Introduction

Plastics have seen a remarkable increase in use since the mid-20th century. However, there is mounting evidence that the leakage of plastics into the environment poses one of the great environmental challenges of the 21st century.

The OECD's first *Global Plastics Outlook: Economic Drivers, Environmental Impacts and Policy Options* (OECD, 2022[1]), released in February 2022, found that plastics production has increased 230-fold from 2 million tonnes (Mt) in 1950 to 460 Mt in 2019. The report concluded that despite recent policy initiatives to close the plastics loop, the plastics lifecycle is only 8% circular.[1] The report found that plastic waste more than doubled from 156 Mt in 2000 to 353 Mt in 2019. However, in 2019 only 15% of plastic waste was collected for recycling and only 9% was actually recycled. Half of the plastic waste was landfilled and close to one-fifth was incinerated. A significant share (22%) of plastic waste was mismanaged (not disposed of adequately), ending up in uncontrolled dumpsites or burned in the open, leading to leakage into the environment. In 2019, 22 Mt of plastic waste leaked into the environment.[2] The vast majority (by weight) of leaked plastics are macroplastics (88%),[3] while the share of microplastics[4] is smaller (12%). As of 2019, an estimated 109 Mt of leaked plastics have accumulated in rivers and 30 Mt in the ocean. The report also found that the COVID-19 pandemic in 2020 temporarily disrupted previous trends in plastics production and waste generation. While certain plastics applications, such as personal protective equipment (PPE), increased, the overall plastics use decreased by 2.2% as a consequence of the fall in economic activity. Nevertheless, the upward trajectory of plastics production and waste generation resumed in 2021 as economic activity picked up again.

Since the release of the first volume of the Global Plastics Outlook, member states of the United Nations have agreed at the United Nations Environmental Assembly (UNEA 5.2) to negotiate an international legally binding instrument by 2024 to end plastic pollution. Meanwhile, global recovery from the COVID-19 pandemic still remains uneven, while the geopolitical outlook is increasingly uncertain in the wake of the war in Ukraine. A key question in this context is: what are the plausible scenarios for the evolution of plastics use, waste and leakage to the environment in the coming decades in the absence of additional measures and, as well, through coordinated policy action to address plastic pollution?

The *Global Plastics Outlook: Policy Scenarios to 2060* provides such a forward-looking perspective. This second volume of OECD's Global Plastics Outlook presents a set of coherent scenarios for plastics to 2060, including plastics use and waste as well as the environmental impacts linked to plastics, especially leakage to the environment. Such an outlook on plastics for the coming decades can help policymakers understand the scale of the challenge to transition to a more sustainable and circular use of plastics and the need for additional policy action to address plastic leakage. By identifying a series of policy packages to bend the plastic curve, the Outlook allows for a better understanding of the environmental benefits and economic consequences of adopting more stringent policies.

Taken together, the two volumes of the Global Plastics Outlook provide a comprehensive roadmap for eliminating plastic leakage and for a more circular plastics lifecycle.

1.2. An overview of the modelling framework

The core of the analysis is based on simulations using the OECD's multi-sectoral, multi-regional dynamic computable general equilibrium (CGE) model ENV-Linkages (Chateau, Dellink and Lanzi, 2014[2]). For this Outlook, ENV-Linkages has been extended to include plastics for 14 polymer categories as well as both primary and secondary (recycled) plastics production (see Annex A).

A strength of CGE models such as ENV-Linkages is that they embed the drivers of sectoral and regional plastics use, such as demand patterns, production modes (including recycling activities) and trade specialisation, into a consistent framework (see Chapter 2). Projections of plastics use already exist in the published literature[5] but this report presents the first projections based on a CGE framework. However, in these studies the projected volumes of plastics follow aggregate economic growth and/or population growth trends, without considering sectoral details. The modelling approach in this report provides a more accurate link between plastics use and economic activities and a more detailed understanding of the consequences of policy action. It considers plastics not only as a final good for consumption, but, above all, as a production input for each sector, thereby taking into account the complexity of the interactions across sectors and regions and along the plastics lifecycle (see Chapter 3).

The ENV-Linkages modelling framework is also used to calculate plastic waste flows. The generation of waste is strongly related to the use of plastics and depends on the average lifespan of each plastic product. The lifespan can be very short, as for packaging, or can span several decades, as for products used in construction (Geyer, Jambeck and Law, 2017[3]). International trade in plastic waste is also modelled, i.e. where plastic waste produced in one country is treated in another.

The ENV-Linkages model has also been enhanced to distinguish the end-of-life fates of plastics, which heavily depend on the waste management capacities and regulations of the location where plastic waste is generated and handled. Four end-of-life fates are modelled: waste can be recycled, incinerated, landfilled (in sanitary landfilling), or mismanaged (which includes uncollected litter) (see Chapter 4).

Finally, this Outlook presents projections to 2060 of the environmental impacts of plastics use and waste. Chapter 5 follows the methodology used in the *Global Plastics Outlook: Economic Drivers, Environmental Impacts and Policy Options* (OECD, 2022[1]), presenting projections of plastic leakage to the environment that combine estimates from four prominent research groups.[6] These experts have refined and customised their analytical approaches to create leakage estimates that are coherent with the projections of economic activities, plastics use and waste from the ENV-Linkages model (see Annex A). Chapter 6 explores other environmental impacts, including greenhouse gas (GHG) emissions from the plastic lifecycle and an analysis of biobased plastics. Finally, a lifecycle analysis (LCA) is used to assess other environmental impacts of plastics.[7]

1.3. Scenario analysis for plastics projections

Projections over long time horizons are, by definition, subject to uncertainties, since it is not possible to foresee with a high degree of accuracy socio-economic changes all the way to 2060. Nevertheless, projections presented here can still highlight the future consequences of current policy choices, and the benefits of more ambitious policy action.

Acknowledging the uncertainties, the Global Plastics Outlook adopts a scenario approach. Specifying and quantifying different scenarios provides a range of possible future developments that are both plausible and internally consistent. Doing so allows for a quantitative evaluation of key economic and environmental developments and in particular the assessment of plastics policies. The modelling provides plastics projections by carefully linking plastic volumes to the consumption and production of plastics in the economy, focusing on the evolution of the sectoral and regional economic drivers of plastics use.

Creating projections of future plastics use, waste and their environmental impacts involves four main steps, as illustrated in Figure 1.1. First, economic flows that drive the use of plastics are projected based on socio-economic trends and various assumptions about policy changes. The second step links plastics use by polymer category and application to different economic activities. The third step provides a link between plastics use and plastic waste, differentiating between waste management techniques. Finally, plastic leakage and key environmental impacts related to the production, use and disposal of plastics are calculated.

The Outlook presents results for a *Baseline* scenario, which is used to show the environmental consequences to 2060 of current policies on plastics and waste management.[8] To highlight uncertainties, alternative *Baseline* scenarios are explored for some of the main trends that drive plastics use and waste in the coming decades.

The policy scenarios, meanwhile, provide a quantification of the environmental benefits and economic consequences of ambitious policy action on plastics, exploring how plastics, use, waste management and environmental impacts vary with the stringency of policy action. Interactions with climate policies are also analysed. These policy scenarios assess the implications of different policy packages that vary in their range and stringency, and are evaluated in comparison to the *Baseline* scenario.

Figure 1.1. The scenario analysis involves four steps

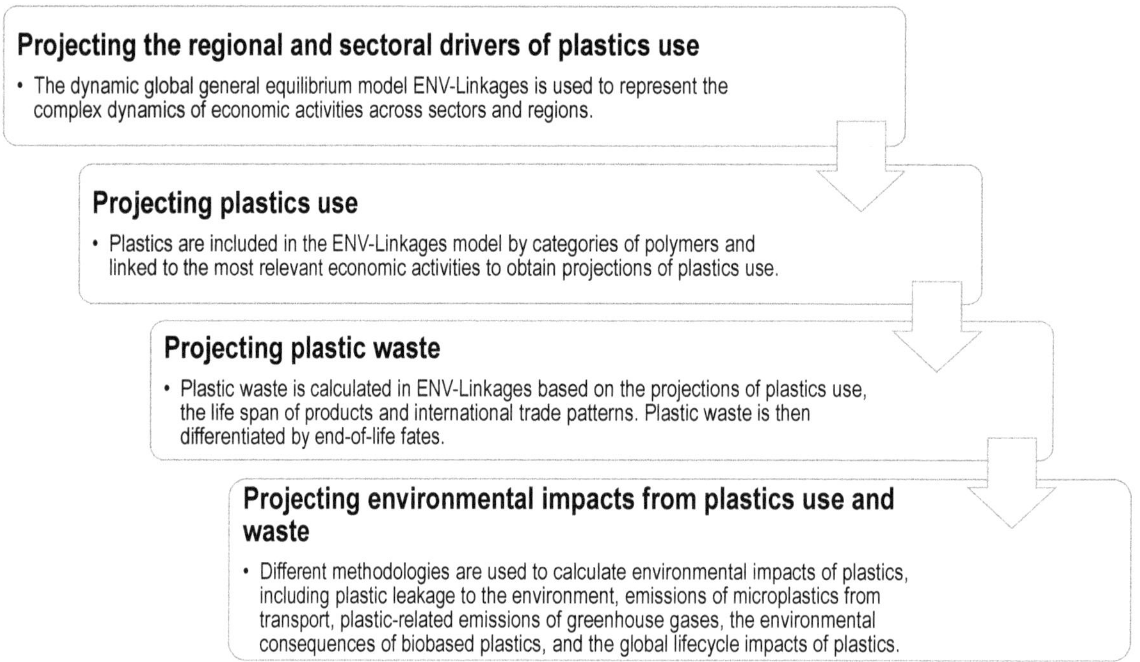

1.4. Projections to 2060 in the Baseline scenario

1.4.1. Global GDP is projected to more than triple by 2060

The global population is projected to reach 10 billion people by 2060. However, there are important differences across countries. Many European countries, Japan, Korea and the People's Republic of China (hereafter 'China') are facing demographic declines. Other countries are likely to experience high population growth, especially countries in Sub-Saharan Africa. Living standards are projected to increase in all countries, with non-OECD countries gradually converging to 2019 OECD-levels by 2060. With growing populations and improving living standards, global gross domestic product (GDP) is projected to more than triple between 2019 and 2060. As economies grow, they also undergo important structural changes. The service sector is projected to experience the fastest growth due to changing household demand patterns as well as changing production patterns. This "servitisation" of economies also has important implications for plastics use, and therefore plastic waste.

Figure 1.2. Without new policies, the plastics lifecycle will only be 14% circular in 2060

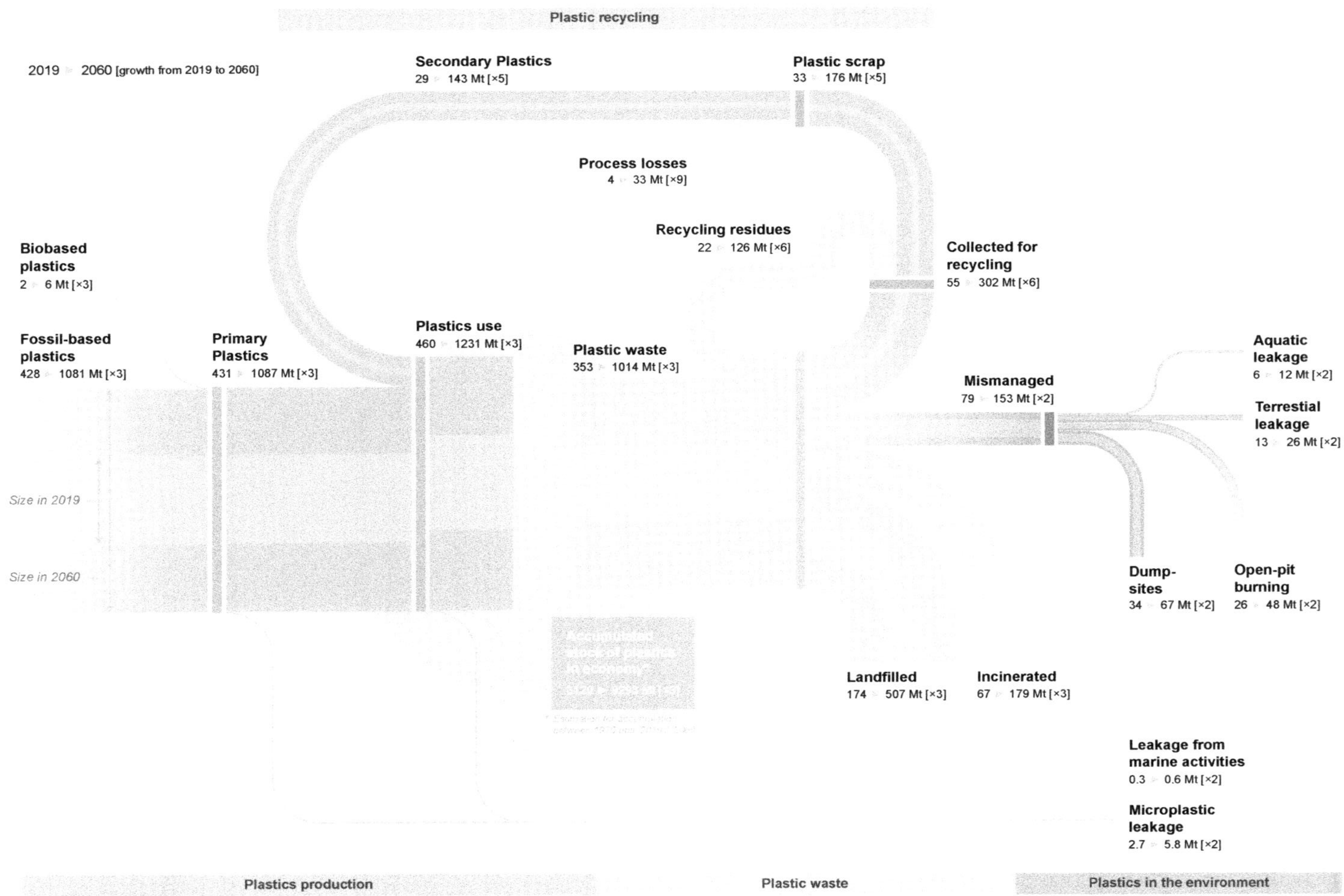

Note: Projections for 2060 suggest that only 143 Mt of the 1014 Mt (14%) of plastics waste generated in 2060 are recycled into new plastics.
Source: OECD ENV-Linkages model.

1.4.2. Plastics use is projected to almost triple by 2060

Plastics use is projected to almost triple, from 460 Mt in 2019 to 1 231 Mt in 2060. In the absence of new policies, the use of plastics will grow at a higher rate than other materials in the same period, except wood and timber. The main driver of this surge is economic growth, but population growth also contributes in important ways. Structural and technology changes, on the other hand, drive down plastics use. Changes in the structure of the economy mean that the global average amount of plastic used to produce 1 USD of GDP is projected to fall by 16% between 2019 and 2060, implying a slight relative decoupling of plastics use and GDP. However, the rate at which economies recover from the COVID-19 pandemic could alter these projections (Box 1.1).

Primary plastics[9] use will continue to dominate (88% in 2060). Even though recycled (secondary) plastics are projected to grow at a faster rate than primary plastics, they are still expected to only make up 12% of the total share of plastics use in 2060.

1.4.3. However, regional growth rates are characterised by important heterogeneities

While OECD countries are projected to double their plastics use, emerging economies are expected to see much more significant increases, from a six-fold increase in Sub-Saharan Africa to a tripling in Asia,[10] as illustrated in Figure 1.3. Despite such fast growth, OECD countries are still set to remain the largest consumers of plastics on an average per capita basis in 2060. Global plastic intensity is expected to decrease between 2019 and 2060 globally, thanks to technology change that leads to lower sectoral plastic intensity and to a shift towards less plastic intensive sectors.

Box 1.1. The effects of the COVID-19 pandemic on plastics use could linger for decades to come

The COVID-19 pandemic and the associated disturbance to economic activity caused a significant contraction of global GDP in 2020, with the annual global GDP growth rate dropping from around +4% in 2019 to -4% in 2020. Many economies have since rebounded, with GDP having returned or exceeded pre-COVID levels. Nonetheless, in many ways the effects will linger. The pandemic is projected to lead to a permanent 2% decrease in both plastics use and plastic waste generation compared to pre-COVID projections. Regional differences abound. Countries experiencing relatively strong growth post-COVID may experience a rebound in plastics volumes, while economies suffering persistent negative impacts from the pandemic could see significant decreases in plastics use and waste in both the medium and in the long term compared to pre-COVID projections. For instance, a slower return to pre-COVID growth rates than projected in the *Baseline* scenario could result in global plastics use and waste generation being as much as 4% lower by 2060.

1.4.4. The growth of plastics across applications and polymers is also heterogeneous

While global plastics use is projected to increase for all applications, the strongest growth is likely to be in the three sectors that currently account for 60% of all plastics use: transportation, such as plastic vehicle components (more than tripling by 2060), construction and packaging (more than doubling by 2060). Consequently, while plastics use increases for all polymers (Figure 1.4), the most substantial increases will be in polymers that are used in these applications. For example, PET (polyethylene terephthalate) and PE (polyethylene) are used for packaging, and their use is projected to more than double by 2060.

Figure 1.3. Plastics use will grow fastest in developing and emerging economies in Africa and Asia

Plastics use in million tonnes (Mt), Baseline scenario

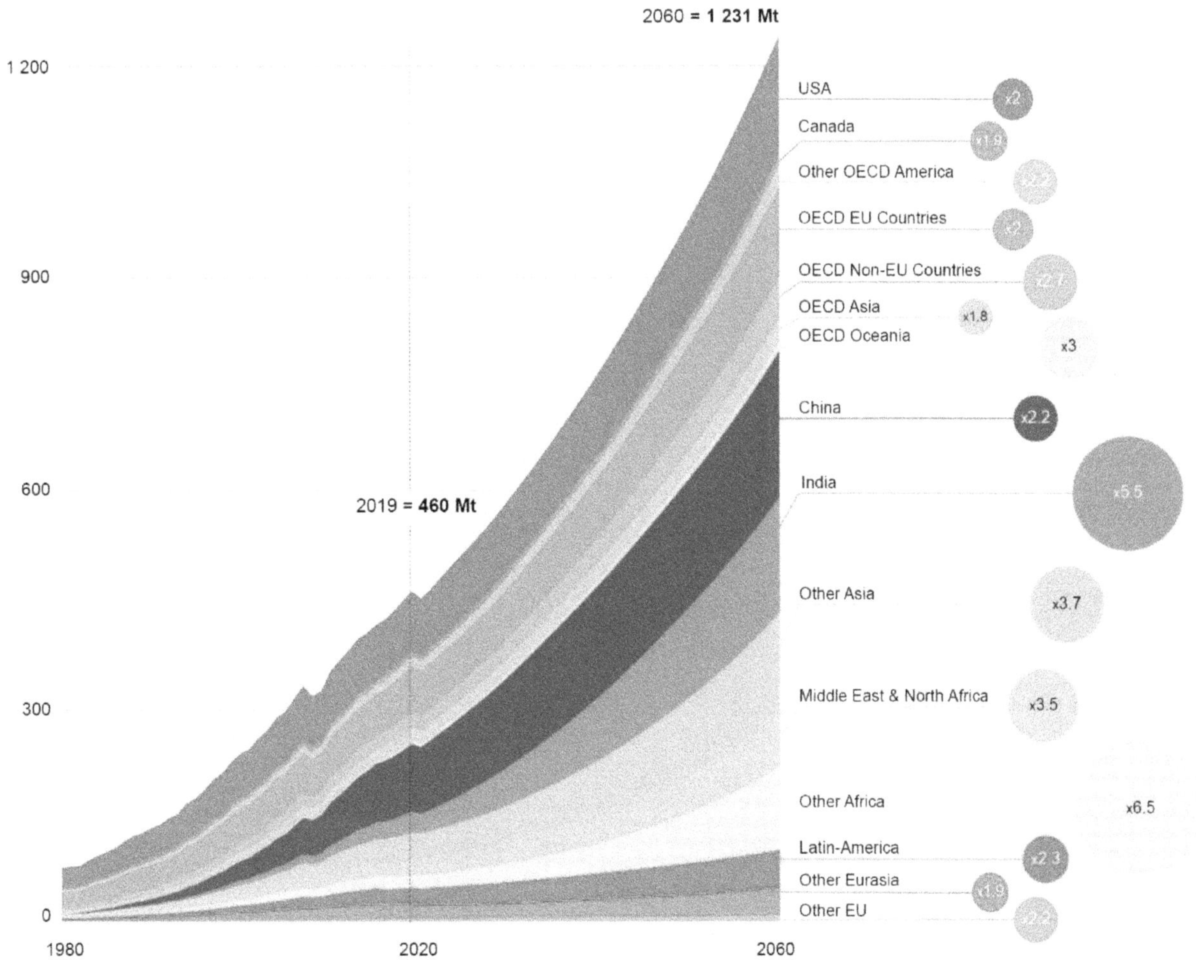

Note: The numbers in the circle on the right–hand side of the graph indicate the growth of plastics use from 2019 (dashed line) to 2060 for each region (e.g. x2 means a doubling of plastics use).
Source: OECD ENV-Linkages model.

StatLink https://stat.link/qrwkca

Figure 1.4. The use of all polymers will significantly increase by 2060

2019-60 increase in plastics use by polymer and application

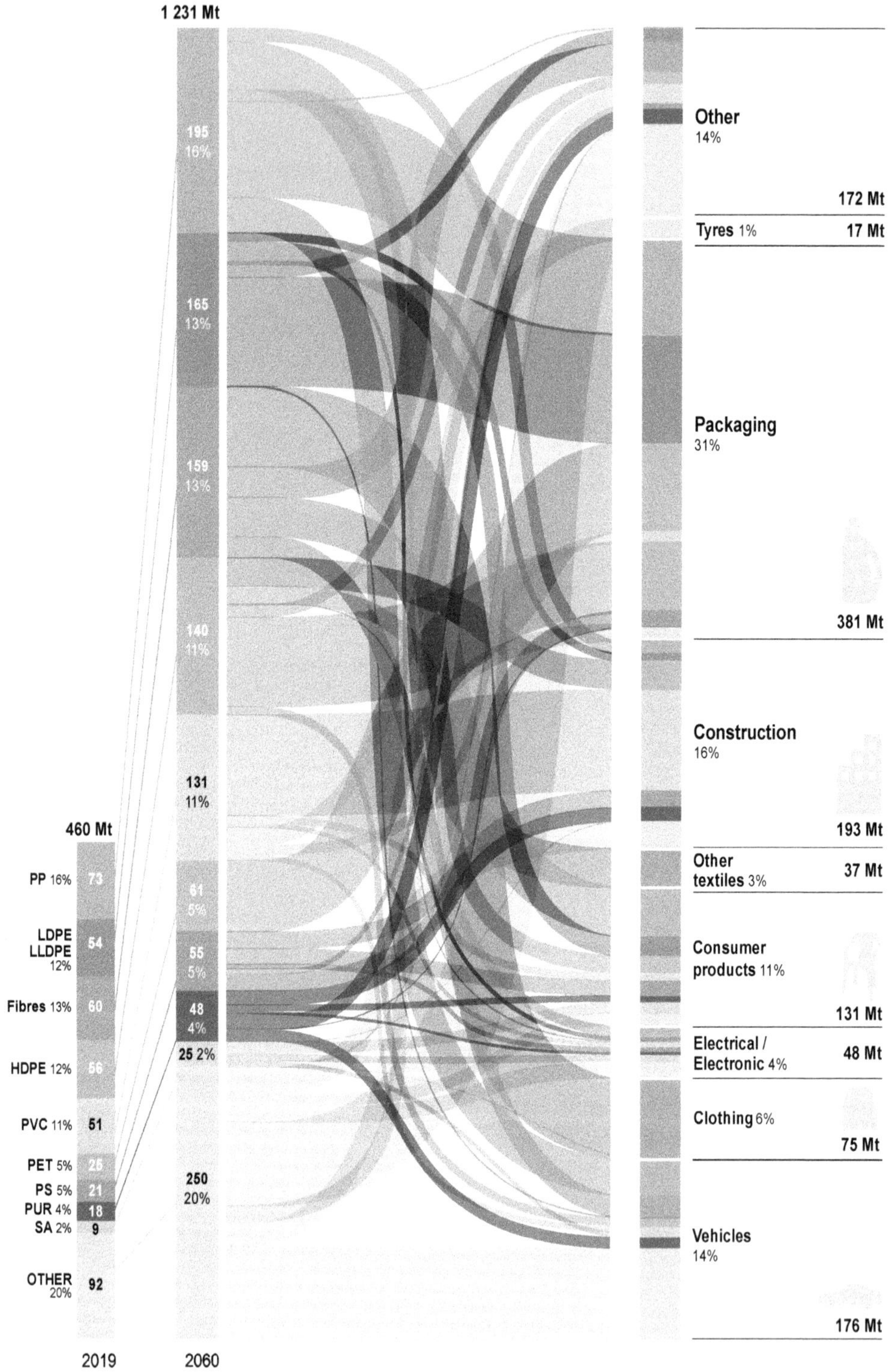

Note: 1. HDPE = high density polyethylene; LDPE = low density polyethylene; LLDPE = linear low-density polyethylene; PET = polyethylene terephthalate; PP = polypropylene; PS = polystyrene; PUR = polyurethane; PVC = polyvinyl chloride; SA stands for ABS, ASA, SAN, where ABS = Ascrylonitrile butadiene styrene; ASA = acrylonitrile styrene acrylate; SAN = styrene acrylonitrile. 2. The figure does not include the application personal protective equipment (face masks and other protection linked to the COVID-19 pandemic) as its use was negligible in 2019.
Source: OECD ENV-Linkages model.

StatLink https://stat.link/01xqn4

1.4.5. Plastic waste is projected to almost triple by 2060, with half of all plastic waste still being landfilled and less than a fifth recycled

Plastic waste is projected to increase almost three-fold – from 353 Mt in 2019 to 1 014 Mt in 2060. Short-lived applications, such as packaging, consumer products and textiles dominate plastic waste streams, accounting for around two-thirds of plastic waste in 2060. Plastic waste from construction and transport applications, such as discarded vehicle components, will also remain sizeable, especially given the rapid economic development in many developing and emerging economies. A large portion of plastic waste will be generated in non-OECD countries (65%), especially in emerging economies in Asia and in Africa, which are projected to see plastic waste grow at the fastest rates.

Recycling is projected to out-pace all other waste management approaches, with recycling rates increasing from 9% in 2019 to 17% in 2060 (Figure 1.5). Even so, recycling will still make up a smaller share of waste management than incineration (18%) and sanitary landfilling (50%).

Despite improvements in waste management infrastructure and litter collection, mismanaged waste is projected to increase in absolute volumes from 79 Mt in 2019 to 153 Mt in 2060. Mismanagement rates of plastic waste decrease to 1% by 2060 in OECD countries, but remain at relatively high levels in non-OECD countries (23%). Large increases in mismanaged plastic waste will be driven by fast economic growth in African and Asian economies, where infrastructure improvements are unforeseen to evolve quickly enough to prevent mismanagement of plastic waste.

Figure 1.5. Half of all plastic waste will continue to be landfilled in 2060

Plastic waste in million tonnes (left-hand axis) by waste management category, after disposal of recycling residues and litter collection

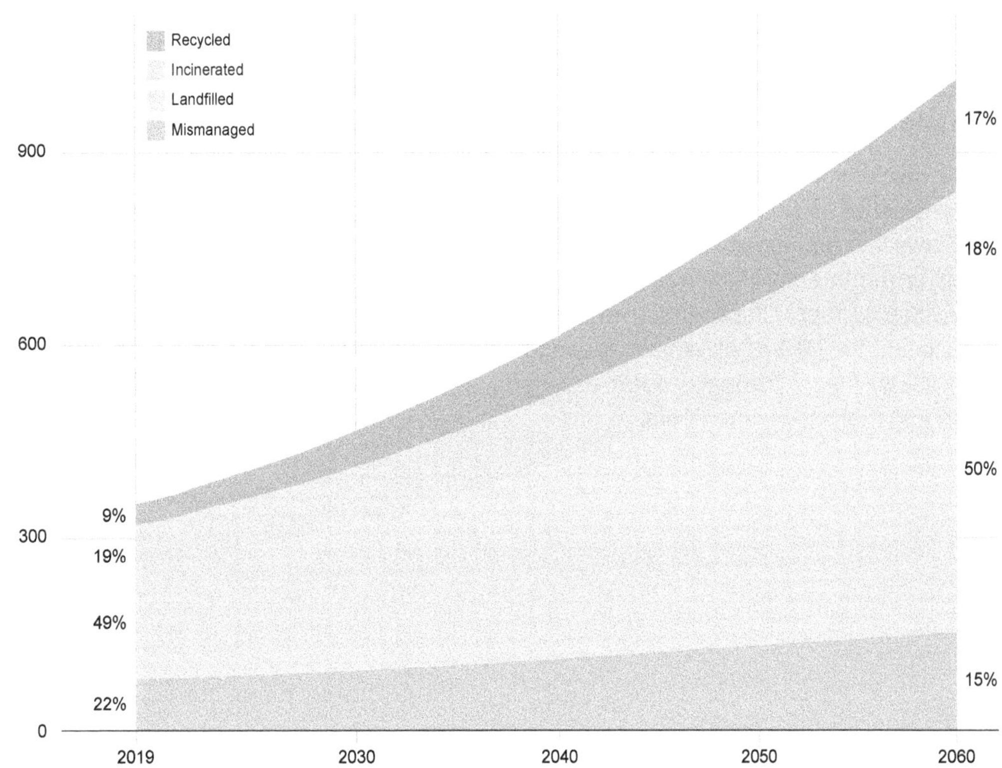

Note: The numbers to the left and right show the share of each fate in 2019 and 2060 respectively.
Source: OECD ENV-Linkages model.

StatLink https://stat.link/d9n0ew

1.4.6. Plastic leakage is projected double, more than tripling the plastic build-up in aquatic environments by 2060

Although some decoupling is projected to occur between plastics use and leakage globally, the leakage of plastics into the environment is still projected to almost double from 22 Mt (16 Mt – 28 Mt) in 2019 to 44 Mt (34 Mt – 55 Mt) in 2060.[11]

Macroplastic leakage will continue to represent a significant share of total leakage (87%) but microplastic leakage is projected to more than double in absolute weight, accounting for 13% of leakage in 2060. While almost 99% of macroplastics will leak from mismanaged waste, microplastic leakage continues to be an issue from a variety of sources, including wastewater sludge, tyre abrasion and road marking wear. Littering is likely to become the fastest growing source of leakage.

As living conditions improve, high-income and middle-income countries are expected to see decreases in volumes of macroplastic leakage, while low-income countries are likely to face increasing macroplastic leakage (Figure 1.6). This is because although plastics use, waste generation and leakage initially increase with rising incomes, as incomes increase further, there is greater demand for better waste management systems and more willingness to deal with visible environmental impacts, such as macroplastic leakage. This trend follows the "Environmental Kuznets Curve", which has also been observed for some other pollutants. Meanwhile, microplastic leakage seems to follow a different trajectory in which leakage continues to increase, although some saturation occurs at higher levels of income. Interventions to address emissions of microplastics (e.g. from tyre abrasion) are generally less advanced, as this form of leakage has not yet received the same level of scrutiny as macroplastics, it occurs all along the lifecycle of products, the cost-effectiveness of mitigation interventions is not yet fully understood, and policy action remains limited currently.

In terms of regional trends, while OECD countries are likely to see plastic leakage fall to 2.5 Mt in 2060, non-OECD countries see leakage increase significantly, to 41.6 Mt, with a major share stemming from mismanaged plastic waste in emerging economies in the Middle East, Africa and Asia. Although all countries contribute to increased microplastic leakage, OECD countries will be responsible for almost one-third of global microplastic leakage in 2060.

Projections are bleak for aquatic environments, such as streams, rivers, lakes, seas and the ocean where the build up of plastics is projected to more than triple from 140 Mt in 2019 to reach 493 Mt in 2060 (Figure 1.7). Flows into aquatic environments are also projected to double over the period, aggravating an already serious environmental challenge. Geographical differences in contributions to aquatic leakage are expected to evolve further. China, India, other non-OECD Asian economies and Sub-Saharan Africa together will account for 79% of all aquatic leakage. While China is projected to be the largest emitter of plastic into freshwater environments, other emerging economies in Asia will contribute significantly to plastic leakage into marine environments.

Figure 1.6. Macroplastic and microplastic leakage show different trajectories when income per capita increases

Per capita leakage (in kg, on y-axis) vs. GDP per capita (in USD, on x-axis), Baseline scenario

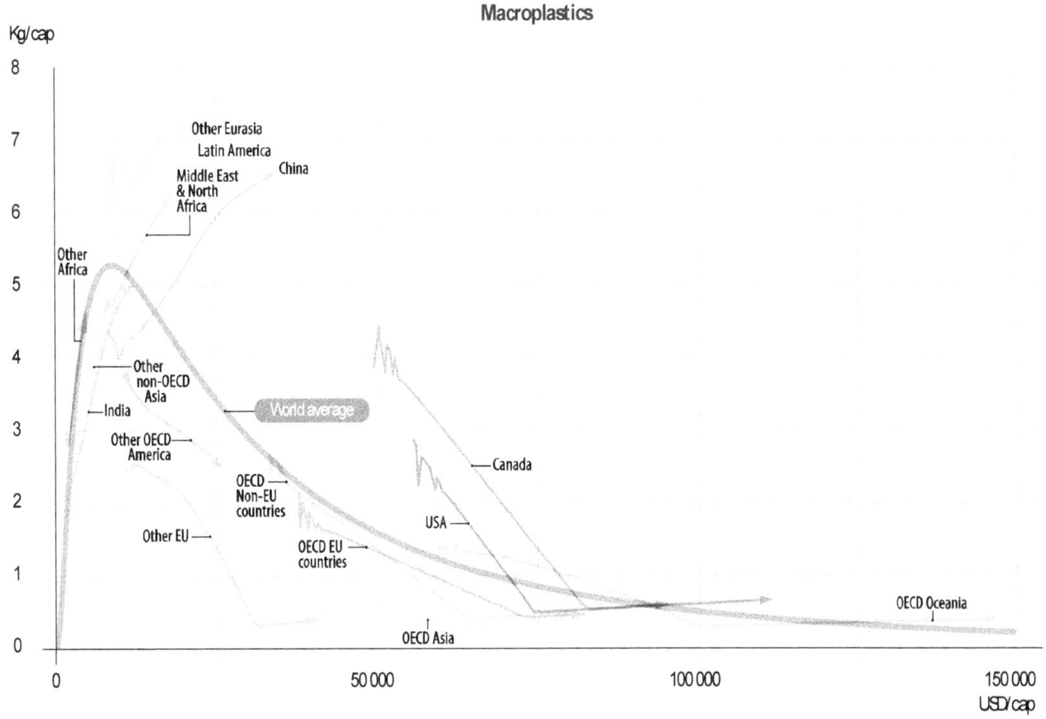

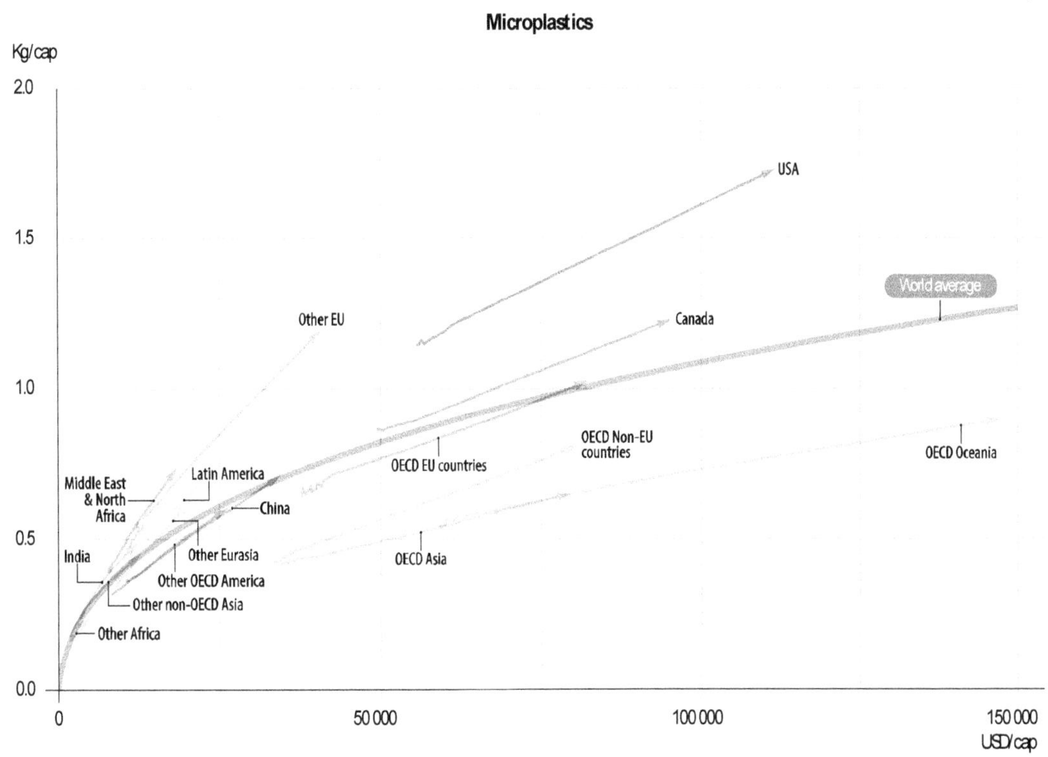

Note: The "world average" line represents regression across time and regions. The data points for each colour represent the evolution of that region between 2019 and 2060, with the arrow pointing towards 2060.
Source: OECD ENV-Linkages model, based on Ryberg et al. (2019[4]), Cottom et. al. (2022[5]) for mismanaged waste.

Figure 1.7. Leakage into aquatic environments is projected to double between 2019 and 2060

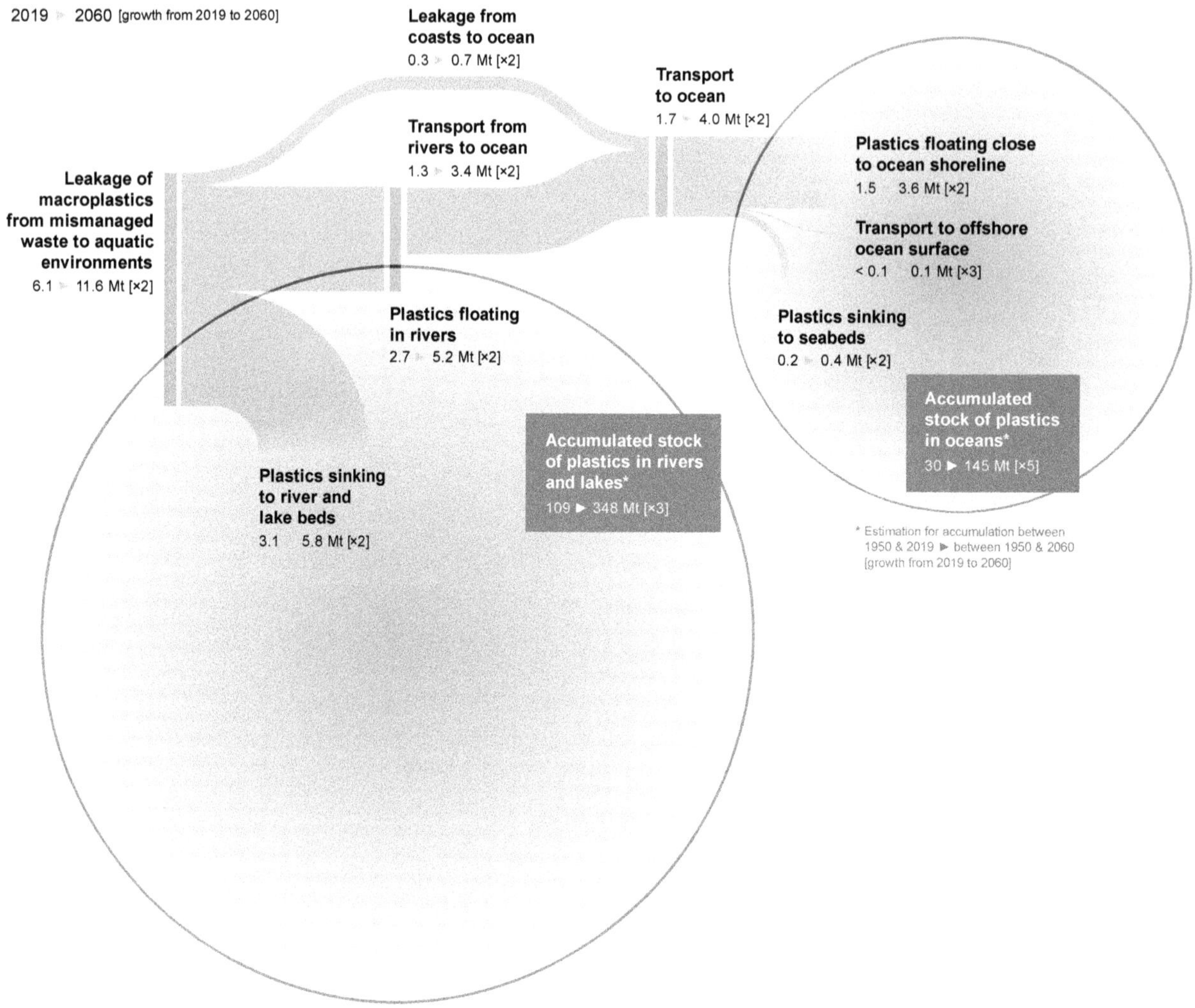

Source: OECD ENV-Linkages model.

1.4.7. The environmental and health impacts of plastics are set to worsen considerably

The entire lifecycle of plastics contributes to GHG emissions in significant ways; this is set to continue in the future in the absence of new policies. Currently, 1.8 gigatonnes of carbon dioxide equivalents (Gt CO_2e) of GHG emissions can be attributed to the plastics lifecycle, but this is expected to more than double to 4.3 Gt CO_2e by 2060. About 90% of these emissions originate from production and conversion, with important differences across polymers: the production of fibres used for textiles is the biggest emitter, followed by polypropylene (PP) and low-density polyethylene (LDPE), which are used for a variety of applications, including for packaging and for vehicles.

Biobased plastics are far from a panacea. Without new policies, they are only likely to represent a fraction of total plastics use in 2060, at around 0.5%. And even if policy measures succeed in increasing the market share to 5% by 2060, the impact on GHG emissions would still be ambiguous. Although the substitution of fossil-based plastic production by biobased plastics would see direct GHG emissions decrease, the additional land required for growing feedstock may see natural areas converted into arable land, which will induce one-off GHG emissions.

The environmental impacts of plastics are not solely limited to plastic leakage and to greenhouse gas emissions. There is a wide-variety of other impacts linked to plastics, such as resource scarcity, land use, ozone formation, eutrophication, ecotoxicity, toxicity and acidification. Figure 1.8 highlights these impacts of different plastic polymers using lifecycle analysis (LCA) of the cradle-to-gate and end-of-life stages. Impacts tend to differ across polymers: for example while polyurethane (PUR) can cause marine eutrophication, polyvinyl chloride (PVC) is carcinogenic for humans. Environmental impacts are projected to more than double to 2060, increasing by 132% to 171%, with land use, as well as marine and freshwater eutrophication seeing the largest increase. The increase in lifecycle impacts is mostly driven by the increase in plastics use and production by 2060. These effects are only partly offset by improvements in waste management that occur by 2060, even in the *Baseline* scenario. For example, the terrestrial acidification impact of plastics production increases 5% less by 2060 than the volumes produced, owing to the increasing market share of secondary plastics. Moreover, the freshwater ecotoxicity impact of the end-of-life stage increases 33% less than plastics use by 2060 thanks to improved waste management practices.

Figure 1.8. Without new policies, the environmental and health impacts of polymers will double in 2060

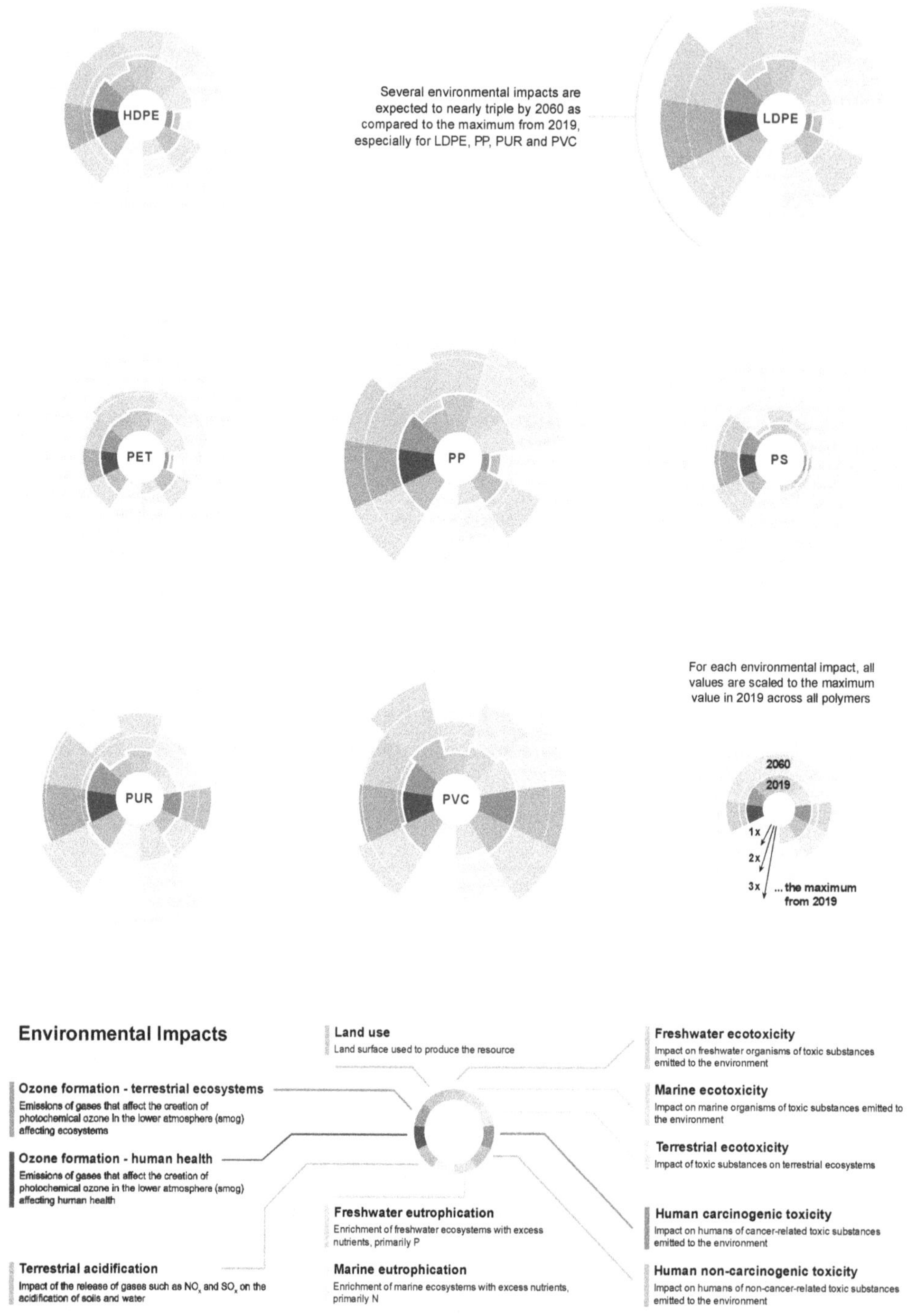

Note: PP=polypropylene; HDPE=high-density polyethylene; LDPE=low-density polyethylene; PVC=polyvinyl chloride; PS=polystyrene; PET=polyethylene terephthalate; PUR: polyurethane.
Source: OECD ENV-Linkages model, based on results from Ghent University.

1.5. Policy packages to eliminate plastic leakage

The previous section paints a bleak picture: without new policies, by 2060 the world will be producing and consuming almost three times as much plastics as today. The environmental impacts of plastics along the entire lifecycle will be more significant than ever. Of great concern is the tripling of quantities of plastic waste generated, which if not managed properly, could lead to a doubling in leakage to the environment and a substantial increase in the stocks of plastics accumulated in rivers and the ocean. Other concerns include the more than doubling of greenhouse gas emissions associated with plastics production and end of life, as well as the substantial increase in other health and environmental impacts along the plastics lifecycle.

In the absence of significantly more stringent and coordinated action, the global community is far from achieving its long-term objective of ending plastic pollution. The plastics issue needs to be tackled systematically, with piecemeal measures replaced by co-ordinated action. This report therefore explores several different policy scenarios that could change the outlook by increasing the circularity of the plastics lifecycle and curb plastic leakage to the environment.

1.5.1. The building blocks of policy packages

More ambitious and co-ordinated policy action is needed along the entire plastics lifecycle, as set out in the policy roadmap in the OECD's first *Global Plastics Outlook: Economic Drivers, Environmental Impacts and Policy Options* (OECD, 2022[1]). The roadmap emphasises the need for regulatory and economic policy instruments that can induce economy-wide behavioural changes. This Outlook builds on this roadmap to develop a range of policy packages that together can alter the foundations of the current plastics economy.

Policies can be categorised into three main pillars: *Restrain plastic demand and enhance circularity*, *Enhance recycling* and *Close leakage pathways*. Each building block includes a number of policy instruments (Figure 1.9):

- *Restrain plastic demand and enhance circularity* is composed of fiscal instruments that disincentivise the production and use of plastics, and other policies that enhance product design to increase their durability and favour reuse and repair. Instruments include a tax on plastics, including on plastic packaging, a set of policies that fosters circular design, such as increasing the lifespan of plastic products, decreasing the final demand for durables, increasing efficiency of intermediate plastics use, and increasing the demand for repair services.
- *Enhance recycling* includes instruments that influence plastics recycling rates, such as recycled content targets, extended producer responsibility (EPR) schemes and region-specific recycling rate targets.
- *Close leakage pathways* aims to decrease and, where possible, eliminate mismanaged plastic waste by investing in waste management infrastructure, and by increasing litter collection rates, thereby substantially reducing leakage of plastics into the environment.

Figure 1.9. The policy packages target the entire plastics lifecycle

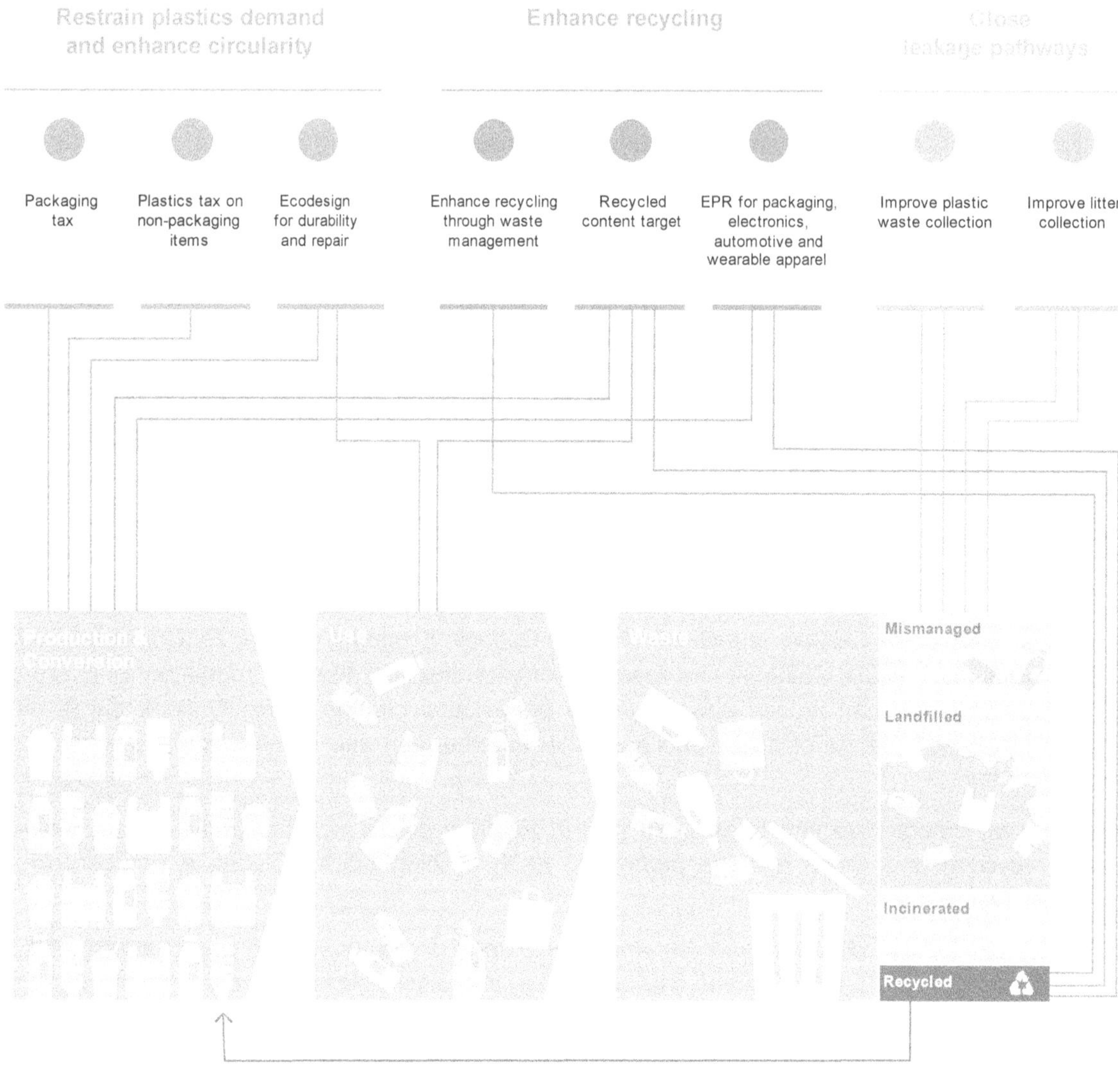

1.5.2. The policy packages modelled vary in their stringency

The Global Plastics Outlook models two scenarios based on the above policies, but with different levels of stringency, to understand their environmental and economic impacts by 2060 (for details see Table 1.1).

The *Regional Action* scenario varies the level of ambition in the policy package to reflect the different circumstances and challenges of OECD versus non-OECD countries. This policy package aims to reduce the plastics volumes at all stages of the lifecycle by 2060, while limiting economic costs.

The *Global Ambition* scenario reflects more co-ordinated effort at the international level, with the level of ambition aiming to reduce plastic leakage to near zero by 2060. This reflects the goals of several international initiatives, including the United Nations Environment Assembly's resolution to develop an international legally binding instrument on plastic pollution, the G20 "Osaka Blue Ocean Vision," as well as voluntary action by the private sector. The package includes the same instruments as the *Regional Action* policy scenario, but with more ambitious targets, and is implemented more rapidly and globally. It would substantially reduce plastics and their environmental impacts along the entire lifecycle though at slightly higher economic costs.

Table 1.1. The policies in the two main scenarios vary in their levels of ambition

Policy pillars	Regional Action	Global Ambition
Restrain Demand	A tax on plastic packaging, increasing linearly from 0 in 2021 to reach USD 1 000/tonne by 2030 in the European Union (EU), by 2040 in the rest of the OECD and by 2060 in (non-EU) non-OECD countries, and staying constant thereafter.	A tax on plastics packaging, increasing linearly from 0 in 2021 to reach USD 1 000/tonne by 2030 globally, then doubling to USD 2 000/tonne by 2060.
	A tax on the use of all other types of plastics (non-packaging), introduced after 2030, starting at USD 25/tonne and reaching USD 750/tonne by 2040 in OECD countries and by 2060 in non-OECD countries. It remains constant thereafter.	A tax on the use of all other types of plastics (non-packaging), reaching USD 750/tonne by 2030 globally, then doubling to USD 1 500/tonne by 2060.
	Policy instruments targeting eco-design, such as an extension of product lifespans by 10%, a 5-10% decrease in intermediate and final demand for durables by 2040, as well as increased demand for repair services.	Policy instruments targeting eco-design, such as an extension of product lifespans by 15%, a 10-20% decrease in demand for durables by 2030, increased efficiency of intermediate plastics use, as well as increased demand for repair services.
Enhance Recycling	Recycled content targets at 40% for OECD and at 20% for non-OECD countries by 2060.	Recycled content target at 40% for all countries by 2060.
	EPR schemes for packaging, electronics, motor vehicles and clothing in OECD and non-OECD EU countries, the remaining countries do not implement EPR.	EPR schemes for packaging, electronics, motor vehicles and clothing in all countries.
	Region-specific recycling rate targets: 60% by 2030 and 70% by 2060 for the EU and the OECD Pacific region, 60% recycling by 2060 for other OECD countries and China, 40% by 2060 for the other countries.	Region-specific recycling rate targets: 60% by 2030 and 80% by 2060 for EU and the OECD Pacific region, 80% recycling by 2060 for other OECD countries and China, 60% by 2060 for the remaining countries.
Close leakage pathways	Investment in mixed waste collection and sanitary landfills, where OECD countries eliminate all mismanaged collected waste while non-OECD countries halve mismanaged waste by 2060.	Investments in mixed waste collection and sanitary landfills, with all countries eliminating collected mismanaged waste by 2060.
	Improvements in litter collection rates to reach 90% for high-income countries.	Improvements in litter collection rates to reach 90% for high-income countries, and collection rates for lower income countries are increased from 65% to 75%.

Source: OECD ENV-Linkages model.

1.5.3. Strengthening domestic policies, even with differentiated regional ambition levels, can deliver substantial environmental gains, but falls short of eliminating leakage

Projections show that the *Regional Action* policy package could see global plastics use decrease by almost one-fifth from the *Baseline* level, from 1 231 Mt to 1 018 Mt by 2060 (Figure 1.10). This is largely due to the effects of taxing plastics use, which restrains demand for and production of plastics. Taxing single-use plastics leads to significant reductions in the use of these short lifespan plastics. Plastic waste would also decrease by about one-fifth below *Baseline*, from 1 014 Mt to 837 Mt, mainly driven by the reduction in demand. Despite these reductions, in 2060 plastics use and waste are still projected to be well above 2019 levels.

As waste management systems undergo important improvements, the global recycling rate would increase to 40% in 2060. Policies that boost demand for plastic scrap and increase the supply of recycled plastics lead to a surge in the market share of secondary plastics, from 12% to 29%. Meanwhile, mismanaged waste would decline by more than 60%, reaching 59 Mt in 2060, even below 2019 levels. A large part of these reductions would be achieved by improving waste management systems in non-OECD countries.

Leakage of macroplastics would fall below *Baseline* projections for 2060, from 38 Mt to 15 Mt. On the other hand, reductions in microplastics would remain relatively small: a 4% decrease from the *Baseline*, from 5.8 Mt to 5.6 Mt. While this policy package halves plastic leakage into the environment, including aquatic environments, it is unable to fully prevent all plastic leakage. This is especially true for non-OECD countries, where additional action and more stringent policies are necessary. This highlights the importance of global ambition and co-operation, as modelled in the *Global Ambition* scenario.

1.5.4. Globally coordinated ambition is required to drastically boost recycling and eliminate leakage to the environment

By 2060, this policy package is projected to reduce both plastics use and waste by one-third compared to the *Baseline* (Figure 1.10). Plastics use would decrease to 827 Mt from 1231 Mt in the *Baseline* scenario, as taxes realign economic activities away from plastic-using sectors, especially in non-OECD countries in Eurasia, the Middle East and Africa. Similarly, compared to *Baseline* projections, plastic waste would decrease to 679 Mt from 1014 Mt in 2060 with policies that restrain demand and production playing an important role.

Recycling would increase to almost 60%, becoming the most common waste management option. The market share of secondary plastics would surge to 41% by 2060, primarily due to important demand-pull policies, such as increased recycled content targets. On the other hand, mismanaged waste would reach near zero levels (6 Mt by 2060 compared to 153 Mt in the *Baseline* scenario). This large decrease can be attributed to massive improvements in waste management infrastructure in non-OECD countries, decreasing mismanaged waste in these regions to 4 Mt.

These improvements will see leakage to the environment substantially curbed by the *Global Ambition* policy package, falling by 85% compared to the *Baseline*, from 44 Mt to 6 Mt, and with macroplastic leakage almost completely eliminated. Aquatic leakage is almost completely eliminated as well, from 11.6 Mt in the *Baseline* projections to 0.2 Mt. Although microplastic leakage is also curbed, it is only reduced by 9% compared to *Baseline* projections. But even with such ambitious global policy measures, however, in the interim, stocks of plastics will continue to accumulate in the aquatic environment, reaching 300 Mt in 2060, which is slightly more than double the 2019 level. This protracted impact on aquatic environments highlights the need for urgent and ambitious policy measures.

The *Global Ambition* policy package also contributes to climate goals, by reducing plastics lifecycle GHG emissions by 2.1 gigatonnes of CO_2 equivalent (Gt CO_2e) in 2060 – a 50% reduction from the *Baseline*. This underlines the positive impact of circular policies on decreasing the GHG emissions of the plastics lifecycle. The important synergies between climate and plastics policies are explored further in Box 1.2.

Figure 1.10. Policies targeting different steps of the plastics lifecycle all contribute to reducing plastic leakage to the environment

Quantities of plastics in million tonnes (Mt)

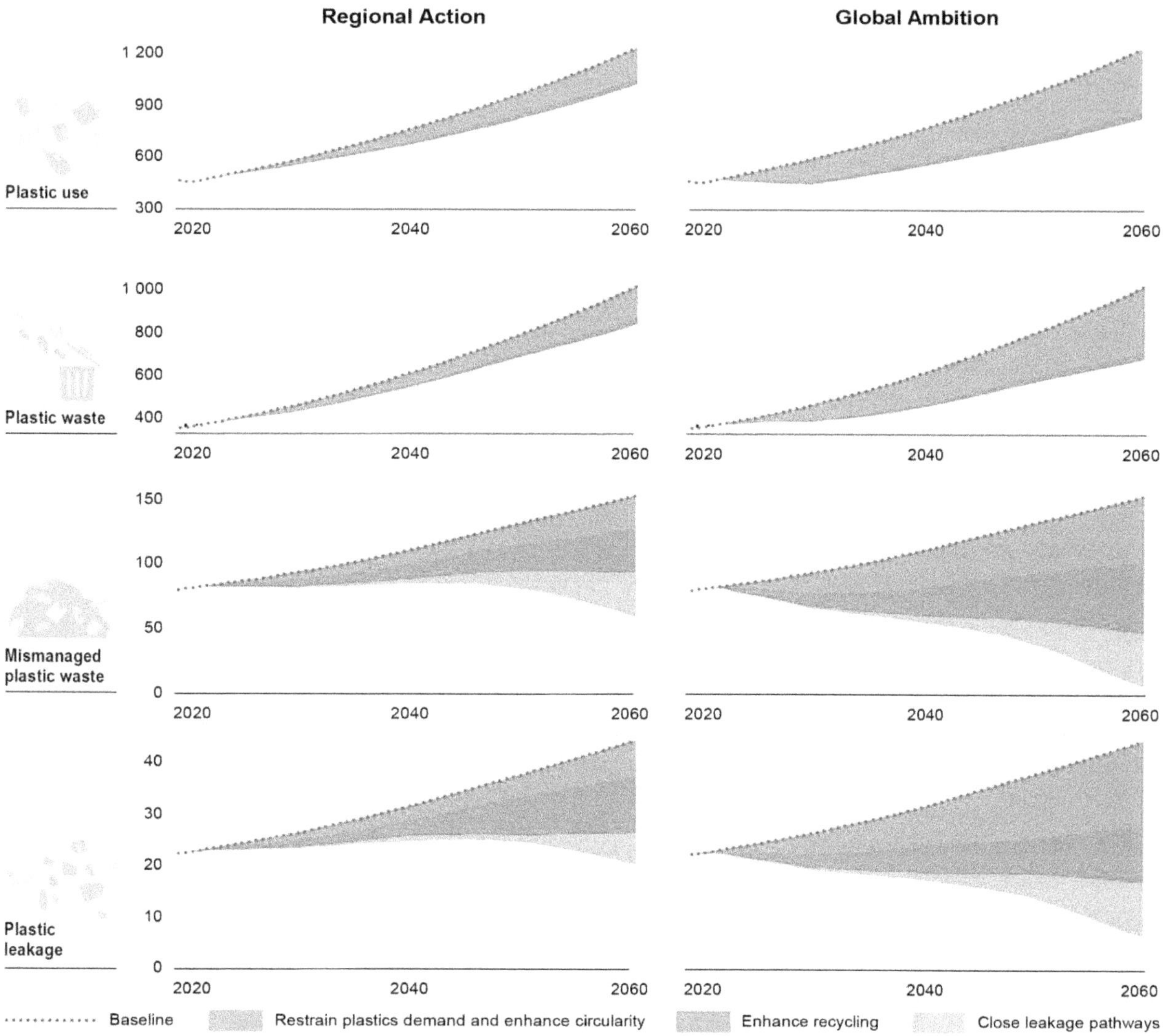

Source: OECD ENV-Linkages model.

StatLink https://stat.link/ykor41

Box 1.2. How does climate mitigation interact with policies to reduce plastics leakage?

The plastics lifecycle is fundamentally linked to climate change. This is because plastics are largely derived from fossil fuels, while plastics production and waste management lead to greenhouse gas (GHG) emissions. Therefore, there are important synergies which policymakers can exploit by tapping into the complementarity of plastics and climate policies.

To examine these interlinkages more closely, a third policy scenario – *Climate Mitigation* – was developed as part of this report. It models the impact of a policy package composed of two instruments: carbon pricing and a structural transformation of the power sector. In this package, the world average carbon price progressively rises to USD 69 in 2060 (USD 155 in the OECD, USD 42 in non-OECD countries). Meanwhile, the transformation of the power sector entails a reduction of the share of fossil-based power generation from 69% in 2019 to 15% in 2060 (compared to 62% in the *Baseline*). This scenario projects that in 2060, global GHG emissions will be reduced by around one-third compared to the *Baseline*, corresponding to a level of global gross emissions of 63 gigatonnes of carbon dioxide equivalent (Gt CO_2e) in 2060.

If the *Global Ambition* policy package is combined with the *Climate Mitigation* scenario, GHG emissions from the plastics lifecycle decrease by two-thirds compared to the *Baseline*, by 2.8 Gt CO_2e. The reduction is achieved by reducing plastics use, shifting energy use in plastics-related activities (production and conversion, and to a lesser extent end-of-life) to less carbon-intensive sources and by reducing indirect GHG emissions from electricity generation.

The combined package not only reduces greenhouse gas emissions from the plastics lifecycle, but also increases even further the share of secondary plastics in total plastics use achieved in the *Global Ambition* scenario: both primary and secondary plastics use decrease, but primary plastics use decreases more than secondary because they are more energy intensive. Therefore, while the combined package does not reduce demand for plastics any further, it does make the plastics lifecycle more circular.

By identifying the synergies that exist in climate and plastics policies, countries would be able to get closer to achieving their climate objectives, while also benefitting from the reduced environmental impacts of plastics. However, there may be conflicts which need careful consideration, such as the potential increase in greenhouse gas emissions through greater use of recycling technologies.

1.5.5. The economic costs of both policy packages are relatively modest, but their implementation will require mechanisms for financial support

Global GDP would be only 0.3% lower than the *Baseline* in 2060 if the *Regional Action* policy package were implemented (Figure 1.11), showing that this policy package can be achieved at a relatively moderate cost to the economy. However, there are important regional differences, with costs ranging from less than 0.1% in China to 1.1% in Sub-Saharan Africa and 1.8% in non-OECD European Union countries.

The *Global Ambition* policy package is estimated to reduce global GDP by less than 1% below the *Baseline*, again showing the rather limited economic cost of even highly ambitious policy action. Macroeconomic costs remain small for OECD EU countries and China, although they are larger for non-OECD EU countries and Africa. Differences in macroeconomic costs are mainly explained by differences in the plastics-intensity of production, as well as shifts in comparative advantages across regions. Comparative advantages emerge as policies that foster eco-design improve efficiency and shift economic activity away from less productive sectors.

Figure 1.11. The costs of both regional and globally coordinated action are less than 1% of global GDP

Percentage change in GDP from Baseline

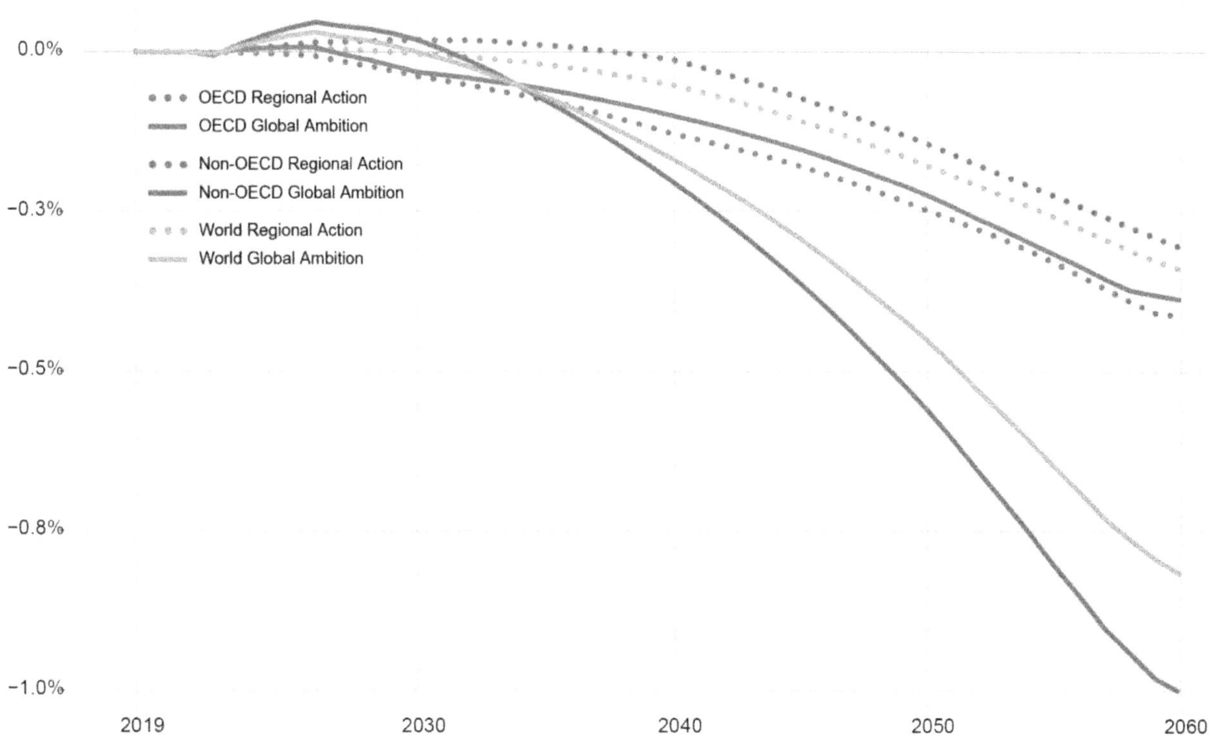

Source: OECD ENV-Linkages model.

StatLink https://stat.link/aqp3g2

A substantial share of the costs of these policies is related to the investment required in waste management systems.[12] In the *Regional Action* policy package investments into waste management systems would amount to USD 320 billion globally. In OECD countries the investment would mainly be in improvements of recycling capacities, while non-OECD countries would need to invest in both recycling and preventing mismanaged waste. Developing economies face higher costs than the global average. Official development assistance (ODA) is already used to support action to address plastics leakage in developing countries, but the financial flows are only a fraction of what is needed and additional sources of funding will be required. Further support will be needed in the form of sharing best practices and existing technologies to support rapidly developing countries in improving their waste management systems.

Meanwhile, despite the drastic reduction in leakage to nearly zero, even in the *Global Ambition* policy package, the stocks of plastics already leaked into the environment would still need to be cleaned up. The environmental benefits of clean-up activities are clear, and the damage avoided could be substantial, including in monetary terms. At the same time, it emerges clearly that pollution prevention makes more economic sense than cleaning up afterwards: having to clean up the full stock of almost 500 Mt plastics in the aquatic environment in 2060 in the *Baseline* scenario, at costs of more than USD 1 000 per tonne, would be much more costly than eliminating leakage via improved waste management. Overall, more ambitious policies that prevent plastic leakage are much more cost-effective than allowing plastics to leak to the environment; however, cleaning up is still more cost-effective than allowing plastics to pollute natural environments.

References

Borrelle, S. et al. (2020), "Predicted growth in plastic waste exceeds efforts to mitigate plastic pollution", *Science*, Vol. 369/6510, pp. 1515-1518, https://doi.org/10.1126/science.aba3656. [9]

Britz, W. and D. van der Mensbrugghe (2018), "CGEBox: A Flexible, Modular and Extendable Framework for CGE Analysis in GAMS", *J Glob Econ Anal*, Vol. 3/2, pp. 106-177. [15]

Chateau, J., R. Dellink and E. Lanzi (2014), "An Overview of the OECD ENV-Linkages Model: Version 3", *OECD Environment Working Papers*, No. 65, OECD Publishing, Paris, https://doi.org/10.1787/5jz2qck2b2vd-en. [2]

Cottom, J. et al. (2022), "Spatio-temporal quantification of plastic pollution origins and transportation (SPOT)" University of Leeds, UK, https://plasticpollution.leeds.ac.uk/toolkits/spot/. [5]

Ellen Macarthur Foundation (2017), *The New Plastics Economy:Rethinking The Future Of Plastics & Catalysing Action*. [10]

Evangeliou, N. et al. (2020), "Atmospheric transport is a major pathway of microplastics to remote regions", *Nature Communications*, Vol. 11/1, https://doi.org/10.1038/s41467-020-17201-9. [16]

Geyer, R., J. Jambeck and K. Law (2017), "Production, use, and fate of all plastics ever made", *Science Advances*, Vol. 3/7, p. e1700782, https://doi.org/10.1126/sciadv.1700782. [3]

Gómez-Sanabria, A. et al. (2018), "Carbon in global waste and wastewater flows – its potential as energy source under alternative future waste management regimes", *Advances in Geosciences*, Vol. 45, pp. 105-113, https://doi.org/10.5194/adgeo-45-105-2018. [7]

Jambeck, J. et al. (2015), "Plastic waste inputs from land into the ocean", *Science*, Vol. 347/6223, pp. 768-771, https://doi.org/10.1126/science.1260352. [6]

Lau, W. et al. (2020), "Evaluating scenarios toward zero plastic pollution", *Science*, Vol. 369/6510, pp. 1455-1461, https://doi.org/10.1126/science.aba9475. [12]

Lebreton, L. and A. Andrady (2019), "Future scenarios of global plastic waste generation and disposal", *Palgrave Communications*, Vol. 5/1, p. 6, https://doi.org/10.1057/s41599-018-0212-7. [11]

Lebreton, L., M. Egger and B. Slat (2019), "A global mass budget for positively buoyant macroplastic debris in the ocean", *Scientific Reports*, Vol. 9/1, p. 12922, https://doi.org/10.1038/s41598-019-49413-5. [14]

Lebreton, L. et al. (2017), "River plastic emissions to the world's oceans", *Nature Communications*, Vol. 8/1, https://doi.org/10.1038/ncomms15611. [13]

OECD (2022), *Global Plastics Outlook: Economic Drivers, Environmental Impacts and Policy Options*, OECD Publishing, Paris, https://doi.org/10.1787/de747aef-en. [1]

Ryberg, M. et al. (2019), "Global environmental losses of plastics across their value chains", *Resources, Conservation and Recycling*, Vol. 151, p. 104459, https://doi.org/10.1016/j.resconrec.2019.104459. [4]

SystemIQ and the Pew Charitable Trust (2020), *Breaking the Plastic Wave: A Comprehensive Assessment of Pathways Towards Stopping Ocean Plastic Pollution*, https://www.systemiq.earth/breakingtheplasticwave/. [8]

Notes

[1] Circularity is calculated as the ratio between secondary plastics (29 Mt) and plastic waste (353 Mt) in 2019, which was 8% in 2019.

[2] Plastic leakage refers to plastics that enter terrestrial and aquatic environments; whereas pollution is broader and refers to all emissions and risks resulting from plastics production, use, waste management and leakage.

[3] Recognisable plastic items, such as littered plastic bottles and packaging. In this report, the use of the term encompasses plastics above 5 mm in diameter.

[4] Solid synthetic polymers smaller than 5 mm in diameter.

[5] Including Geyer, Jambeck and Law (2017[3]), Jambeck et al. (2015[6]), Ryberg et al. (2019[4]), Gómez-Sanabria et al. (2018[7]), Ellen Macarthur Foundation (2017[10]), SystemIQ and the Pew Charitable Trust (2020[8]), Borrelle et al. (2020[9]), Lebreton and Andrady (2019[11]).

[6] Collaborators include: 1) experts from the Technical University of Denmark (DTU) who led the research underlying a study by Ryberg et al. (2019[4]); 2) experts from the University of Leeds who contributed to Lau et al. (2020[12]); 3) Laurent Lebreton, who wrote various research papers on plastic waste generation and leakage (Lebreton et al., 2017[13]; Lebreton, Egger and Slat, 2019[14]; Lebreton and Andrady, 2019[11]), and contributed to the leakage estimations in Borrelle et al. (2020[9]); and 4) Nikolaos Evangeliou from the Norwegian Institute for Air Research (NILU), who developed the Evangeliou et al. (2020[16]) article.

[7] GHG emissions from the plastics lifecycle are calculated in ENV-Linkages. The analysis of biobased plastics is based on the CGE-Box model (Britz and van der Mensbrugghe, 2018[15]). The LCA analysis is based on a methodology developed by the Sustainable Systems Engineering Group of Ghent University. See Annex A for additional information on these methodologies.

[8] The *Baseline* scenario reflects expected trends to 2060 in several key socio-economic variables, including demographic, urbanisation and globalisation trends, and also includes the effects of government policies implemented until 2019 on these projected trends. Policies that were still under discussion in 2022 are excluded from the *Baseline* scenarios presented in this report.

[9] Primary (or virgin) plastics are manufactured from fossil-based (e.g. crude oil) or biobased (e.g. corn, sugarcane, wheat) feedstock that has never been used or processed before.

[10] This refers to the three non-OECD Asian regions (China, India and Other non-OECD Asia), i.e. Asia, excluding Japan and Korea.

[11] It is important to note that due to the lack of robust research on the share of mismanaged waste that is lost to the environment, there are large uncertainties in these estimates (uncertainty ranges are presented in brackets).

[12] Investment is in itself not a cost as it generates value added and contributes to GDP. But less productive investment in waste management at the expense of other expenditures forces shifts in the economy towards less productive activities and these shifts are on balance costly.

Part I
Baseline scenario

2 Economic projections to 2060

There is a strong link between socio-economic development and materials use, including plastics, as materials are an important input for all production processes. This chapter presents the projections to 2060 for socio-economic trends underlying the Baseline scenario, including the evolution in regional populations, gross domestic product, the structure of the economy and production technologies. It also outlines key sources of uncertainty in the economic projections, modelling the impact of slower or faster recovery from the COVID-19 pandemic on economic and sectoral growth.

Key messages

- By 2060 in the *Baseline* scenario, the global population is projected to reach more than 10 billion people. Population is projected to increase more slowly than in the past: at an annual rate of 0.7% on average between 2019 and 2060, compared to 1.8% over the period 1980-2019. Despite a slow population growth rate in most regions, Sub-Saharan Africa will see its population grow at an annual rate of over 3%.
- Gross domestic product (GDP) and living standards are projected to increase gradually in all countries. The GDP of most non-OECD countries is projected to grow faster than OECD countries, gradually converging with current OECD levels. The global economy will thus see major shifts across regions, with non-OECD Asian countries representing an increasingly large share of global economic output. Together, the People's Republic of China (hereafter 'China'), India and other non-OECD Asian countries will contribute almost half of global GDP in 2060.
- The COVID-19 pandemic and government response measures caused a significant contraction of global gross domestic product (GDP) in 2020. Global GDP growth is projected to return to pre-COVID levels before the end of the decade, but GDP levels are likely to remain around 1-2% below the pre-COVID projection, depending on the speed of recovery.
- The increased use of services in manufacturing and consumption ("servitisation") will mean that the plastics sector will grow more slowly than overall economic activity. Plastics production represented 1.3% of the global economy in 2019, and this share is projected to slightly decline to 1.2% by 2060.
- Changes in production technologies lead to a more efficient use of production inputs, including plastics. For instance, the inputs of plastics in the production of manufacturing products are projected to decline from 3% in 2019 to 2% in 2060 on average in both OECD and non-OECD countries.
- This *Baseline* scenario reflects one possible pathway for economic growth, but is subject to uncertainty.

2.1. The global population is projected to increase to 10 billion by 2060, with the strongest growth in Sub-Saharan Africa

World population has been increasing in recent decades and is projected to continue to increase in the coming decades. The *Baseline* scenario projects global population to reach more than 10 billion people by 2060 (Figure 2.1), drawing on the "medium scenario" of the World Population Prospects (UN, 2017[1]) and the Eurostat projections for European countries (Eurostat, 2018[2]). The pace of population growth is projected to slow between 2019 and 2060, in contrast with the strong growth seen over the past 40 years. Over the next four decades (between 2019 and 2060), global population is projected to grow by 0.7% per year on average, compared to the annual growth rate of 1.4% over the period 1980-2019.

This slowdown in population growth applies to all countries. However, population growth trends will vary across countries. Some countries are projected to even face negative growth (many European countries, Japan, Korea, and China). At the other extreme, Sub-Saharan Africa (Other Africa in Figure 2.1) is projected to experience high population growth (over 3% per year over 2019-2060). As a result, more than 26% of world population in 2060 is projected to be in Sub-Saharan Africa, compared to 15% in 2019. In contrast, the OECD share shrinks from 18% in 2019 to 15% in 2060 (Figure 2.1).

Figure 2.1. The world population is projected to keep growing but at a slower pace

Billion people

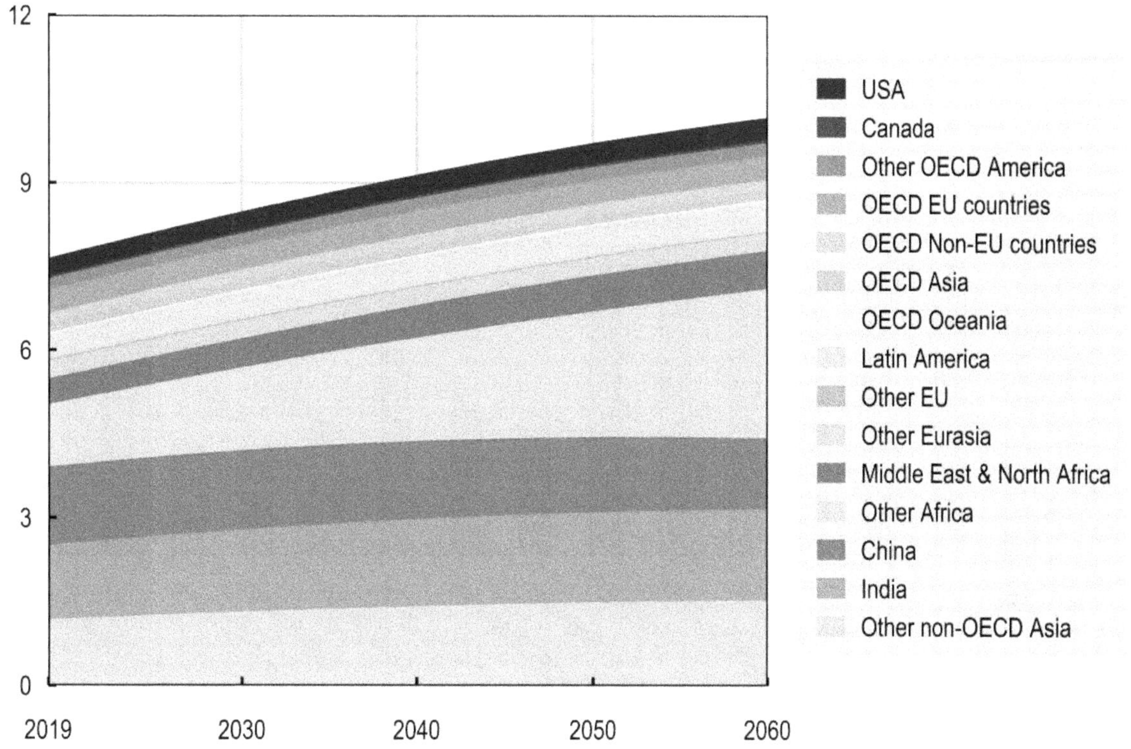

Source: Authors' calculations based on (UN, 2017[1]), *The World Population Prospects: 2017 Revision.*

StatLink https://stat.link/hojd9e

2.2. The engines of economic growth will gradually shift from China to other emerging economies in Asia and Africa

In the coming decades, the global population is not only projected to increase, but to also become wealthier on average. Living standards (measured as GDP per capita) are projected to increase over the entire period, with most countries gradually converging towards OECD levels (Figure 2.2).[1] Global income per capita is projected to reach the OECD 2019 levels by 2060 (USD 41 000). Despite the slower growth, average income in OECD countries more than doubles, from USD 41 000 in 2019 to USD 86 000 in 2060.

The improvements in living standards over the 2019-2060 period (blue bars in Figure 2.2) are projected to be greatest for emerging countries with current low levels of per-capita GDP, and especially for India. Countries that are fossil-fuel exporters, such as those in the Middle East and North Africa region and the "Eurasia" group, which includes the Russian Federation (hereafter 'Russia'), are projected to grow less rapidly than the average non-OECD country, as fossil fuel revenues do not grow as rapidly as other contributing factors to GDP. In contrast, European countries that have recently joined the European Union (EU), especially those labelled as "Other EU" (including for instance Romania and Bulgaria), are projected to grow rapidly. Living standards in developing economies will still be far from those of OECD countries at the end of the time horizon, despite the convergence process, but they will come close to 2019 levels, with the exception of Sub-Saharan Africa ("Other Africa"; see Table A A.2 in Annex A for a list of the regions used in ENV-Linkages).

Figure 2.2. Living standards are projected to increase, especially in lower-income regions

Real GDP per capita in USD trillion (2014 PPP) per person, listed by GDP per capita in 2019, *Baseline* scenario

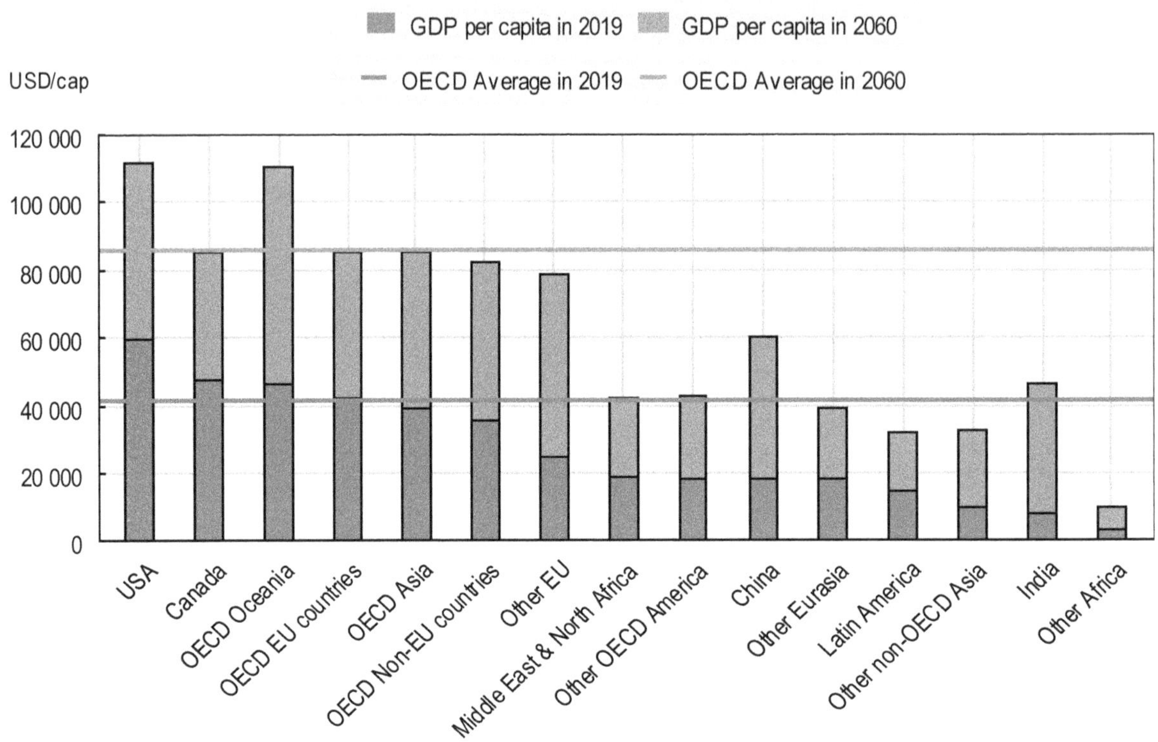

Note: GDP per capita is presented in USD, using 2014 purchasing power parity (PPP).
Source: ENV-Growth model (OECD Environment Directorate) and OECD Economics Department (Guillemette and Turner, 2018[3]), *The Long View: Scenarios for the World Economy to 2060*, https://doi.org/10.1787/b4f4e03e-en.

StatLink https://stat.link/bsdinu

GDP increases in all regions (Figure 2.3), even in countries where population is declining, since the growth of GDP per capita has a larger impact than population changes. Global GDP is projected to more than triple between 2019 and 2060, from USD 131 trillion to USD 418 trillion.

In 2020, the COVID-19 pandemic caused a significant contraction in global GDP, with the annual global GDP growth rate dropping from around +4% in 2019 to -4% in 2020 (Dellink et al., 2021[4]). Increased unemployment, reduced labour productivity, a collapse in demand for certain commodities and higher trade costs all depressed economic activity. In 2021, many countries observe a rebound effect. In the longer run, while GDP growth is projected to return to the levels expected before the COVID pandemic, GDP levels are not.[2]

The *Baseline* scenario projects the global GDP growth rate to slow down and stabilise at about 2.5% after 2030. While India and large parts of Sub-Saharan Africa are projected to record high growth rates and then become important drivers of world growth in the 2019-2040 period, the projected slowdown of the Chinese economy after 2025 dominates. From around 2040, the most dynamic regions are projected to be emerging economies in Asia (India and Other non-OECD Asia in Figure 2.3).

Figure 2.3. Global GDP is projected to grow more slowly, driven by emerging economies

Real GDP by aggregate region in trillion USD (2014 PPP), *Baseline* scenario

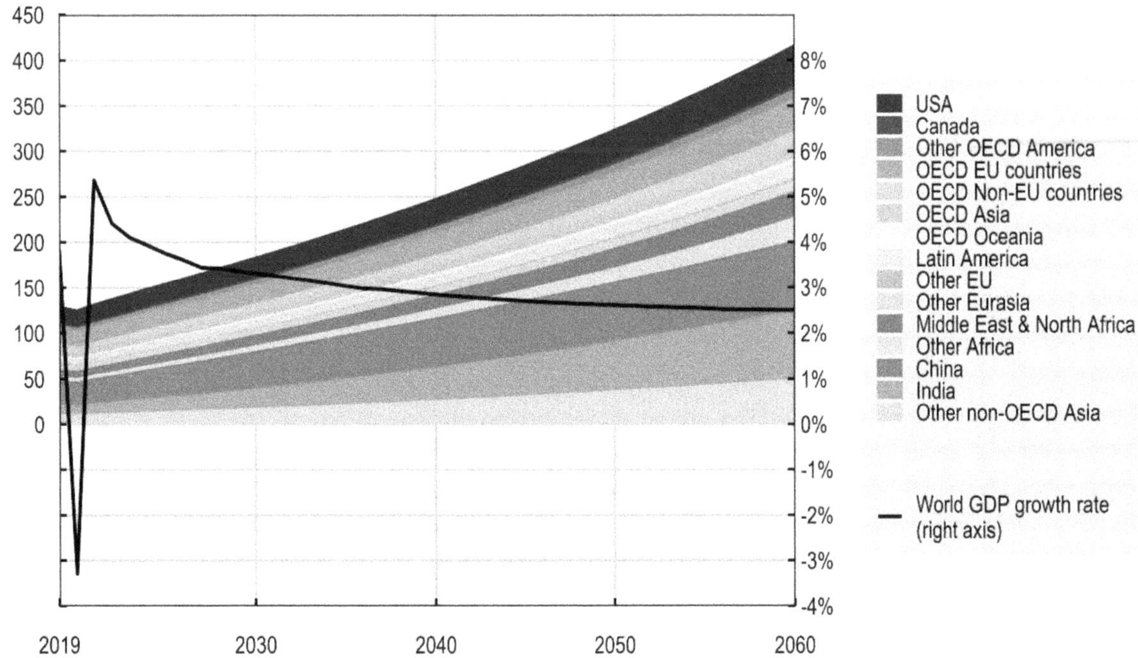

Source: OECD ENV-Linkages model; based on short-term forecasts by OECD Economics Department (OECD, 2020[5]) and International Monetary Fund (IMF, 2020[6]).

StatLink https://stat.link/n0x8at

The share of OECD countries in global GDP in 2060 is projected to fall to 31% from 44% in 2019 (Figure 2.4), since growth rates in non-OECD countries are higher. The importance of the non-OECD Asian countries will increase at the global level (increasing from 37% in 2019 to 48% in 2060). While China will maintain its importance (with a global share of GDP decreasing from 20% in 2019 to 18% in 2060), India and some fast-growing economies in the “Other non-OECD Asia” region - specifically Indonesia and the Philippines - will represent a much larger share of the global economy. In particular, the strong economic growth in India will result in its share of global GDP increasing from 8% in 2019 to 18% in 2060. Within other regions, some countries will become increasingly important in driving economic growth: Egypt in the Middle East & North Africa region, Nigeria in Sub-Saharan Africa (Other Africa) and Peru in Latin America.

Figure 2.4. The regional distribution of GDP will change in the following decades

Share of GDP by region in 2019 and 2060, represented by their area, *Baseline* scenario

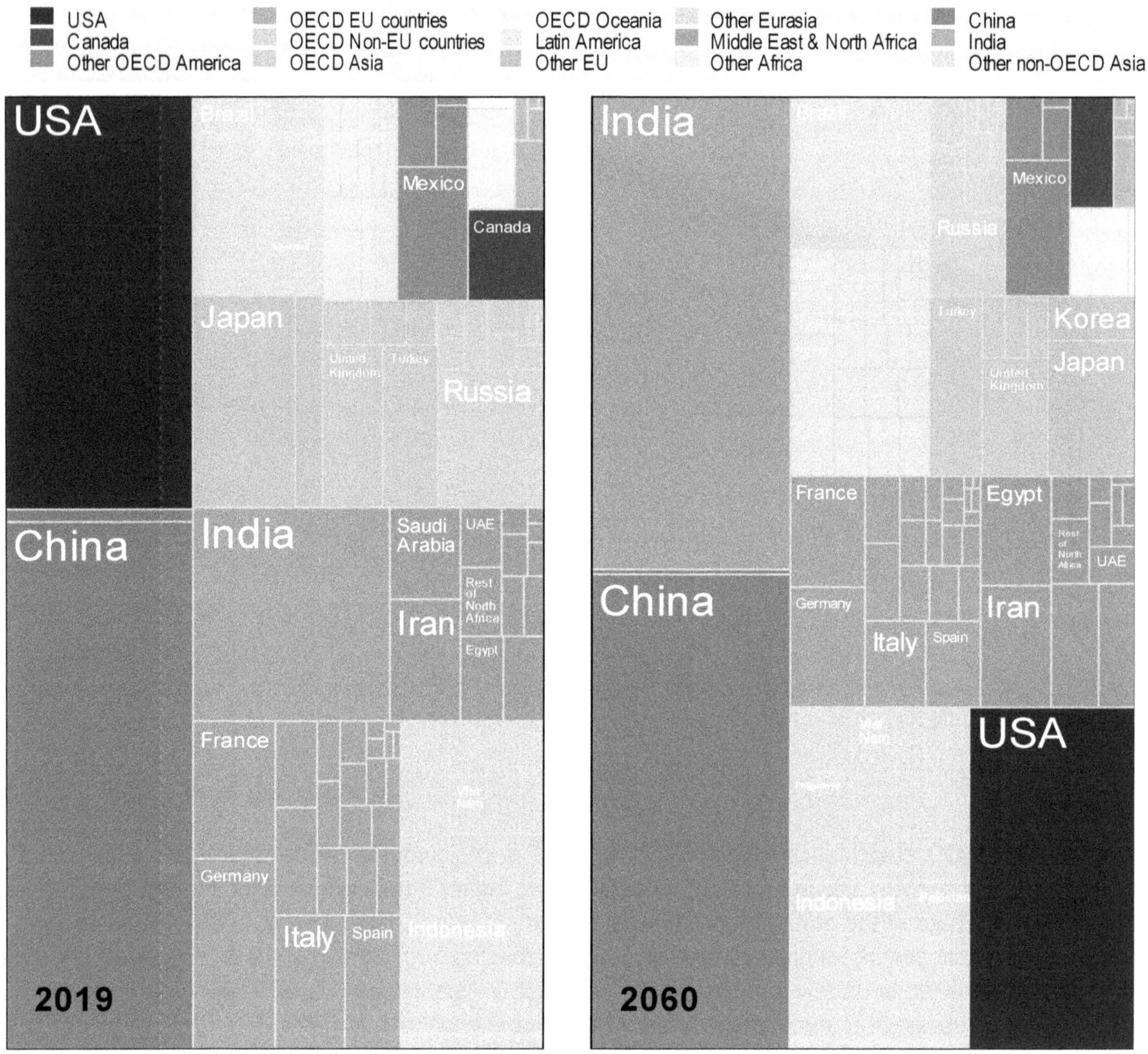

Source: OECD ENV-Linkages model; based on short-term forecasts by OECD Economics Department (OECD, 2020[5]) and International Monetary Fund (IMF, 2020[6]).

StatLink https://stat.link/cdzfox

2.2.1. *Many uncertainties could affect economic projections*

Projecting economic growth is subject to uncertainties. The model is based on long-term projections of key socio-economic drivers, all of which are uncertain. Most notably, future population growth and the speed of convergence across countries can affect long-run economic projections (Box 2.1). Furthermore, while the *Baseline* scenario takes into account the effects of the COVID pandemic, the longer-term effects are still largely unknown. For instance, a slower recovery would imply slower growth in the long-run (Dellink et al., 2021[4]), as explored in Box 2.2. Finally, other uncertain events that can affect regional and global growth are difficult to include in the Baseline. For instance, the recent war in Ukraine will certainly affect regional and global growth (Box 2.3). Nevertheless, due to the high uncertainty of the current situation and in its developments in the coming years, the Ukraine war is not included in the ENV-Linkages economic baseline.

Box 2.1. Uncertainties in projections need to be kept in mind

Projections are not predictions. Models work with a stylised version of reality that omits a long list of factors that can influence future economic and environmental outcomes, such as natural disasters, domestic conflicts and international wars. Several uncertainties need to be kept in mind when evaluating the projections presented in this report. First, the *Baseline* scenario is carefully calibrated to reflect plausible long-term developments, but represents only one possible future pathway. One key source of uncertainty is the development of the socio-economic projections. As highlighted in OECD (2019[7]), changes in population and in the speed of income convergence across countries affect economic projections substantially (Figure 2.5).

Figure 2.5. GDP projections are subject to uncertainty

World real GDP in USD trillion (2011 PPP)

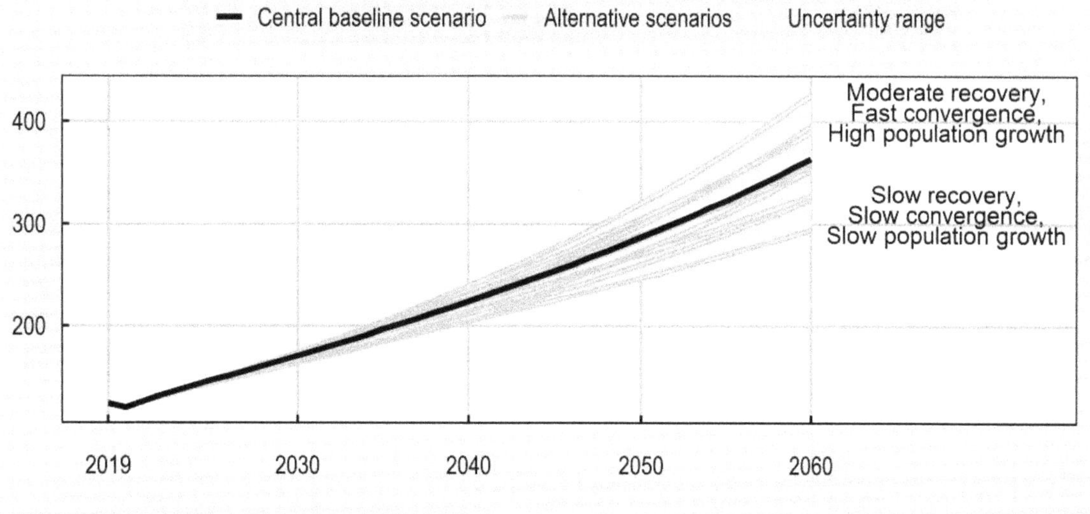

Note: This sensitivity analysis, updated from OECD (2019[7]), explores different assumptions about (i) the recovery from the COVID-19 pandemic, (ii) the speed of income convergence across countries, and (iii) population growth, considering the low and high population scenarios from the UN Population Prospects (2017[1]).
Source: OECD ENV-Linkages model.

StatLink https://stat.link/ds9zym

Box 2.2. What if the global economy recovers more slowly from the pandemic?

The speed at which the global economy will recover from the COVID-19 pandemic is highly uncertain. Therefore, the impacts of the pandemic in the medium term cannot be quantified accurately. The *Slow recovery"* scenario explores the implications of a slower recovery from the pandemic,[1] showing how GDP rebounds more slowly (Panel A in Figure 2.6). By 2040, the global economy is even further below pre-COVID projections compared to the main *Baseline* scenario (which includes COVID-19 impacts). Because the shocks simulated in the *Slow recovery* scenario are assumed to fade at half the speed of the *Baseline* scenario, the effect on economic activity lasts longer and remains twice as strong at least the coming two decades. There are also important differences between regions; the slower recovery is especially detrimental to the Asian economies, not least India (Panel B in Figure 2.6). Box 2.4 explores how a slower recovery might affect plastics production trends.

Figure 2.6. A slower recovery from COVID-19 implies lower GDP levels in the long-run than in the *Baseline* scenario

Deviations from the *pre-COVID* reference projection

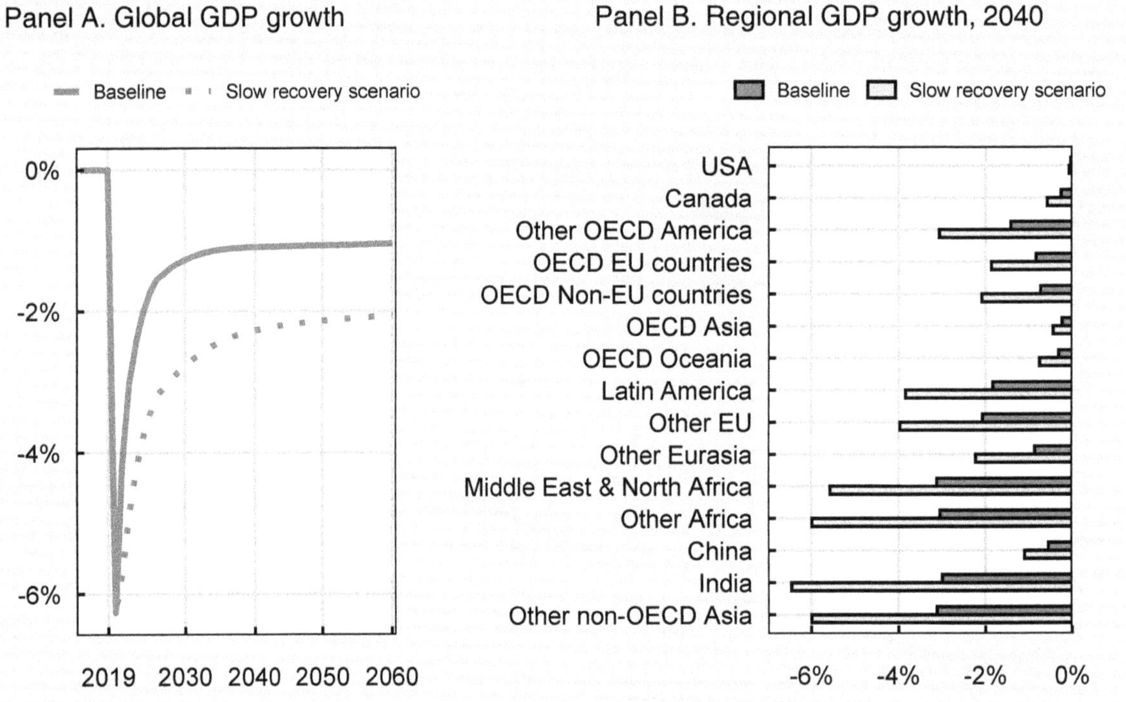

Note: The impacts of these shocks are assessed by comparing the *Baseline* projection with a pre-pandemic projection published in the Global Material Resources Outlook (OECD, 2019[7]).
Source: OECD ENV-Linkages model and Dellink et al. (2021[4]), "The long-term implications of the Covid-19 pandemic and recovery measures on environmental pressures: A quantitative exploration", https://doi.org/10.1787/123dfd4f-en.

StatLink https://stat.link/79j5xc

Box 2.3. The current war in Ukraine will affect economic growth at the global level

At the time of writing (April 2022) the conflict that started at the end of February 2022 in Ukraine is still ongoing. . In March 2022, the OECD Economic Department released an Interim Economic Outlook Report on *Economic and Social Impacts and Policy Implications of the War in Ukraine* (OECD, 2022[8]). This report highlights that the economic consequences will depend on the duration of the conflict and policy responses to the war, such as policy to ensure stable financial market conditions, fiscal support and mitigating the impact of energy price increases on consumers. The war will result in a drag on global growth and significant inflationary pressures.

The report estimates that global GDP growth could be reduced by 1% in the first year and global consumer price inflation could reach 2.5% in the same timeframe, alongside a deep recession in Russia. These estimates are based on the assumption that the commodity and financial market shocks seen in the first two weeks of the conflict remain for at least one year (OECD, 2022[8]).

The war and accompanying sanctions have caused disruptions on a global level given financial and business linkages. The rouble has decreased sharply, while the Central Bank of Russia's interest rate has risen by 10.5 percentage points to 20%. Currency depreciations and risk premia are also occurring in emerging economies, and central and eastern European economies, particularly those with strong business ties to Russia before the conflict.

European economies, particularly those that share a border with Russia or Ukraine are hardest hit. This relates to the gas price rises in Europe and the business and energy ties with Russia and neighbouring countries. Other regions may be affected by the impact of weaker global demand and changes in household income and spending as a result of higher prices. For emerging-market economies, higher food and energy prices push up inflation more than advanced economies.

Other factors and potential shocks may intensify the adverse effects of the conflict and affect economic growth further, such as a cessation of energy exports from Russia to the EU, and further sanctions and boycotts.

While Russia and Ukraine only account for 2% of global GDP, both countries play a large role as major suppliers in a number of commodity markets. Russia and Ukraine account for 30% of global wheat exports; 20% of corn, mineral fertiliser and natural gas exports; and 11% of oil. There are also many supply chains that rely on Russia and Ukraine for metal exports and inert gasses. Ukraine and Russia also play a role in reserves of uranium. Many of these commodities have already seen a price rise since the onset of the war.

A complete stop to wheat exports from Ukraine and Russia would result in shortages in emerging-market and developing economies. In many economies in the Middle East, 75% of the wheat imports come from Ukraine and Russia. Alongside this, the disruption in fertiliser manufacturing risks putting agricultural supply under stress.

Alongside these direct impacts of the conflict, there may also be some longer-lasting impacts, including pressures for higher defence spending, changes to the structure of the energy markets, potential fragmentation of payment systems and changes in the currency composition of foreign exchange reserves.

Source: (OECD, 2022[8]), *OECD Economic Outlook, Interim Report March 2022: Economic and Social Impacts and Policy Implications of the War in Ukraine*, https://dx.doi.org/10.1787/4181d61b-en.

2.3. Services will represent an increasing share of the global economy

The structure of the global economy is evolving as living standards transform preferences; as society adjusts to demographic changes, such as ageing and urbanisation; and also as the nature of production evolves, rely more on digital technologies and services. The main change in the structure of the economy projected for the coming decades is an increase in the demand for services, on the part of households, governments and firms.

As income per capita increases, households spend relatively less on necessary commodities (food and agricultural products) and on manufacturing goods, and more on services, for instance recreational and leisure activities, as well as health and education. Expenditures on durable and equipment goods are also projected to change. For example, they will shift away from paper, towards more electronics and vehicles.

Similar trends in the composition of governments and investment expenditures are also projected, including increasing shares of education and R&D expenditures. Ageing also induces a shift in demand towards more services, especially health and other long-term elderly care expenditures.

The changes in the structure of the economy are also driven by changes in intermediate demand, i.e. demand for produced goods and services by firms. The main structural transformation projected is for the services sectors, and especially the business services sector, to grow faster than the rest of the economy over the period 2019-2060 (Figure 2.7). This effect, referred to as "servitisation", is due to an intensification of services as inputs to all sectors, digitalisation, and the increase of research and development (R&D) expenses.

The structure of regional economies is also influenced by trade patterns, as supply and demand are linked via international trade. In particular, regions can specialise in the production of certain goods and services, while maintaining or expanding a broad availability of goods and services for households and governments.

As a consequence of the servitisation of the economy, the share of the plastics sector grows more slowly than the economy-wide average. However, since plastics are widely used in the economy, the demand for plastics still grows over time, responding to population and economic growth, but also to the fact that business services in particular use plastics, especially for packaging. As illustrated in Figure 2.7, plastics is a small sector of the global economy. Overall, plastics production represented 1.3% of the global economy in 2019, and is projected to slightly decline by 2060 (to 1.2%), with the global monetary value of plastics used in the economy increasing from USD 4.9 trillion in 2019 to USD 12 trillion in 2060. Box 2.4 explores the effects of the COVID-19 pandemic on sectoral production and what it might mean for plastics.

Figure 2.7. The demand for services is projected to increase more than the economy-wide average

Share of total sectoral demand in the economy, *Baseline* scenario

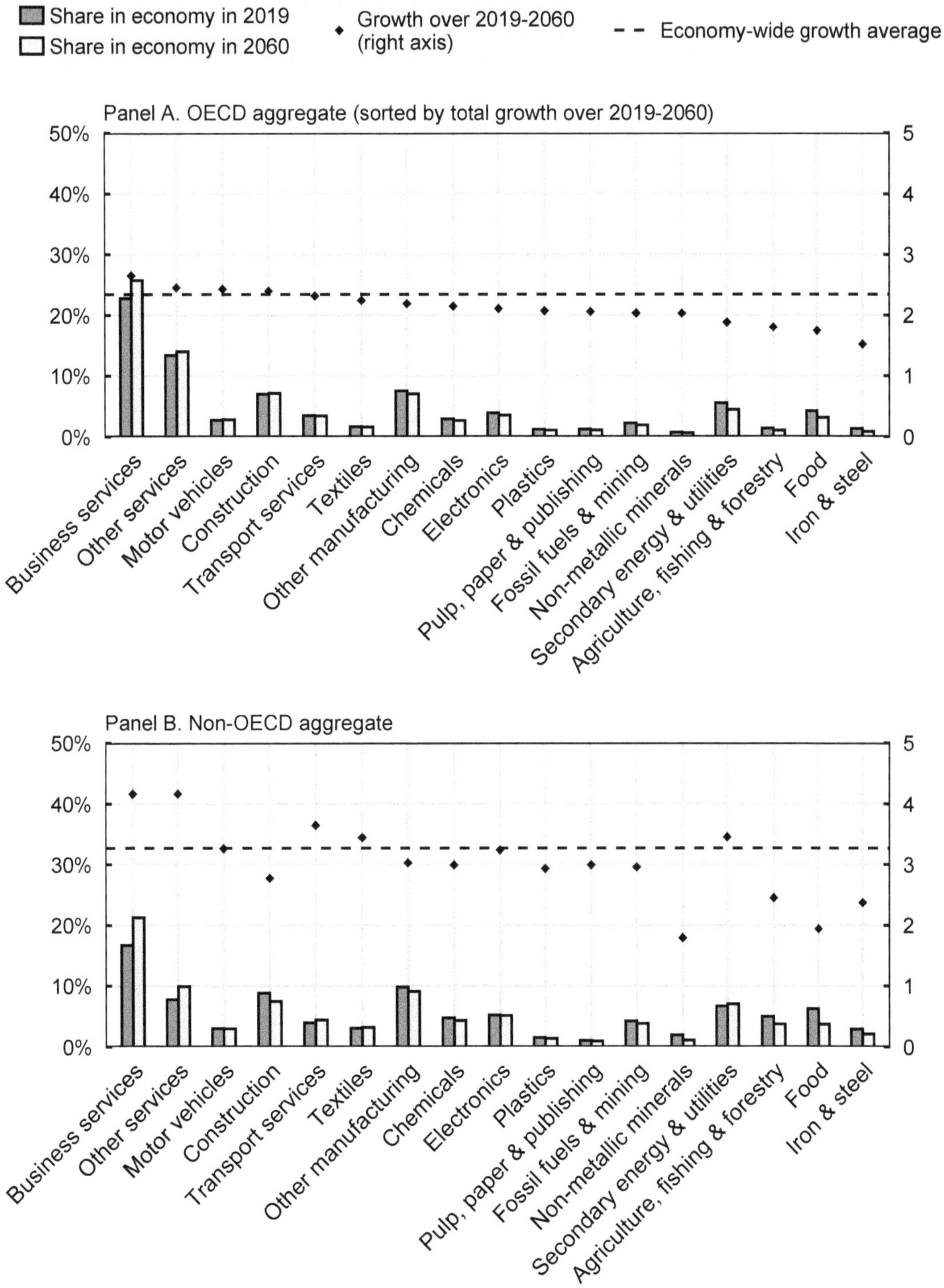

Note: sorted by 2019-2060 sectoral output growth in OECD countries.
Source: OECD ENV-Linkages model.

StatLink https://stat.link/g7f5hr

Box 2.4. How might a slow recovery from the COVID-19 pandemic affect sectoral trends, including plastics?

The COVID-19 pandemic and government response measures will affect the sectoral structure of the economy (Figure 2.8). In the *Baseline* scenario, in the short run (to 2025), most of the burden falls on relatively labour-intensive sectors, including accommodation and food services, transport and construction. In the longer run (to 2040), the effects of the pandemic are felt in capital-intensive sectors, as reduced investment has long-term effects on capital stock. A slower recovery would imply a slower phase-out of the shocks, affecting all sectors negatively. Consequently, although production levels would recover after 2021, they would remain below the pre-COVID *Baseline* projection. This also holds for chemicals and plastics production, the sectors which provide plastics in the modelling framework (see Annex A): while the *Baseline* scenario projects them to see a decrease in production in 2025 of 2.3% and 2.1% respectively, the *Slow recovery* scenario foresees much more persistent effects (although sectoral growth rates are still likely to gradually return to pre-COVID projected levels).

Figure 2.8. A slow recovery from COVID-19 is projected to dampen growth in the plastics and chemical sectors

Deviations from the pre-COVID reference projection, *Baseline* scenario

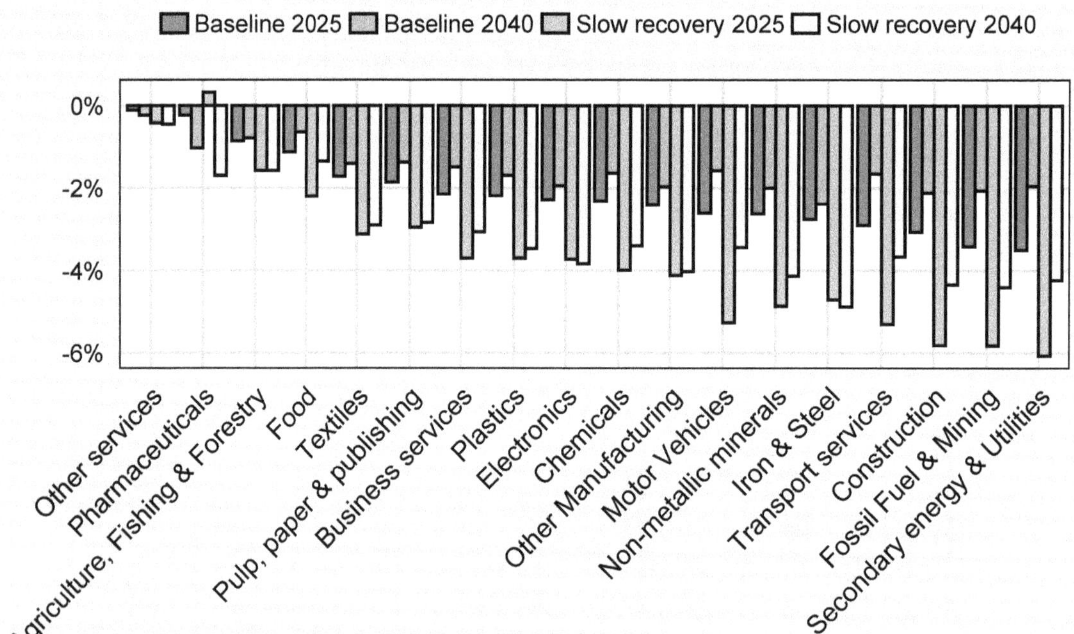

Note: The impacts of these shocks are assessed by comparing the *Baseline* projection with a projection made before the pandemic in the *Global Material Resources Outlook* (OECD, 2019[7]).
Source: OECD ENV-Linkages mode and Dellink et al. (2021[4]), "The long-term implications of the Covid-19 pandemic and recovery measures on environmental pressures: A quantitative exploration", https://doi.org/10.1787/123dfd4f-en.

StatLink https://stat.link/w7t59n

2.1. Production processes will rely on more efficient technologies

Technical progress is a main driver of economic growth. A wide range of evolutions influence technical progress, including continued efforts to optimise production processes, new business models, and the diffusion of best available techniques. The changes in production technologies also imply changes in the input structure (e.g. substitutions of production inputs, labour or capital). Labour efficiency changes over time, driven by country-specific progress in education levels, investment in innovation, and improvement in the quality of institutions and market regulations.

The production of manufacturing goods is an interesting example of these production changes. Table 2.1 illustrates changes over time in the cost structure of aggregate manufacturing goods production for OECD and non-OECD countries. Inputs of services increase, reflecting the servitisation phenomenon described in Section 2.3, while other inputs of goods and services decrease. Thanks to improvements in the efficiency of production technologies, the inputs of plastics in the production of manufacturing goods also decline (from 3% in 2019 to 2% in 2060 on average in both OECD and non-OECD countries).

Table 2.1. The more efficient production of manufacturing goods sees plastics inputs decline

Share of components in production costs of plastics goods

		OECD			Non-OECD		
		2019	2030	2060	2019	2030	2060
Price evolution (index 2017 = 1)		1	1	0.99	1	0.94	0.88
Input composition of production	Capital and resources	13%	13%	14%	10%	10%	10%
	Labour	17%	17%	16%	14%	14%	14%
	Agricultural inputs	4%	4%	4%	9%	9%	9%
	Industrial inputs	44%	34%	30%	51%	50%	50%
	Services inputs	19%	21%	26%	14%	15%	20%
	Plastics	3%	2%	2%	3%	3%	2%

Source: OECD ENV-Linkages model.

In both OECD and non-OECD countries, unit production costs are projected to decline, reflecting higher productivity resulting from technical progress. However, this effect is stronger in non-OECD countries, where a higher rate of convergence also leads to more marked changes in productivity over time. In all regions, production costs shift away from industrial inputs towards more services.

References

Dellink, R. et al. (2021), "The long-term implications of the Covid-19 pandemic and recovery measures on environmental pressures: A quantitative exploration", *OECD Environment Working Papers*, No. 176, OECD Publishing, Paris, https://doi.org/10.1787/123dfd4f-en. [4]

Eurostat (2018), "Population projections", *Eurostat (online data code: tps00002)*, http://ec.europa.eu/eurostat/web/products-datasets/-/tps00002 (accessed on July 2018). [2]

Guillemette, Y. and D. Turner (2018), "The Long View: Scenarios for the World Economy to 2060", *OECD Economic Policy Papers*, No. 22, OECD Publishing, Paris, https://doi.org/10.1787/b4f4e03e-en. [3]

IMF (2020), *World Economic Outlook, October 2020: A Long and Difficult Ascent*, International Monetary Fund, Washington, D.C., https://www.imf.org/en/Publications/WEO/Issues/2020/09/30/world-economic-outlook-october-2020 (accessed on 22 January 2021). [6]

OECD (2022), *OECD Economic Outlook, Interim Report March 2022: Economic and Social Impacts and Policy Implications of the War in Ukraine*, OECD Publishing, Paris, https://doi.org/10.1787/4181d61b-en. [8]

OECD (2020), *OECD Economic Outlook, Volume 2020 Issue 2*, OECD Publishing, Paris, https://doi.org/10.1787/39a88ab1-en. [5]

OECD (2019), *Global Material Resources Outlook to 2060: Economic Drivers and Environmental Consequences*, OECD Publishing, Paris, https://doi.org/10.1787/9789264307452-en. [7]

UN (2017), "World Population Prospects: key findings and advance tables", https://esa.un.org/unpd/wpp/publications/Files/WPP2017_KeyFindings.pdf (accessed on 18 May 2018). [1]

Notes

[1] The macroeconomic projections for OECD and G20 countries match the long-term macroeconomic projections of the OECD Economics Department (Guillemette and Turner, 2018[3]). For the remaining countries, projections are provided by the OECD ENV-Growth model (Annex A).

[2] The implications of the COVID-19 pandemic and government response measures are based on the assessment of a detailed set of shocks to employment, productivity, demand and trade (Dellink et al., 2021[4]), reflecting the macroeconomic implications of the pandemic quantified in the OECD Economic Outlook (2020[5]).

3 Plastics use projections to 2060

The use of plastics is strongly linked to economic growth and other socio-economic factors. This chapter explores these trends in the use of plastics to 2060 through the *Baseline* projection, which assumes that no new policies are implemented. It looks at how plastics use will evolve in the coming decades globally, as well as by region, economic application and polymer. It explores the main drivers of the increases in plastics use, such as rising incomes and populations, and technological change. The chapter also explores alternative baseline scenarios, including changes in oil prices and a slower-than-expected economic recovery from the COVID-19 pandemic.

Key messages

- In the *Baseline* scenario, global plastics use is projected to triple between 2019 and 2060, from 460 million tonnes (Mt) to 1 321 Mt, mainly driven by economic growth. In 2020, the COVID-19 pandemic and its response measures led to a decline in economic activity that put downward pressure on plastics use. By 2060, plastics use is projected to be lower than the pre-COVID projection by 2% or 4% depending on the speed of recovery from the pandemic.
- Thanks to changes in production technologies and, to a lesser extent, changes in the structure of the economy, the global average amount of plastic used to produce 1 USD of GDP is projected to fall by 16% between 2019 and 2060, implying a relative decoupling of plastics use and GDP. Nevertheless, plastics grows faster than other materials, with the exception of wood and timber.
- While plastics use is projected to increase in all regions, it grows fastest in Sub-Saharan Africa and Asia. Driven by strong economic and population growth, in Sub-Saharan Africa, plastics use in 2060 is projected to be over six times larger than in 2019. The strong economic growth in India also leads to a more than five-fold increase in plastics use. Furthermore, in India and other fast-growing Asian economies plastics use grows as output increases in sectors that rely on plastics use, such as the production of motor vehicles and business services. Despite this increase in non-OECD countries, plastics use per person remains higher in OECD countries.
- Plastics use is projected to increase for all applications, but the strongest growth is projected to occur in transportation, construction and packaging, which together make up 60% of total plastics use. Consequently, while plastics use increases for all polymers, the most substantial increases will be in polymers that are used for these applications, such as PET (polyethylene terephthalate) and PE (polyethylene), used for packaging.
- Current policies are insufficient to shift production substantially from primary to secondary or recycled plastics. Nonetheless, secondary plastics grow faster than primary plastics. Their share in overall plastics production is projected to double from 6% to 12% by 2060, indicating a limited but not insignificant increase in the circularity of the economy, even without new policies.

3.1. Plastics use is projected to almost triple by 2060

3.1.1. Economic growth is the main driver of plastics use

Global plastics use is projected to almost triple between 2019 and 2060 in the *Baseline* scenario, increasing from 460 million tonnes (Mt) to 1 231 Mt yearly (Figure 3.1). In this scenario, continued socioeconomic developments and economic growth, including recovery from the COVID-19 pandemic (Chapter 2), see emerging and developing economies catch up with higher income countries.

The projected increase in plastics use is mostly driven by economic growth: more economic activity means more use of plastics, in production and consumption. With global GDP more than tripling between 2019 and 2060, this effect is very strong. While rising income levels lead to a rapid increase in plastics use (to 898 Mt in 2060, shown by the green bar in Figure 3.1), other socio-economic factors also increase the use of plastics. Population growth also leads to an increase in plastics use (light grey bar; +76 Mt). However, its effect is limited because per-capita plastics use is relatively low in the regions with the fastest population growth, most notably Sub-Saharan Africa (see Section 3.2.2). This growth in plastics use will be moderated by changes in the structure of the economy, most notably a shift towards services (purple bar; -66 Mt), and the use of more efficient technologies in production processes (dark grey bar; -136 Mt), which lower the amount of plastics used per dollar of output of plastic-using commodities.

Figure 3.1. Plastics use is projected to almost triple, mostly driven by economic growth

Decomposition of the increase of plastics use between 2019 and 2060 in million tonnes (Mt), *Baseline* scenario

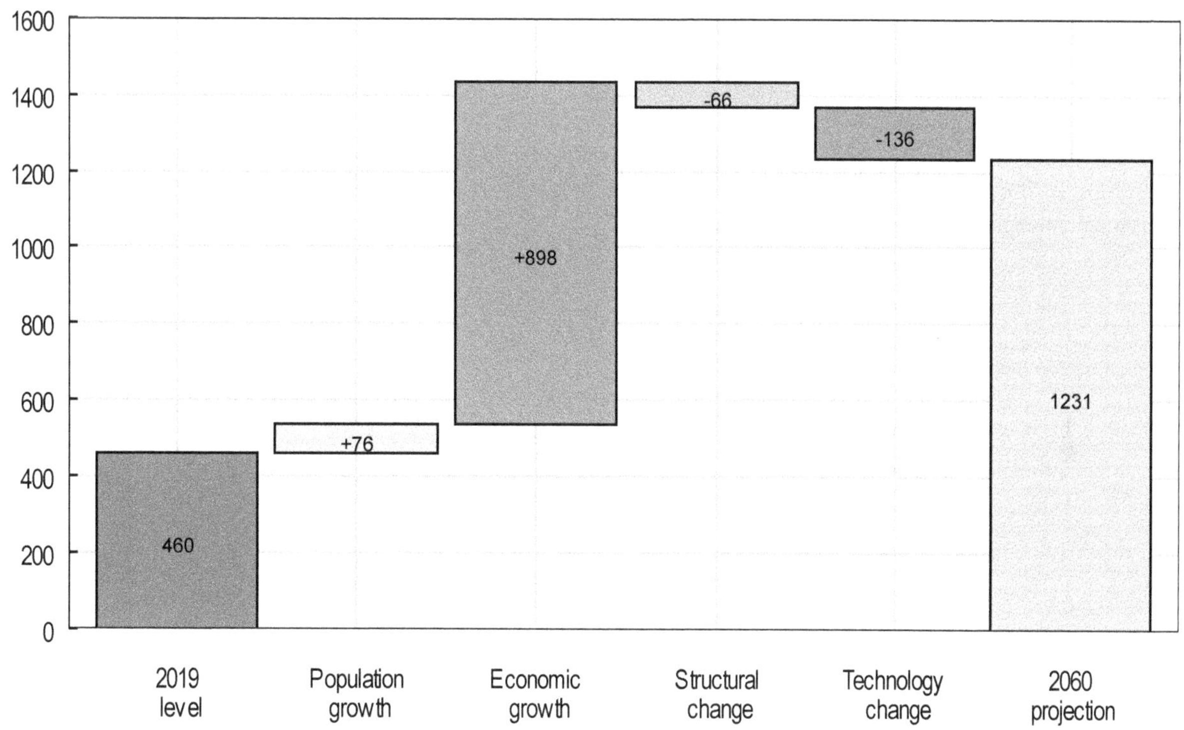

Notes:
Population growth represents a projection in which plastics use is assumed to grow at the same speed as population and in which the regional plastics use per capita stays constant at 2019 levels.
Economic growth represents a counterfactual projection in which plastics use is assumed to grow at the same speed as GDP and in which the regional plastics intensity (the amount of plastic per unit of output) stays constant at 2019 levels.
Structural change identifies the contribution of sectoral shifts to reducing global plastics use by differentiating sectoral growth rates.
Technology change identifies the contribution of technology improvements to reducing global plastics use by differentiating growth rates of plastic inputs to sectoral output. Technology change not only includes technological improvements but also a wider diffusion of existing technologies.
Source: OECD ENV-Linkages model.

StatLink https://stat.link/9ih64z

3.1.2. *Plastics use increases in all regions, but especially Sub-Saharan Africa and Asia*

While plastics use is projected to increase in all regions, the regional contribution to global plastics use has changed enormously over the last century and is projected to continue changing to 2060 (Figure 3.2).

In 1980, OECD countries together accounted for 87% of global plastics use, while Middle East and North Africa and Sub-Saharan Africa ("Other Africa")[1] together accounted for 5%; fast-growing emerging economies in Asia (The People's Republic of China, India and "Other Asia") accounted for only 1% of global plastics use. In 2019, OECD and non-OECD countries contributed almost equally to global plastics use, with the OECD accounting for 46%. China, India and other fast-growing emerging economies in Asia accounted for 35% of global plastics use (China accounting for 20% and India 6%).

Between 2019 and 2060, non-OECD countries are projected to triple their plastics use and, by 2060, will account for 64% of global plastics use. Non-OECD countries in Asia alone will account for 41% of global plastics use in 2060. China remains the region with the highest share in global plastics use, even though its share slightly declines to 17% as the growth in plastics use in the country is lower than the global average growth in plastics use. Plastics use in India is projected to be more than five times larger in 2060 compared to 2019, with its share in global plastics increasing to 13%. Similarly, plastics use increases substantially in other emerging economies in Asia (Other non-OECD Asia). The largest increase in plastics use takes place in Sub-Saharan Africa, where plastics use is more than six times larger in 2060 compared to 2019. Strong population growth in Sub-Saharan Africa, combined with significant income growth (see Chapter 2), contributes to the projected rapid increase of plastics use in that region.

While their share of global plastics use declines, plastics use is projected to double in OECD countries, as well as in the non-OECD regions not mentioned above, which include Latin American and Eurasian countries. In these regions, moderate growth in income and low population growth, combined with minor structural change, limits the growth of plastics use.

Figure 3.2. Plastics use will grow fastest in developing and emerging economies in Africa and Asia

Plastics use in million tonnes (Mt), *Baseline* scenario

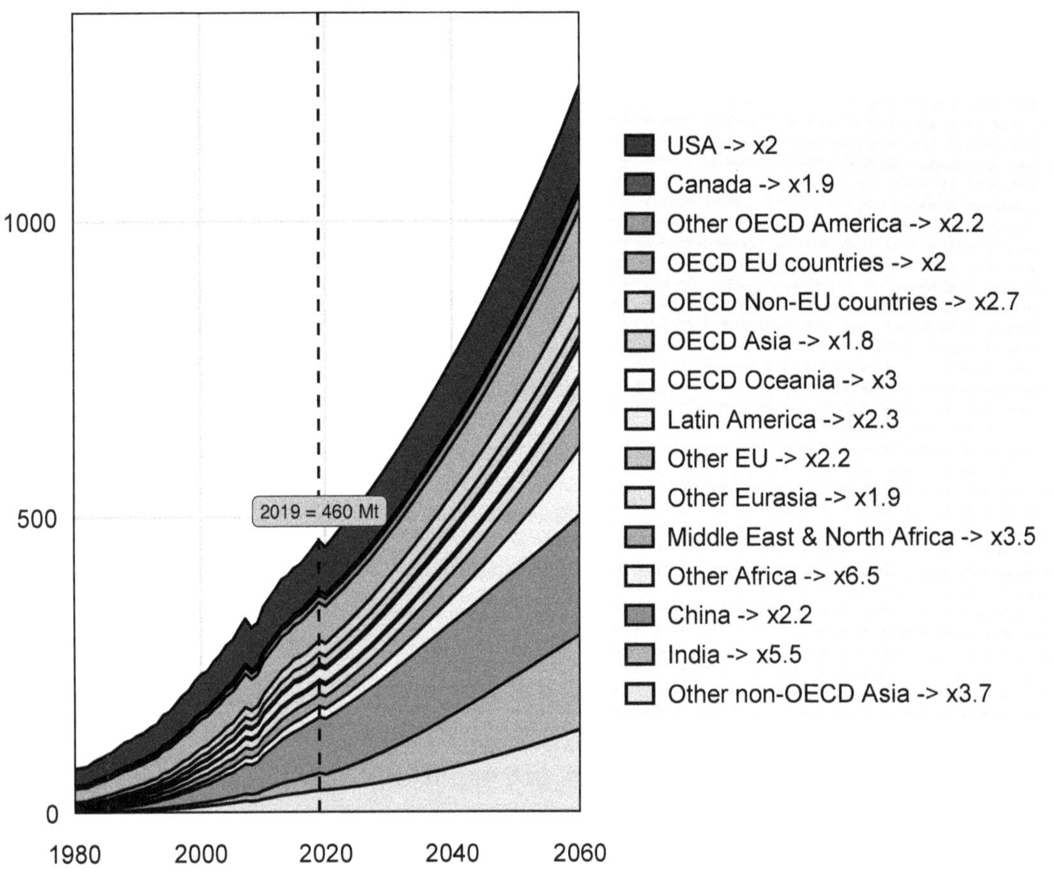

Note: The numbers on the right-handside of the graph indicate the growth of plastics use from 2019 (dashed line) to 2060 for each region (e.g. x2 means a doubling of plastics use). Please see Table A A.2 in Annex A for more details on the regional aggregation of the ENV-Linkages model.
Source: OECD ENV-Linkages model.

StatLink https://stat.link/q2naph

3.1.3. Packaging and transport will drive a large share of the increase in plastics use

Understanding changes in plastics use by application is key to understanding changes in the demand for the different polymers. The ENV-Linkages model maps plastics use by polymer and application to the model sectors.[2] For instance, as PVC (polyvinyl chloride) is mostly used for construction applications, it is linked to the construction sector in the model, while PP (polypropylene) is used for packaging, amongst other applications, and is linked to several sectors, including food products and business services. In general, polymers are used for multiple applications, and applications are also linked to multiple economic sectors, unless they are highly specialised, such as in construction.

Together, packaging, construction and vehicles (which include vehicles for all transport sectors as well as other transport equipment, and marine coatings linked to the production and maintenance of ships) currently account for more than 60% of total plastics use (Figure 3.3, Panel A). By 2060, plastics use is projected to increase for all applications, following increases in production levels across the economy (Figure 3.3, Panel B). Plastics use for the production of vehicles increases most, reflecting a rising demand for transport equipment as economies develop (see Section 3.2.3). Increasing digitalisation and electrification also sees plastics use increase for electrical and electronic products.

While the services sectors have a relatively low plastics intensity (the amount of plastic per unit of output), the servitisation of economies will mean that the services sector will account for the largest share of plastics use. This is reflected in the increase of plastic products frequently used in service sectors, such as packaging and consumer products (e.g. takeaway food containers, health care and medical products, art supplies, credit cards and luggage). The increase in plastics use for packaging shows that policies currently in place are not sufficient to offset the increase in plastics use by key sectors that rely on packaging, including business services, food products and trade.

Plastics use also increases for other applications although to a lesser extent. Plastics use for clothes increases, following an increase in output from the textile sector in non-OECD countries (see Section 3.2.3). Plastics use in construction increases especially in developing and emerging economies as construction activities are linked to investment in infrastructure, which is an essential part of economic development (OECD, 2019[1]). Finally, plastics use for industrial applications and machinery (included in "Other") grows less than other applications thanks to structural shifts away from industry and the continued reliance on steel and other metals by these industries.

Figure 3.3. Plastics use in the transport sector will grow the most by 2060

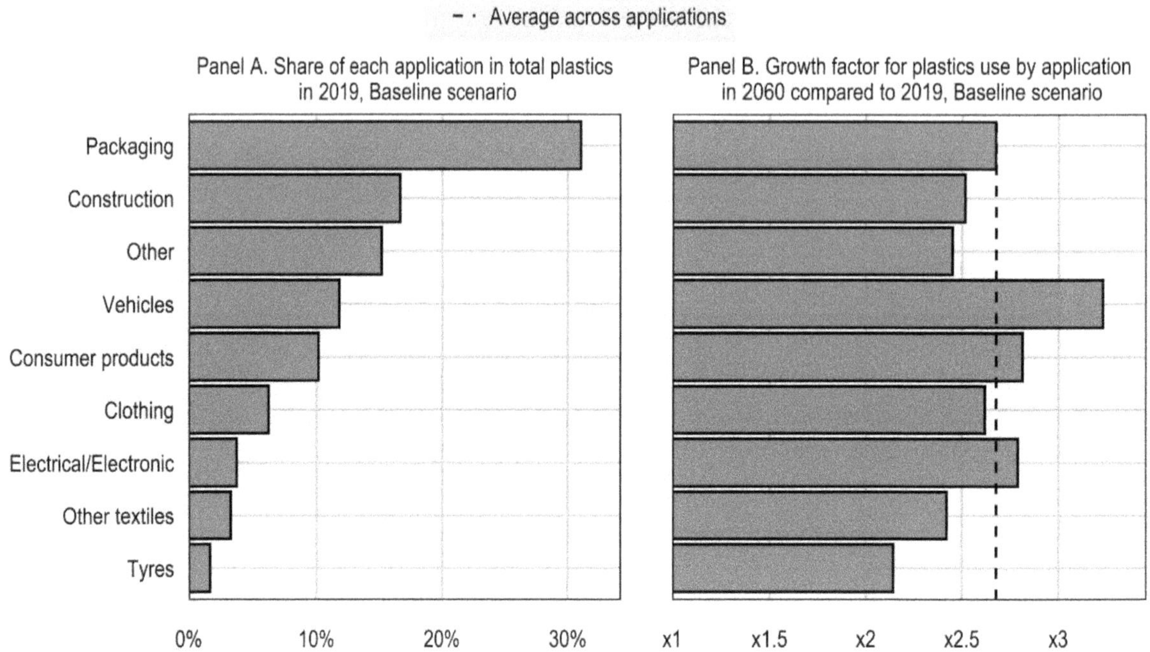

Note: The applications for personal protective equipment linked to COVID-19, and personal care products, are omitted from the graph as the quantity of plastics they use is too small for the calculation to be meaningful.
Source: OECD ENV-Linkages model.

StatLink https://stat.link/sfzren

Plastics use is also projected to increase for all polymers (Figure 3.4), as inputs for the different applications also increase. The links between the different polymers and applications is quite intricate, as the same polymers can be used in different ways in various applications, and some polymers actually represent a wide range of different plastics that are grouped in one category because they share certain characteristics. By 2060, there is projected to be a substantial increase in the use of polymers for packaging. Notably, low-density polyethylene (LDPE, and including linear low-density polyethylene or LLDPE) used in packaging triples compared to 2019; while polypropylene (PP), high density polyethylene (HDPE) and polyethylene terephthalate (PET), all used in packaging, more than double. Polyvinyl chloride (PVC), which is used in construction, increases by 2.6 times. Likewise, fibres, which are used for textiles, are projected to triple. The use of polymers for the production of vehicles, and especially PP, is also projected to increase substantially.

Figure 3.4. The use of all polymers will increase to 2060

Increase in plastics use by polymer and application in million tonnes (Mt) *Baseline* scenario, 2019-60

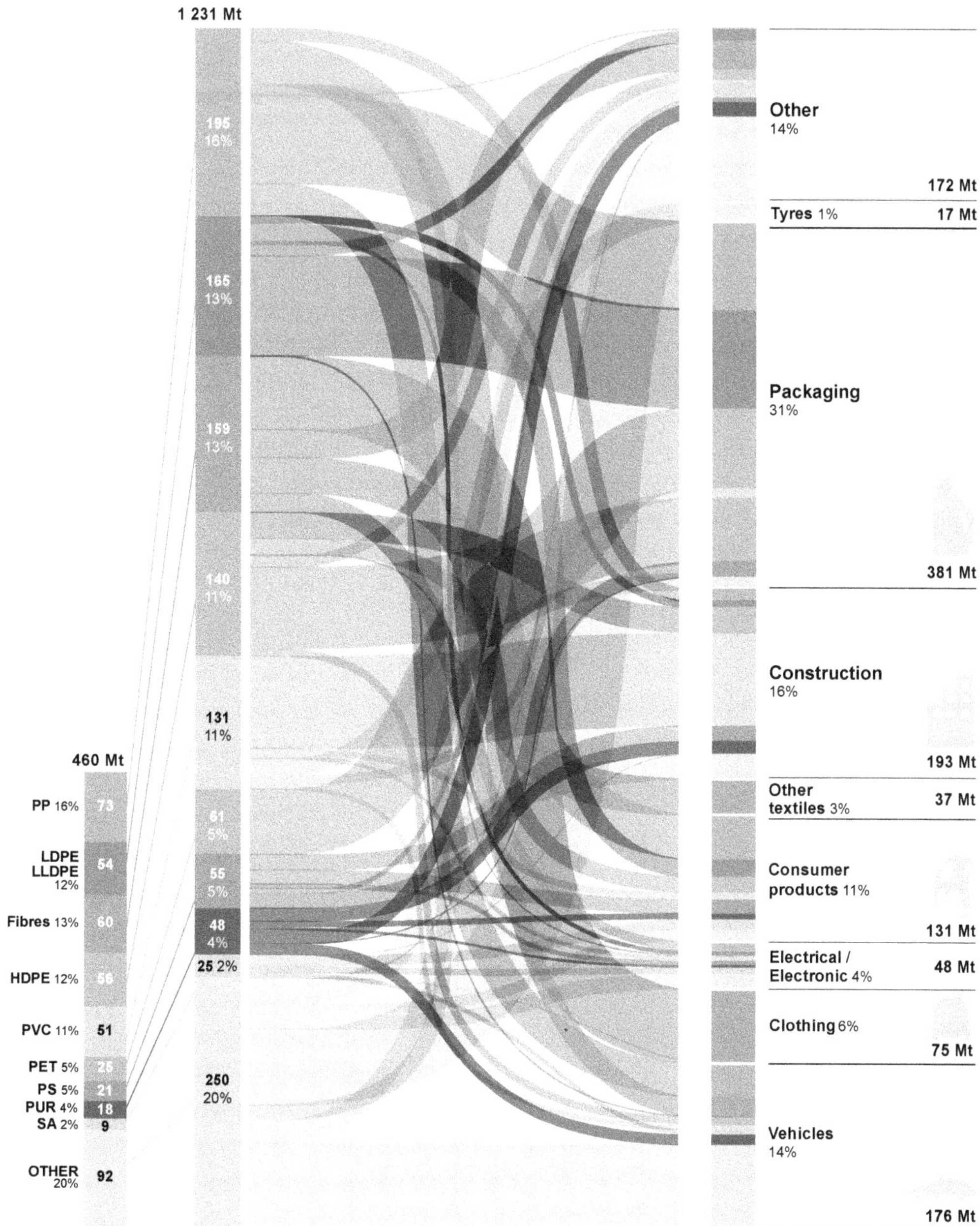

Notes:
HDPE = high-density polyethylene; LDPE = low-density polyethylene; LLDPE = linear low-density polyethylene; PET = polyethylene terephthalate; PP = polypropylene; PS = polystyrene; PUR = polyurethane; PVC = polyvinyl chloride; SA stands for ABS, ASA, SAN, where ABS = acrylonitrile butadiene styrene; ASA = acrylonitrile styrene acrylate; SAN = styrene acrylonitrile.
The figure does not include the application personal protective equipment (face masks and other protection linked to the COVID-19 pandemic) as its use was negligible in 2019.
Source: OECD ENV-Linkages model.

StatLink https://stat.link/3m7s5n

3.1.4. Fossil-based non-recycled plastics will continue to dominate in 2060

The ENV-Linkages model splits plastics production and use into primary plastics and secondary plastics (plastics made from recycled materials). Primary plastics include both fossil-based and biobased plastics, which are a rather small group of plastics with similar characteristics to fossil-based plastics, but are derived from biomass such as corn, sugarcane, wheat or residues from other processes. The estimates for secondary plastics are based on available data on plastics labelled for recycling (i.e. that have labels indicating that they can be recycled). They also take into account losses in the process, such as when plastics are collected for recycling, but cannot be recycled.[3]

In the *Baseline* scenario, the growth in global output of primary and secondary plastics production is similar, with secondary plastics production growing slightly faster than primary. The share of secondary plastics, a key indicator of circularity, is projected to double from 6% to 12% between 2019 and 2060 (Figure 3.5). Secondary plastics use can be boosted in two ways. First, increases in recycling can boost the availability of scrap material for use in secondary plastics production. This supply push effect will be explored in Chapter 4. Second, on the demand side, there is a pull effect from increased demand for plastics as well as increased production costs for primary plastics. The *Baseline* scenario assumes no new policies are introduced to incentivize a shift away from primary plastics, and thus this lever is not very strong. Nonetheless, the share of secondary plastics increases even in the absence of stronger policies, as more scrap becomes available keeping production costs for secondary plastics relatively low so that secondary production can compete better with primary production. The increase is, however, not nearly enough to overcome the strong increase in total plastics demand, leading to a significant increase in primary plastics production.

Figure 3.5. Primary plastics will still make up the lion's share of production in 2060

Primary and secondary plastics production in million tonnes (Mt), *Baseline* scenario, 1950-2060

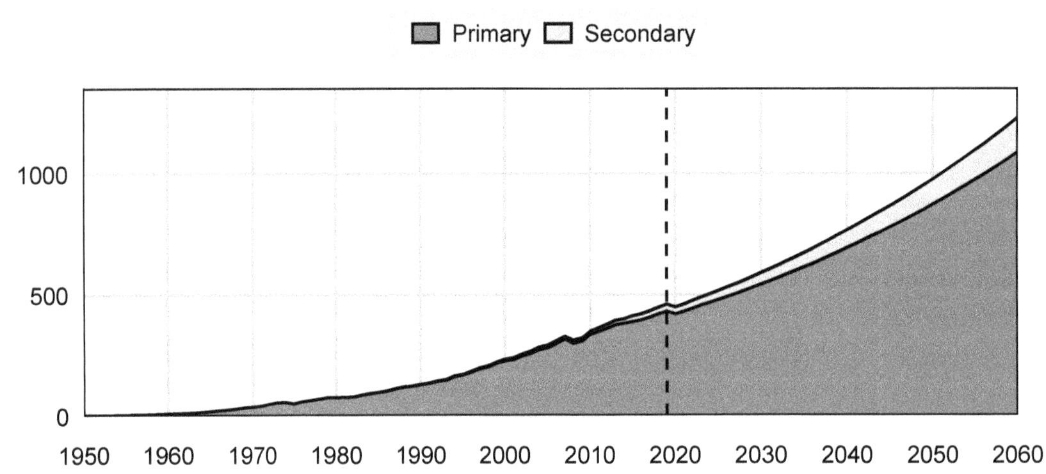

Note: 2019 (dashed line).
Source: OECD ENV-Linkages model.

StatLink https://stat.link/15rn7z

Due to the increasing use of plastics, biobased plastics production is also projected to increase in the *Baseline* scenario, but at a slower rate than total plastics production, and its share remains marginal (at around 0.5% in 2060). The environmental consequences of the growth in bioplastics use are not straightforward to calculate. While the production of biobased plastics is less carbon-intensive than fossil-based plastics, the production of biobased plastics relies on crops, which need extensive land. An increase in demand for biobased plastics could increase the area of cropland needed, potentially driving forest conversion and consequent emission increases (see Chapter 6).

Since fossil fuels are still the main source of plastics, the roles of the energy mix and fossil prices in the *Baseline* scenario are relevant. The *Baseline* projections are based on the energy mix outlined in the current policies ("CPS") scenario of the International Energy Agency's *World Energy Outlook* (IEA, 2018[2]). In the ENV-Linkages *Baseline* scenario, the price of oil is projected to more than double between 2019 and 2060. However, plastics use projections would only change slightly in a scenario with higher or lower oil price profile, partly due to the changes in production prices, but also due to changes in consumption (Box 3.1).

Besides the substitution across different types of plastics, plastics can also be replaced by other materials, depending on the sector and product. For instance, paper and wood are increasingly used for single-use products such as plastic plates, or to turn single-use products in reusable products, as done for instance for reusable water bottles made of metal, which replace single-use plastic ones. However, alternatives to plastics are do not easily available for all product yet. For instance, it will be more difficult to find substitutes for plastics in the production of electronics, where the only current option is to make plastics based on algae. Unfortunately, there is not enough information or data available to create projections to 2060 for these types of alternatives. However, the ENV-Linkages modelling framework takes into account how various materials grow in response to changes in product prices and demand. In the *Baseline* scenario, plastics use is projected to grow faster than most other materials (Box 3.2), highlighting the fact that the economy is increasingly relying on plastics.

Box 3.1. Fossil fuel prices show little impact on plastics use in the long run

Oil and gas are the main raw materials used as feedstock for plastics. For instance, Plastics Europe (2005[3]) estimates that for the production of 1 kilogram of PET bottles, 750 grams of oil and 670 grams of gas are needed. In this context, an uncertainty analysis is used to understand the impact of fossil fuel prices on plastics use and prices and therefore the robustness of the projections of plastics use presented in this report. Figure 3.6 illustrates the impacts of alternative time profiles of oil and gas prices (ranging to an increase or decrease of 15%) on GDP and on the use and price of plastics.[1]

The changes in plastics use then follow the change in overall economic activity caused by the fuel price variations: if plastics become more expensive, their use decreases. Despite fossil fuels being the main natural resource in the production of plastics, changes in fuel prices have a limited effect on plastics use and prices: plastics use changes by less than 2% and the price of plastics by less than 1%. This limited effect, which might appear counterintuitive, is because fossil feedstock is only one input in the production of plastics, which relies largely on labour and capital inputs, as well as chemical products.

The impacts on secondary plastics are lower than on primary plastics as the production of fossil-based primary plastics relies directly on oil and gas inputs. Nonetheless, as primary and secondary plastics compete in the same market, there is only limited room for secondary plastics to deviate as secondary plastics producers are price takers in the plastics market.

Figure 3.6. Changes in fossil fuel prices have little impact on plastics production in the long run

Deviations from the *Baseline* scenario, 2060

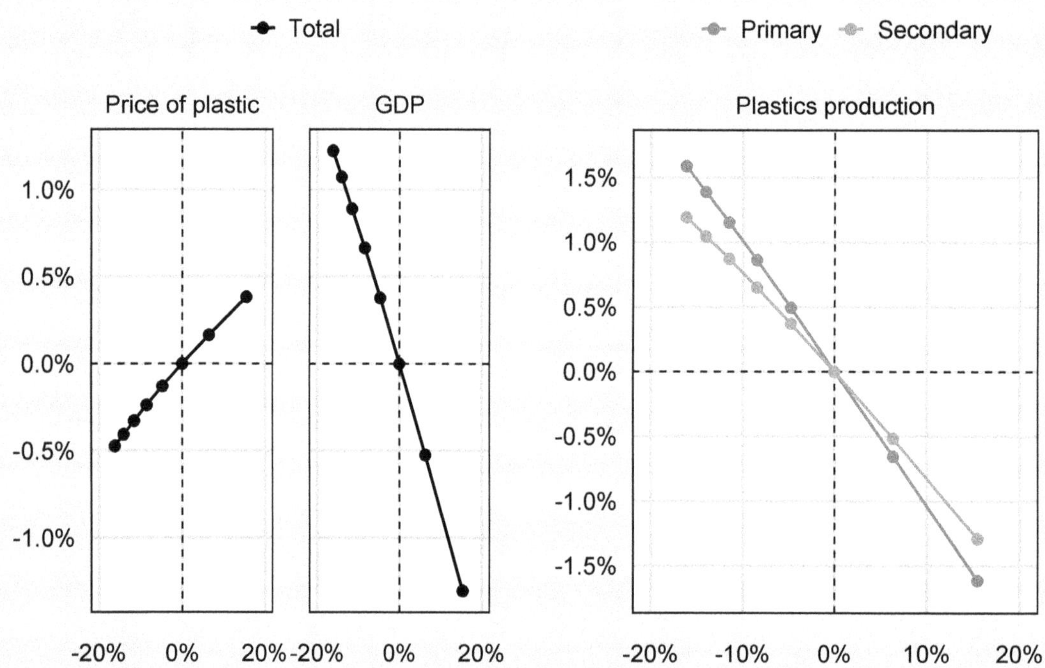

Note: The horizontal axis shows the magnitude of the shock on oil and gas prices compared to the *Baseline* scenario.
[1] In the alternative oil prices scenarios, a shock to oil prices is modelled as a change in the price of natural resources.
Source: OECD ENV-Linkages model.

StatLink https://stat.link/63sa5o

Box 3.2. Plastics grows more than most raw materials

The growth in plastics use can be compared to that of other raw materials used in the economy using the methodology developed in the OECD's *Global Material Resources Outlook to 2060* (2019[1]). The growth rates of materials depend on which economic process they are linked to. The growth in plastics use is projected to outpace all other materials apart from wood and timber (Figure 3.7), which are linked to both industrial activities and construction.

Figure 3.7. Plastics use outpaces most other raw materials in the *Baseline* scenario

Percentage change in 2060 compared to 2019

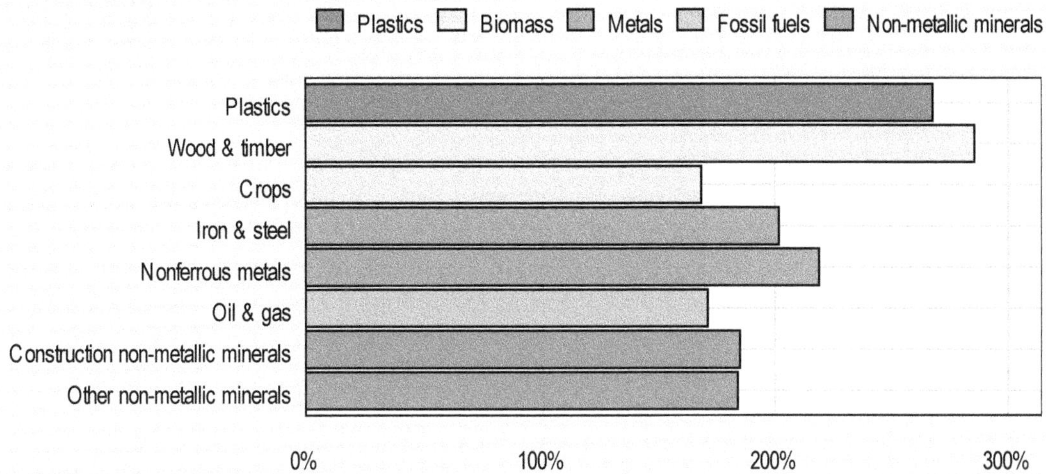

Note: The results presented here differ from OECD (2019[1]), *Global Material Resources Outlook to 2060*, as the *Baseline* scenario includes the effects of the COVID-19 pandemic.
Source: OECD ENV-Linkages model.

StatLink https://stat.link/iqd09m

3.2. The drivers of plastics use vary by region

3.2.1. Population growth and structural and technology changes drive plastics use in some regions

The effects of the four socio-economic drivers of plastics (presented in Figure 3.1) vary by region (Figure 3.8), depending on the characteristics of their economies and the projected regional socio-economic developments (Chapter 2). The large differences in the drivers of plastics use across regions highlight the need to tailor policy action to reduce the environmental impacts of plastics to the specific characteristics of the regional economies.

Economic growth is the main driver of plastics use and leads to an increase in plastics use in all regions. The same does not apply to population growth. In most regions, population growth reflects only a minor share of the total increase in plastics use. This effect is large in Sub-Saharan Africa (Other Africa), which is the region with fastest population growth (see Section 3.2.2). However, in regions with declining populations, which include many Eastern European countries (part of Other EU), Japan, Korea (both part of OECD Asia), and China, demographic changes limit the growth in plastics use.

The effects of structural change also vary by region. In most regions, structural change helps to limit the growth in plastics use. Plastics are used widely in agriculture, industry and services (although the polymers differ). In contrast to the impact on climate change and air pollution, a trend towards servitisation does not automatically imply that plastics use is reduced. Rather, it depends on the specific economic structure of the economy (see Section 3.2.3). Structural change has the strongest effect in China, where the economy is undergoing a process of servitisation and moving towards less material-intensive sectors. In some regions, notably OECD Non-EU countries (which include Turkey and Norway, among other countries), Other EU (which includes some Eastern European countries such as Bulgaria, Croatia and Romania), Eurasia (which includes the Russian Federation) and Sub-Saharan Africa, structural change can drive an increase in plastics use. In these regions, economic development leads to an increase in sectors that rely on plastics inputs, thus leading to an increase in plastics use. While the effect of technology changes limits the increase in plastics use in all regions, this effect is largest in the regions for which structural changes drive plastics use. Therefore, in these regions, economic development leads to the adoption of improved technologies that decrease plastic intensity, but also to an increase in production in more plastic-intensive sectors.

Figure 3.8. The drivers of plastics use vary by region

Relative contribution of the decomposition effects to the overall increase of yearly plastics use between 2019 and 2060 in million tonnes (Mt), *Baseline* scenario

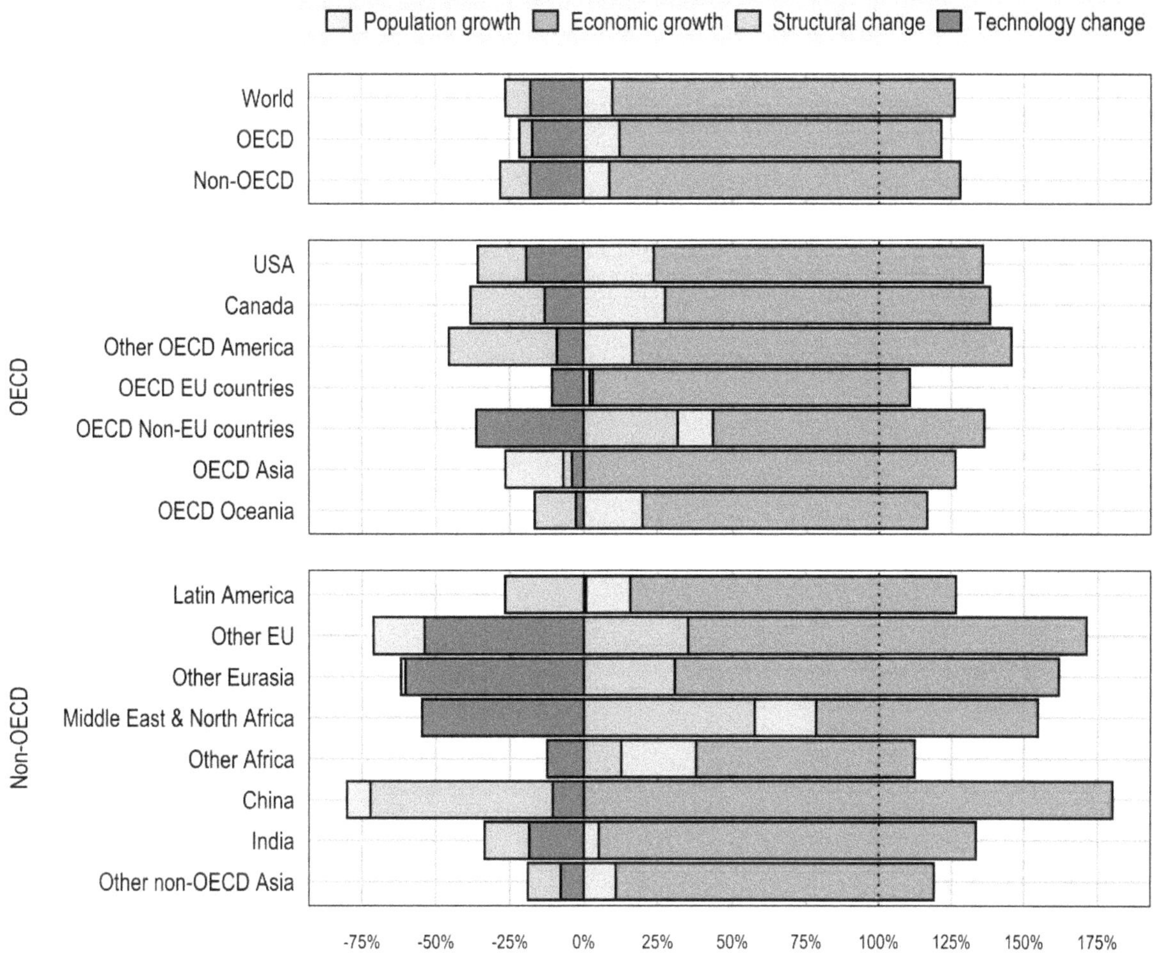

Notes:
The sum of the 4 effects sum up to 100%.
Population growth represents a projection in which plastics use is assumed to grow at the same speed as population and in which the regional plastics use per capita stays constant at 2019 levels.
Economic growth represents a counterfactual projection in which plastics use is assumed to grow at the same speed as GDP and in which the regional plastics intensity (the amount of plastic per unit of output) stays constant at 2019 levels.
Structural change identifies the contribution of sectoral shifts to reducing global plastics use by differentiating sectoral growth rates.
Technology change identifies the contribution of technology improvements to reducing global plastics use by differentiating growth rates of plastic inputs to sectoral output. Technology change not only includes technological improvements but also a wider diffusion of existing technologies.
Source: OECD ENV-Linkages model.

StatLink https://stat.link/1p8jcl

3.2.2. Population and income changes imply limited convergence in plastics use per capita across regions

The effects of population growth on plastics use reflect the projected changes in population from 2019 to 2060 (Figure 3.9). Among all regions, Sub-Saharan Africa (Other Africa) stands out as the region in which population growth drives plastics use the most. Indeed, this is the region with the strongest increase in population (Chapter 2). In the other regions, the growth in plastics use is much stronger than the growth in population, leading to a significant increase in plastics use per capita.

Figure 3.9. Population strongly drives plastics use in Sub-Saharan Africa

Population (millions) and plastics use (Mt) from 2019 to 2060

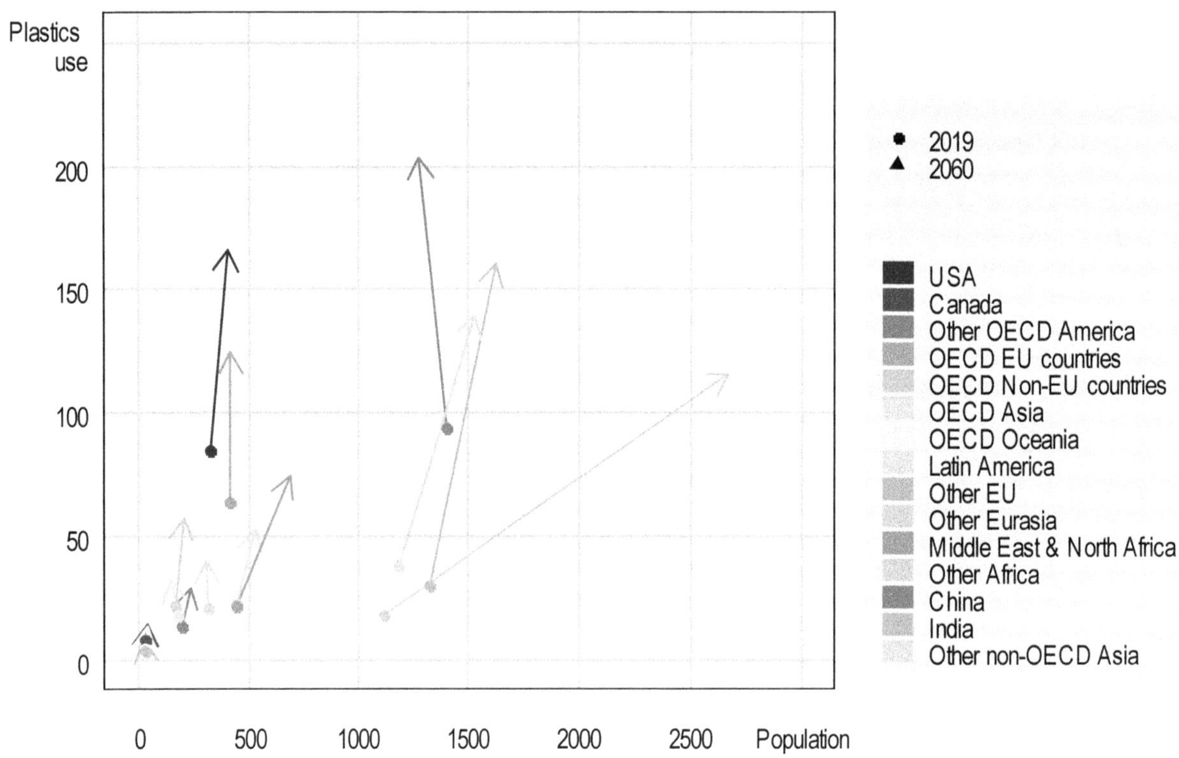

Source: OECD ENV-Linkages model.

StatLink https://stat.link/wvy1n4

Despite economic growth, the strong increase in population growth in Sub-Saharan Africa also implies that, by 2060 this region will still have the lowest levels of plastics use per person (Figure 3.10). On average, plastics use per capita in OECD countries is projected to remain higher than in non-OECD countries. While non-OECD countries are projected to see their plastics use per capita more than Between 2019 and 2060, non-OECD countriesdouble between 2019 and 2060, their projected 2060 levels remain lower than 2019 OECD levels. Thus, there is only very limited convergence in plastics use per capita between OECD and non-OECD countries.

Figure 3.10. Regional income levels drive per-capita plastics use

Plastics use per person (kg/capita) and growth factors between 2019 and 2060, *Baseline* scenario

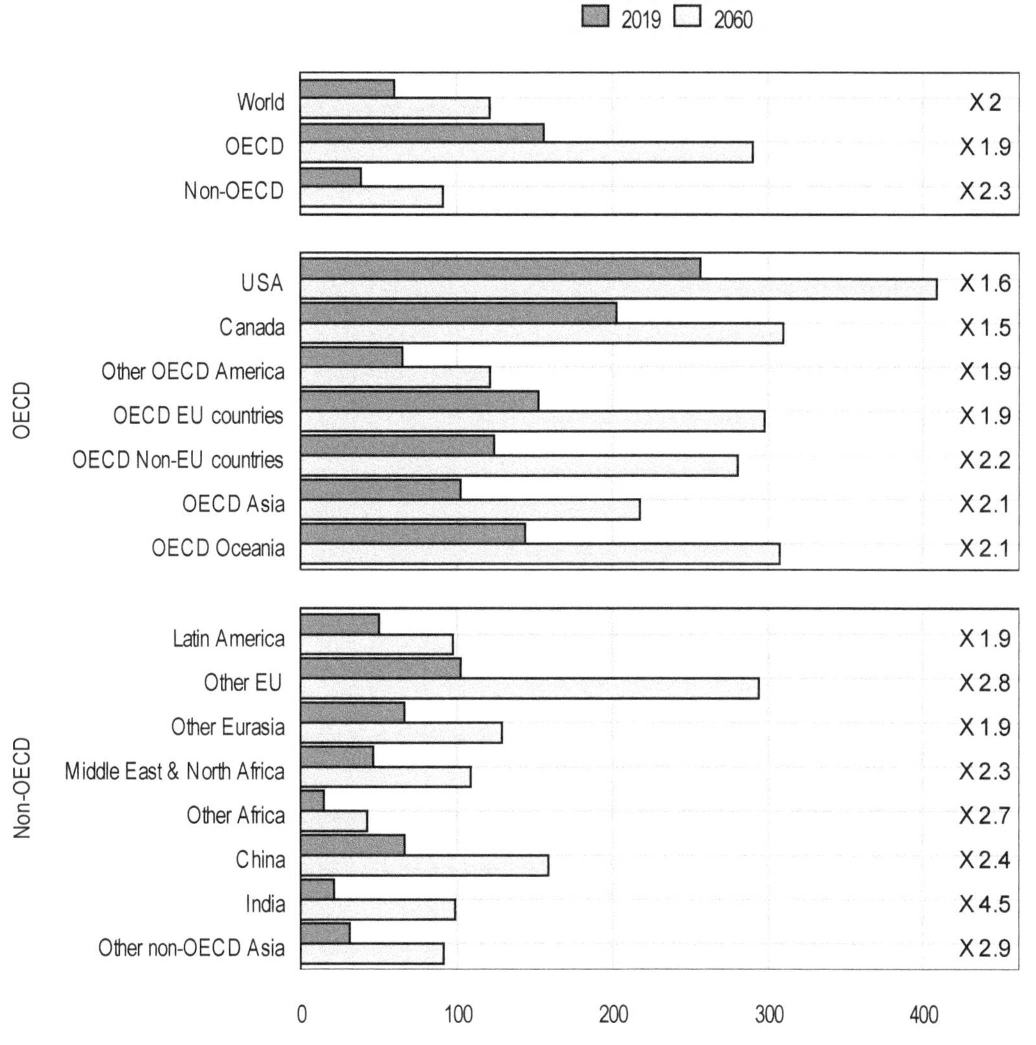

Note: The numbers on the right hand side of the graph indicate the growth of per-capita plastics use from 2019 to 2060 for each region (e.g. x2 means a doubling of plastics use).
Source: OECD ENV-Linkages model.

StatLink https://stat.link/0mjrcu

3.2.3. Changes in plastic intensity depend on structural and technological changes

Despite the growth in plastics use, the global plastics intensity — i.e. the amount of plastics use needed to produce a dollar of GDP -- is projected to fall by 16% between 2019 and 2060.This effect is the result of changes in regional and sectoral production levels as well as increased efficiency in production. The plastic intensity of regional economies depends on changes in the structure of the economy, which determines whether output grows in more or less plastic-intensive sectors; and on changes in production technologies, which influence the plastic intensity of each sector.

Projected changes in technologies imply that plastic intensity decreases in most sectors by 2060 in both OECD and non-OECD countries (Figure 3.11). There are a few exceptions, such as food products in OECD countries, which rely on plastics for packaging, as well as construction in OECD countries, where plastics are increasingly used. Plastic intensity also increases or remains unchanged in some industrial sectors in non-OECD countries (e.g. Other manufacturing). This largely reflects a shift within the sector towards specific commodities that use more plastics, rather than a decline in production efficiency.

Structural change in both OECD and non-OECD countries implies a stronger reliance on services sectors (Figure 3.11). These include government service sectors with very low plastic intensity, such as education and healthcare (Other services), but also services which rely on plastics even limitedly. This is the case for business services, a category which includes trade services that rely heavily on packaging. While business services have relatively low plastic intensity, servitisation implies a large output growth, especially in non-OECD countries (+300%). This effect partly drives the increase in packaging plastics outlined in Section 3.1.3.

Rising living standards and industrialisation in non-OECD countries, and most notably Sub-Saharan African countries, will drive a strong increase in the intensity of plastics use, as consumption leads to strong demand for plastics for construction and (semi-)durables (such as cars or appliances). This effect is particularly evident for transport: as economies grow, they also rely more heavily on transport services and on the use of motor vehicles (Box 3.3). The production of motor vehicles is plastic intensive, especially in non-OECD countries. Hence, the increase in in the share of this sector in the economy also leads to an increase in economy-wide plastic intensity.

Plastic intensity is projected to decline in the textile sector, which relies on the use of fibres.[4] However, while the sector is projected to grow less than the economy average in OECD countries, it is projected to have a large growth in non-OECD countries, thereby also driving the increased use of fibres for used in the production of clothes at the global level.

Figure 3.11. Output growth is fast in some sectors that rely on plastics

Plastic intensity in grams of plastics per unit of sectoral output in USD (g/USD) and sectoral growth, *Baseline* scenario

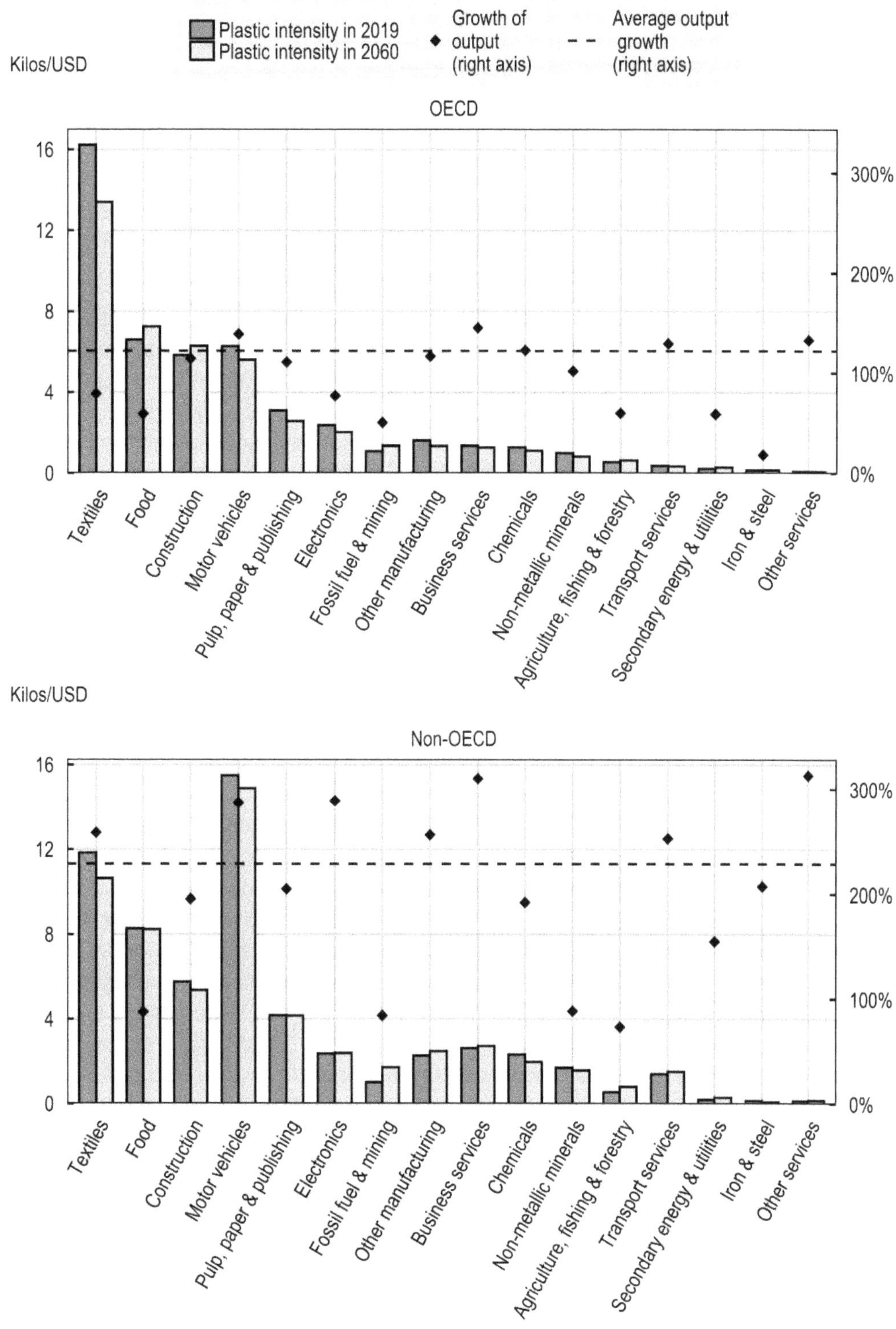

Note: sorted by plastic intensity in 2019 in OECD countries.
Source: OECD ENV-Linkages model.

StatLink https://stat.link/75o9fn

Box 3.3. The increasing use of transport in developing economies affects plastics use

The production of motor vehicles is one of the most plastic intensive sectors. In non-OECD countries, almost 15 grams of plastics were used for each dollar of output in this sector in 2019. In OECD countries, plastics use per unit of output is lower (6 grams/USD) and represents on average a much smaller share of total value of a motor vehicle. This is a typical example of where product quality affects plastics intensity: cars manufactured in OECD countries are on balance at the higher end of the market and thus sell for a higher price than cars that use the same amount of plastics but as they are less luxurious they sell at a lower price.

Moreover, the motor vehicle production sector is projected to grow faster than other sectors, especially in non-OECD countries where it grows by almost 300% between 2019 and 2060. The main reason behind this is the relationship between economic growth and the use of motor vehicles.

The link between increasing income and use and ownership of motor vehicles depends on the level of income. The link is weak or non-existent in countries at very early stages of development, when incomes are too low to purchase a motor vehicle. In high-income countries, changes in income also have limited impact on the use of motor vehicles (Dargay and Gately, 1999[4]), since car ownership is already spread following a progressive saturation of the market. However, car replacement and gasoline prices do affect the use of motor vehicles more than income levels in these countries (Dargay, Madre and Berri, 2000[5]).

For intermediate income levels, changes in income are strongly correlated with car ownership (Dargay and Gately, 1999[4]). Therefore, countries and regions that move from low to middle-income and from middle to high-income are those where the production of motor vehicles grows the most, thus driving plastics use.

3.3. COVID-19 affects plastics use in both the short and long run

The COVID-19 pandemic and associated response measures have affected short-run sectoral output, with a large decrease in economic activity in 2020 and a projected gradual recovery in the coming years (see Chapter 2). The short-term consequences for plastics use are mixed. Some plastics have been used more for specific applications, most notably masks and other personal protective equipment. In response to a shift from in-store shopping to online retail and from restaurant eating to take-away, there has also been a decline in production activities that use plastics, such as construction and motor vehicles manufacturing. On balance, the effect is negative, but relatively small: in 2020 global plastics use is estimated to have declined by around 10 Mt below 2019 levels (see Chapter 3 in OECD (2022[6]). The economic impacts of the pandemic also have longer-term consequences, as economic growth is projected to recover only gradually and economic activity levels remain permanently below the pre-COVID projection (see Boxes 2.2 and 2.4 in Chapter 2).[5]

The medium and long-term implications of the pandemic remain highly uncertain. First, the recovery of the economic and health systems remains fragile at the time of writing, despite increasing vaccination rates in many countries. Second, it is uncertain how government recovery packages are being and will be spent and how this affects plastics use. Third, the behavioural changes induced by the lockdowns, not least the shift to online retail, may either gradually phase out or accelerate over time.

Nonetheless, based on Dellink et al. (2021[7]), which assumes that government recovery packages are not explicitly steered towards recycling or secondary plastics, and that behavioural changes are temporary (in which case demand gradually reverts back to the pre-COVID projection), the modelling captures the effect on future plastics use of changes in economic activity at regional and sectoral level. Based on these assumptions, the *Baseline* scenario suggests that global plastics use remains below the pre-COVID projection in the coming years (Figure 3.12). By 2025, the immediate effects of the early lockdown measures are assumed to have disappeared but the economic impacts are still harshly felt. Thus, plastics use is projected to have recovered to well above 2019 levels, but despite economic growth rates returning to pre-COVID projection rates, use levels remain around 3% below the pre-COVID projection on balance. However, in absolute terms, these effects are small. By 2060, the *Baseline* scenario projects global plastics use in 2060 to be 1 231 Mt, compared to 1 253 Mt had the pandemic not taken place, a difference of less than 2%. Use trajectories will however strongly depend on the actual speed of the recovery from the COVID-19 pandemic (Box 3.4).

Figure 3.12. Overall, the COVID-19 pandemic will reduce regional plastics use projections

Deviations from the pre-COVID projection, *Baseline* scenario

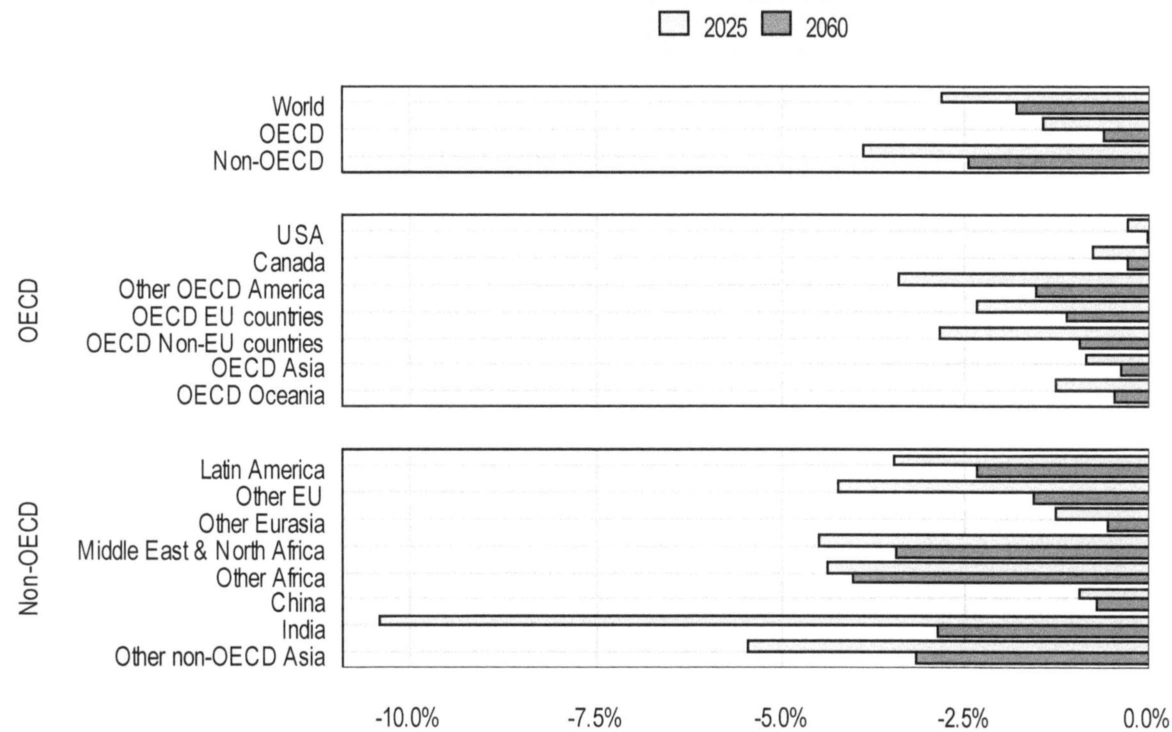

Source: OECD ENV-Linkages model.

StatLink https://stat.link/rwdhvf

The regional differences in the effect of the pandemic on plastics use are driven by changes in local economic activities. In some countries – not least China and the USA – the recovery from COVID-19 is forecast to be rapid (OECD, 2021[8]), and plastics use by 2025 is quite close to the pre-COVID projection. In other regions, most notably India, the negative economic effects of the pandemic are projected still be widespread in 2025, leading to plastics use levels that may be 10% below what they would have been without the pandemic. By 2060, growth rates of plastics use are projected to have recovered in all regions, and levels are at most a few percent below the pre-COVID projection.

Box 3.4. How will the speed of recovery from the COVID-19 pandemic affect plastics use?

The uncertainties surrounding the economic effects of the COVID-19 pandemic (presented in Chapter 2) also apply to plastics use. The projections are clearly influenced by assumptions about the speed of recovery (Figure 3.13; see also Annex B). The *Slow recovery* scenario assumes more prolonged effects of the pandemic. In this scenario, plastics use also recovers much more slowly, and only starts to approach the pre-COVID reference projection after 2030.

Figure 3.13. A slow recovery from COVID-19 will maintain lower global plastics use levels

Deviations from the pre-COVID reference projection

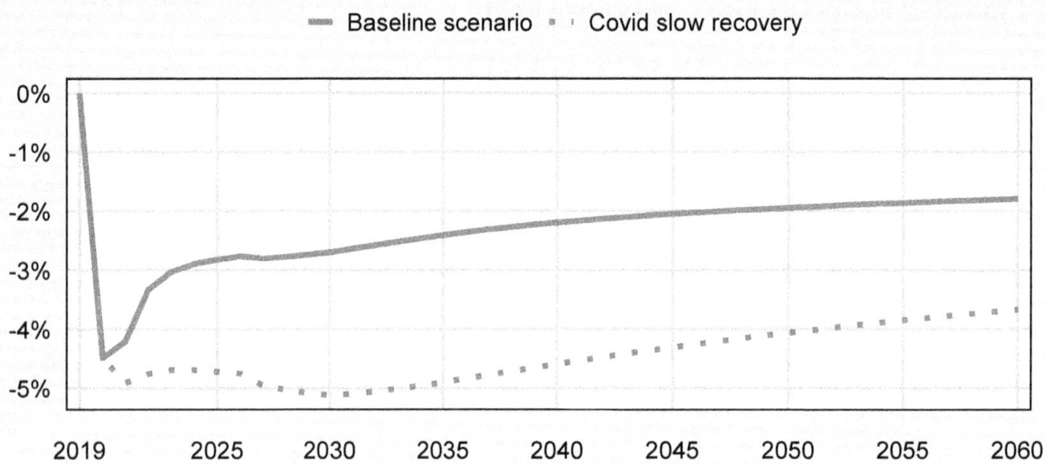

Source: OECD ENV-Linkages model, using the economic projections in Dellink et al. (2021[7]).

StatLink https://stat.link/2951o8

References

Dargay, J. and D. Gately (1999), "Income's effect on car and vehicle ownership, worldwide: 1960–2015", *Transportation Research Part A: Policy and Practice*, Vol. 33/2, pp. 101-138, https://doi.org/10.1016/s0965-8564(98)00026-3. [4]

Dargay, J., J. Madre and A. Berri (2000), "Car Ownership Dynamics Seen Through the Follow-Up of Cohorts: Comparison of France and the United Kingdom", *Transportation Research Record: Journal of the Transportation Research Board*, Vol. 1733/1, pp. 31-38, https://doi.org/10.3141/1733-05. [5]

Dellink, R. et al. (2021), "The long-term implications of the Covid-19 pandemic and recovery measures on environmental pressures: A quantitative exploration", *OECD Environment Working Papers*, No. 176, OECD Publishing, Paris, https://doi.org/10.1787/123dfd4f-en. [7]

IEA (2018), *World Energy Outlook 2018*, OECD Publishing, Paris, https://doi.org/10.1787/weo-2018-en. [2]

OECD (2022), *Global Plastics Outlook: Economic Drivers, Environmental Impacts and Policy Options*, OECD Publishing, Paris, https://doi.org/10.1787/de747aef-en. [6]

OECD (2021), *OECD Economic Outlook, Volume 2021 Issue 1*, OECD Publishing, Paris, https://doi.org/10.1787/edfbca02-en. [8]

OECD (2019), *Global Material Resources Outlook to 2060: Economic Drivers and Environmental Consequences*, OECD Publishing, Paris, https://doi.org/10.1787/9789264307452-en. [1]

Plastics Europe (2005), *Eco-profiles of the European Plastics Industry: Polyethylene Theraphlate (PET) (Bottle grade),*, http://www.inference.org.uk/sustainable/LCA/elcd/external_docs/petb_31116f00-fabd-11da-974d-0800200c9a66.pdf. [3]

Notes

[1] Table A A.2 in Annex A explains the regional groupings used in ENV-Linkages.

[2] Table A A.4 in Annex A summarises the mapping of the economic sectors and plastics applications.

[3] Plastics use and production for 2019 were estimated by calculating the amount of plastics labelled for recycling, minus the plastics lost in the recycling process (during both sorting and conversion). Information on plastics losses was supplied by Leeds University. The evolution of secondary plastics in the *Baseline* scenario was then carefully calibrated to have a match between available plastic waste labelled for recycling (minus losses) and secondary production by region to 2060. See Annex A for details on the methodology and (OECD, 2022[6]) for an overview of base year plastics use.

[4] This sector is slightly more plastic intensive in OECD countries than non-OECD countries. This is a result of the model assumptions that link use of fibres in textiles to the input of chemicals (the sector that creates the fibres). As the model cannot further differentiate between different chemical products, the fibre input is proportional to the input of chemicals in the textile sector.

[5] Furthermore, the short-term reductions in plastics use will only result in changes in waste streams at the end of products timespan; thus reduced plastics use in 2020 will reduce projected plastic waste streams.

4 Plastic waste projections to 2060

The management of the millions of tonnes of plastic waste generated each year is an urgent issue. This chapter presents plastic waste projections in the *Baseline* scenario, which models the effects of current policies on plastic waste generation to 2060. It also looks at how current policies will affect the shares of plastic waste that are recycled, incinerated, landfilled or mismanaged. Finally, the chapter models alternative policy, trade and COVID recovery scenarios to explore their effects on plastic waste and waste management.

Key messages

- Under business as usual, as the use of plastics increases in the coming decades, so too does global plastic waste, rising from 353 Mt in 2019 to 1 014 Mt in 2060. Short-lived applications, such as packaging, will drive this increase, as well as construction in emerging economies.
- The long lifespans of some plastics applications can lock in waste for decades. For instance, for construction, more than 90% of waste up until 2040 will be from plastics produced before 2019.
- While all regions will see an increase in plastic waste, in Asia and Africa it more than quadruples to 2060, linked to population growth and rising living standards. However, OECD countries will still produce much more plastic waste per capita (238 kg on average) than non-OECD countries (77 kg) in 2060.
- The share of recycling as a waste-management practice is projected to rise to 17% in 2060 (176 Mt), up from 9% in 2019 (33 Mt). Sanitary landfilling will remain the most common way of managing plastic waste, accounting for 50% of all waste in 2060 (507 Mt). Landfilling will grow most strongly in non-OECD countries, as they try to move away from the use of dumpsites. The share of incinerated plastic waste will fall slightly, to 18%, as much of the projected growth in plastic waste is located in countries which lack incineration capacity, while incineration stagnates in Europe, Japan, Korea, Australia and New Zealand, due to saturation.
- If today's economic development trends and adoption of waste management policies continue at the same pace, the share of plastic waste that is mismanaged (i.e. not managed through recycling, landfilling or incineration) is projected to fall to 15% by 2060 (down from 22% in 2019), though the amount will still rise to 153 Mt.
- If current waste management practices do not improve between now and 2060, mismanaged plastic waste would increase to almost 270 Mt by 2060, as waste would grow more in countries with less developed waste management systems. This underlines the need to share best practices and existing technologies to support rapidly developing countries in improving their waste management systems to keep up with their growing waste.
- Trade scenarios highlight how policies on the transboundary movement of plastic waste can drastically divert trading patterns and thus have important implications both for regional recycling opportunities and plastic leakage into the environment. To achieve a more circular use of plastics, trade policies and environmental policies need to go hand-in-hand, so that any asymmetries do not result in reduced recycling rates or increased pollution.

4.1. Plastic waste is projected to almost triple by 2060

4.1.1. *The increase in plastic waste is mostly driven by products with short lifespans*

The current use of plastics is far from circular, generating a significant amount of plastic waste that ends up in the environment. Most of this plastic waste is collected with other materials in the form of Municipal Solid Waste (MSW), which contains an important share of plastics. Waste estimates from the ENV-Linkages model include MSW as well as microbeads, waste from road markings and industrial waste, which includes waste from construction and transport activities.

The dynamics of plastic waste differ from those of plastics use as there is a time lag between use and waste, the length of which depends on the lifespan of the product (see Chapter 2 in OECD (2022[1])). For example, on average, plastics used in transport only become waste after 13 years on average, whereas the lifespan of some plastics in construction can be as long as 35 years. Other applications, such as consumer products and packaging, have very short lifespans.

In the *Baseline* scenario, plastic waste is projected to increase substantially in the coming decades, rising from 353 Mt in 2019 to 1 014 Mt in 2060 (Figure 4.1). In this scenario, continued socio-economic developments and economic growth, including recovery from the COVID-19 pandemic (Chapter 2), lead to rapidly rising plastics use (Chapter 3). An important trend is that emerging and developing economies catch up to higher income countries, implying that plastics use increases faster in these countries.

Figure 4.1. Plastic waste is projected to almost triple by 2060

Plastic waste by application in million tonnes (Mt), *Baseline* scenario

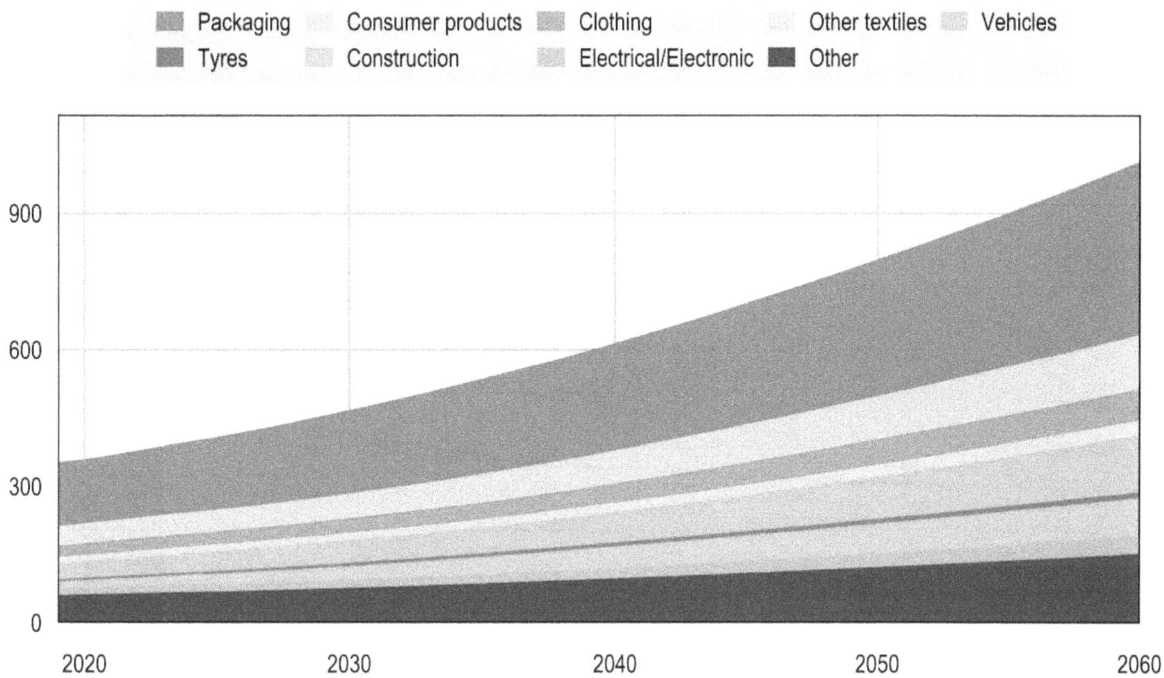

Source: OECD ENV-Linkages model.

StatLink https://stat.link/munclx

In line with the growth in the use of plastics, plastic waste increases for all applications, though not at the same rate. Waste from short-lived plastic products, such as packaging, consumer products and textiles, is projected to increase substantially, but their share in overall waste is projected to slightly decrease, from 63% in 2019 to 59% in 2060, as waste increases at a faster rate for other applications, such as motor vehicles.

One major development is the large increase in plastics use for construction. Growing economies invest in infrastructure and construction (OECD, 2019[2]), driving a rapid increase in the use of durable plastics with long lifespans. These long lifespans mean there is a lag between their production and end of life as waste (Figure 4.2). Indeed, the role of "historical" waste, i.e. waste from applications produced before 2019 is quite substantial for durable products such as those used in the vehicle and construction industries. While for packaging almost all waste generated after 2019 comes from plastics produced in or after 2019, for construction, more than 90% of plastic waste up until 2040 will be from plastics produced before 2019. The lag between plastics use and waste implies that plastics stocks accumulate in the economy and continue to create waste flows beyond 2060 (see Box 4.1).

Figure 4.2. The time lag between plastics use and waste varies by application

Historical and projected plastic waste by application in million tonnes (Mt), *Baseline* scenario

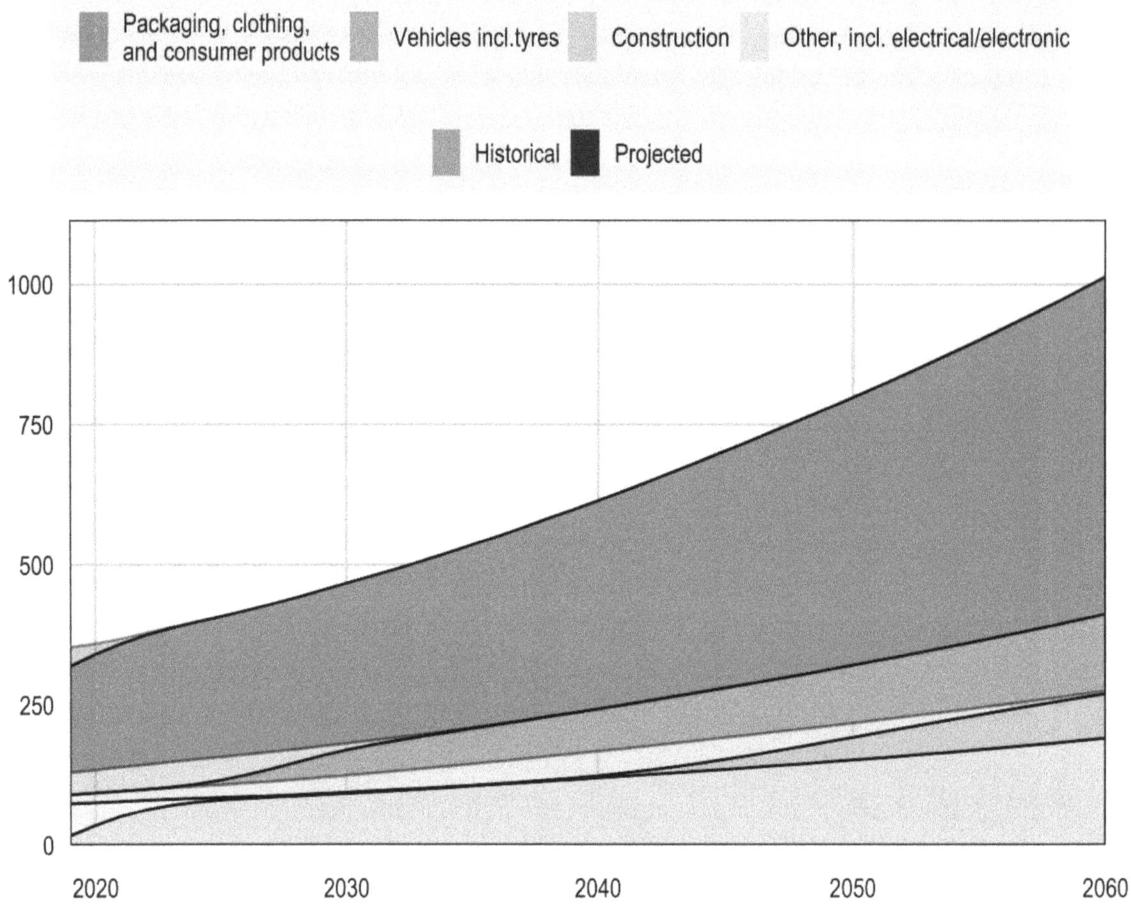

Note: full colours refer to waste from applications produced after 2019 (referred to as "Projected"). The slightly faded colours, further demarcated by the black lines, refer to waste generated by applications produced before 2019 (referred to as "Historical").
Source: OECD ENV-Linkages model.

StatLink https://stat.link/fpdo1w

Box 4.1. Long-lived plastics will contribute to waste levels even after the end of the century

In the ENV-Linkages projections, the waste presented for each year includes both the new waste resulting from the products used and discarded during that year, and the waste from goods produced in the past but not yet discarded. While the time horizon of the model is 2060, ENV-Linkages also calculates waste flows for plastics produced up until 2060 but that remain in use after the model horizon. This plastic stock inevitably becomes waste at some point after 2060. Thus, even if no more plastics were produced after 2060, there would still be an amount of "locked-in plastic waste" corresponding to the pre-2060 plastics use that would be disposed of post-2060. For short-lived applications, such as packaging, this locked-in plastic waste does not last for long after 2060, but for applications with long lifespans these waste streams will materialise over the course of several decades, and for some even into the next century (Figure 4.3). In total, these post-2060 waste streams amount to around 9 gigatonnes (Gt), or roughly one-quarter of the 33 Gt of plastic waste discarded between the first plastic products appeared in 1950 up until 2060.

Figure 4.3. Plastic applications with long lifespans delay waste generation and build up stocks of plastics in the economy

"Locked-in plastic waste" in million tonnes (Mt), *Baseline* scenario

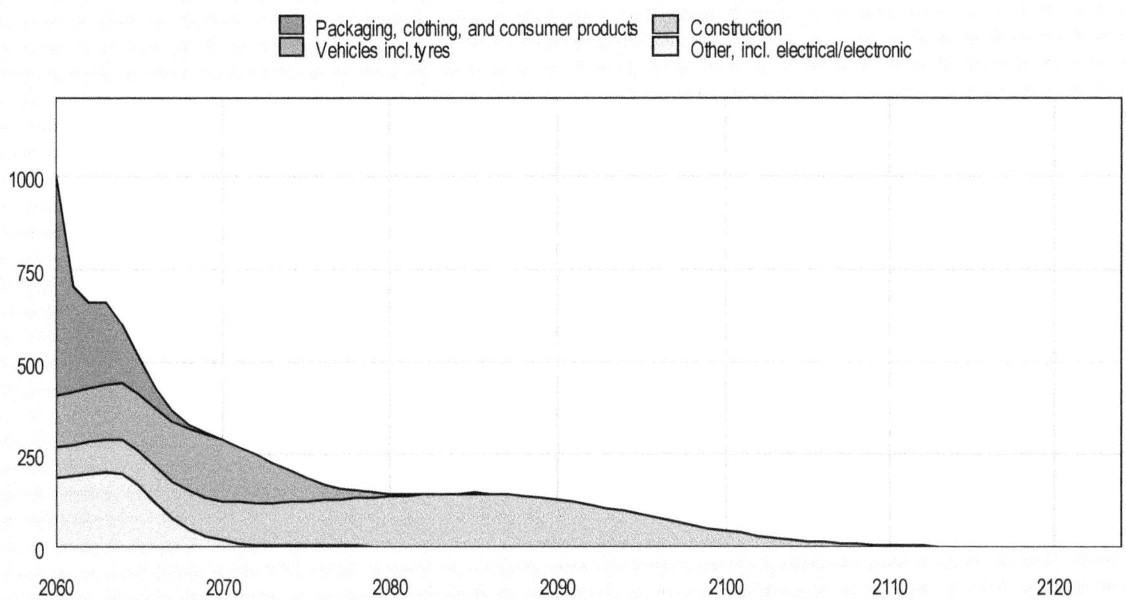

Note: Plastic waste projections after 2060 correspond to plastics that are produced prior to 2060 and are still in use in 2060. Those plastics that end their life beyond the modelling time horizon are referred to as "locked-in plastic waste".
Source: OECD ENV-Linkages model.

StatLink https://stat.link/k6yhwo

4.1.2. *Plastic waste will increase most in Africa and Asia*

Though plastic waste is projected to increase in all regions, it will increase most in non-OECD countries (Figure 4.4), driven by economic growth in emerging economies in Africa and Asia especially. While OECD countries generated roughly half of all plastic waste in 2019, their global share is projected to decrease to one-third in 2060, despite a projected doubling of their plastic waste generation, from 172 Mt in 2019 to 358 Mt in 2060. Non-OECD countries jointly increase their plastic waste production from 181 Mt to 657 Mt. A significant portion of the growth until 2060 already occurs before 2030, especially in currently fast-growing economies like the People's Republic of China (hereafter 'China'), whose share in global waste is projected to increase from 19% to 21%. After 2030, the share of China in global waste declines somewhat (to 18% in 2060), as growth concentrates especially in India, Other non-OECD Asia and Africa.

Figure 4.4. Africa and Asia will see the biggest increase in plastic waste

Plastic waste by region in million tonnes (Mt), *Baseline* scenario

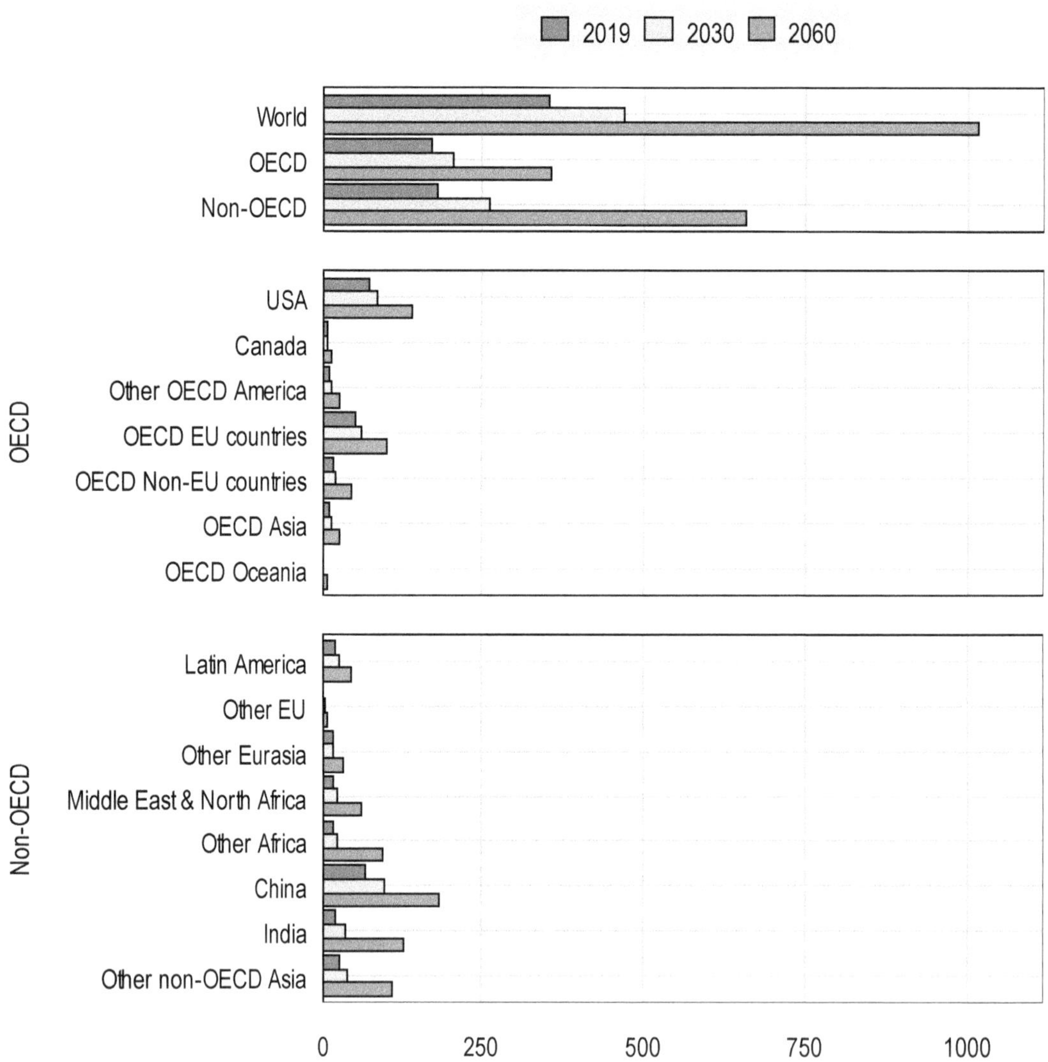

Source: OECD ENV-Linkages model.

StatLink https://stat.link/vi8kc6

The global average amount of plastic waste produced by each person is projected to double by 2060 from 2019 levels (Table 4.1). The highest growth rates for average per-capita waste are in regions that currently use relatively little plastics, such as Africa and Asia. While the growth in per-capita plastic waste is highest in non-OECD countries, they start from much lower levels. Therefore, their average waste per capita is projected to still be much lower than in OECD countries in 2060.

Table 4.1. OECD countries will still use the most plastic waste per capita in 2060

Plastic waste by region in kilogrammes per capita (kg p.c.), *Baseline* scenario

	2019	2030	2060	2060 evolution (index 1 in 2019)
World	46	55	100	2.2
OECD	126	144	238	1.9
USA	221	240	350	1.6
Canada	178	188	268	1.5
Other OECD America	58	63	108	1.9
OECD EU countries	122	142	239	2
OECD Non-EU countries	94	115	221	2.4
OECD Asia	69	86	173	2.5
OECD Oceania	62	83	168	2.7
Non-OECD	29	37	76	2.6
Latin America	43	52	86	2
Other EU	75	108	241	3.2
Other Eurasia	53	57	100	1.9
Middle East & North Africa	38	43	86	2.3
Other Africa	15	15	35	2.3
China	47	67	143	3
India	14	24	79	5.6
Other non-OECD Asia	21	29	71	3.4

Source: OECD ENV-Linkages model.

4.2. Despite better waste management, mismanaged waste will still almost double to 2060

4.2.1. *End-of-life fates of plastic waste*

The end-of-life fates of plastics vary by region, depending on waste management capacity and regulations. The ENV-Linkages model distinguishes between four different waste management categories:[1]

- Recycled: waste that is collected for recycling, processed, and used for the production of secondary plastics. This waste stream excludes the residues from recycling processes (see Box 4.2) that are disposed of using the other waste management categories.
- Incinerated: waste that is incinerated in a state-of-the art industrial facility, either with or without energy recovery.
- Landfilled: waste that is disposed of on the land, in a controlled way and according to state-of-the-art sanitary, environmental and safety requirements.
- Mismanaged: all other waste. This category includes waste that is collected and subsequently burned in open pits, dumped in water or disposed of in dumpsites and unsanitary landfills. It also includes waste that is not captured by waste collection, including e.g. road markings. This category

also includes uncollected litter, i.e. waste that results from littering by individuals or from fly-tipping, and that is not collected via street sweepings or other clean-up actions. It does not include collected litter that is disposed of through one of the other categories.

Box 4.2. The final treatment amounts of waste differ from the amounts collected

Waste management is a chain of consecutive actions. Waste is initially collected and then sorted for specific treatment purposes. During processing, recycling residues will be generated that will need to be disposed of (Box 4.3). Similarly, littered waste may be collected via street sweeping and other clean-up actions and then is partly diverted to other waste management categories. Figure 4.5 presents how waste processing for recycling purposes and litter clean-up affect the distribution between waste management categories. This chapter focuses on the final treatment of waste as this is more important for assessing the environmental burden of plastic waste.

Figure 4.5. Waste collected for recycling and litter flows are partly incinerated, landfilled and mismanaged

Plastic waste by treatment in Mt, year 2060

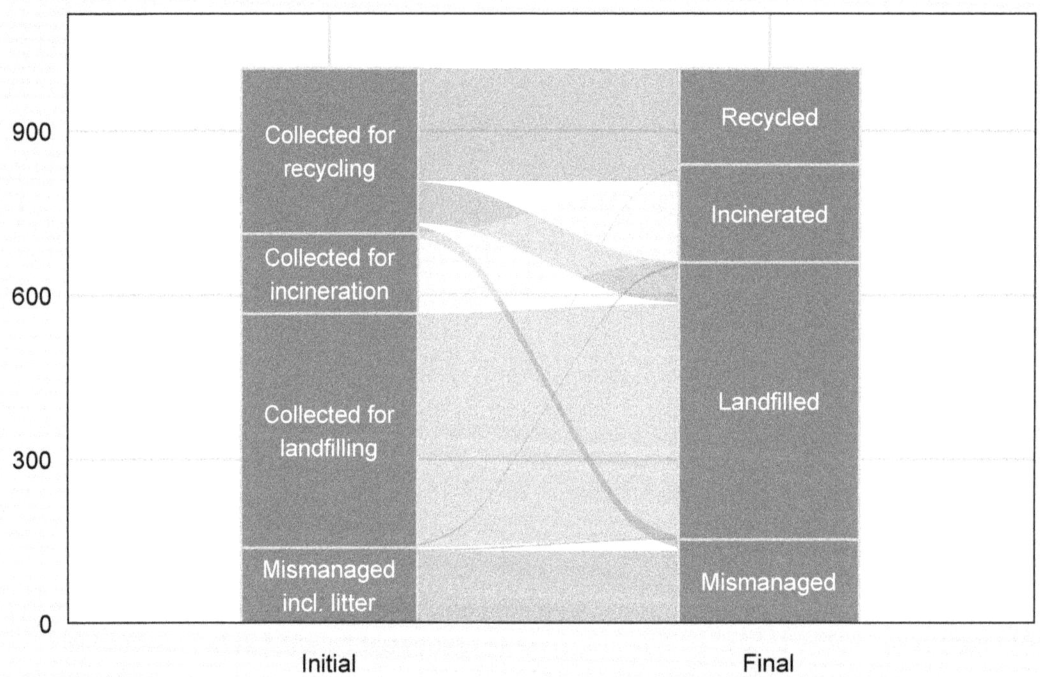

Source: OECD ENV-Linkages model.

StatLink https://stat.link/aixlrq

ENV-Linkages projects the future shares for recycled, incinerated, landfilled and mismanaged waste to 2060. It does so based on a combination of assumptions and cross-country regression analysis that assess the link between waste management categories and gross domestic product (GDP) per capita (see Annex A). One of the underlying assumptions is that the share of plastic waste collected for recycling keeps growing to 2060 at the same average rate as over the last 40 years. Another important assumption is that countries with growing income, invest in better waste collection and treatment as well as in improved litter clean-up, resulting in lower shares of total mismanaged waste.

There are noticeable differences in waste management between regions, reflecting past trends and countries' commitments. For instance, recycling is projected to rise steeply in the OECD EU and OECD Pacific regions, as well as China, following strong policy commitments. The share of incineration is projected to decline in OECD EU and OECD Pacific countries that already have high incineration rates. In contrast, in regions such as the Middle East and Africa and Latin America, the share of incineration is expected to increase, though remaining far below incineration shares in other regions. The share of landfilling decreases in several regions, including OECD EU and OECD Pacific, due to the increase in recycling and incineration. Conversely, the share of landfilling is projected to increase in non-OECD countries thanks to improved basic waste management and slowly declining mismanaged waste shares. However, mismanaged waste remains a large share of plastic waste in non-OECD countries.

Figure 4.6. Waste management improves more substantially in non-OECD countries

Shares of plastic waste by waste management category, *Baseline* scenario

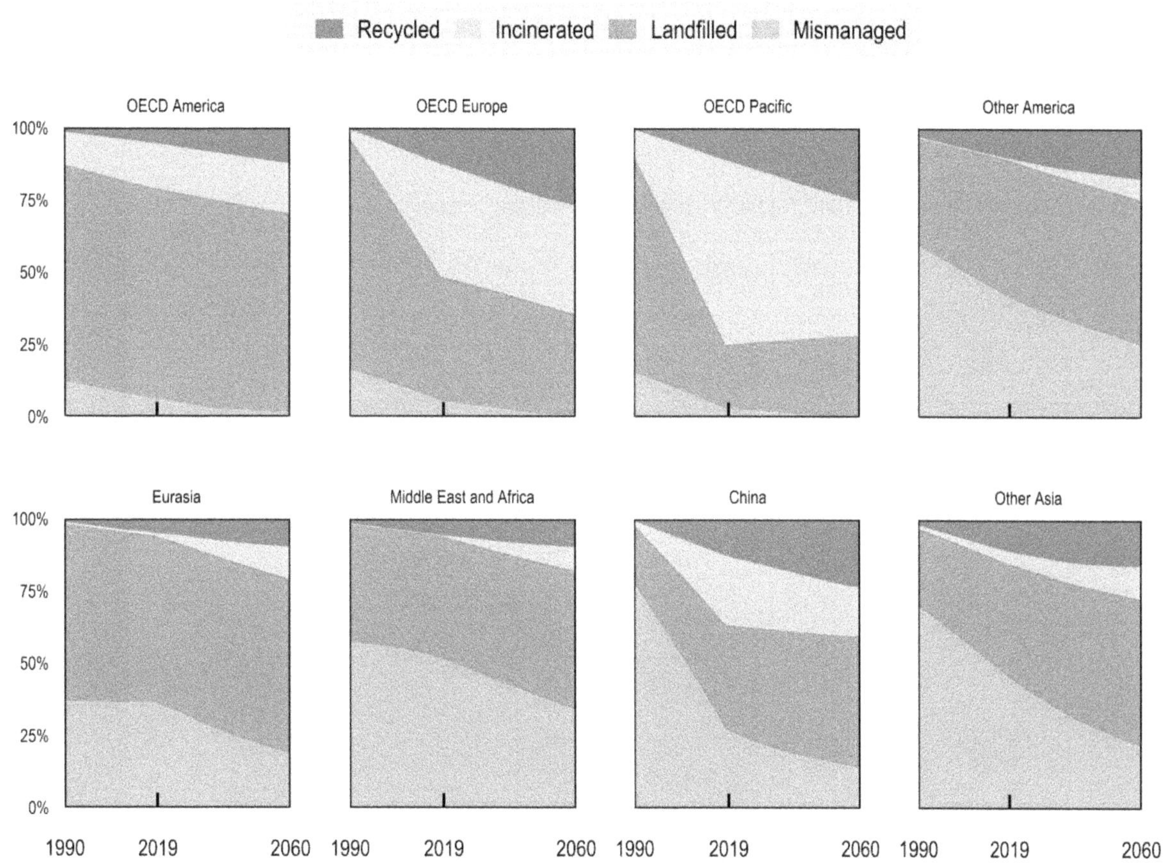

Note: For simplicity, this graph presents a more aggregate version of the ENV-Linkages model regions. OECD America groups the USA, Canada, Mexico, and OECD Latin America (Chile and Colombia). OECD Europe groups OECD EU and non-EU countries. OECD Pacific groups OECD Asia (Japan and Korea) and OECD Oceania (Australia and New Zealand). Eurasia groups Other EU and Other Eurasia. Middle East and Africa groups Middle East and North Africa and Other Africa. Finally, Other Asia groups India and Other non-OECD Asia. See Table A A.2 in Annex A for a detailed description of the regions used in ENV-Linkages.
Source: OECD ENV-Linkages model.

StatLink https://stat.link/m9xio4

4.2.2. *The share of mismanaged waste is projected to be lower in 2060, but its quantity higher*

In the *Baseline scenario*, recycling is projected to grow most, increasing from 33 Mt in 2019 to 176 Mt in 2060 (Figure 4.7). Thus, the share of plastic waste that is recycled almost doubles, reaching 17% of all waste generated, from 9% in 2019. This is a key indicator of circularity, together with the share of secondary plastics in total plastics production presented in Chapter 3, and shows that over time the global plastic economy becomes more circular

Incineration and landfilling also experience steady growth, with landfilling projected to remain the most common waste management category, although regional shares differ widely depending on how scarce land is in the region.[2] The amount of landfilled plastic waste triples from 174 Mt in 2019 to 507 Mt in 2060 while incinerated waste increases from 67 Mt to 179 Mt. Globally, the share of landfilling remains constant at around 50% while incineration accounts for a little less than 20% of plastic waste in 2060.

Mismanaged waste is projected to grow more slowly than other end-of-life fates. This is because recycling absorbs a bigger share of waste, and emerging countries invest part of their additional income in improved waste management facilities and litter collection. Consequently, the share of mismanaged waste decreases from 22% in 2019 to 15% in 2060. However, the amount of mismanaged waste still increases, driven by the growth in waste – nearly doubling from 79 Mt in 2019 to 153 Mt in 2060.

Figure 4.7. Sanitary landfilling will remain the most widespread waste management approach

Plastic waste by waste management category in million tonnes (Mt), *Baseline* scenario

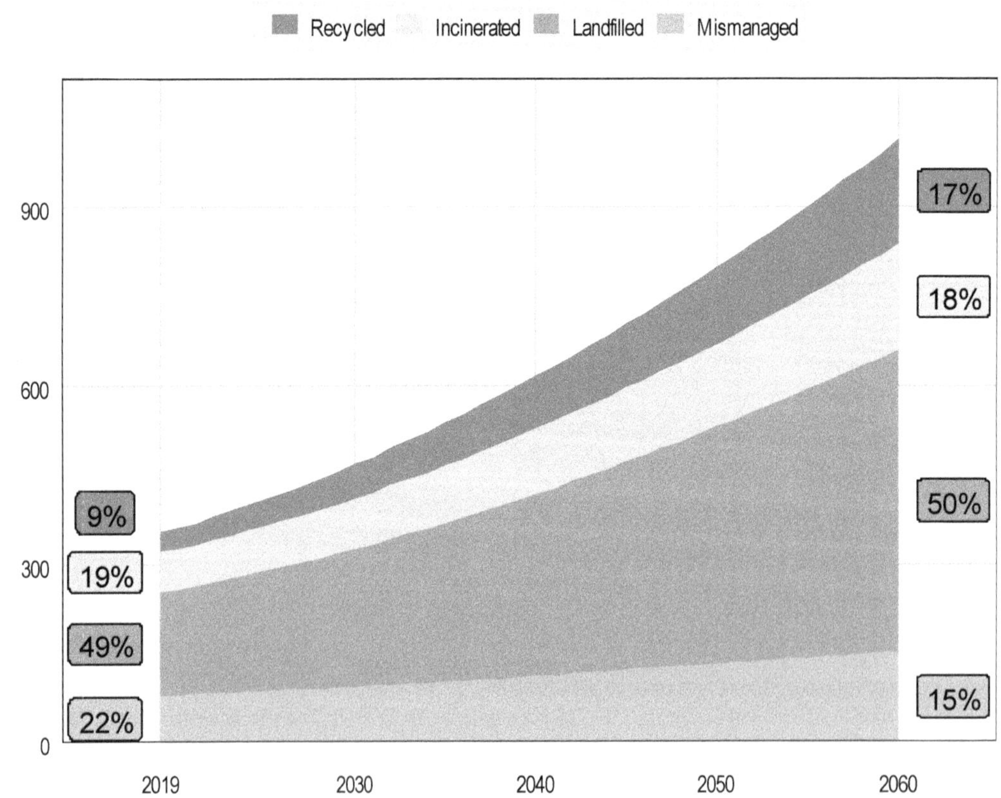

Note: The numbers to the left and right show the share of each fate in 2019 and 2060 respectively.
Source: OECD ENV-Linkages model.

StatLink https://stat.link/9imjey

Both the increased quantity of waste and improved waste management contribute to a strong increase in the amount of waste being recycled (Figure 4.8). Improved waste management takes into account changes in the share of plastic waste collected for recycling, as well as in the share of recycling residues that need to be disposed of (Roosen et al., 2020[3]), as explained in Box 4.3.

Figure 4.8. More plastic waste and better waste management drive the increase in recycled waste

Factors driving the increase in recycled plastic waste in million tonnes (Mt) between 2019 and 2060, *Baseline* scenario

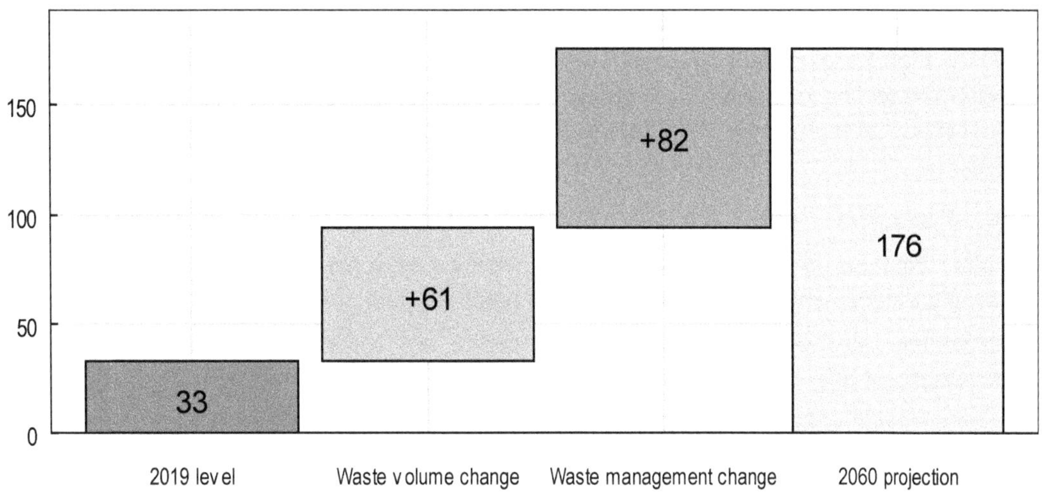

Notes:
Waste volume change represents a hypothetical projection in which all management shares are assumed to be fixed at the 2019 level. Thus, plastic waste collected for recycling is assumed to grow at the same speed as total plastic waste.
Waste management change represents the change in the waste management shares; this reflects a balance between larger shares of waste being generated in emerging and developing economies and improved waste management systems in all countries.
Source: OECD ENV-Linkages model.

StatLink https://stat.link/vb30as

Box 4.3. A large share of waste collected for recycling is lost in the process

The fraction of waste collected for recycling rises from 15% in 2019 to 30% in 2060 in the model, i.e. from 55 Mt to 302 Mt (Table 4.2). This share is assumed to grow linearly following past trends (Geyer, Jambeck and Law, 2017[4]), leading to a doubling in most regions by 2060. However, not all waste collected for recycling will be recycled effectively. For example, there are many plastics that are technically recyclable, but which are not collected in sufficient quantity for economically viable separation and reprocessing. Such "'non-target materials"', as well as impurities and difficult- to- sort mixes of polymers, will end up as recycling residues that need to be disposed of. In 2019, recycling residues represented around 40% of the plastic waste collected for recycling. OECD countries typically have relatively high levels of recycling residues due to the large-scale public collection of recyclables and less informal sorting of waste. Conversely, non-OECD countries have lower levels owing to the selective collection of high- value recyclables and the high-quality sorting by informal waste pickers (OECD, 2022[1]).

Three main factors affect the global share over time (see Annex A):

- Higher amounts of plastic waste allow economies of scale and more experience results in learning effects, which reduce the recycling residues (technology effect).
- Conversely, as more types of low-value plastics are collected, recycling residues increase (development effect).
- Income growth changes consumption patterns. Applications such as packaging and transport contain polymers that are relatively easy to recycle, while polymers in applications such as transport or electronics are more difficult to recycle. Consequently, regions that experience high growth in transport activities (see Section 3.1.3 in Chapter 3) will end up with a higher average rate of plastic recycling residues overall (consumption effect).

At the global level, the three trends more or less cancel each other out so that overall the fraction of recycling residues in collected plastic waste stays approximately constant (40% in 2019 versus 42% in 2060). However, the technology effect dominates in OECD countries (and thus loss rates decline), while outside the OECD the development effect and the consumption effect are stronger (and thus loss rates increase).

Table 4.2. The share of recycling residues decreases in OECD countries but increases in non-OECD countries

		Global	OECD	Non-OECD
2019	Collected for recycling (Mt)	55 Mt	27 Mt	28 Mt
	Recycled (%) / residues (%)	60% / 40%	56% / 44%	65% / 35%
2060	Collected for recycling (Mt)	302 Mt	108 Mt	194 Mt
	Recycled (%) / residues (%)	58% / 42%	64% / 36%	55% / 45%

Source: OECD ENV-Linkages model, based on Cottom et al. (2022[5]).

Improved waste management reduces the amounts of total mismanaged waste, partly offsetting the increase in plastic waste (Figure 4.9). Improvements in waste management systems are projected to be concentrated in emerging and developing economies, which are also the regions with the fastest growth rates of plastic waste (see Section 4.2.2).

Figure 4.9. The increase in mismanaged plastic waste is only partly offset by better waste management

Factors driving the increase in total mismanaged waste in million tonnes (Mt) between 2019 and 2060, *Baseline* scenario

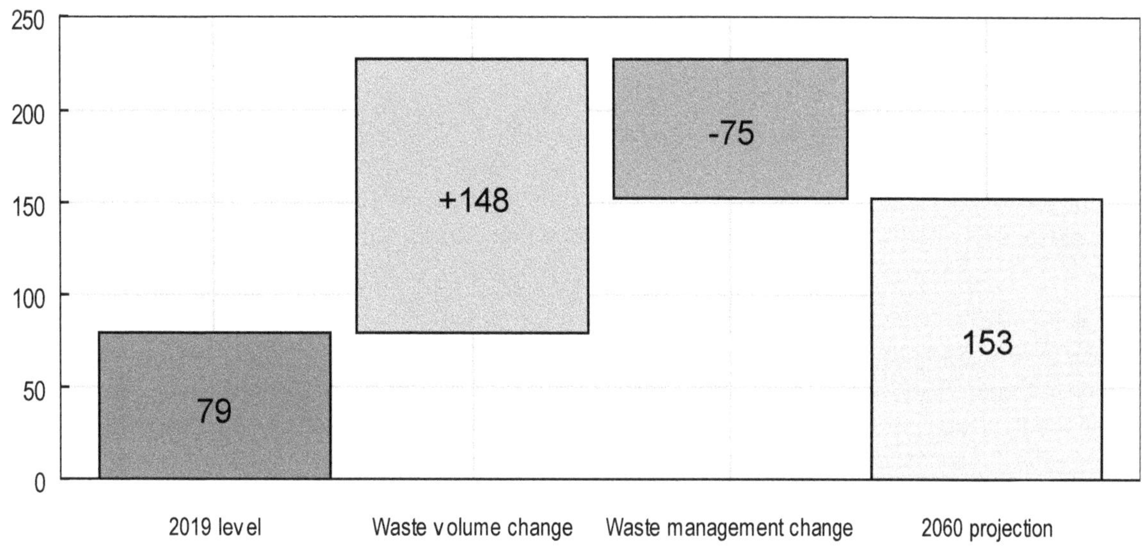

Notes:
Waste volume change represents a hypothetical projection in which all management shares are assumed to be fixed at the 2019 level. Thus, mismanaged plastic waste is assumed to grow at the same speed as total plastic waste.
Waste management change represents the change in the waste management shares; this reflects a balance between larger shares of waste being generated in emerging and developing economies and improved waste management systems in all countries.
Source: OECD ENV-Linkages model.

StatLink https://stat.link/2efnki

The projections of plastics use and waste outlined in this chapter rely on modelling assumptions and choices, which differ in part from those used previously in the literature. They add to the existing literature on plastics projections, confirming certain estimates and challenging others (Box 4.4).

Box 4.4. The wider scope of the OECD projections explains differences with existing studies

The long-term projections for plastics use, waste and mismanaged waste presented in this and the previous chapter are comparable to those of previous studies (Table 4.3). However, there are some differences, explained by the data and methodology used.

Geyer et al. (2017[4]) project global plastics use in 2050 to be higher than in the ENV-Linkages projections. The difference is due to two main factors. First, ENV-Linkages relies on plastics use estimates for the base year (i.e. 2015) from Ryberg et al. (2019[6]), who provide more regional and sectoral detail. Second, while Geyer et al. (2017[4]) mainly extrapolates historical trends, ENV-Linkages also takes into account structural change and technological progress, which reduce the use of plastics in the future. As indicated in Chapter 3, without structural and technology changes, plastics use (and the resulting plastic waste) projections would be around 16% higher in 2060.

ENV-Linkages follows Geyer et al. (2017[4]) and Ryberg et al. (2019[6]) in including fibres (13% of total plastics use) and Geyer et al. (2017[4]) in going beyond plastic waste from municipal sources by also taking into account industrial and construction waste (33% of total plastic waste). This leads to differences in both plastics use and waste compared to projections that exclude fibres and/or only look at municipal waste.

Despite, the larger scope, ENV-Linkages' mismanaged waste projections are lower than those by Lebreton and Andrady (2019[7]) and Lau et al. (2020[8]). Following Ryberg et al. (2019[6]), and municipal solid waste trends from Kaza et al. (2018[9]), ENV-Linkages assumes a significantly lower percentage of mismanaged waste in the projections. Furthermore, the ENV-Linkages projections take into consideration the possible impacts of current policies and marginal improvements on waste management in the coming decades. Without these policies, mismanaged waste would be higher (see Section 4.3).

Table 4.3. Comparison of projections with the existing literature

		2015/2016 (Mt)	2025 (Mt)	2040 (Mt)	2050 (Mt)	2060 (Mt)
Global plastics use	Geyer, Jambeck and Law (2017)[a]	380			1 100	1 371
	Ryberg et al. (2019)[a]	388				
	ENV-Linkages [a]	**413**	**516**	**766**	**976**	**1 231**
Global plastic waste	Geyer, Jambeck and Law (2017)[a]	302			902	
	Ryberg et al (2019)[b]	161				
	Lebreton and Andrady (2019)[b]	181	230	300		380
	Lau et al. (2020)[b]	220		420		
	ENV-Linkages [a]	**308**	**409**	**615**	**799**	**1 014**
Global total mismanaged plastic waste	Jambeck et al. (2015)[b]	37	70			
	Ryberg et al. (2019)[b]	41				
	Lebreton and Andrady (2019)[b]	80	95	155		213
	Lau et al. (2020)[b]	91		240		
	ENV-Linkages [a]	**74**	**86**	**111**	**132**	**153**

Note: Values for Geyer, Jambeck and Law (2017[4]) have been updated from cumulative values. All other yearly values are reported as presented in the respective studies. Where yearly values are not explicitly reported, they are not shown in the table.
a. all plastic.
b. municipal solid waste plastic only.
Source: Jambeck et al. (2015[10]), Geyer, Jambeck and Law (2017[4]), Lebreton and Andrady (2019[7]), Lau et al. (2020[8]), OECD ENV-Linkages model. The Lau et al. (2020[8]) report constitutes the underlying scientific paper for the Breaking the Plastic Wave report (The Pew Charitable Trust; SYSTEMIQ, 2020[11]).

4.2.3. *Improvements in waste management in Africa and Asia will play a key role in limiting mismanaged waste*

In the coming decades, waste management will evolve differently in OECD and non-OECD countries. In OECD countries, recycled waste will increase substantially. Recycling rates will increase from 9% in 2019 to 17% in 2060 (Figure 4.10). While landfilled and incinerated plastic waste will increase, their relative contribution remains stable over time. OECD countries already have a low share of mismanaged waste – 6% in 2019 – and this share is projected to decrease further, to 1.3% by 2060, which relates to a decrease in the amount of mismanaged waste from 10 Mt in 2019 to 4 Mt in 2060.

The changes in waste management will be more substantial in non-OECD countries. Recycled waste will increase, albeit at a slower pace than in OECD countries. Recycling rates will increase from 10% in 2019 to 16% in 2060. As countries become wealthier, the shares of landfilled and incinerated waste are both projected to increase. However, the share of incineration in non-OECD countries remains less than half that of OECD countries, reflecting the high investment cost of this waste management category. While the significant improvements in waste management infrastructure and litter collection result in a decreasing share of mismanaged waste, the yearly amounts of mismanaged waste are still projected to double, from 79 Mt in 2019 to 153 Mt in 2060.

Figure 4.10. Only 17% of global plastic waste is projected to be recycled by 2060

Plastic waste in million tonnes (Mt) and shares (%) of plastic waste by waste management category, *Baseline* scenario

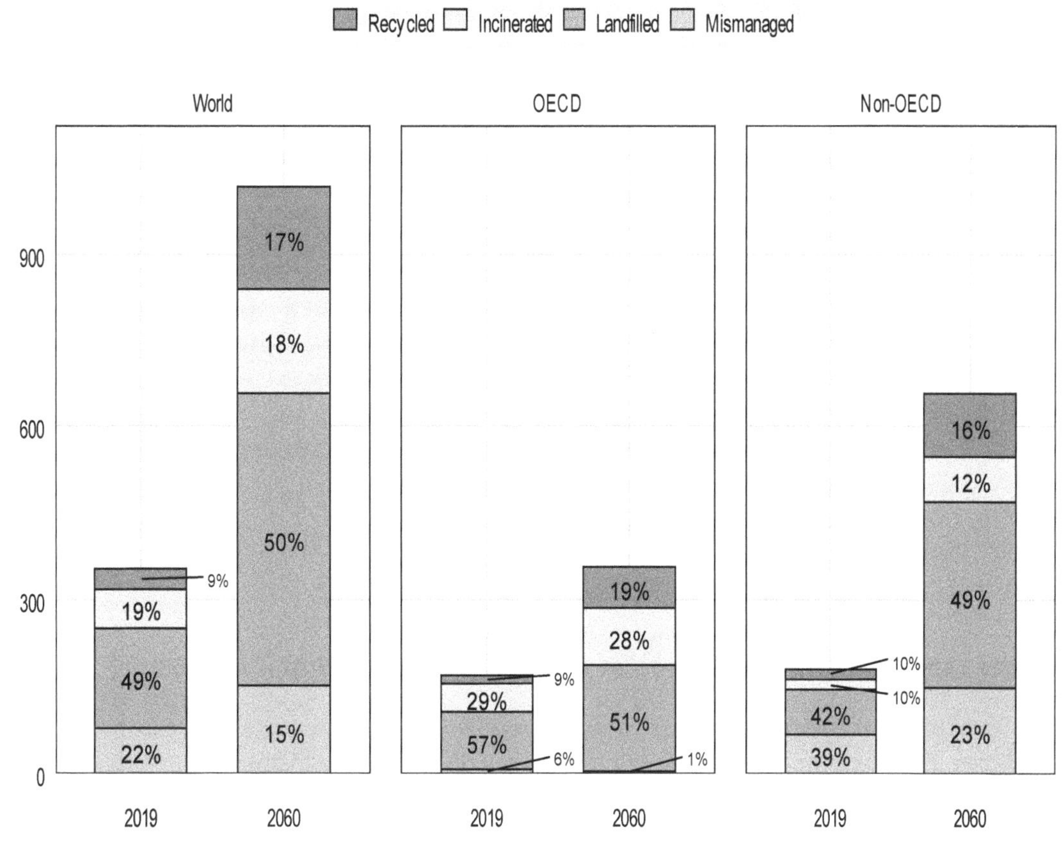

Source: OECD ENV-Linkages model.

StatLink https://stat.link/8d7krb

The increase in mismanaged waste in non-OECD countries is mostly driven by Africa and Asia (Figure 4.11). Economic growth in these regions leads to a strong increase in waste, but waste management systems do not evolve quickly enough to prevent mismanaged waste from increasing substantially. These projected amounts of mismanaged waste stress the urgent need to strengthen domestic policy measures and boost international co-operation further.

Figure 4.11. Mismanaged plastic waste remains a significant issue in most non-OECD regions

Shares (%) of plastic waste in million tonnes (Mt) by waste management category, *Baseline* scenario

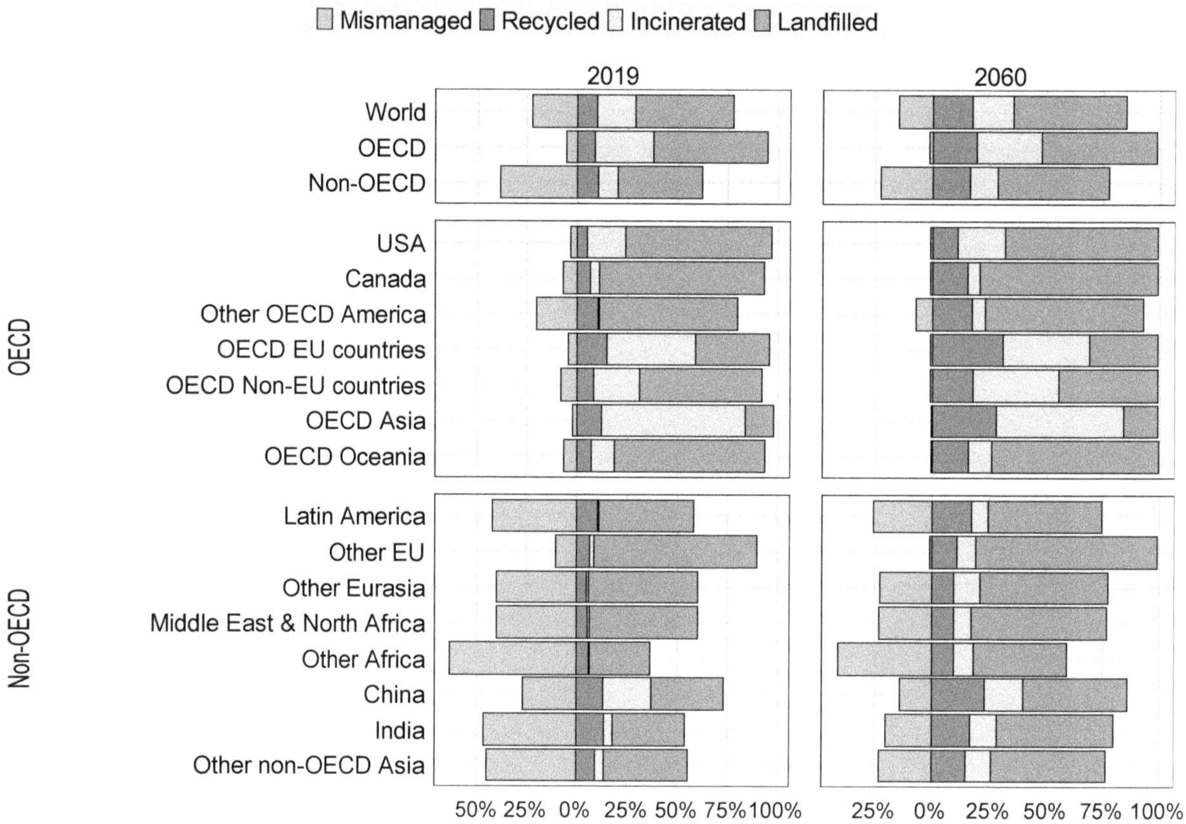

Source: OECD ENV-Linkages model.

StatLink https://stat.link/wer8fl

4.3. Plastic waste projections depend on key uncertainties surrounding waste management, trade and COVID recovery rates

4.3.1. *Waste management is assumed to keep improving – what if it doesn't?*

The evolution of waste management in the *Baseline* scenario takes into account the expected effects of current policies and existing trends in improvements to waste management. This explains why mismanaged waste increases much less rapidly than total plastics use and waste generation. To understand the effect of these waste management assumptions, the *Frozen* waste management policies scenario explores what would happen if there were no improvements in waste management beyond 2025 (Figure 4.12).[3]

The comparison between the *Frozen* and *Baseline* scenarios shows the importance of improvements in waste management systems for limiting the growth in mismanaged waste. If plastic waste management were to see no further improvements, recycling rates would remain limited to around 10% by 2060, while the *Baseline* scenario assumes a continued increase to more than 17%. Furthermore, the amount of plastic waste that would have to be landfilled by 2060 would increase significantly, putting even greater pressure on scarce land, especially near urban centres. But, perhaps most importantly, the amount of mismanaged plastics would increase to 269 Mt by 2060, compared to 153 Mt in the *Baseline*. In other words, the prolonged effects of existing policies (without any new policies to combat plastic waste), would be to avoid 116 Mt of plastic waste being mismanaged in 2060 – a more than 40% reduction.

Freezing the waste management categories at their 2025 levels in each region does not imply fixing the global shares. As growth in plastic waste generation is faster in countries with less developed waste management systems, their weight in global waste management shares increases. Thus, the share of global waste that is incinerated gradually declines in the *Frozen* scenario, and the share of mismanaged waste gradually increases. This emphasises the significant improvements that need to be made in plastic waste management systems in emerging and developing economies just to achieve the limited slowdown in global mismanaged waste growth projected in the *Baseline*. This will require sharing best practices and existing technologies to support rapidly developing countries in improving their waste management systems over time as their income grows.

Figure 4.12. Current policies significantly slow down the growth of mismanaged plastic waste

Plastic waste by waste management category in million tonnes (Mt), *Baseline* scenario

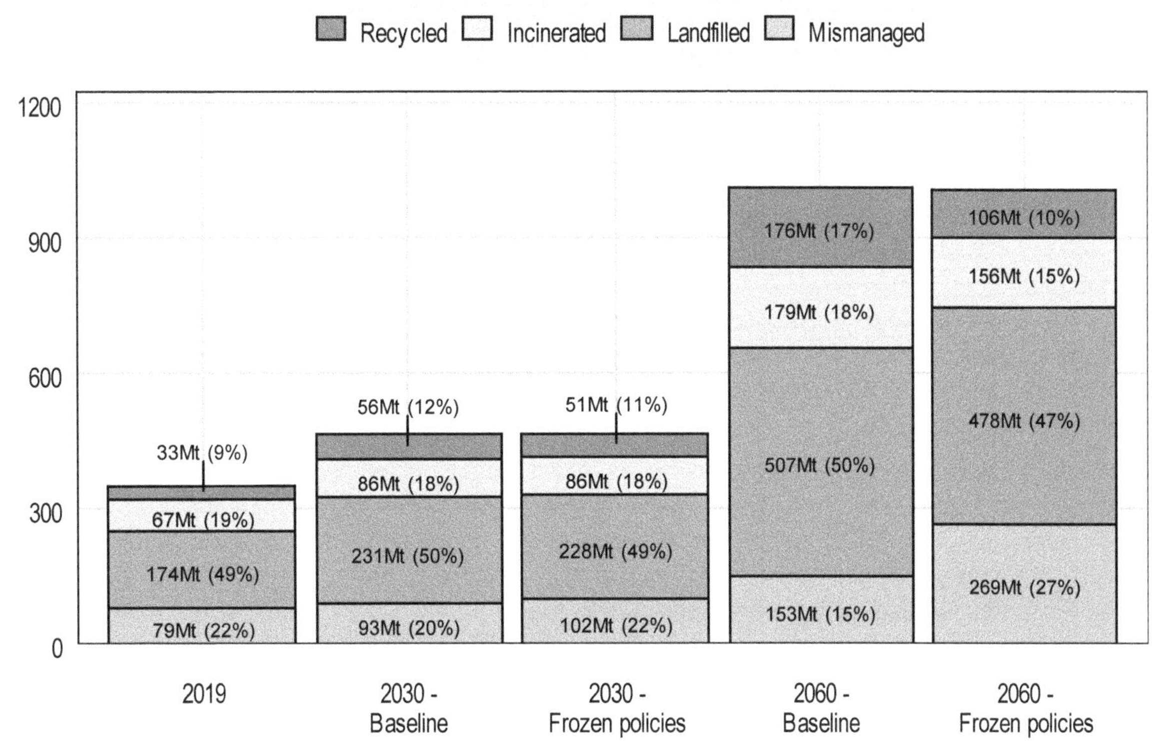

Source: OECD ENV-Linkages model.

StatLink https://stat.link/wlz2da

4.3.2. *Trade in waste is assumed to continue at low levels – what if it doesn't?*

The trade in plastic waste and scrap moves materials to countries with a comparative advantage in recycling plastic. This captures benefits derived from economies of scale and efficient and cheaper processing in the destination country, helps to secure inputs for high quality secondary plastics, and provides opportunities to fill cargo containers (when goods are shipped from one destination to another they can be empty on the way back) (Yamaguchi, 2021[12]; OECD, 2020[13]; Kellenberg, 2012[14]). However, there are concerns about possible negative impacts of the plastic waste trade, leading many countries to reconsider their trade policies and practices over the last few years (Yamaguchi, 2021[12]). These concerns stem from trade motivated by differences in environmental regulations and standards, the illegal trade in waste, and pollution caused by insufficient waste management capacities in the destination country, leading to leakage into the environment.

As a consequence, the international regulatory environment for transboundary trade in plastic waste has changed considerably in recent years (OECD, 2019[2]). Since 2015, traded plastic waste has declined, partly because China – and subsequently several other nations – have imposed restrictions on waste imports (Shi, Zhang and Chen, 2021[15]; Velis, 2014[16]). In addition, the Basel Convention – which regulates trade in plastic waste – has been amended out of concern for some of these impacts of plastics on the environment (Secretariat of the Basel Convention, 2020[17]). How this trade landscape will evolve in the coming years is uncertain and varies by region (Box 4.5). While the *Baseline* scenario assumes that current waste trade patterns will continue, this section investigates two extreme alternative baseline scenarios: (1) *No waste trade* scenario: strict policy measures eliminating all trade in plastic waste; and (2) *2015 Waste trade* scenario: a return to 2015 trade patterns.

Box 4.5. What if trade flows of plastic waste evolved differently?

The *No waste trade* scenario assumes that after 2019, all international trade in plastic waste between regions ceases.[1] In the *Baseline* scenario, total inter-regionally traded plastic waste in 2060 is projected to reach 10.9 Mt. In this hypothetical alternative baseline, this amount drops to 0.1 Mt. Obviously, exports and imports are reduced in all countries.

The *2015 Waste trade* scenario explores what could happen if the trade changes in 2015 had not occurred. Projections of inter-regional trade patterns of plastic waste in this scenario start from the 2015 bilateral trade flows and are then projected for the coming decades.[2] This has two effects. First, global inter-regional trade in plastic waste is projected to grow to more than 24 Mt by 2060, i.e. more than double the *Baseline* scenario. Second, the bulk of exported plastic waste is assumed to go towards China. As was the case in 2015. Although in reality the geography of this trade shifted away from China between 2015 and 2019 (Wen et al., 2021[18]; OECD, 2022[1]), the *2015 Waste trade* scenario assumes this shift does not take place.

An important caveat in this analysis is that the modelling framework only represents trade between the 15 model regions, and excludes any trade within these regions. Thus, for example trade between one of the countries in the OECD EU region with one of the countries in the non-OECD EU region is included, but intra-regional trade among any of the 22 OECD EU countries is excluded. As a consequence, total traded volumes are significantly smaller than when measured at the national level: the global trade volume equalled 14 Mt in 2015 and 7.5 Mt in 2019 (OECD, 2022[1]), while the inter-regional trade volume in the modelling framework accounts for 8.7 Mt in 2015 and 4.9 Mt in 2019, i.e. roughly one-third of total trade is aggregated (hidden) as intra-regional flows of the model. Nonetheless, comparing the alternative trade scenarios with the *Baseline* gives a feeling for the plausible range of traded plastic waste volumes in the coming decades, as well as their impacts on the volume of mismanaged waste and available plastic scrap for producing secondary plastics.

1. The modelling assumes that some trade between the two modelled regions of OECD-EU and non-OECD EU remains possible.
2. This includes a counterfactual development between 2015 and 2021, i.e. all post-2015 trade flows are adjusted.

The extent to which changes in plastic waste trade affect global volumes of mismanaged waste and available scrap depends on the waste management systems of the exporting and importing countries. Although a large share of the traded volumes concerns recyclable materials and can thus contribute to scrap for secondary plastics production, some imported waste will be mismanaged and eventually leak to the environment. In line with the *OECD Global Plastics Outlook Economic Drivers, Environmental Impacts and Policy Options* (OECD, 2022[1]), the modelling framework assumes that half of the traded plastic waste can be recycled, and that the other half end up in domestic waste streams, i.e. some is incinerated, some landfilled and some mismanaged, depending on the waste management system in the destination country (see Annex A).

Given the small volumes of waste traded inter-regionally, the improvements in waste management in the *Baseline* scenario, and the assumption that a significant share of the waste in the traded volumes can be recycled, the abolishment of plastic waste trade in the *No waste trade* scenario only slightly changes the total mismanaged waste in 2060 compared to the *Baseline* (a fall of less than half a percent, or less than 1 Mt), with most of the reductions occurring in the non-OECD Asian economies (Figure 4.13).[4]

The *2015 Waste trade* scenario, which assumes higher trade volumes, projects a slight increase in global mismanaged waste by 2060 (Figure 4.13). The increase in China more than compensates the decrease in other non-OECD Asian economies. Given that waste management systems tend to be more developed in China than in the other non-OECD Asian economies, the net global effect on mismanaged waste is small: an increase of less than 1 Mt compared to the *Baseline*. Thus, while inter-regionally traded volumes double compared to the *Baseline* scenario, the global volume of mismanaged waste is projected to remain unchanged.

Thus, the changes in plastic waste trade regimes within the range given by these two scenarios – and under the assumption that half of the traded waste is recycled – will affect trade patterns. But only if trade and environmental policies go hand in hand and the imported waste is properly managed will the consequences for leakage be limited.[5] More drastic changes to trade patterns, such as unlimited exports of plastic waste to countries with less developed waste management systems, i.e. waste dumping, would lead to significant increases in plastic leakage. Such a scenario would, however, be at odds with recent developments.

Figure 4.13. Alternative waste trade scenarios have limited impact on global mismanaged plastic waste and available scrap, masking regional shifts

Deviations from the *Baseline* scenario in 2060, waste trade scenarios

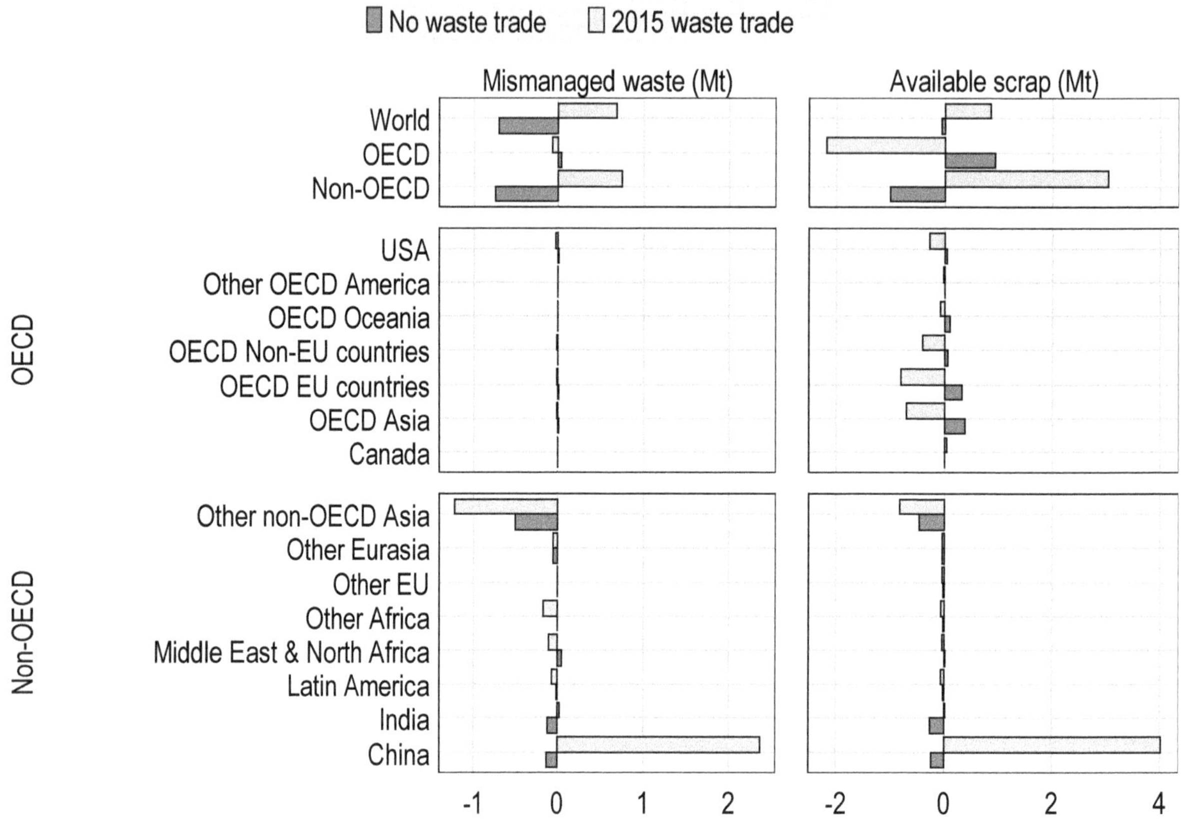

Source: OECD ENV-Linkages model.

StatLink https://stat.link/3w2mtn

By ensuring the imported recyclable material is indeed recycled and not diverted to open dumps or other mismanaged treatments, increasing imports of plastic waste can increase domestic stocks of plastic scrap available for secondary plastics production. In the *No waste trade* scenario, the recyclable material is no longer exported, and thus the countries that export plastic waste in the *Baseline* scenario, including most OECD countries, increase their domestic scrap. The importers (including most non-OECD countries) are confronted with less scrap available for secondary plastics production. The global effect is roughly zero: the materials do not disappear but are treated in the exporter countries, where recycling facilities are at least as advanced as in the importer countries. However, given that this is a baseline scenario where no ambitious policies to boost secondary production are implemented, the additional scrap in OECD countries may not be turned into more secondary plastics, but instead may only lead to higher recycling loss rates (and thus higher recycling residues) when the scrap is discarded. Furthermore, recycling capacity constraints may imply that in the short run more recyclable material is discarded until new recycling capacity becomes available.

Global scrap availability is not independent of plastic waste trade. When the trade flow is diverted to regions with less developed waste management systems and specifically lower recycling rates, less scrap is retrieved from the waste stream. The alternative *2015 Waste trade* scenario, which reverts trade flows to their 2015 patterns, suggests that developments between 2015 and 2019 may indeed have induced a decline in the global availability of scrap. In this scenario, more waste is exported to China, which has fairly high recycling rates and can better transform the waste into scrap (Figure 4.13). This increase more than outweighs the decrease in plastic scrap produced by other emerging economies in Asia. Such an increase in global scrap availability does not scale proportionally with the volume of traded waste because the higher exports of OECD countries lead to lower available scrap there. However, when the material is exported from an OECD country with lower recycling rates than China, then more scrap can be retrieved by export to China than when trade is restricted, and thus more plastics can be recycled.

Although the scenarios in this analysis are highly stylised, they shed light on how policies on the transboundary movement of plastic waste can drastically divert trading patterns with important implications both for regional recycling opportunities and plastic leakage into the environment. Specifically, if plastics trade were to be opened up to further divert plastic waste trade to countries with less waste management capacities, this would risk a greater increase of plastic leakage into the environment. It is therefore important to keep in mind that trade policies can drastically change the landscape of plastic waste in a relatively short period of time (which was the case for the introduction of Chinese import bans as well as the Basel Convention amendments on plastics), whereas developing recycling and waste management capacities is a long-term process, requiring investment and development plans, as well as inclusive frameworks to work with the informal sector in certain countries. To achieve a more circular use of plastics, trade policies and environmental policies need to go hand-in-hand in a co-ordinated fashion, so that any asymmetries do not result in reduced recycling rates or increased leakage into the environment.

4.3.3. *Recovery from the COVID-19 pandemic could take longer than assumed*

As outlined in Chapter 3 of OECD *Global Plastic Outlook: Economic drivers, environmental impacts and policy options* (OECD, 2022[1]), the COVID-19 pandemic was estimated to have led to a reduction in global plastics use in the short term. This decrease results from the economic slowdown, which had a stronger effect than the increase in the use of plastics for personal protective equipment.

In the coming decades, while the effect of the COVID-19 pandemic is projected to fade, it will nevertheless lead to a reduction in global plastic waste in the *Baseline* scenario compared to pre-pandemic waste projections (Figure 4.14). The effect on plastic waste in 2025 is much smaller than the effect on plastics use (Chapter 2), as a significant share of plastics lasts for many years. There are, however, concerns about the large share of plastics for personal protective equipment, especially face masks, that are either littered or leak into the environment (OECD, 2022[1]). The regional differences in changes in plastic waste roughly reflect the changes in plastics use.

Figure 4.14. The effects of COVID-19 on plastics use and waste remain noticeable even in 2060

Deviations from the pre-COVID projection in percentage change (%), *Baseline* scenario

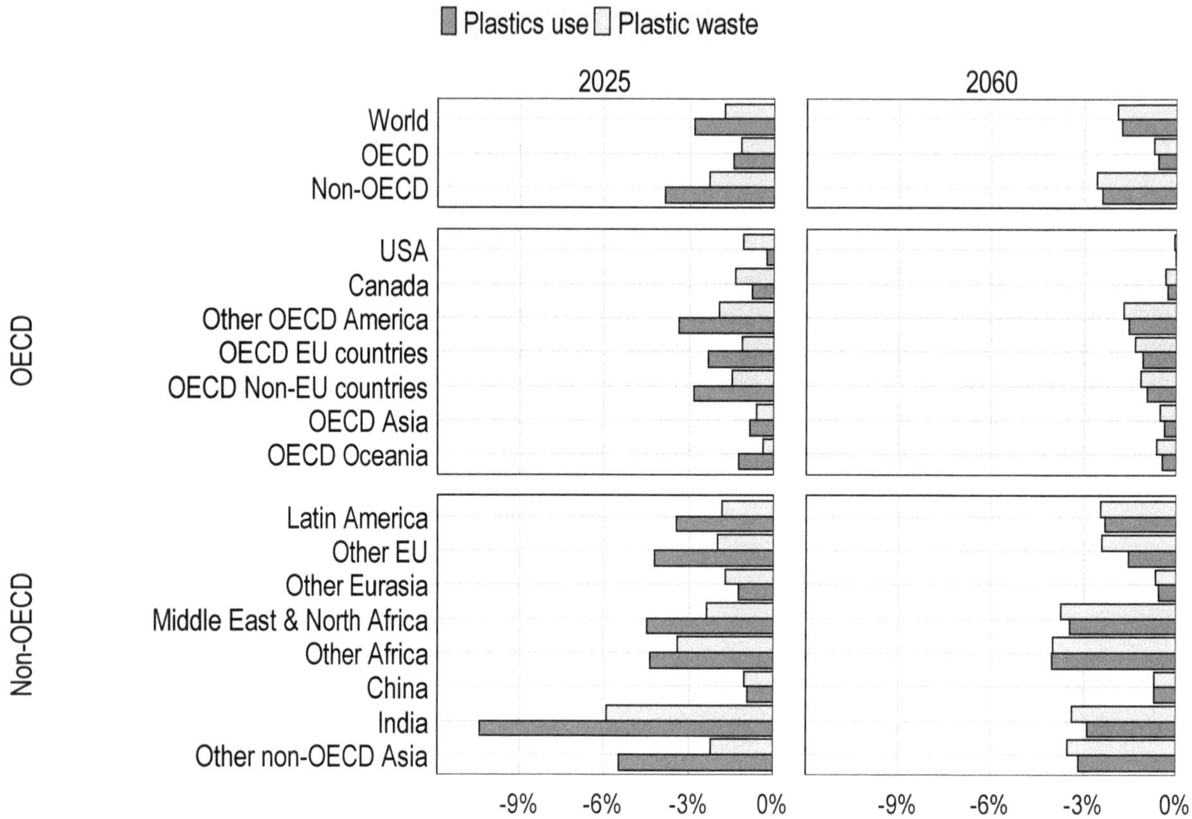

Source: OECD ENV-Linkages model.

StatLink https://stat.link/qs3gzv

Over time, the effects on plastic waste catch up with the effects on plastics use, and by 2060 reductions in plastics use and waste are similar. The *Baseline* projections for plastics use and waste are still below the pre-COVID projections in almost all countries, as the result of lower levels of economic activity over the long term.[6] Assumptions about the speed of recovery from COVID-19 further affect these waste projections (Box 3.4).

The specific sectoral drivers – especially the different lifespans of plastics applications – affect how quickly the COVID-19 pandemic has consequences for projected plastic waste (Figure 4.15).[7] Taken together ("Total" effect in Figure 4.15), the largest impacts on plastic waste occur around 2035 and gradually phase out afterwards. The type of polymer used also has an effect. In some cases, notably polyethylene terephthalate (PET), the effects on plastic waste have very small delays and largely follow the economic impacts, whereas polyvinyl chloride (PVC), for example, has a more staged effect as the various applications that use PVC (e.g. in construction) tend to have much longer lifespans. Regarding the applications, there is a huge time difference between plastic waste from packaging and waste from construction. The effects of the lifespan of plastics are much more visible in the projections for the applications than for the polymers, highlighting that most polymers are used in multiple applications, some with longer lifespans than others.

Figure 4.15. The impact of COVID-19 on plastic waste depends on the polymer and application

Deviations from the pre-COVID projection of plastic waste in percentage change (%), *Baseline* scenario

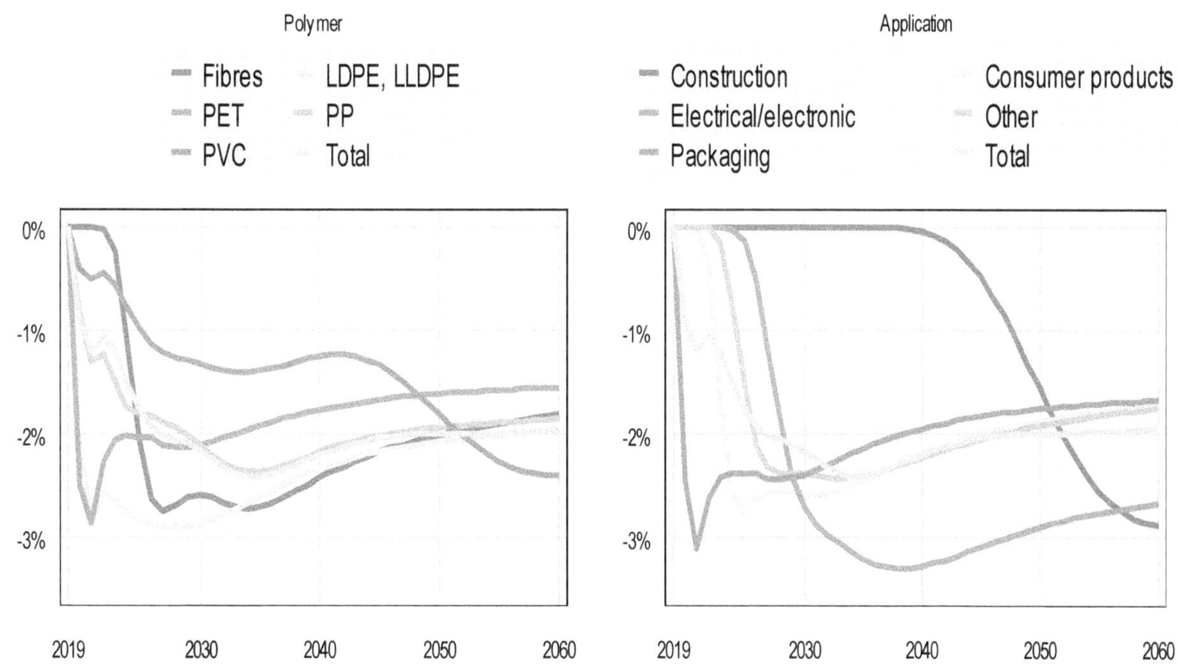

Note: PET = polyethylene terephthalate; PVC = polyvinyl chloride; LDPE = low-density polyethylene; LLDPE = linear low-density polyethylene ; PP = polypropylene. This assessment is only based on the effects of the COVID-19 pandemic on plastics use and ignores changes in the composition of waste induced by the pandemic, such as a permanent shift to single-use plastics.
Source: OECD ENV-Linkages model.

StatLink https://stat.link/y4g13u

Box 4.6. How would a slow recovery from COVID-19 affect plastics use and waste?

Assumptions about the rate of recovery determine the timeframe and level at which plastics use and waste stabilise compared to the pre-COVID projection, i.e. when growth rates fully recover back to their pre-COVID reference projection levels. A *Slow recovery* scenario was modelled to explore this (see Annex B). Whilst the impact on global plastic waste stabilises at around 2% below pre-COVID levels in the *Baseline* scenario by 2060, it stabilises at around 4% below for the *Slow recovery* scenario. In both settings, the COVID-19 related impacts on plastic waste lag significantly behind the impacts on plastics use; in the *Baseline* scenario they catch up around 2035, but with slow recovery this delay extends to 2045.

Figure 4.16. A slow recovery from COVID could lower global plastics use and waste by 4% in 2060

Deviations from the pre-COVID reference projection in percentage change (%)

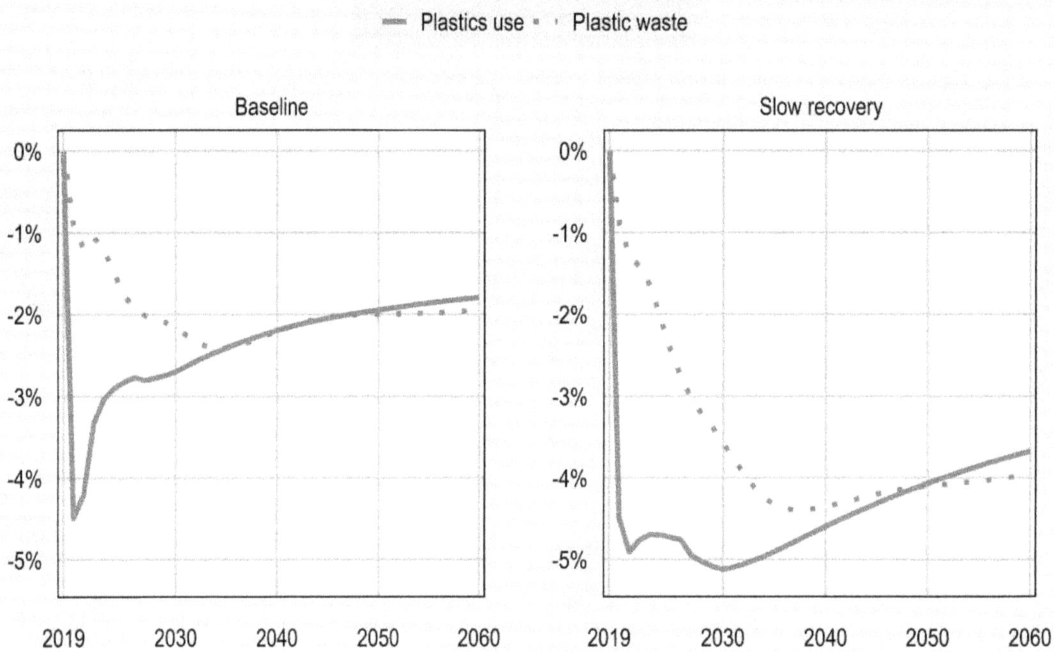

Note: The small spike in 2023 in the plastic waste projection for the *Baseline* scenario is linked to a quick rebound in the use of PET, which has a very short lifespan (Figure 4.15).
Source: OECD ENV-Linkages model, using the economic projections in Dellink et al. (2021[19]).

StatLink https://stat.link/0gaez8

References

Cottom, J. et al. (2022), "Spatio-temporal quantification of plastic pollution origins and transportation (SPOT)" University of Leeds, UK, https://plasticpollution.leeds.ac.uk/toolkits/spot/. [5]

Dellink, R. et al. (2021), "The long-term implications of the Covid-19 pandemic and recovery measures on environmental pressures: A quantitative exploration", *OECD Environment Working Papers*, No. 176, OECD Publishing, Paris, https://doi.org/10.1787/123dfd4f-en. [19]

Geyer, R., J. Jambeck and K. Law (2017), "Production, use, and fate of all plastics ever made", *Science Advances*, Vol. 3/7, p. e1700782, https://doi.org/10.1126/sciadv.1700782. [4]

Jambeck, J. et al. (2015), "Plastic waste inputs from land into the ocean", *Science*, Vol. 347/6223, pp. 768-771, https://doi.org/10.1126/science.1260352. [10]

Kaza, S. et al. (2018), *What a Waste 2.0: A Global Snapshot of Solid Waste Management to 2050*, Washington, DC: World Bank, https://doi.org/10.1596/978-1-4648-1329-0. [9]

Kellenberg, D. (2012), "Trading wastes", *Journal of Environmental Economics and Management*, Vol. 64/1, pp. 68-87, https://doi.org/10.1016/j.jeem.2012.02.003. [14]

Lau, W. et al. (2020), "Evaluating scenarios toward zero plastic pollution", *Science*, Vol. 369/6510, pp. 1455-1461, https://doi.org/10.1126/science.aba9475. [8]

Lebreton, L. and A. Andrady (2019), "Future scenarios of global plastic waste generation and disposal", *Palgrave Communications*, Vol. 5/1, p. 6, https://doi.org/10.1057/s41599-018-0212-7. [7]

OECD (2022), *Global Plastics Outlook: Economic Drivers, Environmental Impacts and Policy Options*, OECD Publishing, Paris, https://doi.org/10.1787/de747aef-en. [1]

OECD (2020), *OECD Workshop on International Trade and Circular Economy – Summary Report*, OECD Publishing, Paris, https://www.oecd.org/env/workshop-trade-circular-economy-summary-report.pdf. [13]

OECD (2019), *Global Material Resources Outlook to 2060: Economic Drivers and Environmental Consequences*, OECD Publishing, Paris, https://doi.org/10.1787/9789264307452-en. [2]

Roosen, M. et al. (2020), "Detailed Analysis of the Composition of Selected Plastic Packaging Waste Products and Its Implications for Mechanical and Thermochemical Recycling", *Environmental Science & Technology*, Vol. 54/20, pp. 13282-13293, https://doi.org/10.1021/acs.est.0c03371. [3]

Ryberg, M. et al. (2019), "Global environmental losses of plastics across their value chains", *Resources, Conservation and Recycling*, Vol. 151, p. 104459, https://doi.org/10.1016/j.resconrec.2019.104459. [6]

Secretariat of the Basel Convention (2020), *Basel Convention Plastic Waste Amendments*, http://www.basel.int/Implementation/Plasticwaste/PlasticWasteAmendments/Overview/tabid/8426/Default.aspx. [17]

Shi, J., C. Zhang and W. Chen (2021), "The expansion and shrinkage of the international trade network of plastic wastes affected by China's waste management policies", *Sustainable Production and Consumption*, Vol. 25, pp. 187-197, https://doi.org/10.1016/j.spc.2020.08.005. [15]

The Pew Charitable Trust; SYSTEMIQ (2020), *Breaking The Plastic Wave: A Comprehensive Assessment of Pathways Towards Stopping Ocean Plastic Pollution*, https://www.systemiq.earth/wp-content/uploads/2020/07/BreakingThePlasticWave_MainReport.pdf. [11]

Velis, C. (2014), *Global recycling markets – plastic waste: A story for one player – China. Report prepared by FUELogy on behalf of ISWA Globalisation and Waste Management Task Force*, International Solid Waste Association, Vienna, https://doi.org/10.13140/RG.2.1.4018.4802. [16]

Wen, Z. et al. (2021), "China's plastic import ban increases prospects of environmental impact mitigation of plastic waste trade flow worldwide", *Nature Communications*, Vol. 12/1, https://doi.org/10.1038/s41467-020-20741-9. [18]

Yamaguchi, S. (2021), "International trade and circular economy - Policy alignment", *OECD Trade and Environment Working Papers*, No. 2021/02, OECD Publishing, Paris, https://doi.org/10.1787/ae4a2176-en. [12]

Notes

[1] Additional information on waste management modelling is provided in Annex A.

[2] Landfilled waste implies an increased demand for suitable landfilling sites, putting additional pressure on land use. However, by taking the land density into account in the projection of the share of landfilling in the region, the largest increases in area required for landfilling are in regions that have relatively ample space available. However, landfilling often occurs close to city centres, which could still pose problems. Furthermore, the environmental implications of increased land use for waste management could not be taken into account in the analysis.

[3] In particular, under this hypothetical scenario the shares of the different waste management categories are set constant beyond 2025, allowing for a three-year lag to account for the continued impact of current policies.

[4] The change in global mismanaged waste depends on the relative difference in mismanagement shares across exporters and importers: the waste is still treated, but in a different location.

[5] The environmental implications of other waste treatment methods also matter: if for example the exported waste is landfilled rather than incinerated in the destination country, there is no energy recovery and there is also potential for pollution.

[6] While GDP growth rates fully recover, GDP levels remain somewhat below the *Baseline* projection; see (Dellink et al., 2021[19]).

[7] While the *Baseline* scenario presented in this report includes the impacts of COVID-19 on economic activity, lack of robust data meant it was not linked to the impacts on particular types of plastics, apart from plastics for face masks and other personal protective equipment (see Chapter 3 in (OECD, 2022[1])).

5 Projections of plastic leakage to the environment to 2060

Plastic leakage to the environment causes wide-ranging impacts on the environment and human health, and is a key concern for policy makers. With plastics use and waste projected to triple by 2060, this chapter explores the projected trends for leakage to the terrestrial and aquatic environments in the *Baseline* scenario, which assumes no new policy measures are taken. The chapter also quantifies projected trends in airborne microplastics pollution from tyre and brake wear.

Key messages

- The leakage of plastics into terrestrial and aquatic environments is substantial and increasing. In 2019, 22 million tonnes (Mt) of plastics leaked into the environment globally; the *Baseline* scenario projects this to double to 44 Mt by 2060. This projection is highly uncertain, with low and high estimates ranging from 34 to 55 Mt.
- The share of leaked plastics from OECD countries halves to 6% by 2060, with projections suggesting that the share of OECD countries in macroplastic leakage will reduce from 11% in 2019 to 2% by 2060. However, their contribution to microplastic leakage remains high, despite falling from 35% in 2019 to 28% in 2060. In non-OECD countries, the combination of population and economic growth and less developed waste management systems are projected to drive substantial growth in the leakage of both macro- and microplastics, especially in Asia and Africa.
- Mismanaged waste (waste not disposed of adequately) is by far the largest source of leaked macroplastics, accounting for 86% of all plastic leakage in 2019. Though it will remain the main source of leakage to 2060, leakage from marine activities and of microplastics are projected to grow quickly in the coming decades, highlighting the need to also address the sources of these flows.
- The flow of plastics leaking from mismanaged waste into aquatic environments (streams, rivers, lakes and the ocean) is projected to increase by 91% to 2060, reaching 11.6 Mt per year in 2060 from 6.1 Mt per year in 2019. Other sources of leakage, including marine activities and microplastics, more than double. Although the upward trend is clear, there is substantial uncertainty around the magnitude of the leakage, which could range between 6.2 Mt and 16.8 Mt.
- These continuous inflows of plastic waste drive up the accumulated stocks of plastics in aquatic environments to a staggering 493 Mt by 2060, more than three times from 2019 levels. As macroplastics break down into microplastics in the environment very slowly, the annual amount of microplastics generated by this degradation is limited to less than 1 Mt in 2060. However, the process will continue beyond 2060, implying a permanent inflow of microplastics into the seas and the ocean.
- By 2060, 145 Mt of plastics will have accumulated in the ocean. The ocean is projected to receive an annual inflow of 4 Mt of mismanaged waste plastics from rivers and coastlines by 2060, more than double the inflows of 1.7 Mt in 2019. Ambitious policies with global reach will be needed to reduce the additional leakage to the ocean to zero as put forward by the G20 in the Osaka Blue Ocean Vision, and ultimately end plastic pollution, as articulated in the UNEA Resolution 5/14.

5.1. Plastic leakage the environment presents a wide range of environmental and human health hazards

Plastic leakage – i.e. the flows of plastics into the environment – and the accumulation of plastics in the environment are problems of increasing concern for ecosystems and human health. The presence of plastics has now been documented in all the major ocean basins, on beaches, in rivers and lakes, as well as in terrestrial and aerial environments (OECD, 2021[1]). Even pristine environments such as the Arctic and remote mountain areas have been found to be contaminated with plastics (Obbard et al., 2014[2]; Allen et al., 2019[3]).

The majority of plastic materials that enter the environment will persist for a long time. Large items (usually referred to as macroplastics), such as bottles or fishing nets (OECD, 2021[4]), can also slowly degrade and fragment into microplastics – i.e. particles, fragments or fibres smaller than 5 mm in diameter[1] – and potentially into nanoplastics,[2] amplifying the likelihood of exposure and risks for ecosystem and human health (Andrady, 2011[5]). Removing plastics from the environment may be difficult and costly (see Section 8.4.2 in Chapter 8), if not virtually impossible in certain cases (e.g. microplastics or debris in the deep ocean and sediments).

The impacts of marine plastic pollution on wildlife have been widely reported. Plastics harm many species (e.g. mussels, turtles, fish, sea birds, marine mammals) via ingestion or entanglement. Entangled organisms may be hindered in their ability to feed, breathe, move, and avoid predators, while ingestion of plastics can lead to suffocation, intestinal blockages, or starvation. At least 550 wildlife species are known to be affected by either entanglement in or ingestion of plastic debris, with negative implications for biodiversity, ecosystem health and the sustainability of fisheries (Kühn, Bravo Rebolledo and van Franeker, 2015[6]).

Owing to their small size, microplastics are particularly likely to be ingested by aquatic species, either directly or by feeding on contaminated species. Microplastics have been found in the digestive tracts of several marine and freshwater species (OECD, 2021[1]). Particle ingestion may result in physical injuries inducing inflammation and stress, obstruct feeding organs and reduce the feeding activity and efficiency (SAPEA, 2019[7]). Laboratory experiments have shown that exposure to microplastics may result in reduced feeding efficiency, starvation, reduced growth rates, physical deterioration, and increased mortality rates (Wright, Thompson and Galloway, 2013[8]). Humans may also be exposed to microplastics, for instance by consuming contaminated food and drinks or by inhalation.

There are also concerns that plastic materials may play a role in exposing wildlife and humans to suspected hazardous chemicals. The possible health effects of exposure to hazardous chemicals include carcinogenicity, reproductive health effects, developmental toxicity, and mutagenicity (causing genetic mutations). Certain additives used during production, such as Bisphenol A, polychlorinated biphenyls (PCBs), phthalates, and some brominated flame retardants are suspected endocrine disruptors, i.e. chemicals with thyroid-disrupting effects (WHO, 2019[9]). Plastics may also act as a sink and transportation media for chemicals and persistent organic pollutants (POPs) that accumulate on their surface while in the water. Generally, the exposure of organisms to these chemicals may vary widely, depending on concentrations of pollutants and local circumstances (GESAMP, 2015[10]).

Assessing the risks from plastic leakage for ecosystems and human health requires a better understanding of the current and projected levels of leakage. To date, estimates of the amounts of plastics that leak into the environment and spread to land, water and air have been based on substantial assumptions due to a lack of knowledge about elements that affect leakage, such as the mobility of leaked plastics, weather patterns and the rate of degradation. To improve the knowledge base, four research groups were mobilised as part of the OECD's plastics work (see Box 5.1).

Box 5.1. How is plastic leakage quantified in the Global Plastics Outlook?

The OECD ENV-Linkages model is used in the analysis to create economic projections (Chapter 2) and link them to plastics use (Chapter 3) and waste, including a distinction between different waste management categories (Chapter 4). This information on economic growth, plastics use and waste from ENV-Linkages is then used as input for external models that calculate the leakage to the environment. The estimates of plastic leakage presented in this report combine the work of four research groups, each looking at complementary aspects:

- experts from the Technical University of Denmark (DTU), who led the research underlying the Ryberg et al. (2019[11]) study, quantified plastic leakage to the environment;
- experts from the University of Leeds, who contributed to Lau et al. (2020[12]), quantified macroplastic leakage to terrestrial and aquatic environments;
- Laurent Lebreton, who contributed to the leakage estimations in Borrelle et al. (2020[13]), quantified plastic leakage to and mobility of plastics in aquatic environments;
- Nikolaos Evangeliou from the Norwegian Institute for Air Research (NILU), who developed the Evangeliou et al. (2020[14]) study, quantified microplastics from brake and tyre wear that leak directly to the atmosphere.

In this Outlook, as well as in the previous *Global Plastics Outlook: Economic Drivers, Environmental Impacts and Policy Options* (2022[15]), the estimates for plastic leakage to the environment are produced by combining the estimates from DTU and Leeds University and providing a range (low, central and high estimates). DTU provides estimates for macroplastic leakage coming from mismanaged waste (municipal solid waste or MSW, non-MSW and litter) and marine activities, as well as microplastics. Leeds University provides estimates for leakage from mismanaged waste only. For mismanaged waste (representing the bulk of the leakage), the central estimates are calculated as the average of the two estimates provided by DTU and Leeds University. High and low then correspond to the higher and lower values between the values produced by DTU and Leeds University. For the leakage of marine activities and microplastics, the values of DTU are used as central estimates.

Aquatic leakage is quantified based on the central projection. In Section 5.3 on aquatic leakage, to account for uncertainties in estimating emissions at regional level, confidence intervals are given with low and high emission probability ranges derived from the midpoint emission estimate and respectively subtracting and adding the standard deviations of lower and higher country-scale emission probabilities as provided by Borrelle et al. (2020[13]) and weighted by country population size.

Annex A describes the approach used to estimate current leakage, which is also presented in the OECD *Global Plastics Outlook: Economic Drivers, Environmental Impacts and Policy Options* (2022[15]), and to provide projections for the future.

Although the combination of approaches draws on state-of-the-art expertise on this topic, the results should be interpreted with care as there is still significant uncertainty surrounding certain parameters used in the modelling.

5.2. Plastic leakage to the environment is projected to double by 2060

The global annual plastics leaked to the environment is projected to double, from 22 million tonnes (Mt) in 2019 to 44 Mt in 2060 (Figure 5.1) in the *Baseline* scenario. In this scenario, continued socio-economic developments and economic growth, including recovery from the COVID-19 pandemic (Chapter 2), lead to rapidly rising plastics use (Chapter 3) and plastic waste (Chapter 4). An important trend is that emerging and developing economies catch up with higher income countries.

The lack of robust knowledge surrounding certain critical factors, such as the share of mismanaged waste that is lost to the environment, means these estimates have wide uncertainty ranges depending on the assumptions employed, with the high estimate being almost 55 Mt and the low estimate 34 Mt in 2060 (16 Mt – 28 Mt in 2060). Despite the uncertainty, the projections show that in the *Baseline* scenario, plastic leakage will increase over time and add to the plastic stocks already accumulated in the environment. The rest of this section focuses on the central estimates in Figure 5.1.

Figure 5.1. All estimates agree that global plastic leakage is growing, though magnitudes vary

Plastic leakage to the environment in million tonnes (Mt), *Baseline* scenario

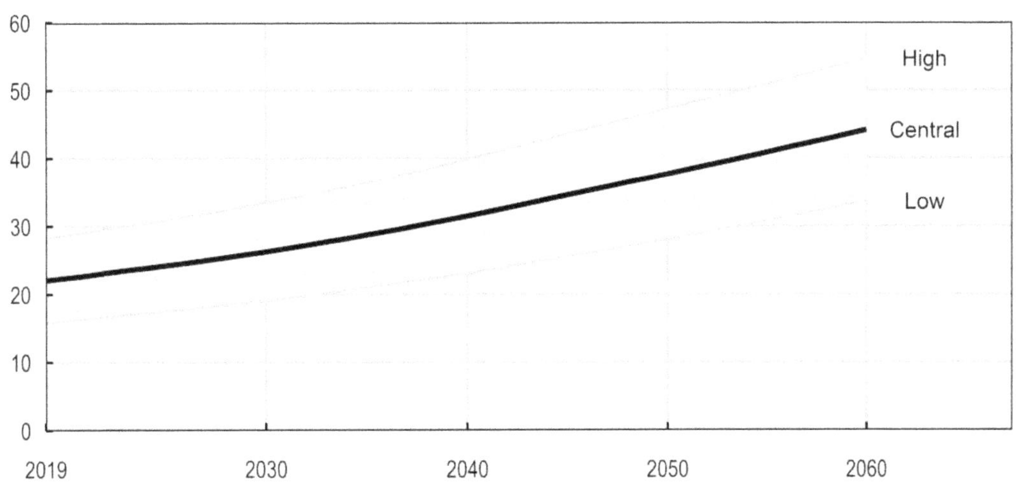

Source: OECD ENV-Linkages model, based on Ryberg et al. (2019[11]) (high estimate) and Cottom et al. (2022[16]) (low estimate).

StatLink https://stat.link/dgc9yp

Leakage of both macroplastics and microplastics is projected to double between 2019 and 2060 (Figure 5.2). The annual leakage of macroplastics increases from 19.4 Mt in 2019 to 38.4 Mt in 2060, while the leakage of microplastics doubles, to reach 5.8 Mt in 2060.

Not all regions will see the same rates of increase. The global increase in plastic leakage is largely driven by non-OECD countries, following the increase in mismanaged waste discussed in Chapter 4. While OECD countries see a fall in annual plastic leakage, from 3.2 Mt in 2019 to 2.5 Mt in 2060, plastic leakage more than doubles in non-OECD countries, from 18.9 Mt to 41.6 Mt (Figure 5.2). The region with the highest increase in leakage is Sub-Saharan Africa (Other Africa), where waste management systems do not evolve quickly enough to match the socio-economic changes that drive plastics use and waste. Leakage also increases substantially in Asia, where the largest increase in the region is in India and Other non-OECD Asia.[3]

While the share of OECD countries in overall macroplastic leakage decreases, from 11% in 2019 to 2% in 2060, they continue to contribute a high share of leaked microplastics (28% in 2060, compared to 35% in 2019). Leakage of microplastics increases substantially both in OECD and non-OECD countries, suggesting that microplastic leakage is an increasingly important issue for the whole world.

Figure 5.2. Leaked macro- and microplastics will double, with regional differences

Plastic leakage to the environment by region in million tonnes per year (Mt), *Baseline* scenario

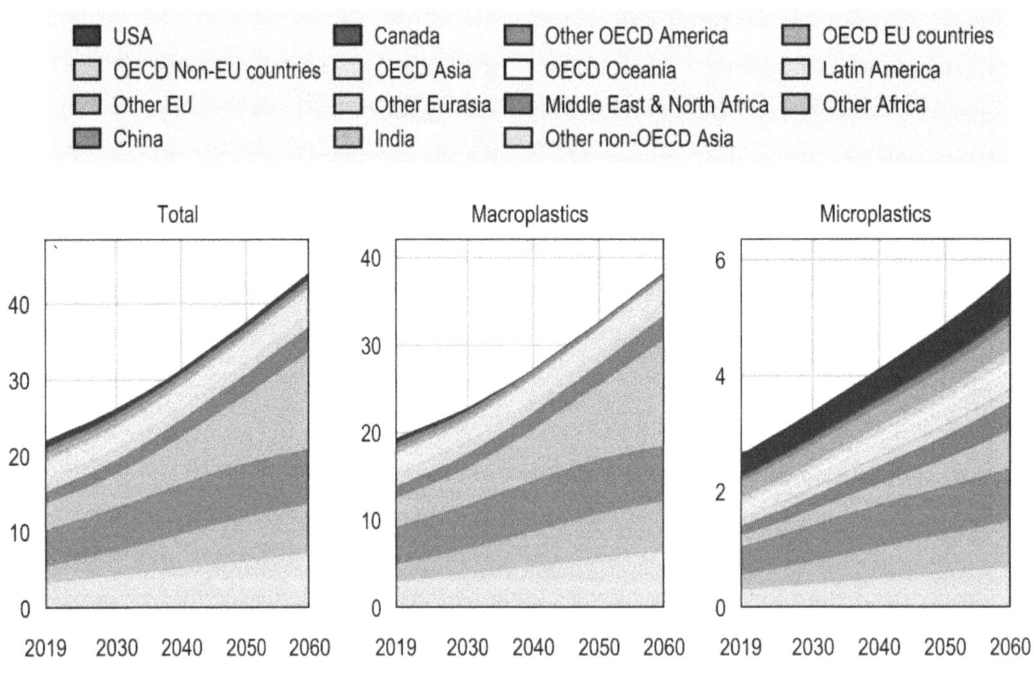

Source: OECD ENV-Linkages model, based on Ryberg et al. (2019[11]) and Cottom et al. (2022[16]).

StatLink https://stat.link/hqarij

Mismanaged waste is by far the main source of macroplastic leakage to the environment (OECD, 2022[15]), making up 99% of leaked macroplastics by 2060 (Figure 5.3), and mainly originating in non-OECD countries (Chapter 4). The annual leakage from mismanaged waste excluding litter in non-OECD countries doubles to 35.4 Mt in 2060, compared to 0.1 Mt in 2060 in OECD countries. Littering is the fastest growing source of macroplastic leakage and reaches an annual amount of over 2.3 Mt globally in 2060. Leakage from marine activities (mostly fishing nets, but also dolly ropes[4]) – the only source of macroplastic leakage included in the scope that does not originate from mismanaged waste – more than doubles globally to reach 0.6 Mt in 2060, 17% of which originates from OECD countries.

While macroplastic leakage to the environment can be reduced by focusing on mismanaged waste, the leakage of microplastics is a more pervasive and complex problem and it is increasing in all regions. The largest assessed sources of leaked microplastics in 2060 are wastewater sludge[5] (30%), tyre abrasion (24%), and microplastic dust[6] (19%):

- Leakage of microplastics from waste water sludge is projected to more than double in OECD countries, from 0.4 Mt in 2019 to 0.9 Mt in 2060. However, it will quintuple in non-OECD countries, following the development of waste water treatment plants (WWTPs) in many countries, and it is projected to reach 0.8 Mt in 2060. Thus, while OECD countries represent 72% of the global leakage for this category in 2019, their share is projected to decrease to about half in 2060. While an increase in WWTPs will prevent the direct leakage of microplastics into rivers, the resulting sludge – containing microplastics and other chemicals – needs to be dealt with.[7]
- Microplastic leakage from tyre and brake abrasion is projected to double globally, following a projected increase in road transport. In many non-OECD countries, this growth is stronger as economic development drives an increasing demand for transport (Chapter 3). In addition to leaking microplastics to terrestrial and aquatic environments, tyre and brake abrasion also emits microplastics to the air (see Section below).
- Microplastic dust is projected to increase globally from 0.8 Mt a year in 2019 to 1.1 Mt in 2060. Over 90% of the leakage in this category (1 Mt) is projected to occur in non-OECD countries.

Figure 5.3. Plastic leakage comes from a wide range of sources

Plastic leakage to the environment in million tonnes per year (Mt), *Baseline* scenario

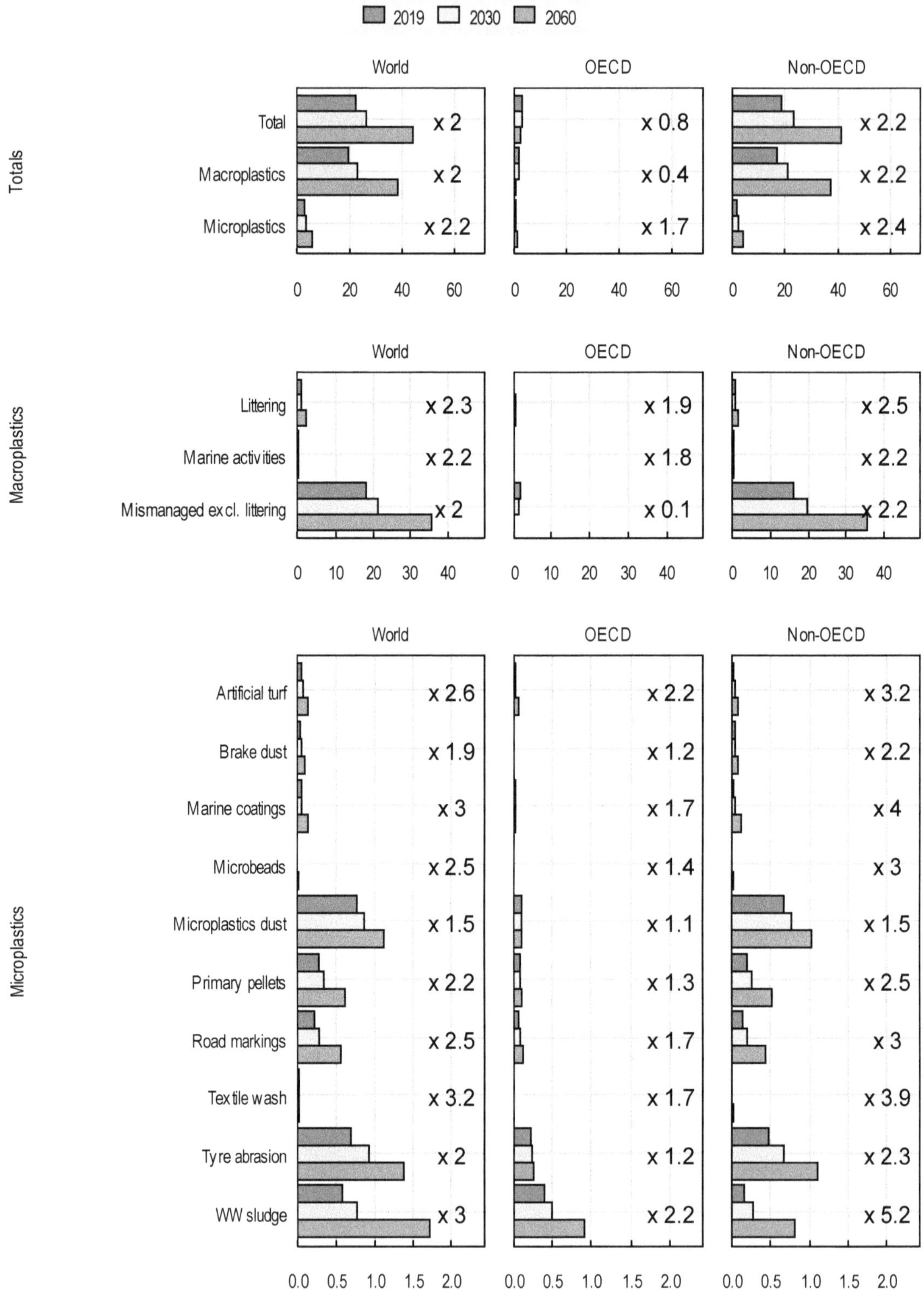

Note: The numbers on the right of each graph show the increase between 2019 and 2060. WW = waste water
Source: OECD ENV-Linkages model, based on Ryberg et al. (2019[11]) and Cottom et al. (2022[16]).

StatLink https://stat.link/mx4pez

The changes in macro- and microplastics over time are strongly linked to socio-economic developments. As income and plastics use increase, plastic leakage per person increases steadily at the global level, from 2.9 kg/cap in 2019 to 4.3 kg/capita in 2060 (Figure 5.4). This is largely accounted for by growth in non-OECD countries, where plastic leakage per capita increases from 3 kg/cap in 2019 to 4.8 kg/cap in 2060. The profile of OECD countries is different: plastic leakage per capita initially decreases, from 2.3 kg/cap in 2019 to 1.6 kg/cap in 2050, before increasing again to reach 1.7 kg/cap in 2060. The decrease to 2050 stems from the sharp fall in macroplastic leakage following a near phasing out of mismanaged waste (while microplastic leakage keeps increasing). However, after 2050, the growth in macroplastic littering and microplastic leakage, driven by the effect of population growth and economic growth on plastics use, implies that total leakage stabilises and even increases slightly again to 2060. This evolution highlights that policy measures that aim at curbing plastic leakage to the environment need to go beyond waste management and also take into account the quantities of plastics produced and discarded.

As economies develop and improve their waste management systems, the ratio between plastic leakage and GDP decreases from 0.24 g/USD (grams per USD) in 2019 to 0.17 g/USD in 2060. Although the ratio is expected to decrease in all regions, in the absence of additional policy intervention non-OECD countries will not catch up with OECD countries as macroplastic leakage from mismanaged waste remains a major source of leakage in non-OECD countries. The OECD average more than halves, from 0.06 g/USD in 2019 to 0.02 g/USD in 2060, while the non-OECD average halves from 0.53 g/USD to 0.33 g/USD mainly driven by changes in macroplastic leakage. Microplastic leakage per dollar of output decreases slightly following the close link between microplastic leakage and plastics use, and the slowly decreasing plastics intensity of the economy (see Section 3.2.3 in Chapter 3).

As waste management systems improve, plastic leakage decouples from plastics use, as indicated by the leakage-to-plastics use ratio (Figure 5.4). Globally, the ratio decreases from 4.8% in 2019 to 3.6% in 2060. This ratio decreases in both OECD and non-OECD countries, despite a disparity in levels. The OECD ratio is projected to decrease the most, from 1.5% to 0.6%, with a near absence of mismanaged waste by the end of the projection horizon. In contrast, in non-OECD countries the ratio decreases, but from 7.6% to 5.3%. This underlines the importance of improving waste management practices all over the world and especially in low and middle-income countries.

Overall, the projections show that the dynamics of macro- and microplastic leakage change as economies develop and improve their waste management systems. Macroplastic leakage follows an "Environmental Kuznets Curve" (Grossman and Krueger, 1995[17]) (Figure 5.5, top panel): leakage initially rises but then starts falling at higher income levels. The growth in plastics use and waste generation initially dominates and causes leakage to grow. However, as countries develop further, there is greater demand for better waste management systems and more willingness to deal with visible environmental impacts, such as macroplastic leakage. Thus, they invest in better waste management infrastructure, leading to lower rates of mismanaged waste and therefore declining macroplastic leakage. Microplastic leakage is projected to increase with GDP per capita, regardless of the level or region (Figure 5.5, bottom panel), although some saturation occurs at higher levels of income. Microplastics are not as visible as macroplastics, and therefore initiatives to curb leakage are less likely to be promoted.

Figure 5.4. While plastic leakage per capita increases, leakage rates will decouple from GDP and plastics use levels

Baseline scenario, to 2060

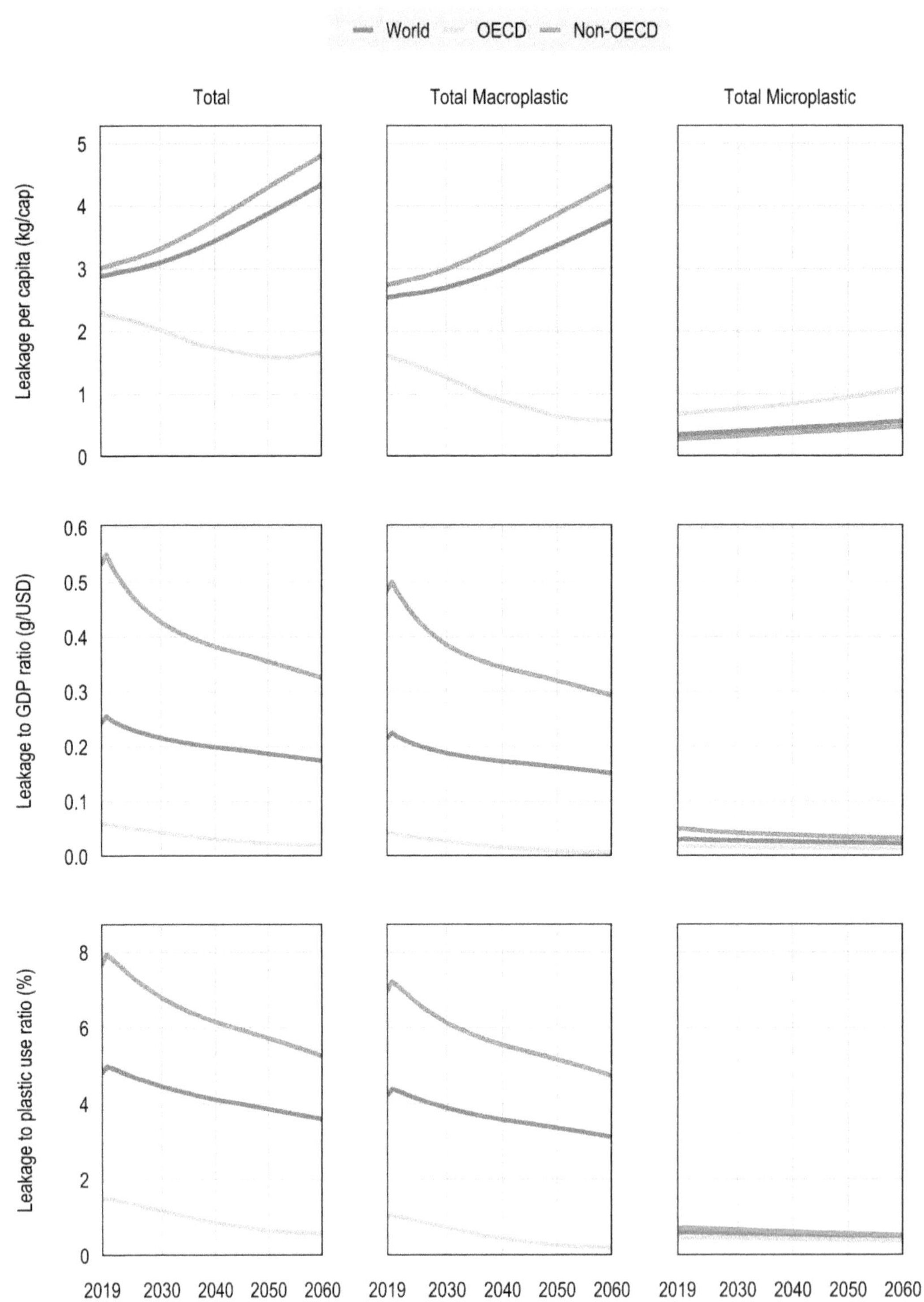

Source: OECD ENV-Linkages model, based on Ryberg et al. (2019[11]) and Cottom et al. (2022[16]).

StatLink https://stat.link/akb6uq

Figure 5.5. Macroplastic and microplastic leakage show different trajectories when income per capita increases

Per capita leakage (in kg, on y-axis) vs. GDP per capita (in USD, on x-axis), *Baseline* scenario

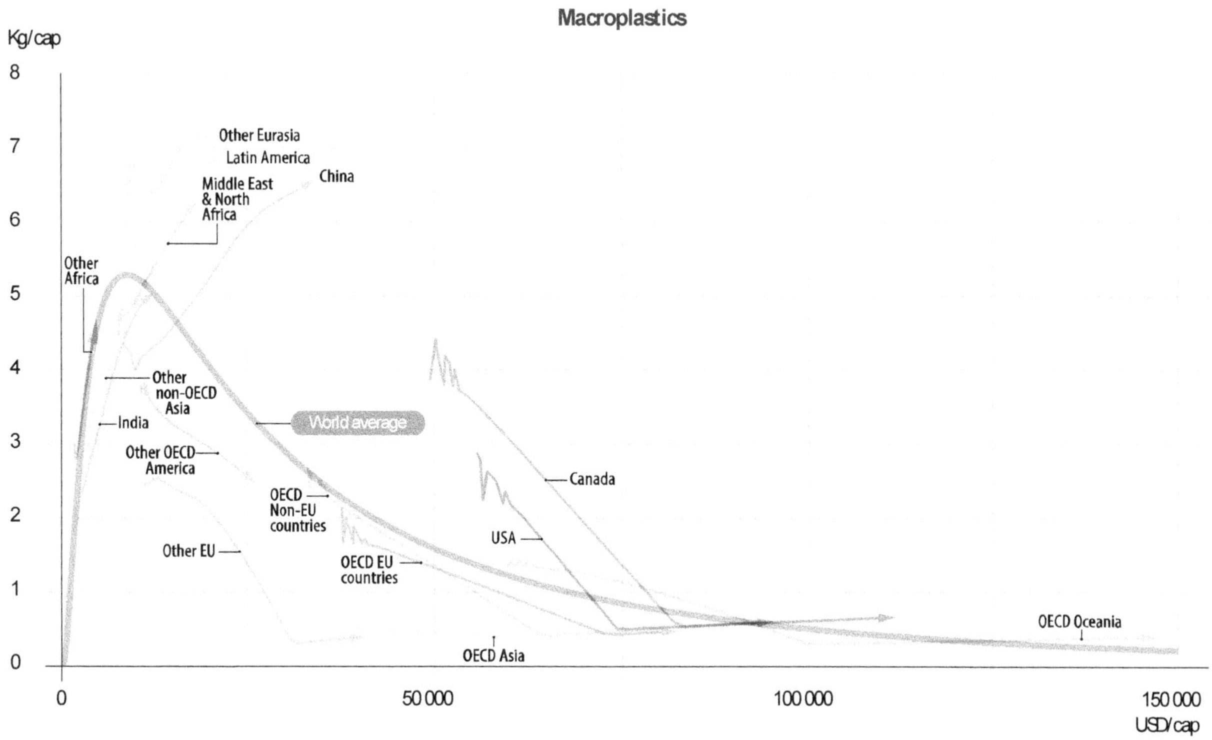

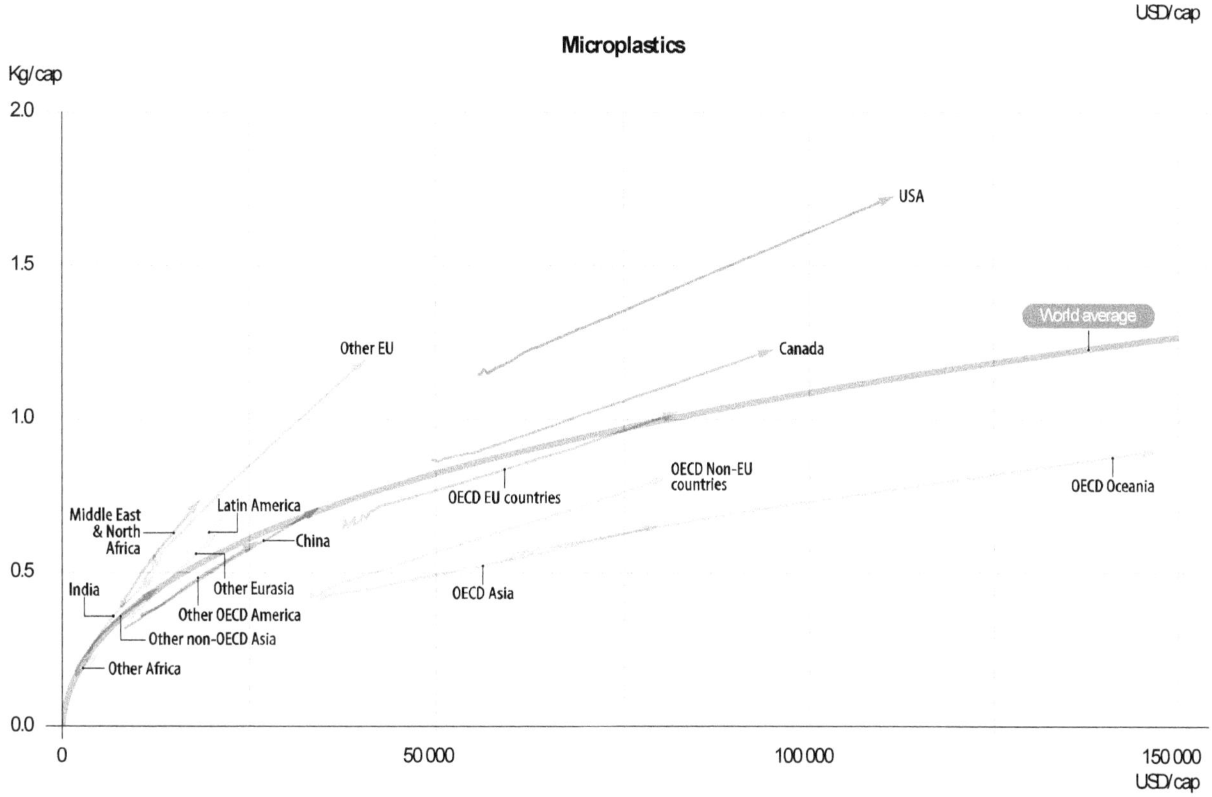

Note: The data points for each colour represent the evolution of that region between 2019 and 2060, with the arrow pointing towards 2060.
Source: OECD ENV-Linkages model, based on Ryberg et al. (2019[11]) and Cottom et al. (2022[16]).

5.3. Plastic leakage into aquatic environments is projected to almost double by 2060

While some leaked plastics will remain on land (terrestrial leakage), others will reach aquatic environments: streams, rivers, lakes, seas and the ocean. As outlined in detail in Section 2.5.1 of the *Global Plastics Outlook: Economic Drivers, Environmental Impacts and Policy Options* (2022[15]), plastic aquatic environments is influenced by spatial elements, such as proximity of rivers and coasts, weather patterns and plastics' characteristics (weight, flexibility). Some polymers and plastic products are more easily transported, and thus have a higher risk of ending up in an aquatic environment. Also, local elements such as the presence of dams affect the transport of plastics in rivers and the inflow into the ocean. This section focuses on the behaviour of macroplastics, starting from the leakage estimates for mismanaged and littered waste discussed in the previous section. Considering the multitude of elements to be taken into account and the uncertainty around these aspects, these estimations are only indicative and need to be interpreted with care.

Annual global plastic leakage into aquatic environments is projected to almost double, from 6.1 Mt in 2019 to 11.6 Mt in 2060 ("Central estimate" in Figure 5.6). The wide range, with a low estimate of 6.2 Mt and a high estimate of 16.8 Mt, emphasises the substantial uncertainty given the lack of empirical data. To further underline the uncertainty, the dots in Figure 5.6 represent estimates provided by Leeds University to check and corroborate the OECD methodology (Box 5.1) and leakage to water results. The numbers from Leeds University are lower than the OECD central estimate but fall within the uncertainty range at the lower end, starting from 4.1 Mt in 2019 to 8 Mt in 2060. Regardless of the size of the estimate, however, the trend indicates that the increasing use of plastics, only partly abated by the slow improvement of global waste management, will steadily drive up the annual amounts of plastics leaked to aquatic environments.

Figure 5.6. Global leakage to aquatic environments could at least double by 2060

Plastic leakage to aquatic environments in million tonnes per year (Mt), *Baseline* scenario

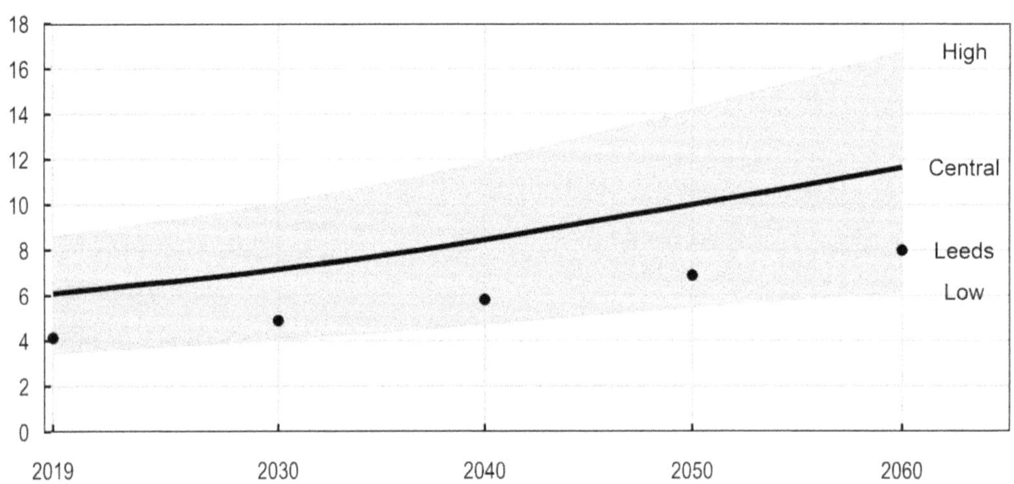

Note: High and low correspond to low and high emission probability ranges (see Box 5.1). The dots correspond to Leeds University estimates.
Source: OECD ENV-Linkages model, based on Lebreton and Andrady (2019[18]), Lebreton, Egger and Slat (2019[19]) and Cottom et al (2022[16]).

StatLink https://stat.link/dl9yof

A few previous studies have also made projections about plastic leakage to water. Lau et al. (2020[12]) estimated that a business-as-usual scenario without any policy intervention after 2020 would lead to approximately 29 Mt of aquatic leakage annually in 2040. Borrelle et al. (2020[13]) estimated that, without any structural change or additional ambitious policies, between 20 and 90 Mt would enter aquatic environments by 2030. Although comparing these estimates with the OECD central estimate presented in Figure 5.6 is difficult due to different definitions, assumptions and methodologies, the OECD estimates of annual leakage to aquatic environments seem significantly lower.

A first reason for this difference is that ENV-Linkages estimates lower amounts of mismanaged waste (see Box 4.5 in Chapter 4). Lau et al. (2020[12]) estimate mismanaged waste in 2040 to be more than double the amount projected by ENV-Linkages for that same year (Table 4.3 in Chapter 4). This difference directly relates to the more detailed modelling of the evolution of waste management in ENV-Linkages (see Chapter 4). Less mismanaged waste means less leaked plastics. Secondly, ENV-Linkages builds on an in-depth analysis of the fate of mismanaged waste (OECD, 2022[15]) that splits the mismanaged waste into four categories: waste deposited in dumpsites, open burning, leakage to terrestrial environments and leakage to aquatic environments. The analysis suggests that only around 8% of mismanaged waste ultimately ends up in aquatic environments, which is lower than the 12% share assumed by Lau et al. (2020[12]). Thirdly, to estimate the leakage to water, ENV-Linkages focused on macroplastics owing to the importance of this category for leakage and the availability of exploratory models and data. Microplastics are not included in the scope, but are an emerging concern for which more research on risks and potential policy measures is needed. Clearly, adding microplastic leakage to the estimates for leakage to water would increase the amounts. Thus, the estimates put forward in this chapter are likely to be conservative.

Ultimately, the estimation of plastic leakage is secondary to the intrinsic message from all these studies: plastic leakage is a major environmental problem and is getting worse over time. The urgency with which policy makers and other societal decision makers must act is high.

Thanks to improvements in waste management, plastic leakage to aquatic environments is projected to decrease over time until 2060 in OECD countries (Figure 5.7).[8] However, in absence of additional policies, aquatic leakage increases substantially in non-OECD countries. Plastic leakage to aquatic environments predominantly comes from non-OECD regions (Figure 5.7). The biggest contributors in 2019 were Asian countries, with the People's Republic of China (hereafter 'China') emitting 1.3 Mt, followed by other emerging economies in Asia (Other non-OECD Asia) at 1 Mt. These countries are projected to be the second-largest contributor by 2060, with 2.4 Mt emissions per year while India and China follow, with a projected 2 and 1.7 Mt per year by 2060 respectively. Sub-Saharan African countries (Other Africa) were responsible for almost 0.8 Mt in 2019, but by 2060 are projected to top the chart, at 2.9 Mt per year. The rapid increase in plastic leakage from the African continent reflects population growth and economic development, combined with immature waste management systems.

Figure 5.7. By 2060 non-OECD countries will be the main source of plastic leakage into aquatic environments

Plastic leakage to aquatic environments by region million tonnes (Mt), *Baseline* scenario

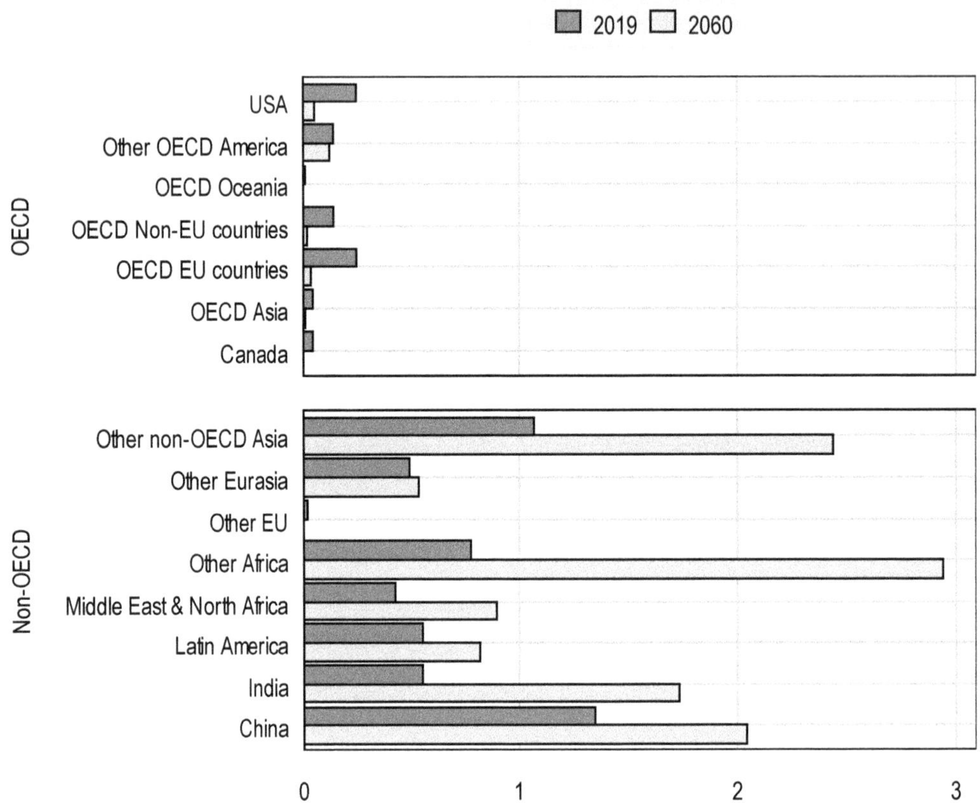

Source: OECD ENV-Linkages model, based on Lebreton and Andrady (2019[18]).

StatLink https://stat.link/i3dzvh

Projections for the coming decades suggest a clear geographical shift in the main regional sources of plastics in freshwater and marine environments (Figure 5.8). Advanced economies such as the United States and OECD Europe were primarily responsible for leaked plastics until the 1990s. Since 2000 the contribution of Asian and African countries has increased strongly, driven by growing plastic demand in developing economies. By 2060, over 66% of plastics accumulated in aquatic environments are projected to have come from four regions: Sub-Saharan Africa (Other Africa), as well as China, India and other developing Asian countries. By 2060, China is projected to be the biggest emitter of plastics to freshwater environments, while other emerging economies in Asia (Other non-OECD Asia) are the primary source of plastic leakage to marine environments. This difference can be explained by the greater probability of leaked plastics reaching the ocean from island nations, where populations are mostly coastal and the monsoon season implies a greater risk of direct emissions to the ocean.

Figure 5.8. Regional contributions to plastics leaking into aquatic environments shift over time

Percentage share of plastic leakage to global freshwater environments and the ocean, *Baseline* scenario

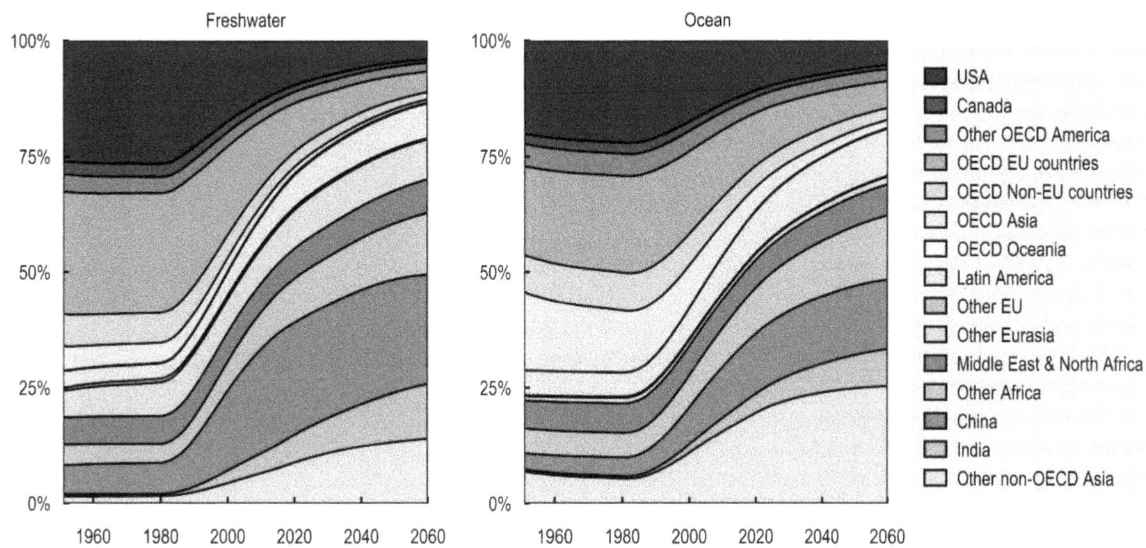

Source: OECD ENV-Linkages model, based on Lebreton and Andrady (2019[18]).

StatLink https://stat.link/phez3t

Once plastics reach an aquatic environment, their fates depend on their characteristics and on the environment itself. Only 5% of plastics leaking to aquatic environments arrive directly in the ocean from the coast (Figure 5.9). Most plastics leak into freshwaters, i.e. rivers and lakes. When plastics are denser than water, they tend to sink rapidly to the bottom (representing 50% of the total plastic leaked to aquatic environments). The remainder floats (either because they are less dense than water or their shape traps air) and can potentially be transported downstream (44% of the total plastic leaked to aquatic environments). For instance, applications like packaging, which use high amounts of light-weight polymers (e.g. PE and PP) and heavier polymers (e.g. PET) in less dense plastic products (like plastic bottles), are much more likely to contribute to the "plastic soup" in the ocean. Each of these flows into aquatic environments is projected to increase substantially by 2060.

Figure 5.9. Only a small share of leaked plastics reaches the ocean via the coast

Plastic leakage to aquatic environments in million tonnes per year (Mt), *Baseline scenario*

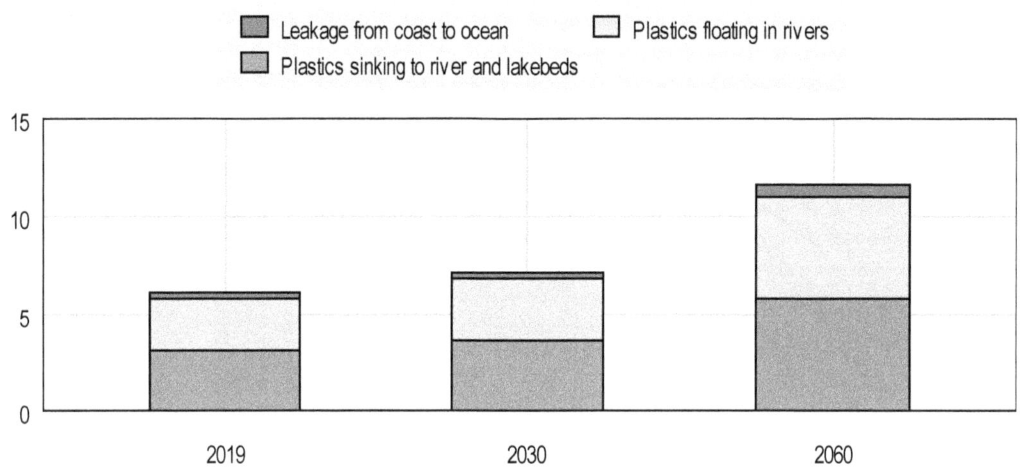

Source: OECD ENV-Linkages model, based on Lebreton and Andrady (2019[18]).

StatLink https://stat.link/4anjru

Plastics have been accumulating in the aquatic environment since the onset of plastic mass production in the 1950s. By 2019, an estimated total of 140 Mt of plastics had found their way into the aquatic environment globally (Figure 5.10). Of this, only 22% had reached the ocean due to the large share of plastics that sinks to river or lake beds and the slow transport of floating plastics downstream. A much larger share (78%) was still in freshwater systems. [9] With the *Baseline* scenario projecting a near doubling of plastic inputs to aquatic environments globally from 2019 to 2060, the outlook is bleak for these environments: a staggering 493 Mt of plastics will have accumulated by 2060, 29% of which will have reached the ocean.

Figure 5.10. There are more leaked plastics stored in freshwater systems than in the ocean

Plastic leakage accumulated in aquatic environment in million tonnes (Mt), *Baseline* scenario

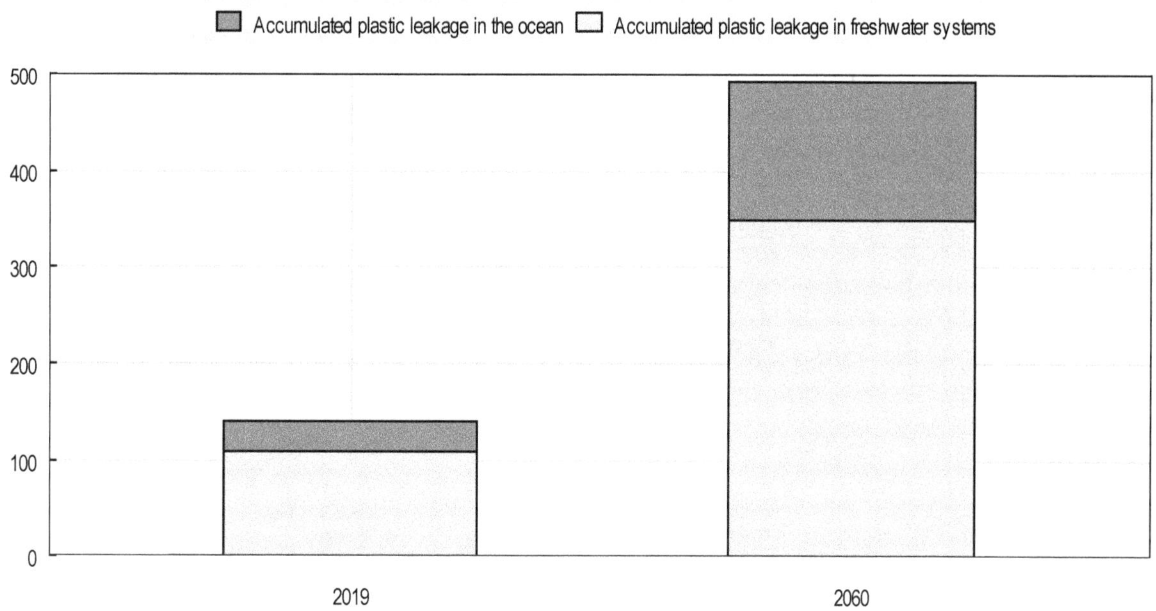

Source: OECD ENV-Linkages model, based on Lebreton and Andrady (2019[18]).

StatLink https://stat.link/knfa07

The slow rate at which plastics move through rivers means that accumulated plastics in rivers keep on flowing towards the ocean decades after they enter an aquatic environment. Moreover, part of the stock is slowly broken down to microplastics, which are more likely to be ingested by aquatic species, thus increasing the related environmental risks. Figure 5.11 shows some of the dynamics occurring in aquatic environments. The estimated total annual inflows of macroplastics into the ocean were 1.7 Mt in 2019; by 2060 they are projected to be 4.0 Mt. Degradation of macroplastics to microplastics is a slow process, estimated at 0.3 Mt annually in 2019, rising to 0.8 Mt in 2060, with most degradation occurring in the large, accumulated stocks in rivers. However, these dynamics are strongly influenced by local conditions such as weather patterns, river morphology and biological degradation processes. However, limited current understanding of these influences and capabilities makes it challenging to model the overall picture, so the errors in each of these numbers could be substantial. Nonetheless, it is clear that additional policies are needed to achieve the target of net-zero leakage to the ocean from the G20 as put forward by the Osaka Blue Ocean Vision, and to ultimately end plastic pollution, as articulated in the UNEA Resolution 5/14.

Figure 5.11. The flow of macroplastics into rivers and lakes is substantially larger than outflows to the ocean

Plastic leakage in million tonnes per year (Mt), *Baseline* scenario

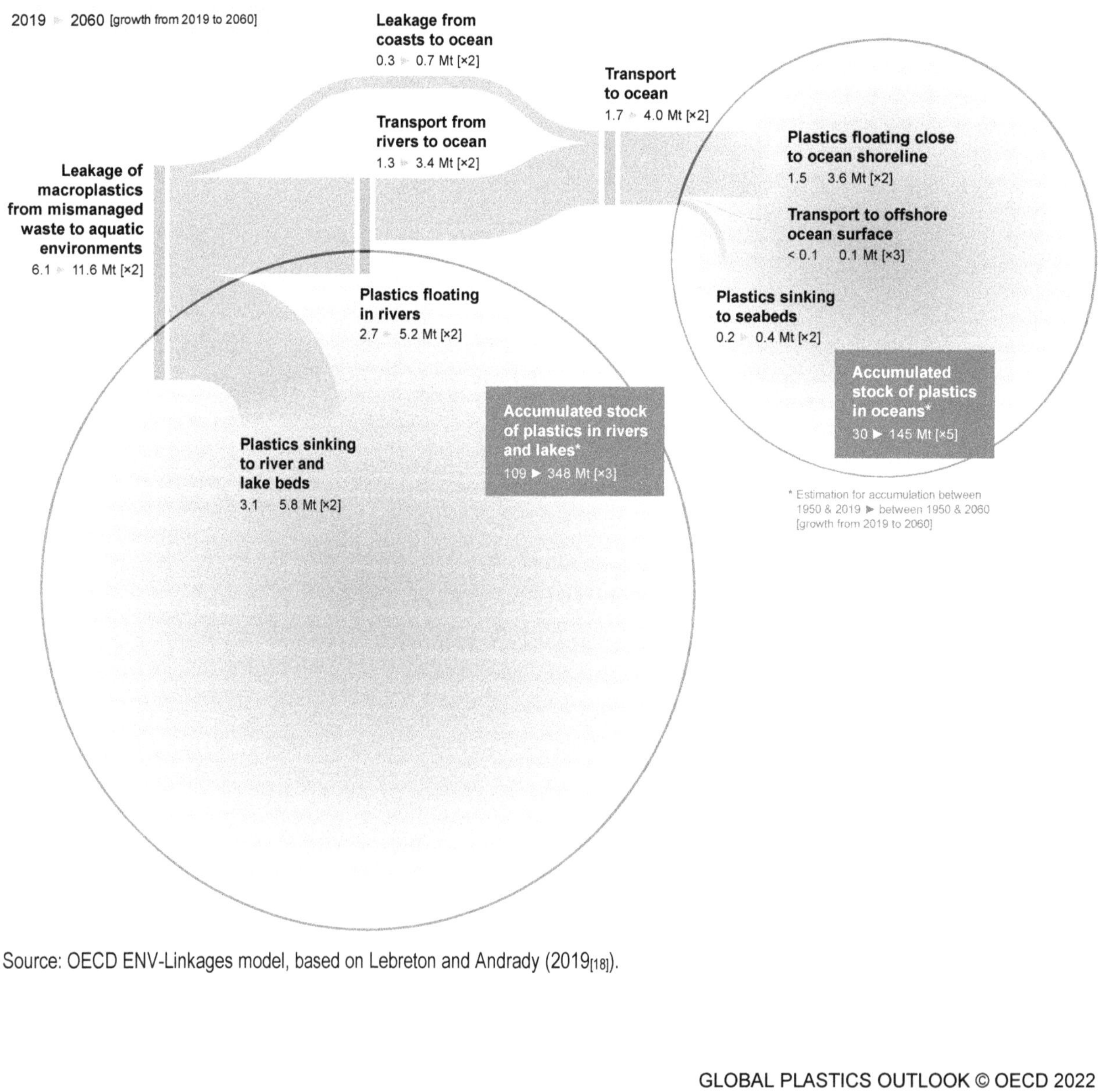

Source: OECD ENV-Linkages model, based on Lebreton and Andrady (2019[18]).

5.4. The projected increase in transport will lead to more airborne microplastics

Some microplastics become airborne and can be transported long distances before being deposited on the land or in aquatic environments. Road transport, and in particular the wear of tyres and brake pads, is one of the main sources of aerial microplastic pollution, in the form of particulate matter (PM) (OECD, 2022[15]). Airborne emissions from road transport are mostly due to the abrasion of tyres, with emissions from tyres 16 times larger than emissions from brakes in 2019. However, brake abrasion is responsible for a larger share of fine particulate matter ($PM_{2.5}$, i.e. particles with a diameter below 2.5 micrometres), which may have more severe health impacts (Evangeliou et al., 2020[14]). Road transport-related microplastics are emitted mainly in large urban agglomerations, such as the eastern part of North America, continental Europe and Northeast Asia.

The majority of airborne microplastic emissions tends to remain close to their source, where they increase the concentration levels of PM at ground level. This is the case for highly populated and industrialised areas in North America, Europe and East Asia. However, some particles can travel long distances and end up far beyond these source areas, depending on the location and atmospheric conditions. Microplastics can even reach fragile environments such as the Arctic (Figure 5.12), highlighting the global scale of the plastic challenge.

The increase in road transport projected to 2060 will lead to further growth in airborne microplastics, their deposition in the environment and impacts on air quality. In North America and Europe the depositions of microplastics are projected to steadily increase by 2060, while in China, depositions are projected to more than double, and in other emerging economies such as India, they are projected to nearly quadruple.

Figure 5.12. Deposition of airborne microplastics from tyre and brake abrasion will increase

Deposition of airborne microplastics, *Baseline* scenario

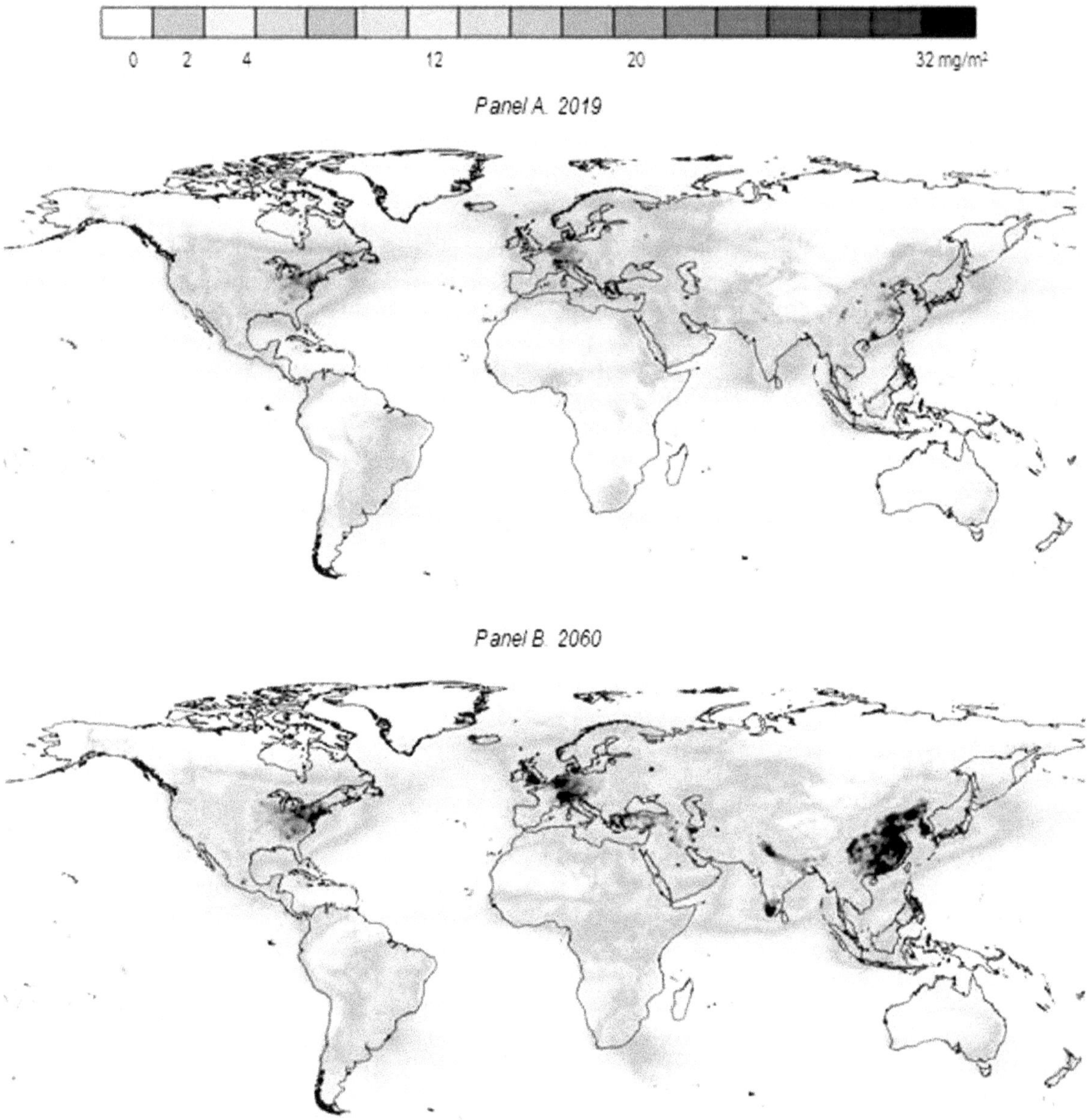

Source: OECD ENV-Linkages model, based on Evangeliou et al. (2020[14]).

References

Allen, S. et al. (2019), "Atmospheric transport and deposition of microplastics in a remote mountain catchment", *Nature Geoscience*, Vol. 12/5, pp. 339-344, https://doi.org/10.1038/s41561-019-0335-5. [3]

Andrady, A. (2011), "Microplastics in the marine environment", *Marine Pollution Bulletin*, Vol. 62/8, pp. 1596-1605, https://doi.org/10.1016/j.marpolbul.2011.05.030. [5]

Borrelle, S. et al. (2020), "Predicted growth in plastic waste exceeds efforts to mitigate plastic pollution", *Science*, Vol. 369/6510, pp. 1515-1518, https://doi.org/10.1126/science.aba3656. [13]

Cottom, J. et al. (2022), "Spatio-temporal quantification of plastic pollution origins and transportation (SPOT)" University of Leeds, UK, https://plasticpollution.leeds.ac.uk/toolkits/spot/. [16]

Evangeliou, N. et al. (2020), "Atmospheric transport is a major pathway of microplastics to remote regions", *Nature Communications*, Vol. 11/1, https://doi.org/10.1038/s41467-020-17201-9. [14]

GESAMP (2015), *Sources, fate and effects of microplastics in the marine environment: a global assessment*, IMO/FAO/UNESCO-IOC/UNIDO/WMO/IAEA/UN/UNEP/UNDP Joint Group of Experts on the Scientific Aspects of Marine Environmental Protection), http://www.imo.org. [10]

Grossman, G. and A. Krueger (1995), "Economic Growth and the Environment", *The Quarterly Journal of Economics*, Vol. 110/2, pp. 353-377, https://doi.org/10.2307/2118443. [17]

Kühn, S., E. Bravo Rebolledo and J. van Franeker (2015), "Deleterious Effects of Litter on Marine Life", in *Marine Anthropogenic Litter*, Springer International Publishing, Cham, https://doi.org/10.1007/978-3-319-16510-3_4. [6]

Lau, W. et al. (2020), "Evaluating scenarios toward zero plastic pollution", *Science*, p. eaba9475, https://doi.org/10.1126/science.aba9475. [12]

Lebreton, L. and A. Andrady (2019), "Future scenarios of global plastic waste generation and disposal", *Palgrave Communications*, Vol. 5/1, p. 6, https://doi.org/10.1057/s41599-018-0212-7. [18]

Lebreton, L., M. Egger and B. Slat (2019), "A global mass budget for positively buoyant macroplastic debris in the ocean", *Scientific Reports*, Vol. 9/1, p. 12922, https://doi.org/10.1038/s41598-019-49413-5. [19]

Obbard, R. et al. (2014), "Global warming releases microplastic legacy frozen in Arctic Sea ice", *Earth's Future*, Vol. 2/6, pp. 315-320, https://doi.org/10.1002/2014EF000240. [2]

OECD (2022), *Global Plastics Outlook: Economic Drivers, Environmental Impacts and Policy Options*, OECD Publishing, Paris, https://doi.org/10.1787/de747aef-en. [15]

OECD (2021), *Policies to Reduce Microplastics Pollution in Water: Focus on Textiles and Tyres*, OECD Publishing, Paris, https://doi.org/10.1787/7ec7e5ef-en. [1]

OECD (2021), "Towards G7 action to combat ghost fishing gear: A background report prepared for the 2021 G7 Presidency of the United Kingdom", *OECD Environment Policy Papers*, No. 25, OECD Publishing, Paris, https://doi.org/10.1787/a4c86e42-en. [4]

Ryberg, M. et al. (2019), "Global environmental losses of plastics across their value chains", *Resources, Conservation and Recycling*, Vol. 151, p. 104459, https://doi.org/10.1016/j.resconrec.2019.104459. [11]

SAPEA (2019), *A scientific perspective on micro-plastics in nature and society*, https://doi.org/10.26356/microplastics. [7]

WHO (2019), *Microplastics in drinking water*. [9]

Wright, S., R. Thompson and T. Galloway (2013), "The physical impacts of microplastics on marine organisms: A review", *Environmental Pollution*, Vol. 178, pp. 483-492, https://doi.org/10.1016/j.envpol.2013.02.031. [8]

Notes

[1] Microplastics are sometimes split further into three categories: 1) primary microplastics, i.e. plastics that are by design smaller than 5 mm in diameter; 2) secondary microplastics generated from abrasion during the use of synthetic products, such as tyre wear particles; and 3) secondary microplastics that are formed by the fragmentation of macroplastics that have already leaked into the environment.

[2] Nanoplastics are plastics with a size below 1 or 100 nanometre, depending on the definition used (OECD, 2021[1]).

[3] See Table A A.2 in Annex A for a list of the regions used in ENV-Linkages.

[4] Black, orange or blue polyethylene strings used in bottom trawling, a method of fishing that involves dragging heavy weighted nets across the sea floor.

[5] Of the microplastics removed in wastewater treatment plants, a share may be reintroduced to the environment via the spreading of sewage sludge on agricultural fields. The relative importance of this pathway varies across countries, depending on the effectiveness of the wastewater treatment process at retaining microplastics and on the type of sludge disposal method. The remainder of the microplastics are disposed via incineration or landfilling, from which no losses to the environment are reported. Further details on the assumptions made on the fate of microplastics in wastewater are given in Annex B.

[6] Microplastic dust refers to the unintentional and uncontrolled releases of microplastics throughout the lifespan of various products through abrasion, either by weathering or direct human activities. In this model, we accounted for five such sources: household textile dust, interior paints, exterior paints, exterior construction and demolition, and shoe sole abrasion. This is not an exhaustive list, but represent those microplastics dust sources for which there is sufficient literature.

[7] Microplastics which end up in sewage waste water come from a variety of sources: tyre abrasion (24% of the total mass), microplastics dust (21%), artificial turf (20%), pellets from plastics production (16%), road markings (10%), and textile microfibres (5%).

[8] Canada has made preliminary estimates for plastics production, waste and leakage available on request in November 2021. The information is available on https://www150.statcan.gc.ca/n1/daily-quotidien/211109/dq211109e-eng.htm. Though the results differ from the results from the OECD ENV-Linkages model for Canada, the differences are small overall, taking into account uncertainties for several key parameters.

[9] Though it is important to note that as the model did not account for any removal mechanisms, a share of this accumulated waste could have in fact been recovered by now.

6 Projections of the environmental impacts of the plastics lifecycle to 2060

The entire lifecycle of plastics, from their production through to their disposal, has many and varied environmental and health impacts. This chapter explores how these impacts evolve to 2060 in the *Baseline* scenario, i.e. in the absence of any new policies. It models the greenhouse gas emissions from all stages of the plastics lifecycle, and compares them with two scenarios for the use of biobased plastics. It also assesses the lifecycle environmental impacts of seven common polymers, projecting impacts to 2060 on aspects ranging from human carcinogenic toxicity to acidification, eutrophication and land-use change.

Key messages

- By 2060, an improvement in the greenhouse gas (GHG) emissions intensity of plastics production over time fails to compensate for the large rise in emissions from increased plastics use and waste. Overall, plastics lifecycle emissions are projected to increase from 1.8 Gt CO_2e in 2019 to 4.3 Gt CO_2e in 2060, growing from 3.7% to 4.5% of global emissions.
- Policies that promote biobased plastics can reduce GHG emissions from the production of plastics, but there are concerns that the increasing demand for agricultural land to grow the biomass required may lead to loss of natural areas. Modelling the effects of increasing bioplastics' market share to 5% by 2060 finds only a small impact on GHG emissions. Finding ways to reduce the need for agricultural feedstock could significantly improve the potential of biobased plastics to mitigate global plastics lifecycle GHG emissions.
- Using life cycle analysis (LCA) to model the plastics lifecycle shows that the production and waste management of seven commonly used polymers have wide-ranging negative impacts on the environment and human health, including on land use, ozone formation, eutrophication, ecotoxicity, toxicity and acidification. These impacts will all double or triple by 2060, with land use and eutrophication increasing most, driven mainly by the production of plastics. Limiting the growth in plastics use is urgent to limit these harmful impacts.

6.1. Plastics use and waste contribute to climate change

6.1.1. Greenhouse gas emissions from fossil-based plastics are projected to more than double by 2060

Plastics generate greenhouse gas (GHG) emissions all along their lifecycle, from their production from fossil fuel feedstock transformed through highly energy-intensive processes, to their management as waste, which requires energy and generates direct emissions. The OECD ENV-Linkages model estimates that in 2019, total GHG emissions related to fossil-based plastics were 1.8 gigatonnes of carbon dioxide equivalent (Gt CO_2e), or 3.7% of global emissions.[1] As plastics use and waste increase in the *Baseline* scenario, these emissions are projected to more than double to 2060, reaching 4.3 Gt CO_2e (Figure 6.1), or 4.5% of global GHG emissions in 2060. While the plastics sector grows at roughly the same rate as the economy-wide average over the period, the growth of the services sectors (which have relatively low emissions intensity) exceeds the average, to represent a large share of the economy. Meanwhile, some very emission-intense sectors – such as iron and steel, non-metal minerals, mining and livestock production – are projected to have below average growth (Chapter 2). This explains why the percentage of plastic emissions increases over time.

Emissions from producing polymers and converting them into products account for around 90% of the lifecycle emissions of fossil-based plastics, both in 2019 and 2060. However, the level of emissions varies depending on the polymer (OECD, 2022[1]). The largest contributors to emissions are fibres used for textiles and clothes, followed by polypropylene (PP), used for a large variety of applications, including food packaging and moulded parts in vehicles. Production of low-density polyethylene (LDPE), used for instance in plastic bags or dispensing bottles, is the third-highest emitter. The increase in emissions between 2019 and 2060 is largely driven by these polymers.

End-of-life emissions account for the remaining lifecycle emissions (about 10%) and vary significantly by disposal option. Incineration accounts for more than 70% of the total end-of-life emissions, both in 2019 and 2060, followed by recycling. Recycling however enables the production of secondary plastics that can reduce overall GHG emissions by substituting for primary plastics. The GHG emissions avoided by recycling and the subsequent production of secondary plastics depends on the polymer and region (mostly on the energy mix of the region's recycling sectors). However, the average reduction of GHG emissions across regions amounts to at least 1.8 tonne of CO_2e for a tonne of polymer produced or a reduction of more than two-thirds compared to the production of the primary equivalent. The impact of plastic leakage on greenhouse gases is not incorporated, but recent research (Shen et al., 2020[2]) based on experimental data by Royer et al. (2018[3]) estimated that degradation in the environment and non-sanitary landfilling leads to methane emissions of roughly 2 Mt CO_2e per year.

Figure 6.1. Greenhouse gas emissions from fossil-based plastics are projected to more than double by 2060

GHG emissions from the plastics lifecycle in gigatonnes of CO_2 equivalent ($GtCO_2e$), *Baseline* scenario

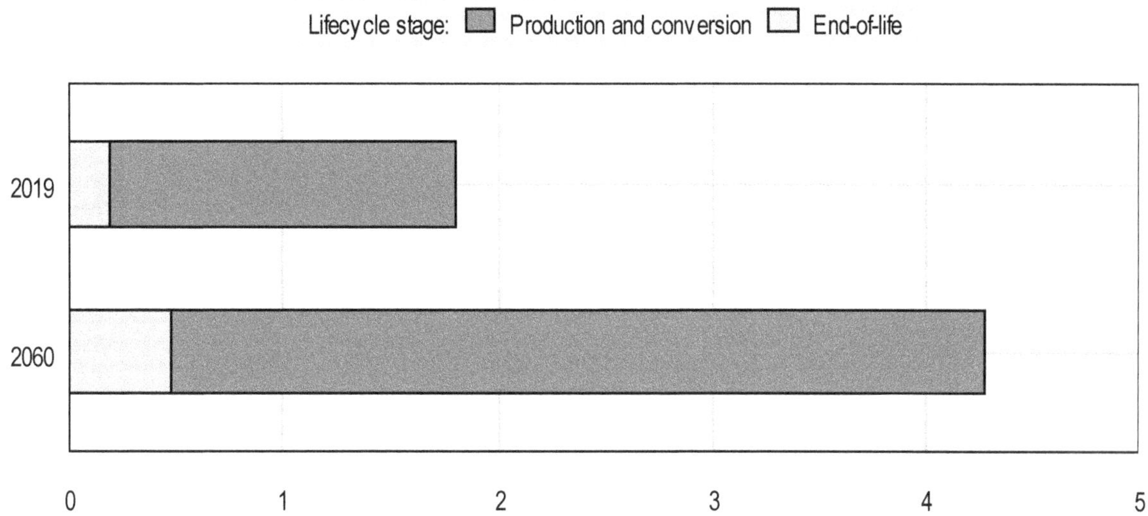

Note: End-of-life includes recycling, incineration, landfilling and mismanaged waste.
Source: OECD ENV-Linkages model.

StatLink https://stat.link/hd6is8

The large growth in GHG emissions from 2019 to 2060 is driven by several factors (Figure 6.2). The increase in the production and conversion of fossil-based plastics accounts for the majority of new emissions (+2.4 Gt CO_2e), while the increase in waste contributes a further 0.4 Gt CO_2e. Projected changes in polymer and waste management (including recycling) have almost negligible effects. The only factor to sizeably mitigate the emissions over time in the *Baseline* scenario is the reduction in the GHG intensity of plastics production and conversion (around -0.3 Gt CO_2e), and, to a lesser extent, of waste (-0.1 Gt CO_2e).

These results suggest that the most straightforward way of mitigating GHG emissions from the plastics lifecycle is to slow down the increase in global plastics use and waste. Other mitigation options include increasing the availability and use of secondary plastics; decarbonising production and conversion; as well as waste treatment processes, by, among others, an increased use of electricity as a replacement for fossil fuels, combined with a decarbonisation of electricity generation.

Figure 6.2. Growing plastics use and waste drives the increase in plastics GHG emissions

Factors contributing to the change in plastics lifecycle GHG emissions between 2019 and 2060 in gigatonnes of CO_2 equivalent (Gt CO_2e), *Baseline* scenario

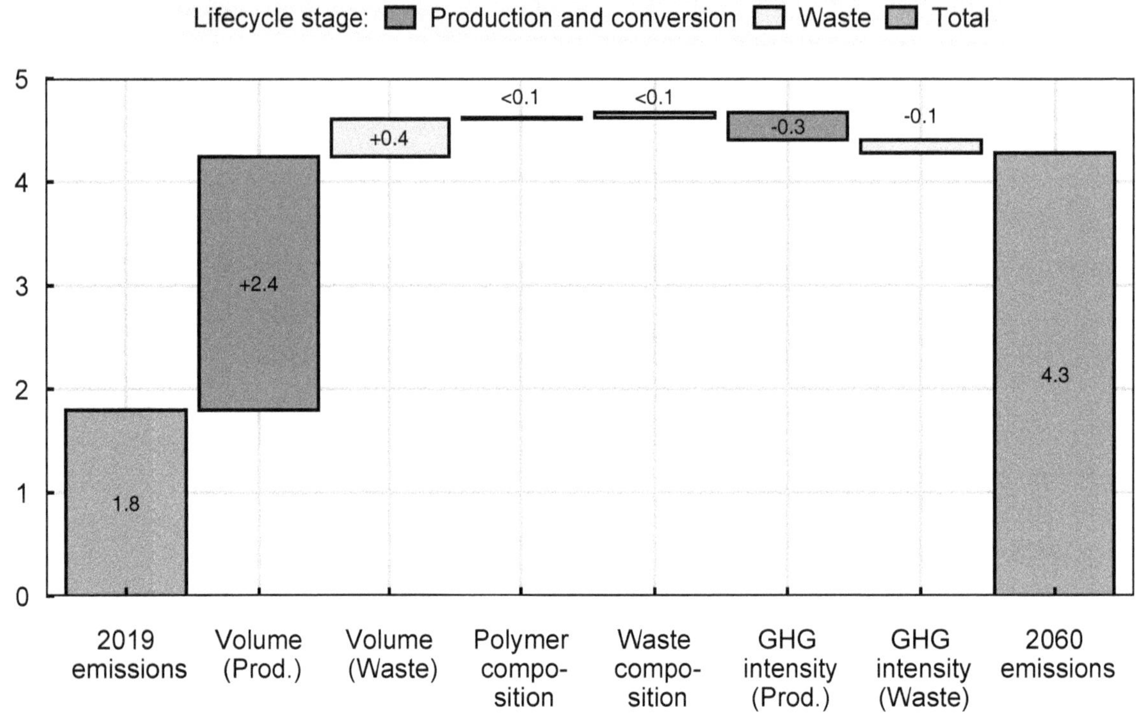

Note: This waterfall chart depicts the 2019 plastics lifecycle GHG emissions (far left bar), and the 2060 plastics lifecycle GHG emissions (far right bar). The bars in between show the contributions of the various drivers to the change in plastics lifecycle emissions between 2019 and 2060. Production refers to the emissions generated from production of raw polymers, while conversion refers to the emissions from their conversion to plastics products. Waste refers to emissions from plastics end of life (incinerated, recycled or landfilled plastics). Waste refers to emissions from end-of-life (incinerated, recycled or landfilled plastics). The details of the driver bars are as follows (from left to right, see Annex A for details):

1. "Volume (Prod.)" shows the change in emissions from total plastics use to 2060 assuming 2019 emission factors and composition.
2. "Volume (Waste)" shows the change in emissions from total plastic waste generated to 2060 assuming 2019 emission factors and composition.
3. "Polymer composition" adds the effect of the projected change in plastics use composition between 2019 and 2060.
4. "Waste composition" adds the effect of the projected change in the composition of end-of-life fates between 2019 and 2060, including the shift between primary and secondary plastics and the changes in incineration (without accounting for waste-to-energy processes impacts).
5. "GHG intensity" adds the changes in emission factors between 2019 and 2060 (due to the changes in the production structure in ENV-Linkages), both for production and conversion ("Prod.") and waste ("Waste").

Source: OECD ENV-Linkages model.

StatLink https://stat.link/dqx6sw

As with any long-term exercise, these projections are subject to uncertainty. The *Baseline* scenario in ENV-Linkages assumes a gradual decrease in the GHG intensity of production over time due to the increase in fossil fuel prices relative to electricity. These assumptions are important, given the reliance of plastics production on fossil fuels and its link to the global market for fossil fuels (see Box 6.1). Furthermore, ENV-Linkages assumes general energy-efficiency improvements will be made over the period, without considering any technological breakthrough that would drastically change lifecycle emissions of plastics, While this assumption is plausible for mature technologies for which the emission profile is not likely to change much, it can be challenged for emerging technologies. For instance, chemical recycling could replace or complement mechanical recycling, affecting the GHG emissions from recycling significantly (Civancik-Uslu et al., 2021[4]). However, these emerging technologies are by definition in the early stages, so their efficiency improvements and penetration are too uncertain to quantify soundly their evolution in the coming decades.

Box 6.1. Emissions from the plastics lifecycle are closely linked to fossil fuel prices

Plastics production relies on fossil fuels (oil and gas) as inputs, as well as sources of energy for the production process – either directly through combustion on site, or indirectly through their contribution to power production. Changes in fossil fuel prices can therefore affect plastics production and related GHG emissions. Two scenarios are compared to the *Baseline* (Figure 6.3): a low oil and gas price scenario (around 15% below the *Baseline* in 2060) and a high price scenario (about 15% above). Box 3.1 in Chapter 3 describes the two scenarios in more detail.

Figure 6.3. High fossil fuel prices reduce the GHG emissions of plastics significantly

Factors contributing to the change in plastics lifecycle GHG emissions compared to the *Baseline* in gigatonnes of CO_2 equivalent (Gt CO_2e), 2060

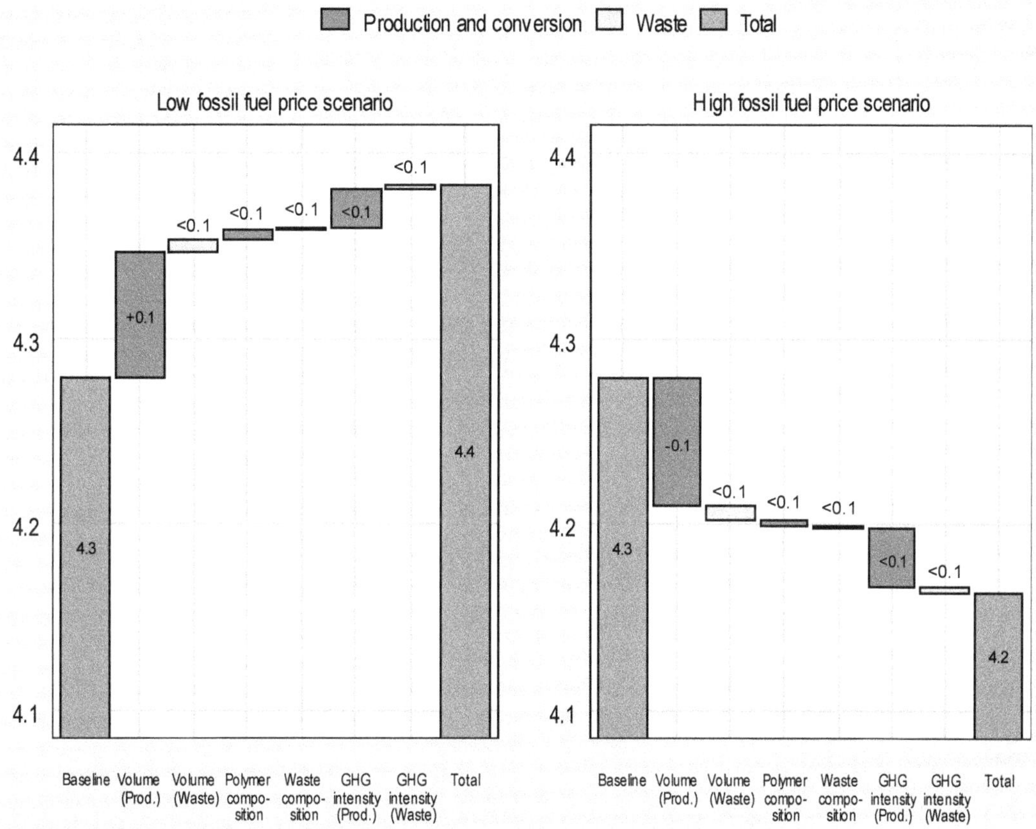

Note: This waterfall chart depicts the plastics lifecycle GHG emissions in the *Baseline* (far left bar) and fossil fuel price (far right bars) scenarios. The other bars show the contributions of the various drivers to the change in plastics lifecycle emissions between the scenarios and the *Baseline*. Production refers to the emissions generated from the production of raw polymers, while conversion refers to the emissions from their conversion to plastics products. Waste refers to emissions from plastics' end of life (incinerated, recycled or landfilled plastics). The details of the driver bars are as follows (from left to right, see Annex A for details):

1. "Volume (Prod.)" shows the change in emissions from total plastics use assuming *Baseline* emission factors and composition.
2. "Volume (Waste)" shows the change in emissions from total plastic waste generated assuming *Baseline* emission factors and composition.
3. "Polymer composition" adds the effect of the projected change in plastics use composition.
4. "Waste composition" adds the effect of the projected change in the composition of end-of-life fates, including the shift between primary and secondary plastics and the changes in incineration (without accounting for waste-to-energy processes impacts).
5. "GHG intensity" adds the changes in emission factors (due to the changes in the production structure in ENV-Linkages), both for production and conversion ("Prod.") and waste ("Waste").

Source: OECD ENV-Linkages model.

StatLink https://stat.link/25f4ej

Overall, lower fossil fuel prices lead to a 2.4% increase in plastics lifecycle emissions compared to the *Baseline*. Fossil fuel prices affect plastics lifecycle emissions through two main channels: by changing the volume of production and by changing the GHG intensity of production (Figure 6.1). A decrease in fossil fuel prices leads to a decrease in the price of plastics, through less expensive fossil inputs and less expensive energy, hence increasing demand. Low fossil fuel prices also increase GDP (see Chapter 3), thus increasing demand for all goods, including plastics. Lower fossil fuel prices also favour fossil fuels as an energy source over other, often less emissions-intensive, energy sources, thereby also increasing the GHG intensity of both plastics production and recycling. The exact same mechanisms are at play when higher fuel prices are considered, but in the opposite direction, leading to a decrease in plastics lifecycle emissions by 115 Mt CO_2e in 2060 compared to the *Baseline* (-2.7%).

A change in fossil fuel prices would also affect emissions not related to plastics. At the global level, lower fossil fuel prices result in more economic activity (around +1% in GDP, see Chapter 3) as well as an increase in the GHG-intensity of economic activity. This results in an increase in global emissions of around 4.7%, which is twice the percentage change in plastics lifecycle emissions. Therefore, the share of plastics lifecycle emissions slightly decreases from 4.5% in the *Baseline* scenario to 4.4%. Conversely, higher oil prices decrease global emissions by 4.1% and slightly increase the share of plastics emissions in global emissions to 4.6%.

6.1.1. Biobased plastics can only reduce GHG emissions if land use impacts are avoided

Biobased plastics are derived from biomass such as corn, sugarcane, wheat or residues of other processes. Their production therefore generates fewer greenhouse gas emissions than fossil-based plastics. In the *Baseline* scenario, the use of biobased plastics[2] is projected to increase but remains limited. The biobased plastics market share is projected to remain around 0.5% in 2060, with the use of plastics from biobased feedstock increasing from around 2 Mt in 2019 to 6 Mt in 2060.

The net environmental effects of the substitution of fossil-based plastics by biobased plastics are not straightforward, as explored in Box 2.2 in Chapter 2 of the OECD *Global Plastics Outlook: Economic Drivers, Environmental Impacts and Policy Options* (2022[1]). In particular, any additional demand for land for growing the feedstock for biobased plastics might drive land use changes such as deforestation that could lead to significant GHG emissions, as well as biodiversity loss, eutrophication and acidification (referred to as indirect land use effects). Furthermore, production of biobased plastics often relies on additives, whose production also contributes to GHG emissions and other environmental impacts (Zimmermann et al., 2020[5]).

This section compares the evolution of biobased plastics in the *Baseline* scenario with two alternative scenarios (the *Mandate* and the *Efficiency* scenarios). In these scenarios, policy makers take additional measures to pursue a 5% market share of biobased plastics in five economic regions that together represent 60% of global biobased plastics production – People's Republic of China (hereafter 'China'), the United States, the EU, Brazil and Thailand. A market share of 5% in these regions therefore translates into a global market share of around 3%. The *Mandate* and the *Efficiency* scenarios differ in the way that the higher share of biobased plastics is achieved. The *Mandate* scenario taxes the consumption of fossil-based plastics while subsidizing the consumption of bioplastics. In the *Efficiency* scenario, investment in technology increases the factor productivity for agricultural raw materials and reduces the land needed for biobased plastics production (Table 6.1). These improvements reflect the upscaling of technologies that enhance biomass utilization efficiencies, for example via pathways based on non-food feedstock (e.g. algae, perennial crops or waste) or cascading uses and closed-loop approaches (e.g. in integrated biorefineries). The scenario comparison uses the computable general equilibrium model CGE-Box (Britz and van der Mensbrugghe, 2018[6]) and builds on earlier research by Escobar and Britz (2021[7]) (see Annex B for methodological details).

Table 6.1. Policy measures can boost the market share of biobased plastics, but environmental consequences vary

Details	*Mandate scenario*	*Efficiency scenario*
	Description	
Market share of biobased plastics targeted in the 5 selected regions*	5%	Larger for Brazil (17.6%) and Thailand (6.3%), which are using sugarcane (the most cost-effective feedstock). Around 4% for China, USA and OECD Europe.
Market share of biobased plastics targeted globally	3%	3%
Drivers used to increase market share of biobased plastics	Combination of taxes on fossil fuels and subsidies for biobased plastics.	Investments in technology reduce the agricultural feedstock and land needed for biobased production. Global real GDP is kept constant imposing taxes on fossil-based plastics.
	Results (compared to Baseline)	
Impact on global GDP compared to *Baseline*	-0.02%	0%
Impact on global primary plastics production	-2.0%	-2.8%
Impact on global cropland area	+0.3%	+0.1%
Impact on global GHG emissions from plastics use, including indirect land use effects	+0.2%	-1.1%

* The five regions are China, the United States, the EU, Brazil and Thailand.
Source: CGE-Box model (Britz and van der Mensbrugghe, 2018[6]), based on OECD ENV-Linkages *Baseline*.

In both scenarios, biobased plastics production expands at the cost of fossil-based plastics. The effect is larger in the *Efficiency* scenario as this scenario reflects the use of technologies that make the production of biobased plastics more efficient and thus biobased plastics more competitive. This scenario leads to regional shifts in biobased production, while the *Mandate* scenario only targets the specified biobased production of 5% in each of the concerned regions. In both cases, the economic consequences of achieving a higher share of biobased plastics are very small. These small GDP losses are driven by the contraction of fossil fuel sectors, while production factors are shifted towards agriculture and livestock production, which have lower value added.

The higher demand for biobased plastics increases global demand for feedstock crops, driving up cultivated land (Figure 6.4, Panel A). This comes at the expense of both managed land uses (pasturelands and forest plantations, shown in Panel B in Figure 6.4) and unmanaged land uses (e.g. natural forests, shown in Panel C in Figure 6.4). But an additional effect emerges: as crop prices increase due to the increased demand for cropland, livestock feed becomes more expensive, leading livestock producers in Arctic regions, central Asia and some tropical zones to extensify their production, i.e. use more land for pasture. Thus, the pressure on unmanaged land comes from both crop and livestock production. Global cropland area increases most in the *Mandate* scenario, especially in the United States and the EU, but also in major grain-producing regions such as Canada, Australia and New Zealand, which export grains internationally, mainly to China and the EU (Figure 6.4, Panel A).

Figure 6.4. Changes in land use with higher penetration rates of biobased plastics

Land area changes (% change between 2015 and 2060), *Baseline* scenario

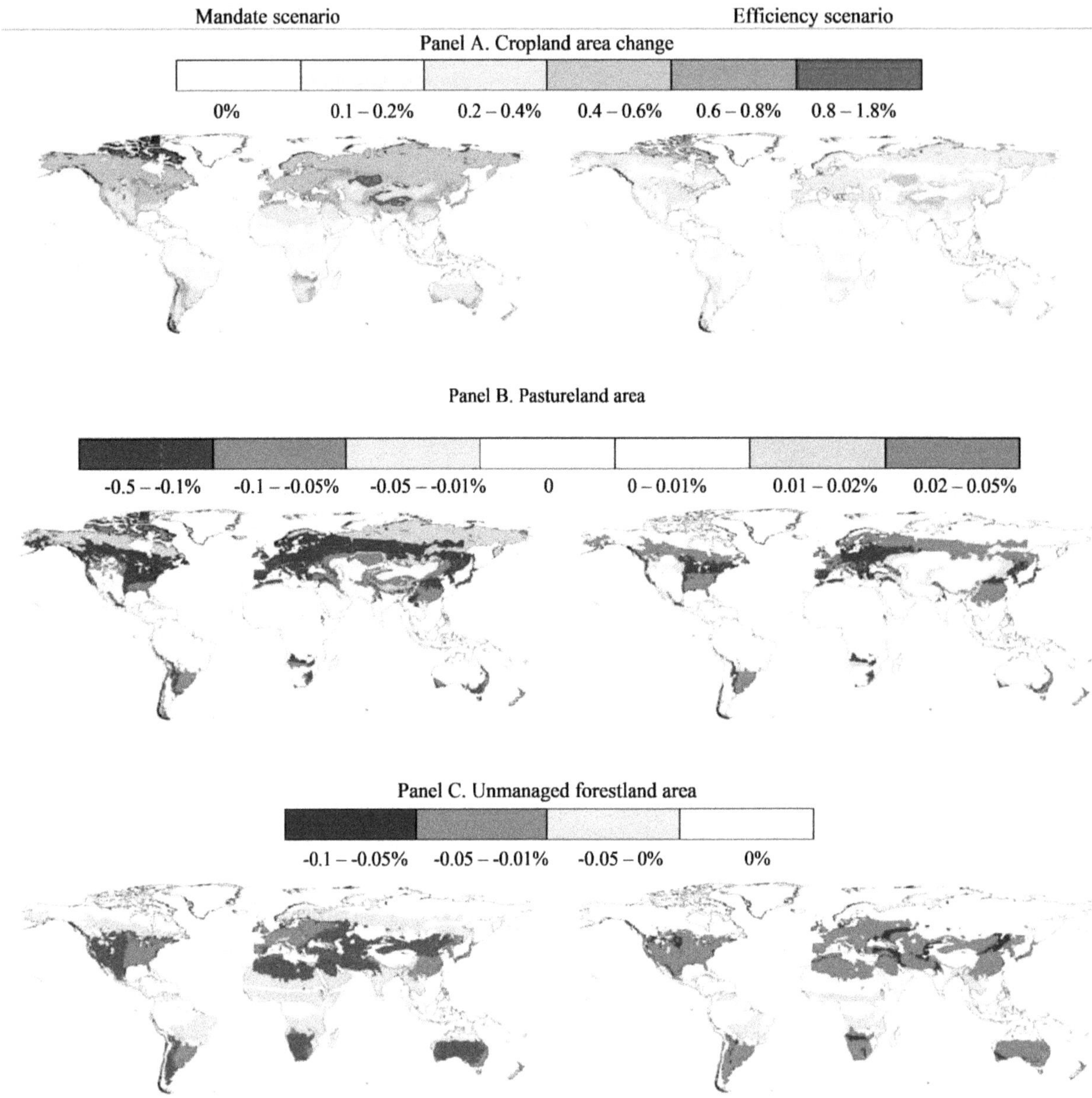

Source: CGE-Box model from Britz and van der Mensbrugghe (2018[6]).

The overall impact on global GHG emissions is small. The *Mandate* scenario sees a small net increase in emissions, while the *Efficiency* scenario sees a slightly larger net decrease (Figure 6.5). In both the *Mandate* and the *Efficiency* scenarios, the main increase in GHG emissions comes from land use change, while the main decrease comes from lower CO_2 emissions due to the substitution of fossil-based plastics. Another small increase in emissions in both scenarios is due to the additional use of fertilisers in agricultural production. In the *Mandate* scenario the increase in emissions from land use (43 Mt CO_2e by 2060) is projected to largely offset the emissions reductions from lower production of fossil-based plastics and the associated reductions in fossil fuel production (40 Mt CO_2e). Conversely, in the *Efficiency* scenario GHG emissions decrease overall (Figure 6.5). In this scenario, while direct CO_2e emission reductions from plastics production (44 Mt CO_2e) are similar to the *Mandate* scenario, GHG emissions from increased land use are limited to 15 Mt CO_2e globally, mostly coming from the loss of unmanaged forest.[3]

Figure 6.5. The *Efficiency* scenario leads to a decrease in GHG emissions

Annualised GHG emissions in gigatonnes of CO_2 equivalent ($GtCO_2e$) in 2060

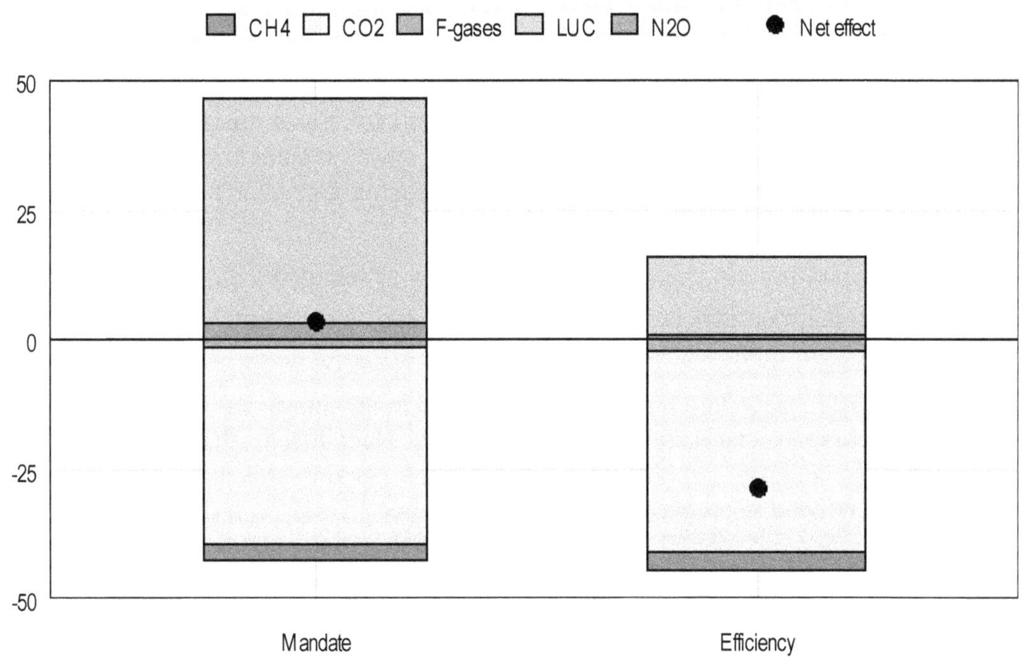

Note: CH_4=methane; CO_2= carbon dioxide; F-gases: fluorinated gases; LUC=land use change; N_2O=nitrous oxide.
The annual greenhouse gas emissions from land-use change are computed assuming carbon remains sequestrated for 30 years.
Source: CGE-Box model (Britz and van der Mensbrugghe, 2018[6]), based on the OECD ENV-Linkages baseline.

StatLink https://stat.link/cbuvs5

The analysis highlights that any policy approach to stimulate biobased plastics must be chosen carefully to limit implications for land use and GHG emissions. The overall environmental outcome of upscaling biobased plastics will only be positive when a combination of global commitments and locally enforced regulatory measures succeeds in restraining the conversion of natural areas into agricultural land. Moreover, investing in research into more efficient biobased plastics production pathways that reduce the amount of agricultural feedstock used could significantly improve the potential to mitigate global GHG emissions.

6.2. The environmental impacts of the plastics lifecycle are wide and significant

In addition to plastic leakage to the environment and GHG emissions, the plastics lifecycle is linked to a variety of other environmental and human health pressures. This section presents the results of a life cycle assessment (LCA) carried out by the Sustainable Systems Engineering Group of Ghent University[4] (see Annex A for the methodology). LCA is a widely recognised methodology for assessing environmental impacts associated with the different stages of a product's lifecycle (Eunomia, 2020[8]). It involves a thorough inventory of the energy and materials required across the industry value chain of a product, process or service, and calculates the corresponding impacts on the environment.

The assessment includes the global production from cradle to gate and the end-of-life stage of seven commonly used polymers (polypropylene, PP; high-density polyethylene, HDPE; low-density polyethylene, LDPE; polyvinyl chloride, PVC; polystyrene, PS; polyethylene terephthalate, PET; and polyurethane, PUR), which make up for 65% of total plastics use. The analysis excludes the environmental effects relating to the manufacturing or use of products derived from these polymers. It also does not take into account any future technological changes related to the production of these polymers. The LCA considers numerous environmental impacts, including land use, ozone formation, eutrophication, ecotoxicity, toxicity and acidification (see Annex A for a description).

Owing to the multitude of environmental aspects related to the lifecycle of plastics, not all environmental impacts can be calculated from databases commonly used for LCA. Since the database used (Ecoinvent 3.6) only contains sufficient information on recycling across environmental impact categories for HDPE (relying on data for polyethylene) and PET, Figure 6.6 presents the environmental impacts of these polymers for the following two lifecycle stages:

- Production: the polymer can be produced from primary or secondary material.
- End-of-life: the polymer can be mechanically recycled, incinerated without energy recovery, landfilled, dumped or burned in an open pit.

The most circular lifecycle, secondary plastic that is recycled at its end of life, scores best for almost all environmental impact categories for both polymers (Figure 6.6). Nonetheless, this circular lifecycle still has considerable impacts on land use and both freshwater and marine eutrophication. These impacts mainly come from the energy needed to prepare, process and transport plastics in a circular loop (see also the plastics lifecycle GHG emissions related to recycling as presented in Section 6.1.1). Since eutrophication comes from emissions such as NO_x from the energy combustion, improvements in clean energy production and energy efficiency would reduce the environmental impacts of circular plastics further. The impact on land use is driven by the relatively high levels of biomass feedstock in the energy mix of the countries with the highest recycling rates. As discussed in Section 6.1.1, research to limit the land use needed for biobased fuels and materials could improve their environmental footprint considerably.

In the 'transition to a circular economy', most plastics are still made from primary plastics while recycling increases steadily. Unfortunately, primary plastics that are recycled not only score worse for most impact categories than secondary plastics that are recycled, but also than the primary plastics that are landfilled or incinerated. Indeed, the energy needed to collect, sort and pre-process end-of-life plastics is taken into account, but the gains of using secondary plastics are not. This highlights the importance of high quality recycling and closing material loops.

Primary plastics that are landfilled tend to score better than when incinerated for most impact categories, apart from land use and marine eutrophication. The impact on land use is logically related to the land needed to operate the landfills. The eutrophication impact is higher for landfilling than for incineration because the used Ecoinvent database does not include any direct marine eutrophication emissions from incinerating or burning plastics. It is also important to note that the energy recovered from incineration in waste-to-energy plants and the related environmental benefits are only accounted for as part of the overall energy mix, and are not allocated to the incinerating category. Consequently, the incineration results are only representative for incineration without energy recovery.

Figure 6.6. The plastics lifecycle is linked to a variety of environmental and human health pressures

LCA impacts per million tonne (Mt) of polymer in 2060, *Baseline* scenario

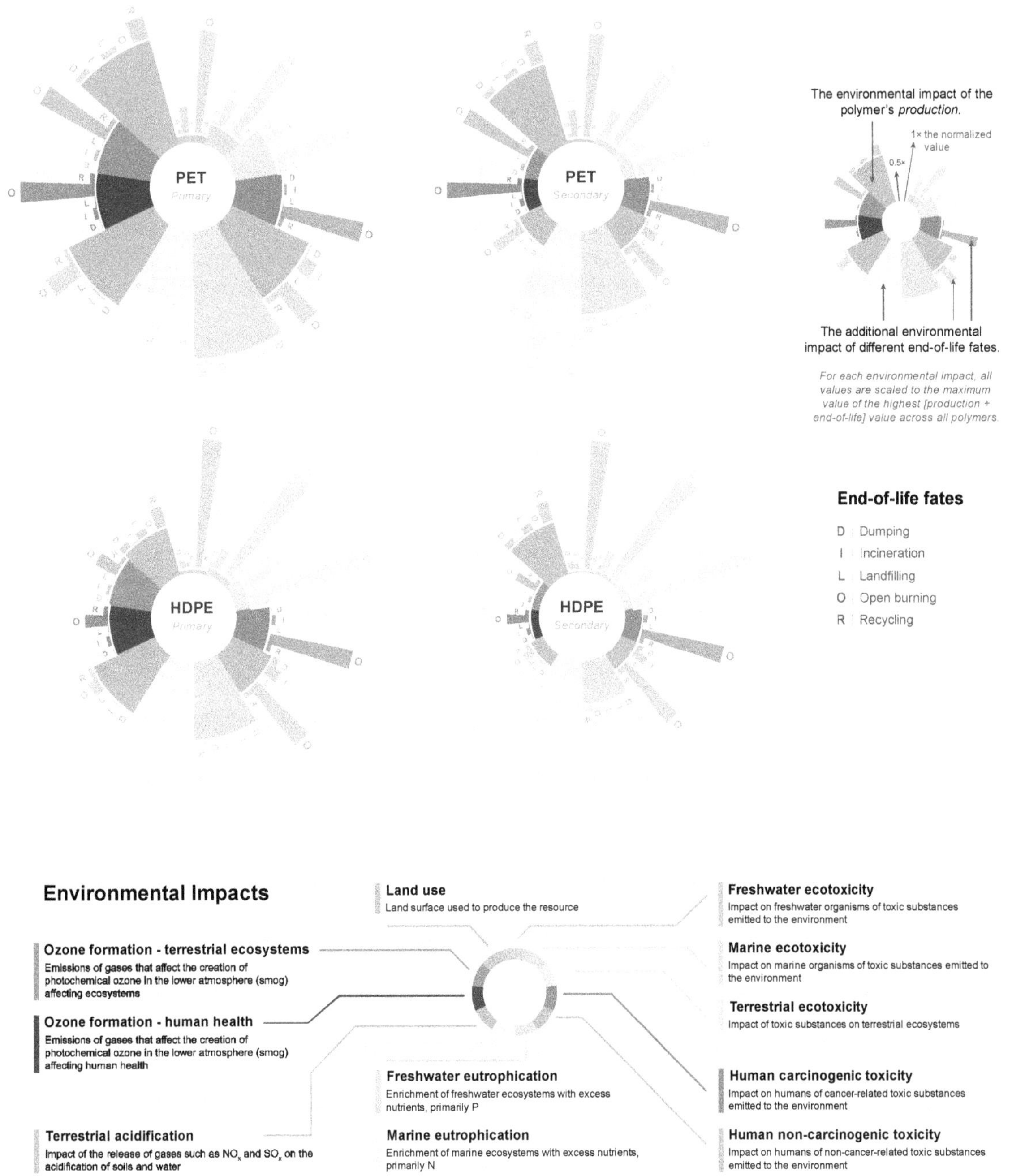

Source: OECD ENV-Linkages model, based on results of Ghent University.

Unsurprisingly, dumping and burning have worse environmental effects than the properly engineered disposal alternatives, landfilling and incinerating. However, they score slightly better than landfilling and incinerating for environmental categories where the benefits of having well-managed infrastructure are low due to the energy needed to manage waste in a proper way. For example, land use for a landfill or dumpsite will be similar, but the energy needed to build and operate a sanitary landfill will generate some small additional impacts on land use elsewhere in the supply chain. Since the data on pathways and impacts of leaked plastics are still scarce in LCA (Boulay, Verones and Vázquez-Rowe, 2021[9]), leakage to the environment originating from improper or informal waste collection is not taken into account. Nevertheless, Chapter 5 shows that dumping and generally mismanaging waste are the main sources of plastic leakage to the environment.

Projections for seven polymers that make up 65% of all plastics use (Figure 6.7 and Figure 6.8) show the potential negative impacts of plastics on a wide range of health and environmental areas. They also stress that impacts will worsen substantially between 2019 and 2060. This trend is driven by the increase in plastics use, with the total use of the seven polymers almost tripling (with growth of around 170%) by 2060 (Chapter 3). The biggest increase is for LDPE, which triples; while HDPE and PET see the slowest growth (about 150% growth to 2060). In line with these trends, the environmental impacts of all polymers worsen, but the impacts of LDPE are worse than for HDPE and PET. These trends confirm that restraining plastics use is a key lever to address the environmental challenges related to plastics.

As waste management will improve between now and 2060 even in the *Baseline* scenario, some mismanaged waste will be reduced by more recycling and safe disposal options. As secondary plastics have lower impacts overall than their primary equivalents (Figure 6.6), the shift towards more recycling means that the environmental impacts grow more slowly than plastics use. For example, the terrestrial acidification impact of production increases 5% less by 2060 than the volumes produced owing to the increasing market share of secondary plastics. Moreover, the shift away from mismanaged waste reduces impacts such as Ecotoxicity, ozone formation, carcinogenic toxicity and non-carcinogenic toxicity following the reduction of open-pit burning and less dumping. For instance, the freshwater ecotoxicity effects of the end-of-life stage increases 33% less than plastics use by 2060 thanks to improved waste management practices. These results highlight the importance of speeding up investments in recycling and safe waste management.

PET and PS have relatively low total impacts (Figure 6.7). However, these two polymers only represent around 5% of plastics use each in 2060. PP (16%), LDPE (13%), HDPE (11%) and PVC (11%) are a larger part of production (see Chapter 3) and have therefore more environmental impacts overall. PP, the most produced polymer, generates per tonne less environmental impacts than the average assessed polymer for each of the categories. In contrast, only 4% of all plastics are made of PUR but in this sample of seven polymers, it is a relatively large contributor to eutrophication, acidification and ozone formation. However, comparing the environmental impacts of these polymers or drawing conclusions with respect to the potential effect of substitution of polymers, is challenging because the polymers are used for different applications.

Figure 6.7. With no new policies, the environmental and health impacts of seven common plastics polymers will be substantial in 2060

Total LCA impacts by polymer, *Baseline* scenario

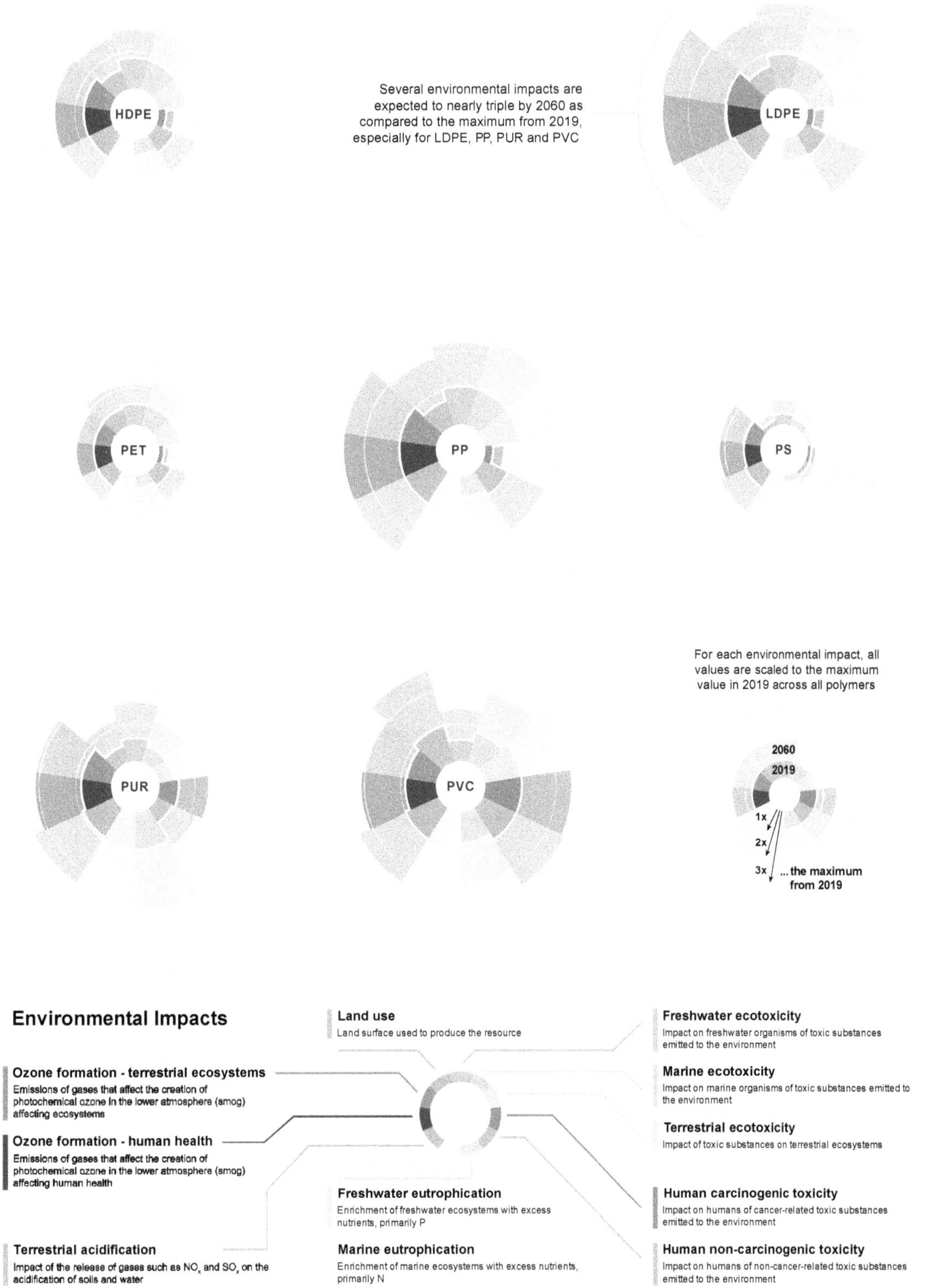

Source: OECD ENV-Linkages model, based on results of Ghent University.

Production drives the results for most impact categories (Figure 6.6 and Figure 6.8). By 2060, production is responsible for more than 85% of the impacts on ozone formation, acidification, human non-carcinogenic toxicity and land use. However, for freshwater ecotoxicity the end-of-life stage contributes more than 40% of the lifecycle impact, due to mismanaged waste and, to a lesser extent, incineration. In particular, the relatively high impacts of mismanaged PUR waste and of incinerating PET drive up the end-of-life impacts on freshwater toxicity. Similarly, the end-of-life stage makes up a quarter of the terrestrial ecotoxicity impact and one-third of the marine ecotoxicity impact. The end-of-life stage also contributes 39% to the total human carcinogenic toxicity impact due to the effect of mismanaged waste, and especially mismanaged PVC waste. PUR also contributes strongly to this impact category, but is mainly driven by production.

The resulting evolution of the total environmental impacts shows an increase to 2060 that ranges from 132% –i.e. a value of 2.32 in 2060 – to 171% – i.e. a value of 2.71 – depending on the impact (Figure 6.8). The largest overall increases are seen for indicators related to the energy needed for increased share of recycling in 2060, which also causes GHG emissions (Section 6.1.1). Bioenergy in the energy mix means that more energy consumption leads to a greater impact on land use, while combustion of fossil fuels leads to more eutrophication. The indicators that benefit most from more circular waste management practices, such as freshwater and marine ecotoxicity, experience the lowest increases. Nonetheless, these strongly increasing environmental impacts underline the need for policy action.

Figure 6.8. All environmental impacts included in the analysis more than double by 2060

Evolution of total LCA impacts in 2060 compared to 2019 (index 1 in 2019), *Baseline* scenario

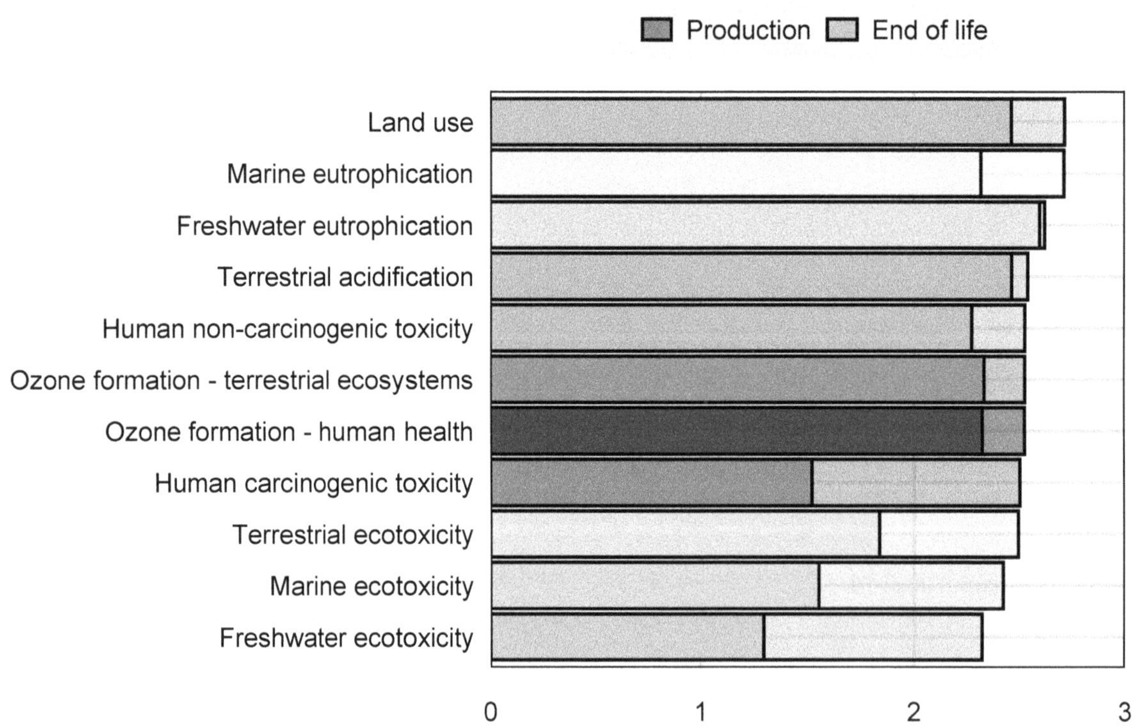

Source: OECD ENV-Linkages model, based on results of Ghent University.

StatLink https://stat.link/c9s1yr

References

Boulay, A., F. Verones and I. Vázquez-Rowe (2021), "Marine plastics in LCA: current status and MarILCA's contributions", *The International Journal of Life Cycle Assessment*, Vol. 26/11, pp. 2105-2108, https://doi.org/10.1007/s11367-021-01975-1. [9]

Britz, W. and D. van der Mensbrugghe (2018), "CGEBox: A Flexible, Modular and Extendable Framework for CGE Analysis in GAMS", *J Glob Econ Anal*, Vol. 3/2, pp. 106-177. [6]

Civancik-Uslu, D. et al. (2021), "Moving from linear to circular household plastic packaging in Belgium: Prospective life cycle assessment of mechanical and thermochemical recycling", *Resources, Conservation and Recycling*, Vol. 171, p. 105633, https://doi.org/10.1016/j.resconrec.2021.105633. [4]

Escobar, N. and W. Britz (2021), "Metrics on the sustainability of region-specific bioplastics production, considering global land use change effects", *Resources, Conservation and Recycling*, Vol. 167, p. 105345, https://doi.org/10.1016/j.resconrec.2020.105345. [7]

Eunomia (2020), *Plastics: Can Life Cycle Assessment Rise to the Challenge? How to critically assess LCA for policy making*, Eunomia, Bristol. [8]

IPCC (1995), *Climate Change 1995: A report of the Intergovernmental Panel on Climate Change - IPCC Second Assessment*. [10]

OECD (2022), *Global Plastics Outlook: Economic Drivers, Environmental Impacts and Policy Options*, OECD Publishing, Paris, https://doi.org/10.1787/de747aef-en. [1]

Royer, S. et al. (2018), "Production of methane and ethylene from plastic in the environment", *PLOS ONE*, Vol. 13/8, https://doi.org/10.1371/journal.pone.0200574. [3]

Shen, M. et al. (2020), "(Micro)plastic crisis: Un-ignorable contribution to global greenhouse gas emissions and climate change", *Journal of Cleaner Production*, Vol. 254, p. 120138, https://doi.org/10.1016/j.jclepro.2020.120138. [2]

Zimmermann, L. et al. (2020), "Are bioplastics and plant-based materials safer than conventional plastics? In vitro toxicity and chemical composition", *Environment International*, Vol. 145, p. 106066, https://doi.org/10.1016/j.envint.2020.106066. [5]

Notes

[1] The ENV-Linkages model uses the energy and factor intensity of economic sectors, along with their process emission intensity, to estimate the greenhouse gas emissions in the economy. This generic approach is complemented with information on plastics lifecycle emissions factors. Based on these calculations the greenhouse gases are aggregated using 100-year global warming potentials from the IPCC 2nd Assessment Report (IPCC, 1995[10]).

[2] Biobased plastics are derived from biomass such as corn, sugarcane, wheat or residues of other processes. Their production generates fewer greenhouse gas emissions than fossil-based plastics.

[3] These results depend on modelling assumptions, in particular the ease with which industries can replace fossil-based plastics with biobased plastics. The responsiveness of land conversion to price can affect the results on land use and GHG emissions. A higher responsiveness of land-use conversion to price changes would imply more GHG emissions, since cropland would expand more and imply larger losses of natural areas. A higher level of substitution between fossil-based and biobased plastics would imply a higher increase in biobased plastics, as well as in global cropland and GHG emissions.

[4] The analysis used Simapro v9.1, Ecoinvent database 3.6, cut-off model and lifecycle impact assessment methods: Recipe 2016 Midpoint (H) v1.04 and Cumulative Energy Demand (CED) v1.11.

Part II

Policy scenarios to bend the plastics curve

7 The *Regional Action* policy scenario

Policies to curb plastics demand, increase product lifespans through repair and reuse, and improve waste management and recyclability can all help to reduce plastic leakage to the environment. This chapter explores the *Regional Action* policy scenario, in which a policy package is implemented to improve the circularity of plastics use and diminish the environmental impacts of plastics. The package comprises a mix of fiscal and regulatory policies targeting all phases of the plastics lifecycle, but with different policy ambitions for OECD and non-OECD countries.

Key messages

- The *Regional Action* policy package combines policies that aim to restrain plastic demand and production, enhance recycling, and close leakage pathways. This package ensures that economic growth can continue without increasing plastic leakage to the environment. Policies are more stringent for OECD countries than for non-OECD countries.
- Applied globally, the policy package is projected to see global plastics use fall by almost 20% below the *Baseline* projection, to 1 018 million tonnes (Mt) in 2060, instead of 1 231 Mt. A large part of this effect is achieved by taxing plastics use.
- Plastic waste is projected to decrease by a similar percentage, reaching only 837 Mt annually by 2060, instead of 1 014 Mt in the *Baseline*. Higher tax rates for single-use plastics allow for rapid waste reduction in the short term, which slows in later years as plastics lifespans are prolonged.
- The policies in the *Regional Action* package stimulate secondary (recycled) plastics markets by boosting demand for scrap, while also boosting the supply of recycled plastics. The share of waste that is recycled increases from 17% to 40% at the global level, while the share of secondary plastics in global production increases from 12% in the *Baseline* to 29% in the *Regional Action* scenario.
- All policies in the *Regional Action* scenario help to reduce mismanaged waste (waste that is not disposed of adequately); global mismanaged waste is projected to be 26% below 2019 levels in 2060, or 63% below the *Baseline* levels, reaching 59 Mt in 2060 instead of the 153 Mt projected for 2060 in the *Baseline*. The decrease in mismanaged waste is mostly driven by improvements in waste management in non-OECD countries.
- The *Regional Action* scenario primarily targets macroplastic leakage to the environment, which is projected to be 62% lower in 2060 compared to the *Baseline* scenario (falling to 15 Mt in 2060, versus 38 Mt in the *Baseline*). Microplastic leakage is also projected to decrease in the *Regional Action* scenario, although only by 4% relative to the *Baseline* scenario (falling to 5.6 Mt, versus 5.8 Mt), highlighting the need for more policies targeting microplastic leakage.
- Annual plastic leakage to aquatic environments will fall by 60% below the *Baseline* in 2060. Despite these large gains, net inflows of plastics to marine environments will persist in the coming decades and stocks are still expected to almost triple by 2060.
- The macroeconomic impacts of the *Regional Action* scenario are limited, costing 0.3% of global GDP by 2060 (a little more than USD 1.4 trillion globally). However, there are important regional differences, with the People's Republic of China (hereafter 'China') slightly benefitting (less than 0.1%) but higher costs in other regions: 1.1% in Sub-Saharan Africa and 1.8% in non-OECD European Union countries. As plastics are linked to many economic activities, the shift away from plastics can become particularly costly in some cases.
- Plastics are an important input for many economic activities, and a cost-effective policy package will have to consist of a combination of reductions in plastics use with properly managing the residual plastic waste.
- Waste treatment investment costs induced by the policy package are significant, but an order of magnitude smaller than the macroeconomic costs. The cumulative additional investment required to achieve the *Regional Action* policy objectives amounts to USD 320 billion (bn) between 2020 and 2060. In OECD countries this investment is almost entirely in additional recycling (USD 160 bn), whereas non-OECD countries need to invest USD 100 bn in recycling and USD 60 bn in improved waste collection to allow adequate disposal. These costs are on

top of the *Baseline* plastic waste management costs; at global level the investments required in 2060 represent 20% of total waste management costs in that year.

- Despite its positive impacts, plastics use and waste are projected to still more than double by 2060 from 2019 levels in the *Regional Action* scenario. Although the policy package could see a partial decoupling of plastics use and waste from economic growth, stocks of plastics in the environment continue to build up.

7.1. The policy package in the *Regional Action* scenario is broad and regionally varied

The results from the *Baseline* scenario outlined in Part I highlight how socioeconomic developments, economic activity (Chapter 2), plastics use (Chapter 3), plastic waste (Chapter 4) and plastic leakage (Chapter 5) are intrinsically linked. These links can be weakened or even broken by making plastics use more circular – i.e. by using more recycled plastics – and by improving how we deal with any remaining plastic waste. Achieving this requires a comprehensive set of policies.

This chapter explores the consequences of a *Regional Action* policy scenario, in which a policy package is implemented to reduce plastic leakage to the environment and to enhance the circularity of plastics use throughout their lifecycle. The policy package builds on the policy roadmap presented in the *OECD Global Plastics Outlook: Economic drivers, environmental impacts and policy options* (OECD, 2022[1]), and addresses each step of the plastic lifecycle, from production, use and reuse to waste management – including recycling. It involves a gradual approach that can be implemented over time to achieve increasingly ambitious policy objectives (Figure 7.1).

Figure 7.1. A policy roadmap for more circular use of plastics

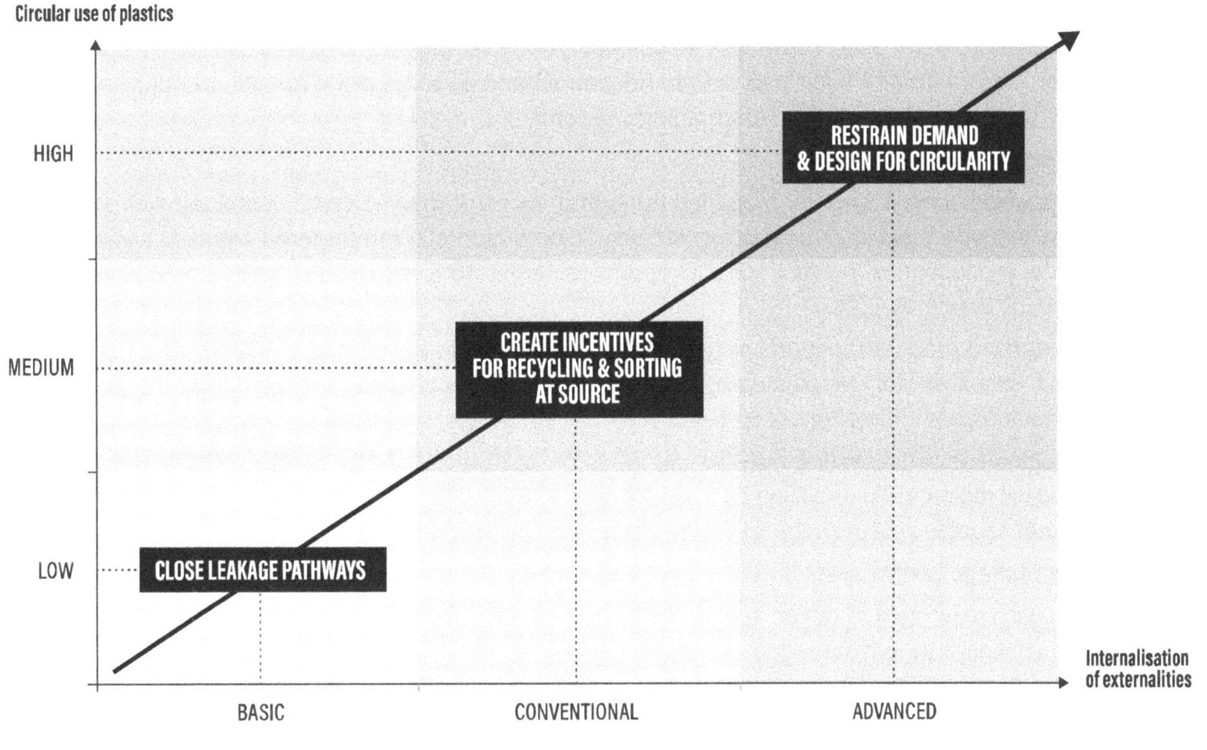

Source: (OECD, 2022[1])

The *Regional Action* policy package models the roll-out from 2022 (or in some cases from 2030) of flagship instruments put forward in the policy roadmap while taking into account the differences in capabilities across regions and the complexity of ramping up policy ambition. For example, not all countries can be expected to put in place advanced Extended Producer Responsibility (EPR) schemes (Box 7.1). Furthermore, the European Union has already advanced legislative action to implement plastics taxes, so is in a better position to quickly ramp these up than other countries. And countries that currently have very low recycling rates cannot be expected to reach the same targets as countries that already have set up high-capacity recycling facilities, not least the European Union and he OECD Pacific countries (Japan and Korea). In contrast, some technological advances, such as improved design for durability and reparability, can diffuse globally once they have reached a certain level of maturity.

In this *Regional Action* scenario, OECD countries undertake ambitious action, while non-OECD countries undertake more moderate action. Although these policies are aimed at reducing leakage of plastic to the environment significantly, they fall short of completely eliminating plastic leakage to the environment. Chapter 8 focuses on a more ambitious policy package, which aims at achieving global ambitions to reduce plastics leakage to the environment.

The *Regional Action* policy package includes a range of policy instruments, grouped into three main pillars (Figure 7.2). The various policies are designed to work together, rather than independently (see Annex B for details of the modelling):

- **Restrain plastics production and demand and enhance design for circularity**:
  - A tax on plastic packaging, increasing linearly from 0 in 2021 to reach USD 1 000/tonne by 2030 in the European Union (EU), by 2040 in the rest of the OECD and by 2060 in (non-EU) non-OECD countries.[1] It remains constant thereafter.
  - A tax on the use of all other types of plastics, introduced after 2030, starting at USD 25/tonne and reaching USD 750/tonne by 2040 in OECD countries and by 2060 in non-OECD countries. It remains constant thereafter.
  - Policy instruments to increase circularity and encourage more durable and repairable design of plastics. This includes (i) an extension of product lifespans by 10% to reflect durability, (ii) a decrease in intermediate (i.e. industrial and commercial) and final demand for durables of 5-10% by 2040 to reflect the longer lifespans of products, (iii) an increase in the demand for repair services calibrated such that overall household and government expenditures are unaffected by the policy. These policies are applied globally.
- **Enhance recycling:**
  - Recycled content targets, modelled through a tax on primary plastics combined with a subsidy on secondary plastics, as a proxy for regulation to achieve the targeted share of secondary in total production of plastics. OECD countries target 40% recycled content by 2060 and non-OECD countries 20%.
  - Extended producer responsibility (EPR; see Box 7.1), implemented by OECD and non-OECD EU countries for all packaging, electronics, motor vehicles and clothing; the remaining countries do not implement EPR.
  - Region-specific recycling rate targets; 60% by 2030 and 70% by 2060 for EU and the OECD Pacific region; 60% recycling by 2060 for other OECD countries and China; 40% by 2060 for the other countries. As with the EPR, the associated investment needs are included in the model.
- **Close leakage pathways:**
  - Public investment in mixed waste collection and sanitary landfills; this allows OECD countries to eliminate all mismanaged collected waste (e.g., dumped or burned in open pits) by 2060, and non-OECD countries to halve their share of mismanaged waste by 2060.
  - Policies to improve litter collection: litter collection rates increase more rapidly with income and reach 90% for high income countries (versus 85% in the *Baseline* scenario)

Figure 7.2. The policy package of the *Regional Action* scenario

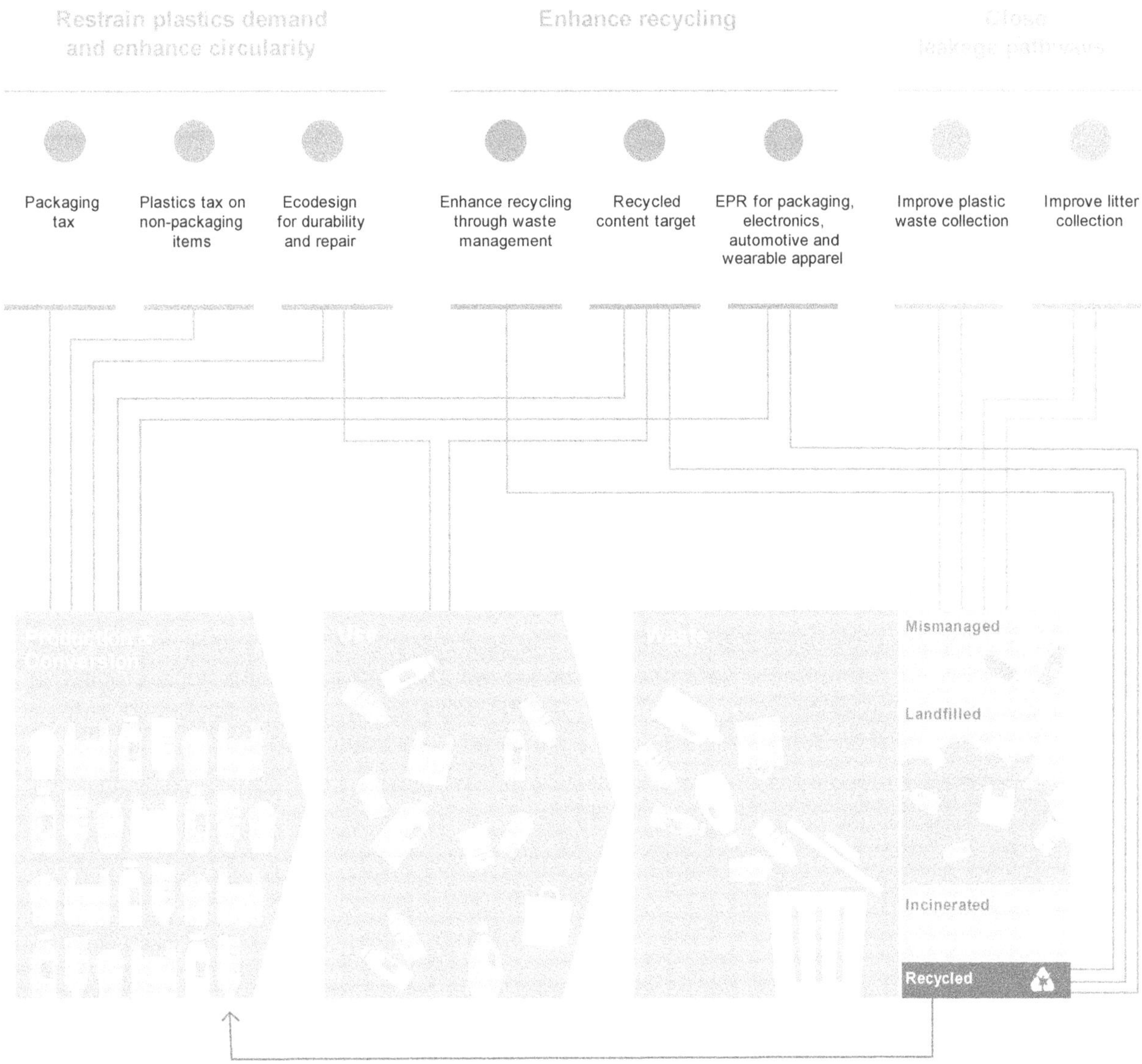

Box 7.1. How can the impacts of Extended Producer Responsibility schemes be modelled?

Extended Producer Responsibility (EPR) is a policy approach under which producers are given a significant responsibility for the treatment or disposal of post-consumer products. Assigning such responsibility could in principle provide incentives to prevent wastes at the source, promote product design for the environment and support the achievement of public recycling and materials management goals.

The EPR policy in the enhance recycling pillar (Figure 7.2) can be modelled through a stylised representation in a general equilibrium framework such as ENV-Linkages:

1. The increase in production costs is represented by a tax on plastics inputs for the affected sectors. In line with current costs of EPR schemes (Laubinger et al., 2021[2]), the level of the tax increases linearly to reach USD 300/tonne in OECD and non-OECD EU countries in 2030, and remains constant thereafter.
2. The increase in waste collected for recycling is modelled through a subsidy on the waste sector – including recycling activities – so that the EPR instrument is budget neutral. In this way, the modelling assumes that the government is an independent broker between producers and waste handlers; this is a proxy for a direct negotiation between both parties and should have very limited effects on the modelling results.
3. Recycling rates are increased to reflect that the policy targets recycling rather than all waste management. The policy is assumed to increase recycling rates by 20 percentage points by 2060, based on evidence on the impact of EPR schemes on plastics packaging in three European countries (Watkins et al., 2017[3]; European Commission, 2014[4]).
4. Investment in recycling facilities and waste collection for recycling is adapted to account for the increased recycling rates (see Section 7.4.2).

7.2. The *Regional Action* policy package limits growth in plastics use and waste

7.2.1. All instruments in the policy package help to reduce mismanaged waste

The *Regional Action* scenario reduces plastics quantities throughout the plastic lifecycle compared to the *Baseline* scenario, including plastics use, waste generation and mismanaged waste (Figure 7.3).

Globally, plastics use is projected to fall by 18% below the *Baseline* projection, reaching 1 018 million tonnes (Mt) in 2060 instead of 1 231 Mt (Panel A in Figure 7.3). It still represents a more than doubling from the 460 Mt in 2019. Most of the decrease in plastics use is, as expected, achieved by restraining demand (175 Mt of plastics use is avoided), mainly by taxing plastics use. Plastics use also decreases thanks to policies that aim at improving product design for circularity, such as increasing product lifespans and enhancing reuse. These policies prolong the lifespan of durable goods, reducing their demand. Downstream policies aimed at improving plastic waste management, including enhancing recycling and closing leakage pathways, have little effect on plastics production and use, although enhancing recycling does induce a switch in production from primary to secondary plastics.

Plastic waste generation is projected to decrease by a similar percentage (-18%), reaching 837 Mt by 2060, compared to 1 014 Mt in the *Baseline* (Panel B). As eventually all plastics that are used end up as waste, these reductions in plastic waste follow from the reduction in plastics use driven mostly by policies to restrain plastics demand; extension of product lifespans further postpones waste generation.

Overall, the three pillars of the *Regional Action* policy package are projected to reduce mismanaged waste by more than half (-63%), reaching 59 Mt by 2060, instead of 153 Mt in the *Baseline* (Panel C in Figure 7.3). This is 26% lower than the 79 Mt in 2019. The policies to restrain demand reduce the scale of the waste management problem, avoiding 26 Mt of mismanaged waste, but do nothing to decrease the share of waste that is mismanaged. Adding policies to enhance recycling take out another 34 Mt, including those that improve waste collection and sorting to increase recycling rates. Finally, closing leakage pathways by implementing waste management policies to increase the use of sanitary landfills, rather than dumpsites, reduce mismanaged waste by another 34 Mt. However, there are significant interaction effects at play here: when total waste is already reduced by the "restrain demand" pillar, and larger shares of waste are recycled due to the policies in the "enhance recycling" pillar, there is relatively little scope to also avoid mismanaged waste by closing leakage pathways. Alternatively, relying solely on closing leakage pathways as a stand-alone policy, and not implementing the policies in the other pillars, could avoid 73 Mt of mismanaged waste (Box 7.2), but would require significantly higher waste treatment investment. Thus, the third pillar can be quite effective, but the need for waste management investment is lower when the other pillars are also implemented.

Plastics use and waste are projected to still more than double by 2060 in the *Regional Action* scenario, compared to 2019, despite the implemented policies. Two key elements play a role here. First, population and economic growth, as well as regional development, imply a significant increase in plastics use in the *Baseline* scenario. Although the *Regional Action* scenario achieves a partial decoupling of plastics use from economic growth, this does not necessarily imply a reduction in plastics use in absolute terms. Second, plastics are an important input for many economic activities, and avoiding all mismanaged waste through upstream demand policies only would be very difficult and costly to achieve. It is cheaper to combine policies to restrain demand with policies that boost recycling and ensure that remaining waste is managed properly.

Mismanaged waste is projected to be reduced from 2019 levels, implying an absolute decoupling of mismanaged waste from economic activity. This decrease in mismanaged waste results in lower plastic leakage to the environment, despite a continued growth in plastics use and total waste levels.

Figure 7.3. The combined pillars of the *Regional Action* scenario bring plastics use, waste and mismanaged waste below *Baseline* projections

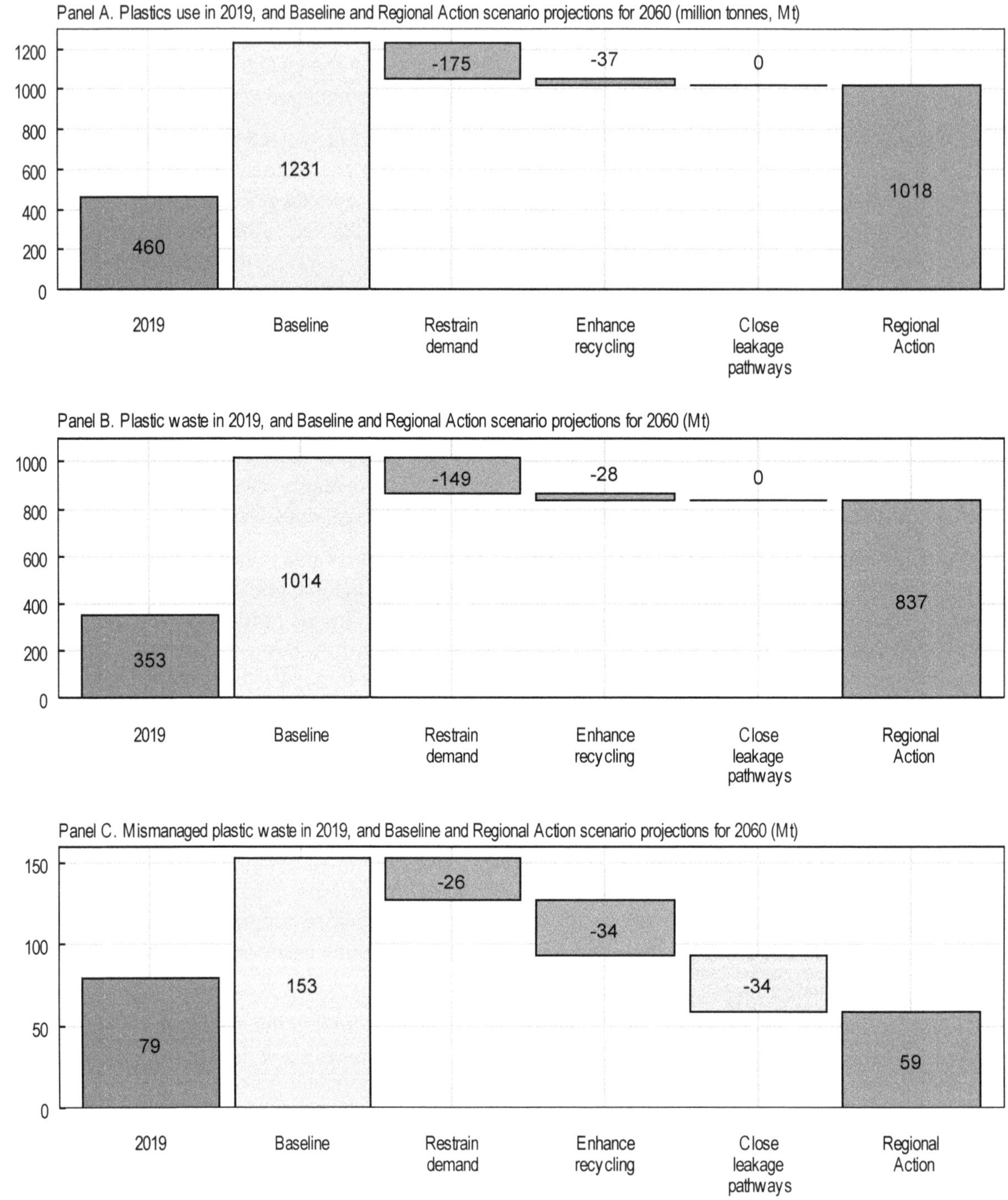

Source: OECD ENV-Linkages model.

StatLink https://stat.link/4a2kfi

Box 7.2. The interactions between the three pillars in the policy package are significant

The numbers presented in Figure 7.3 are based on the incremental implementation of the pillars; the right-hand panel of Figure 7.4 repeats these. Thus, for example the "enhance *recycling*" bar shows the effect of adding the enhanced recycling policy instruments to those of the "restrain *demand*" pillar. The left-hand panel of Figure 7.4 shows that if the policies to enhance *recycling* were introduced alone (grey bars), their effect could be somewhat stronger, as – in absence of the restrain demand pillar effects (blue bars) – they would act on a larger quantity of plastics use, waste and mismanaged waste. The same holds for the "close *leakage pathways*" pillar (green bars), albeit only for mismanaged waste as these policies do not aim at plastics use or total waste. In other words, as part of the policy package the contribution of the close leakage pathways pillar amounts to 34 Mt of avoided mismanaged waste while the policies in this pillar on their own would reduce mismanaged waste by 73 Mt.

Figure 7.4. The combined effect of the policy package is smaller than the sum of the three pillars implemented individually

Change compared to *Baseline* in million tonnes (Mt), 2060

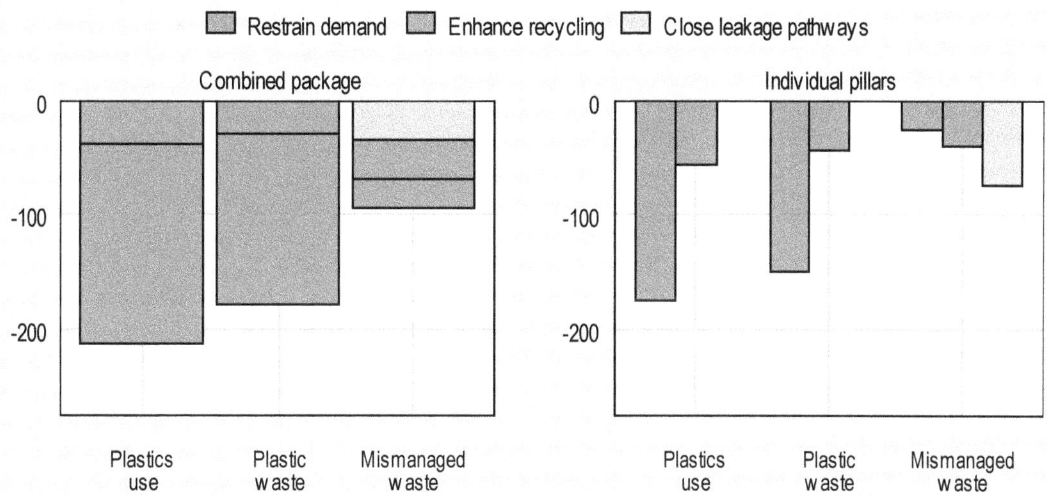

Source: OECD ENV-Linkages model.

StatLink https://stat.link/zaqfg9

7.2.2. The growth in plastics use slows down

The introduction of the *Regional Action* policy package is projected to curb the growth of plastics use in all regions (Figure 7.5). By 2060 in OECD countries, plastics use is projected to fall by 16% (69 Mt) compared to the *Baseline,* and by 18% (144 Mt) in non-OECD countries. But the time profile of plastics use reductions is different: in the OECD regions, action in the *Regional Action* scenario occurs in the short to medium term, and most policies are assumed to be fully in place by 2040. Thus, plastics use declines by 14-17% below *Baseline* levels by 2040 (reflecting a small increase in absolute levels, as plastics use increases significantly in the *Baseline*). After 2040, no further decoupling takes place and the difference with the *Baseline* remains constant. In contrast, the policies in non-OECD countries are assumed to be implemented more gradually, leading to a slower but steadier reduction in plastics use from the *Baseline.*

The exception is the non-OECD European Union group of countries , which are assumed to adopt the same high plastic packaging tax as the OECD EU Member States, causing significant reductions in the use of plastics for packaging in that region.

Given the rapid growth of *Baseline* plastics use, this still represents an increase in absolute levels of plastics use compared to 2019, in line with the discussion above. Outside the OECD, the most significant reductions below the *Baseline* are projected for the regions that have a high plastics-intensity (see Table 2.4 in OECD (2022[1])).[2] Sub-Saharan Africa (Other Africa) and Other Eurasia realise a 26% and 24% reduction below *Baseline* levels, respectively. In these regions, the high volume of plastics use for every dollar of commodity production implies that a tax of USD 1 000 per tonne translates into a relatively strong increase in the price of plastics inputs in production, thus driving a stronger substitution away from plastics inputs (as well as a loss of competitive position in these commodities on the global market).[3] As a result, these regions lower their plastics use below the *Baseline* trajectory at similar levels to OECD countries by 2030, and beyond them by 2060.

Figure 7.5. The more plastics-intensive non-OECD regions see the largest reductions in plastics use in the *Regional Action* scenario

Percentage change in plastics use compared to the *Baseline* scenario, 2060

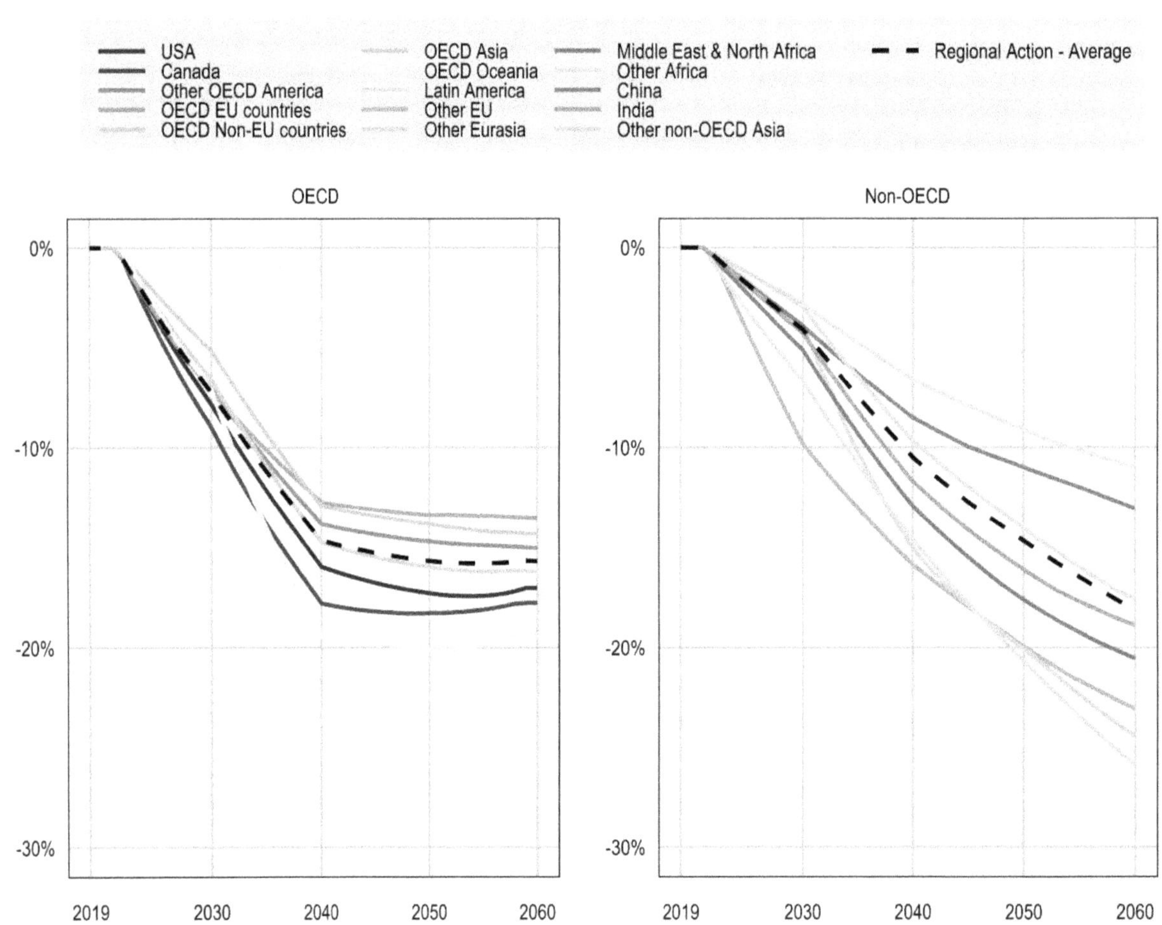

Source: OECD ENV-Linkages model.

StatLink https://stat.link/igqrd7

The implementation of the policy package causes the price of plastics to rise, altering production and consumption patterns and driving substitution by paper or glass, where available and economically feasible. Furthermore, as plastics-intensive sectors (such as motor vehicles) pass on their rising production costs to consumers, consumption shifts away from these sectors. Plastics demand declines more in the most plastics-intensive sectors (Figure 7.6). A particular case is business services, which includes accommodation and food services, as well as wholesale and retail trade, insurance and real estate. This sector does not have a very high plastics-intensity but is very large and thus uses very large amounts of plastics (not least in food services and trade) and are projected to decrease plastics demand by 75 Mt (22%) in 2060 compared to the *Baseline*. Motor vehicles, construction and food products (including packaging) follow. For motor vehicles, the economic impact on OECD countries is projected to be relatively small, as changes in competitive position induce a shift in production towards OECD countries, as their use of plastics makes up a relatively small share of total car manufacturing production costs, when compared to car manufacturing in non-OECD countries.

Figure 7.6. Business services contribute most to plastics use reductions in the *Regional Action* scenario

Difference in sectoral plastics use between *Regional Action* and *Baseline* scenarios in Million tonnes (Mt), 2060

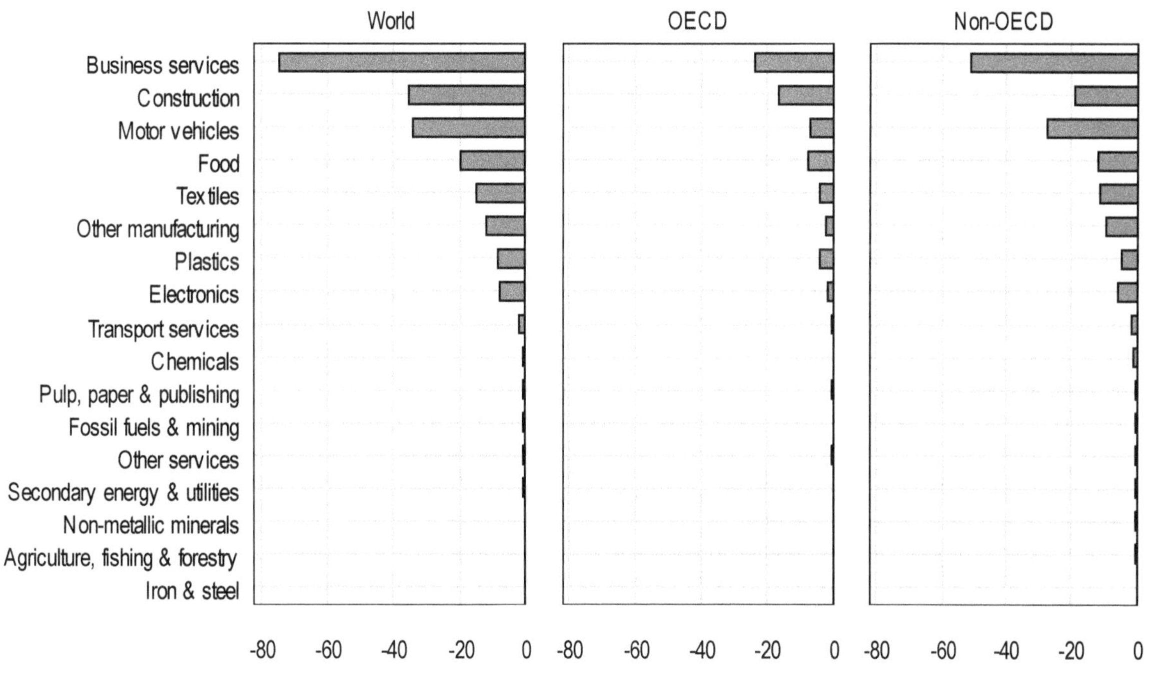

Source: OECD ENV-Linkages model.

StatLink https://stat.link/l0gn2q

The *Regional Action* scenario will result in a strong rise in secondary plastics use (Figure 7.7), with their 2060 share increasing to 29% from 12% in the *Baseline* and 6% in 2019. This reflects a more than tenfold increase in the global amount of secondary plastics use from 2019 levels (from 29 Mt to 297 Mt). However, the increase in secondary plastics is not strong enough to satisfy the full increase in plastics demand, and primary plastics continue to grow, albeit much more slowly than in the *Baseline* (on average 1.3% per year versus 2.3% in the *Baseline*). However, as secondary production starts from a much smaller base in 2019, the absolute increase in primary plastics between 2019 and 2060 (291 Mt) is still larger than the corresponding increase in secondary plastics use (268 Mt).

Secondary plastics production is affected by interactions among the three pillars. On one hand, the taxes on plastics in the "restrain demand" pillar reduce secondary plastics use. On the other hand, secondary plastics require scrap as input, which is generated by recycling plastic waste, which is boosted by the "enhance recycling" pillar. By reducing the amount of plastic waste, less scrap will be available for secondary production. The different pillars work in tandem as a 'push-pull' set of measures to stimulate secondary plastics markets: the recycled content targets boost demand for scrap (pull), while the recycling policies boost supply (push).

Figure 7.7. Secondary plastics use grows faster than primary plastics in the *Regional Action* scenario

Global plastics use in million tonnes (Mt) and share of secondary plastics

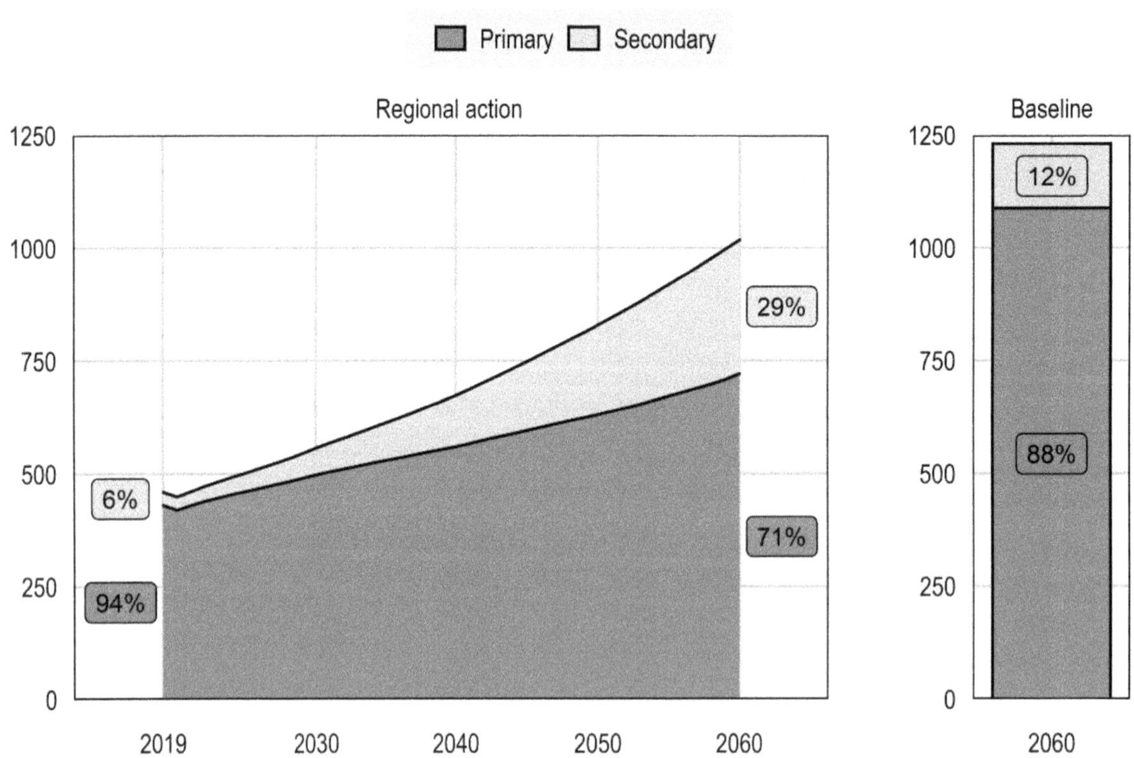

Source: OECD ENV-Linkages model.

StatLink https://stat.link/qixvnu

7.2.3. Recycling is boosted and waste management improves

The evolution of plastic waste generation largely follows the evolution of plastics use (Figure 7.8). At the global level both decline by around 18% compared to the *Baseline* scenario, while still more than doubling in absolute levels compared to 2019. Given the short lifespan of many plastics applications, and the large impact of plastic taxes on packaging, the lag between the effects on plastics use and plastic waste is fairly short on average. With stronger action in OECD countries, these effects are more visible in the OECD than in non-OECD countries.

In the first years after the policy package is introduced, the emphasis on taxing single-use plastics leads to more significant reductions in plastics use for applications with short lifespans. Thus, plastic waste declines more rapidly than plastics use compared to the *Baseline*. After 2030, when the policies that prolong lifespans start to kick in, more plastics are retained in the economy, and the reductions in plastic waste stall.

The extension of product lifespans as part of the "restrain demand" pillar delays the generation of waste. Applications for which plastics last longer before being discarded, such as building and construction, industrial machinery and transportation, will see longer extensions, while short-lived products such as packaging and personal care products are projected to have shorter lifespan extensions.[4] As a result, at least for a transitory period, waste generation is substantially postponed as the lifespans of applications are gradually prolonged as a result of the policy package. However, all plastics eventually become waste in the long run.

Figure 7.8. Changes in plastic waste largely follow changes in plastics use in the *Regional Action* scenario

Percentage change compared to the *Baseline* in 2060

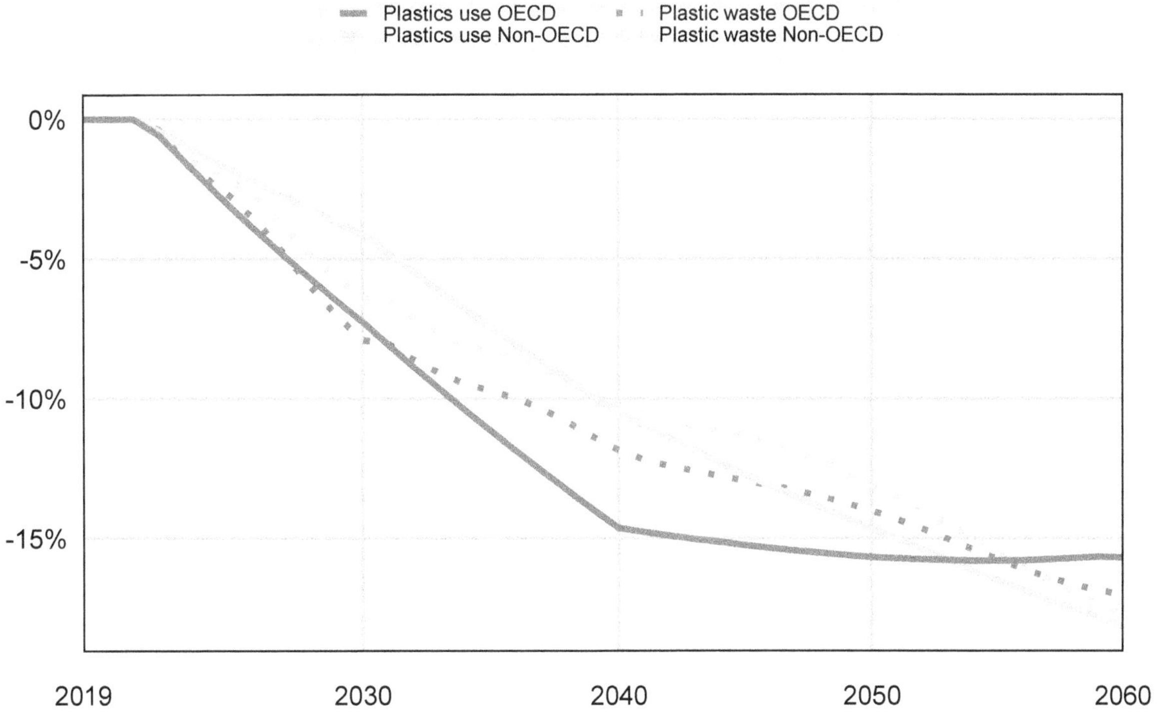

Source: OECD ENV-Linkages model.

StatLink https://stat.link/oqvdk1

Overall, the full package is projected to increase recycled plastic waste by 162 Mt in 2060 compared to the *Baseline*, while reducing mismanaged waste by 94 Mt (Figure 7.9). The policy package affects waste management, and therefore the amount of recycled and mismanaged waste, through two channels: (i) by altering the amount of waste generated (the "restrain demand" pillar); and (ii) by improving the way waste is treated (the "enhance recycling" and "close leakage pathways" pillars). Both channels ultimately result in less mismanaged waste, but only the latter boosts recycled plastics. As shown in Figure 7.9, the "restrain demand" pillar (second column) reduces mismanaged waste by 25 Mt in 2060 compared to the *Baseline* but does not directly boost recycling; therefore total recycling quantities decrease more or less in proportion to the change in total waste generation. The policies in the "enhance recycling" pillar significantly boost the share of recycling (from 17% to 40%, i.e. an increase of 188 Mt); consequently, these policies reduce mismanaged waste by another 34 Mt. Lastly, the "close *leakage pathways*" pillar (added in the last step) is projected to decrease the share of mismanaged waste by another 34 Mt in 2060. Thus, the overall result of the full *Regional Action* package (fourth column) is to reduce mismanaged waste from 153 Mt in the *Baseline* to 59 Mt (a decline of 94 Mt), while increasing recycling from 176 Mt in 2060 in the *Baseline* to 338 Mt (+162 Mt) in the policy scenario, representing a substantially larger piece of a substantially smaller pie.

Overall, the share of plastic waste that is recycled, a measure of circularity, increases from 9% in 2019 to 17% in 2060 in the *Baseline* scenario and 40% in the *Regional Action* scenario. This implies a significant improvement in the circularity of the economy, but is far from sufficient to avoid further growth in the use of primary plastics in production.

The decrease in mismanaged waste is mostly driven by changes in non-OECD countries (). In OECD countries in the *Baseline* scenario, mismanaged waste declines to 2060 driven by existing policies. The *Regional Action* policies have limited effect in the OECD on average, reducing mismanaged waste from 4.5 Mt in the *Baseline to* 2.3 Mt in 2060, as the levels of mismanaged waste are already projected to be low in the *Baseline* scenario. By far the largest reduction is achieved in Other OECD America, which has a higher share of mismanaged waste in the *Baseline* scenario than other OECD regions. In contrast, in non-OECD countries, while the picture is more mixed across individual countries, on balance there is a significant increase in mismanaged waste in the *Baseline* scenario. As non-OECD countries already account for 88% of global mismanaged waste in 2019, this difference in regional performance will grow wider over time unless more stringent global policies are introduced. As a result of the *Regional Action* scenario, non-OECD countries will exhibit a significant decline in mismanaged waste, falling to 56 Mt (-62%) in 2060 from 148 Mt in the Baseline.

Importantly, this also implies a significant drop in the total amount of global mismanaged waste compared to 2019 levels: from 79 Mt to 59 Mt. However, while the policy package in the *Regional Action* scenario does prevent any further growth in the coming decades and roughly stabilises mismanaged waste levels over time,[5] it does not eliminate mismanaged waste entirely.

Figure 7.9. The *Regional Action* scenario induces a significant shift from mismanaged to recycled waste

Plastic waste in million tonnes (Mt), 2060

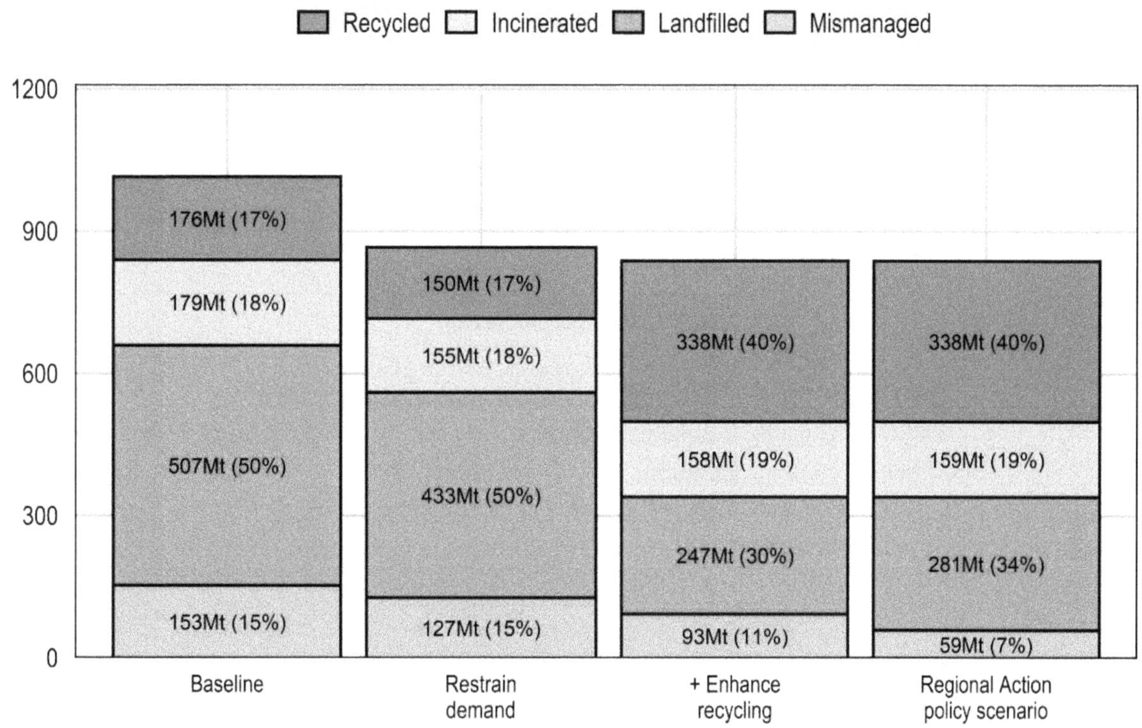

Note: As in other figures, the chart presents the cumulative impacts of the individual policy packages from left to right such that the right column corresponds to the *Regional Action* scenario, including the "restrain demand", "enhance recycling" and "close leakage pathways" policy pillars.
Source: OECD ENV-Linkages model.

StatLink https://stat.link/beoh8f

Figure 7.10. Mismanaged waste volumes are projected to fall most in non-OECD countries in the *Regional Action* scenario

Mismanaged plastic waste in million tonnes (Mt)

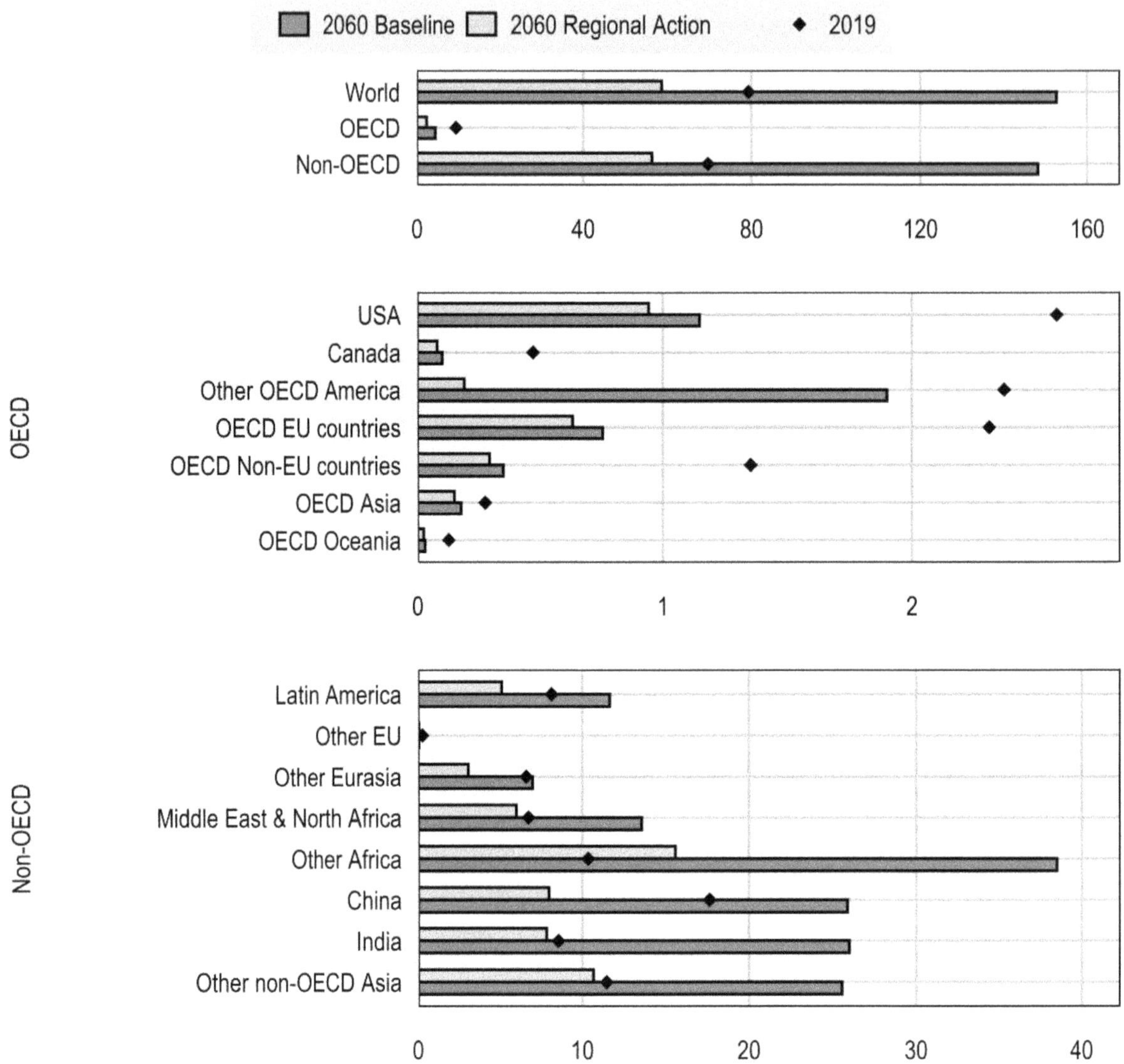

Source: OECD ENV-Linkages model.

StatLink https://stat.link/2o59br

7.3. The environmental benefits of policy action are clear, but plastic leakage to the environment continues

7.3.1. Plastic leakage to the environment remains significant despite policy action

The *Regional Action* scenario substantially curbs the leakage of plastics to the environment (Figure 7.11.). By 2060, global annual plastic leakage to the environment is projected to decrease by 55% compared to the *Baseline* scenario, from 44 Mt to 20 Mt. All three pillars in the policy package work together to ensure that plastic leakage does not grow, and eventually drops below the 2019 level of 22 Mt. The effectiveness of the pillars in reducing leakage is linked to their impact on curbing mismanaged waste.

The policies that restrain demand and enhance recycling limit the total waste produced and improve waste treatment respectively, thus reducing the amount of mismanaged waste, avoiding 18 Mt of leakage to the environment by 2060. Additional waste management policies aimed at closing leakage pathways explicitly target the reduction of mismanaged waste, further reducing leakage by 6 Mt in 2060 (Figure 7.11). As highlighted in Section 5.2 in Chapter 5, the estimations of leakage are surrounded by considerable uncertainties. However, in terms of percentage reductions, the outcomes are similar as these uncertainties affect both the *Baseline* and the *Regional Action* scenarios. In particular, across all estimates the package is expected to more than halve (-52% to -56%) annual plastic leakage to the environments by 2060.

Figure 7.11. All pillars contribute to reducing plastic leakage to the environment

Plastic leakage to the environment in million tonnes (Mt)

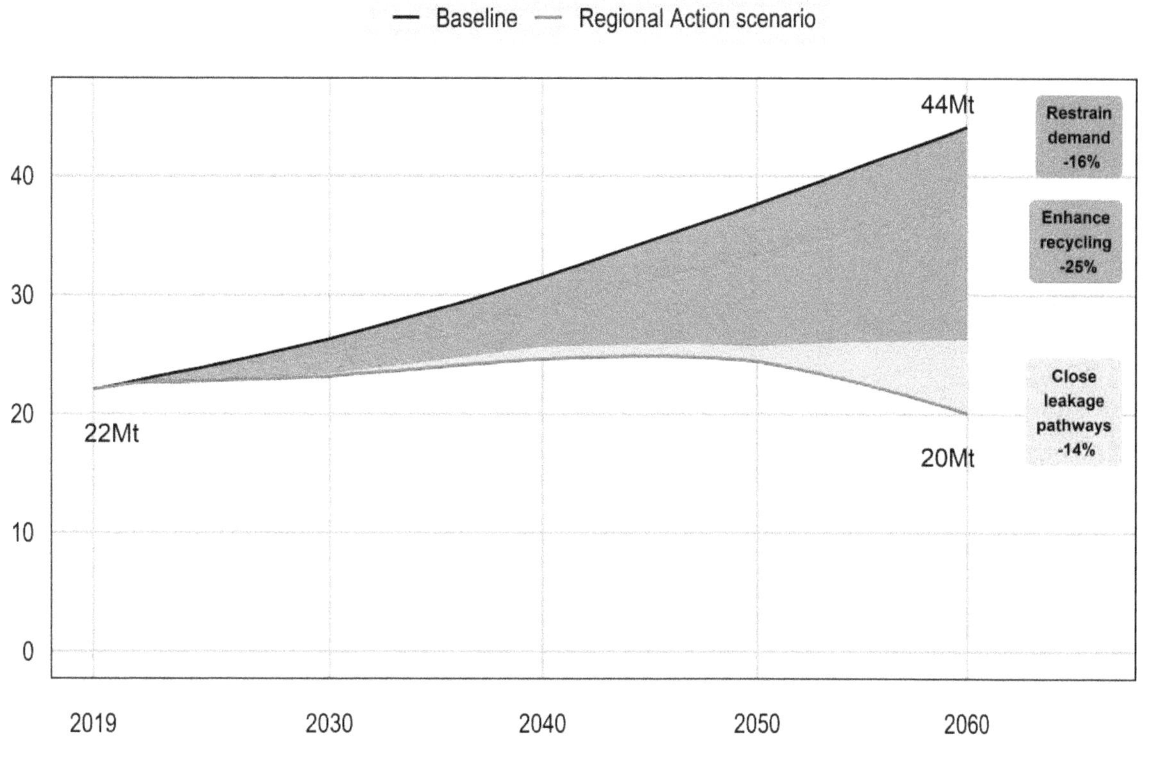

Source: OECD ENV-Linkages model, using the methodology adapted from Ryberg et al. (2019[5]) and Cottom et al. (2022[6]).

StatLink https://stat.link/nctsdg

Overall, the *Regional Action* scenario reduces plastic leakage per capita and further contributes to decoupling leakage from population growth (Figure 7.12, left panel). Plastic leakage per capita is expected to fall below 2019 values for both OECD and non-OECD countries once the policy package kicks in, primarily due to the decline in plastics use and the increase in recycling rates compared to *Baseline*. But reductions in plastic leakage per capita become even more significant after 2050, reflecting the inertia in the system: policies are gradually ramped up, it takes on average several years before reductions in plastics use translate into reductions of plastic waste, and shares of mismanaged plastic waste only gradually decline. Consequently, the ratio of leakage to plastics use also declines significantly over time (Figure 7.12, middle panel).

Furthermore, the amount of plastics leaked to the environment varies across activities and types of plastic waste. For instance, uncollected litter fully leaks to the environment, while waste collected in open dumps only partially leaks. The policy package achieves significant reductions in the amount of mismanaged waste, but other sources of leakage continue unabated. Especially leakage from microplastics, such as those from wastewater sludge and tyre abrasion, continue to grow. Therefore, the share of microplastics in leakage grows, especially in the longer run (Figure 7.12, right panel).

Figure 7.12. The *Regional Action* scenario will lower plastic leakage per capita, and decouple leakage from GDP and plastics use

Plastic leakage to the environment

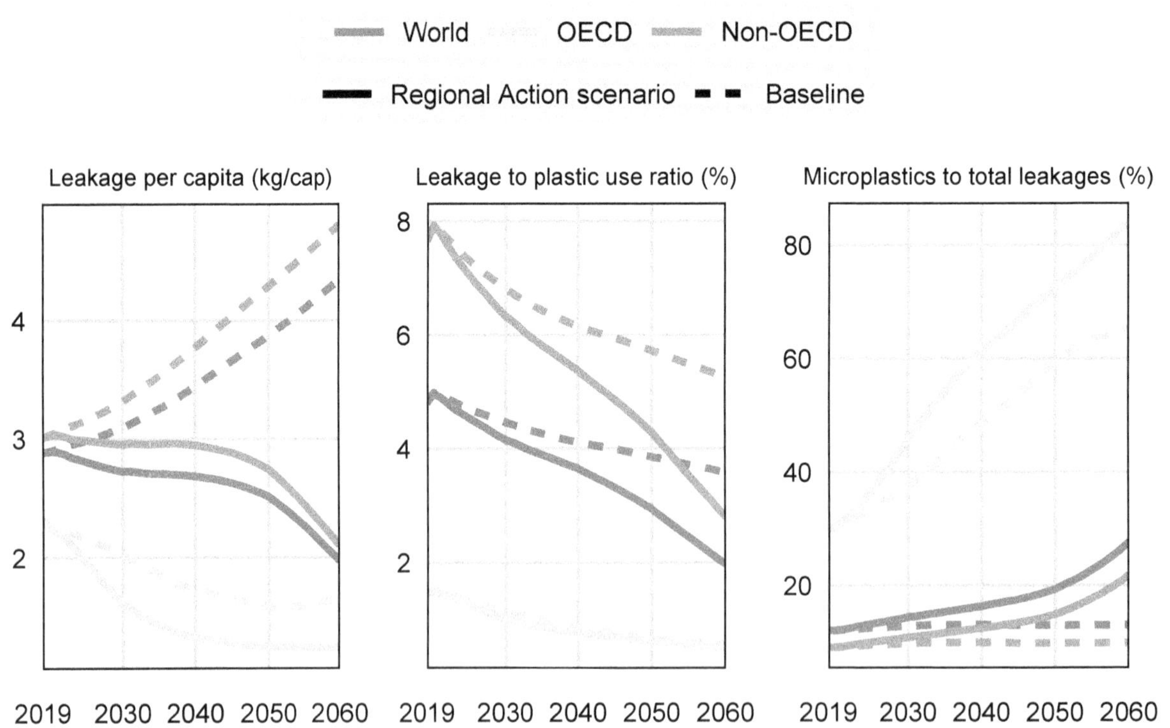

Source: OECD ENV-Linkages model, using the methodology adapted from Ryberg et al. (2019[5]).

StatLink https://stat.link/lsmbtv

The *Regional Action* scenario targets the leakage of macroplastics into the environment,[6] which is projected to be 62% lower in 2060 than in the *Baseline* scenario (falling to 15 Mt, from 38 Mt in the *Baseline*). Macroplastics make up for 87% (in terms of weight) of plastics leaked to the environment in

2060 in the *Baseline* scenario. The reduction in leakage of macroplastics is mainly driven by the reductions in mismanaged waste, which is projected to fall by 65% by 2060. Leakage from marine activities, such as ghost fishing gear, also contribute to macroplastic leakage, but are not significantly reduced in the policy scenario. In terms of the regional distribution, the largest absolute reductions in leakage are projected to be in non-OECD countries (23 Mt in 2060, corresponding to -62%), mostly in Sub-Saharan Africa (Other Africa) and the non-OECD Asian regions (Figure 7.13). These reductions largely follow the reductions in mismanaged waste (). In relative terms, reductions in total plastics leakage are projected to be limited in most OECD countries, except for Other OECD America, where mismanaged waste is stable at fairly high levels in the *Baseline* scenario, but reduced to almost zero in the policy scenario, leading to a large percentage decline in leakage. Reductions tend to be larger in most non-OECD regions, except for Other EU, which experiences a similar trend as OECD countries as they have rapidly reducing shares of mismanaged waste already in the *Baseline* scenario.

Leakage of microplastics into the environment is also projected to decrease in the *Regional Action* scenario, albeit by only 4% (to 5.6 Mt, from 5.8 Mt in the *Baseline* scenario), and with the largest reductions occurring in OECD countries. This result reflects more on the lack of policies to reduce microplastics considered in the package than a fundamental inability to reduce microplastic leakage. The reductions that do occur are mostly driven by the lower use of all plastics in the economy, which will reduce microplastics leaking from primary pellets, wastewater sludge and road markings. These results, which do not reflect the additional microplastics from the degradation of leaked macroplastics, highlight that policy measures specifically targeting microplastic leakage to the environment are needed.

Figure 7.13. The *Regional Action* scenario reduces macro- and microplastic leakage in all regions

Difference from *Baseline* in million tonnes (Mt) and percentage change, 2060

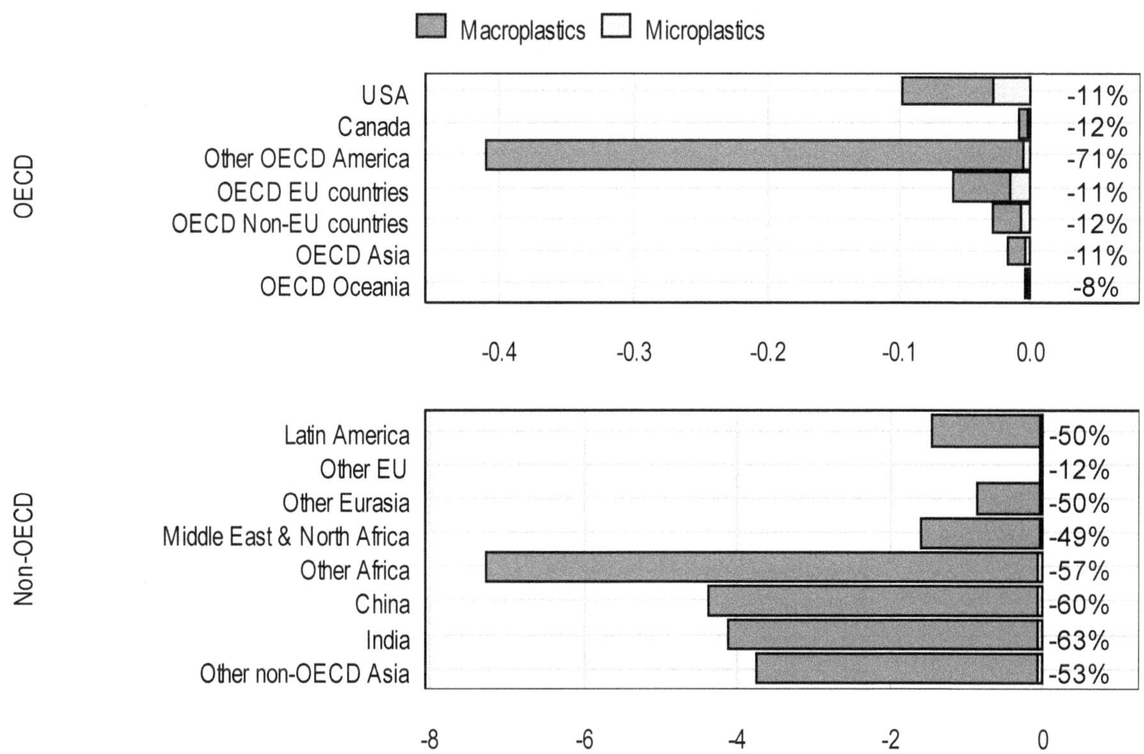

Source: OECD ENV-Linkages model, using the methodology adapted from Ryberg et al. (2019[5]).

StatLink https://stat.link/fr6jlg

7.3.2. Less plastics will be leaked to the aquatic environment

Thanks to the overall reduction in plastic leakage to the environment, the *Regional Action* scenario is projected to also curb plastic leakage to aquatic environments by 2060. In the *Baseline*, the net inflows into aquatic environments are projected to reach 11.6 Mt in 2060; the *Regional Action* scenario could reduce these inflows by 60% (a 4.6 Mt reduction in 2060). This decrease is largely driven by policies that directly target waste management and reduce mismanaged waste (Section 7.2) and thus total leakage to the environment.

The largest reductions are projected to occur in non-OECD countries (6.8 Mt below the *Baseline* projections; Figure 7.14), which are currently – as well as in 2060 in the *Baseline* scenario – the main contributors to the projected rise in leakage to aquatic environments. Overall, the *Regional Action* package more than halves leakage to aquatic environments from Sub-Saharan Africa (Other Africa), and the Other non-OECD Asia region, while leakage in India and China are expected to fall by almost two thirds. OECD countries see substantial reductions in leakage to aquatic environments compared to 2019 levels, but a key difference with many non-OECD countries is that – with the exception of Other OECD America – reductions are also foreseen in the *Baseline* scenario and thus do not rely on the policies in the *Regional Action* scenario.

Figure 7.14. Non-OECD countries will see greatest reductions in plastic leakage into aquatic environments in the *Regional Action* scenario

Plastic leakage into aquatic environments in million tonnes per year (Mt/year)

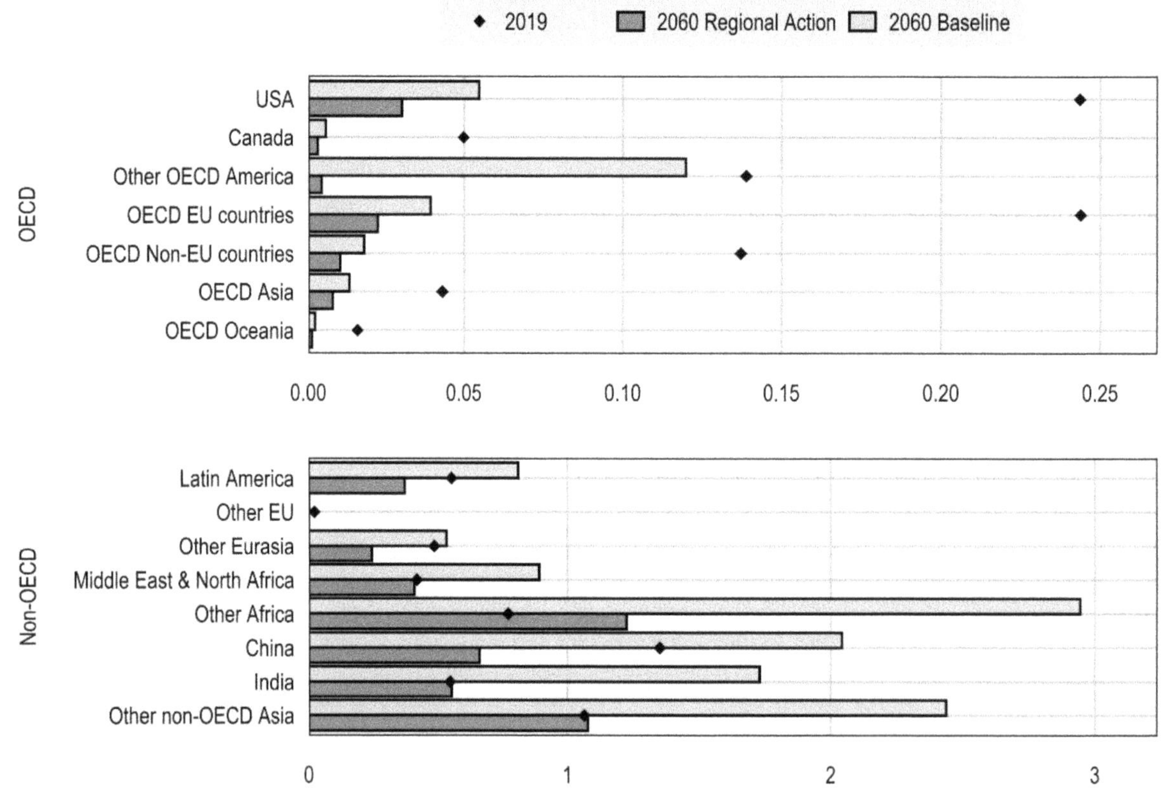

Source: OECD ENV-Linkages model, adapted from (Lebreton and Andrady, 2019[7]).

StatLink https://stat.link/jz6qke

The reductions in leakage to aquatic environments caused by the *Regional Action* policies substantially reduce the plastics accumulated in rivers and the ocean by 2060 compared to the baseline. But until leakage pathways are completely closed and flows fall to zero, accumulated stocks of plastic in rivers and the ocean continue to build up. As it takes 40 years in the *Regional Action* scenario to reduce mismanaged waste to low levels, significant flows of plastics continue to leak to the environment, with sizable mounts ending up in aquatic environments, especially in non-OECD countries. Consequently, total accumulated plastics in aquatic environments will still almost triple by 2060 in this scenario (Figure 7.15) and reach 388 Mt. These stocks are 105 Mt lower than in the Baseline, where 493 Mt accumulates in rivers and the ocean between 2019 and 2060. More ambitious policy action at the global level, and especially ramping up short-term policy ambitions, is necessary to further reduce plastic leakage to the ocean.

Figure 7.15. The *Regional Action* scenario still leads to a tripling of accumulated plastic leakage stocks

Accumulated plastic leakage in million tonnes per year (Mt/year)

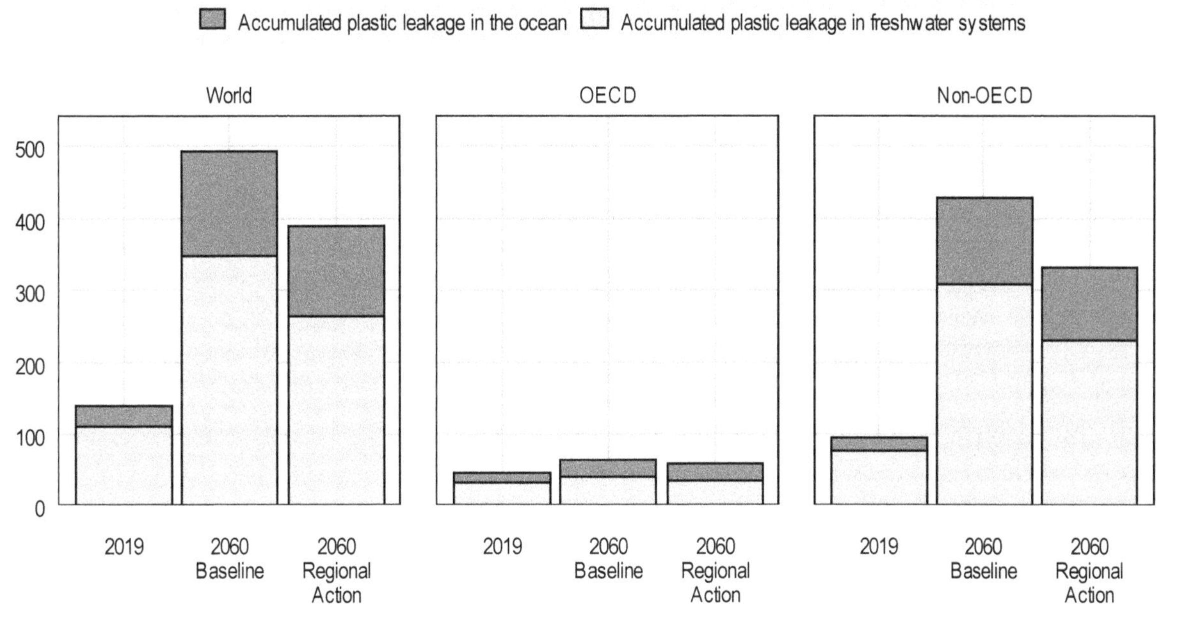

Source: OECD ENV-Linkages model, adapted from (Lebreton and Andrady, 2019[7]).

StatLink https://stat.link/ymudtp

7.4. The macroeconomic impacts of the *Regional Action* scenario are small

7.4.1. The policies reduce GDP levels slightly below those in the Baseline

The macroeconomic impacts of the *Regional Action* scenario are limited.[7] The macroeconomic costs are determined through several interacting mechanisms. First, although the fiscal instruments (such as the taxes in the "restrain demand" pillar) increase costs for plastics users, they simultaneously create revenues that can be used to finance public expenditure, such as on waste management. Also, producers faced with increased costs of plastics inputs as a result of these taxes will shift towards other inputs, boosting value added in those activities. The net macroeconomic effect is thus the difference in productivity between these different inputs, rather than the gross value lost in the plastics production sectors.

Second, several policies in the *Regional Action* package deal with regulations that combine a cost with a benefit for firms and households. For example, the ecodesign policies increase commodity prices but prolong plastics lifespans. Similarly, less frequent replacement of commodities by stimulating repair leads to value creation in the repair sector.[8] Such instruments largely entail a shift in expenditures while the macroeconomic effects are very limited overall. The macroeconomic effects of such shifts are determined by the difference in productivity between the sectors (plus some indirect effects from changing prices etc.). For instance, if repair services have a higher productivity than the production of consumer goods, then increased repair can boost GDP even if it leads to reduced demand for consumer products. The EPR instrument in the "enhance recycling" pillar entails a cost for producers, but creates an income source for the waste management sector that carries out the waste collection.

Third, the "enhance recycling" and "close leakage pathways" pillars imply additional investments in waste collection, sorting and treatment. These investment costs can be significant, although it is again the cost difference that is relevant: waste that is incinerated in the *Baseline* but recycled in the *Regional Action* scenario entails recycling costs, but simultaneously generates cost savings from avoiding incineration. Furthermore, investment is an economic activity that generates value added and thus contributes to GDP: new value added is created in recycling activities and – where relevant – in construction.

Fourth, the increase in waste management costs is moderated by the reduction in waste generated compared to the *Baseline* scenario. As overall plastic waste declines in the *Regional Action* scenario – at least compared to the *Baseline* projection – a higher treatment share for recycling and landfilling to reduce mismanaged waste does not translate proportionately into higher investment costs.

Overall, while these marginal shifts in economic activity and increases in waste management expenditures do have a macroeconomic cost, this macroeconomic impact is much smaller than a partial accounting of gross implementation costs would suggest. Compared to the *Baseline* projection, GDP (measured in constant prices using purchasing power parities as exchange rates) is projected to decrease by 0.3% globally (Figure 7.16). This equals more than USD 1.4 trillion, and reflects value added that is not generated in the policy scenario.

Figure 7.16. The *Regional Action* policy package reduces plastics use much more than regional GDP

Percentage change in 2060 compared to the Baseline

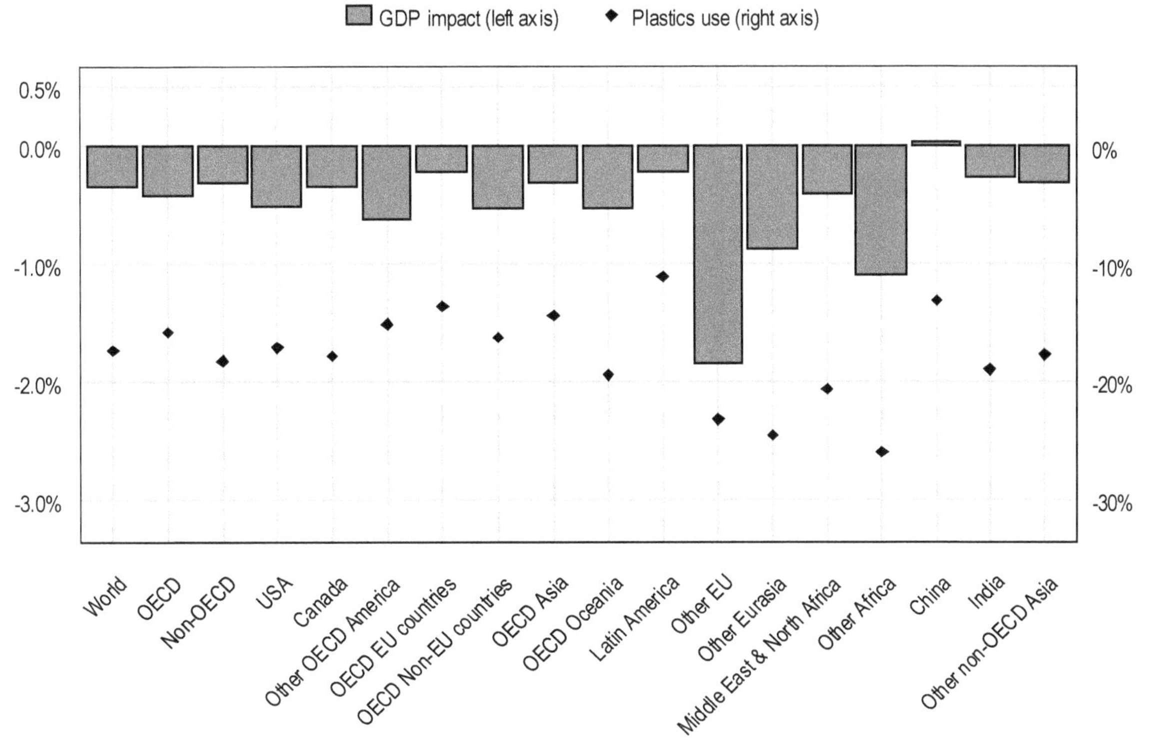

Source: OECD ENV-Linkages model.

StatLink https://stat.link/d80cuk

The macroeconomic costs of implementing the policies are below 1% in most regions. Overall, the implementation of the *Regional Action* policy package will curb plastics use, and waste, at moderate economic costs. As plastics use decreases more than GDP, plastics intensity (the ratio of the two) drops substantially across regions.

In the short run, as the policies gradually ramp up, the costs associated with the policies are small. In some cases they can actually boost GDP, when economic activity shifts towards more productive activities, as discussed above. Over time, the impact of the policy package on GDP increases as policies are intensified and the effects on the economy, not least on capital stocks, accumulate. Thus GDP levels decline further below the *Baseline* over time, while still growing in absolute values.

Furthermore, some non-OECD countries, most notably China, can benefit from an increase in competitiveness vis-à-vis their OECD competitors as the OECD countries accelerate their policies before non-OECD countries, which also have lower targets for some policies. The smaller increase in production costs for exporting sectors in Asia thus improves their competitive position. This causes a small shift in production from OECD to non-OECD – or at least the non-OECD Asian – countries.[9] Of all regions, the smallest change in GDP is projected for China, which is projected to be able to increase GDP above *Baseline* levels by less than 0.1% of GDP. Box 7.3 teases out these trade and competitiveness impacts in more detail.

However, the countries that are most severely affected by the policy package are also outside the OECD (Figure 7.16). The highest costs are projected for the Other EU region (-1.8%), which is assumed to harmonise part of its policy package, notably the packaging plastics tax, the EPR and the recycling rate targets, with the OECD EU countries. As the region has relatively high plastics intensity, this leads to a more significant reduction in economic activity and GDP. The losses in Africa (-1.1%) and non-OECD Eurasia (which includes the Russian Federation; -0.9%) are also relatively large. In these most strongly affected regions, plastics use reductions are also somewhat larger than in other regions. While a higher plastics-intensity of domestic production leads to stronger plastics use reductions from taxing plastics use, it also implies a stronger negative effect on the region's competitive position. Thus, a substantial part of the costs stems from worsening trade relations rather than from the implementation of the domestic policies.

Box 7.3. Domestic effects and trade effects both matter for the macroeconomic costs of the *Regional* Action scenario

The effects of the policy package on GDP depends on (i) the domestic costs of implementation of the policies, (ii) international trade effects caused by the effects of the domestic policies on prices and thus on comparative advantage vis-à-vis foreign competitors, and (iii) effects on trade from the policies implemented abroad. To shed further light on these effects, Figure 7.17 compares the *Regional Action* scenario with a hypothetical alternative where only OECD countries implement their policies, and there are no domestic policies in non-OECD countries.

Figure 7.17. Plastics use reductions are driven by domestic policies, but GDP is also affected by policies implemented abroad

Percent change compared to *Baseline* scenario, 2060

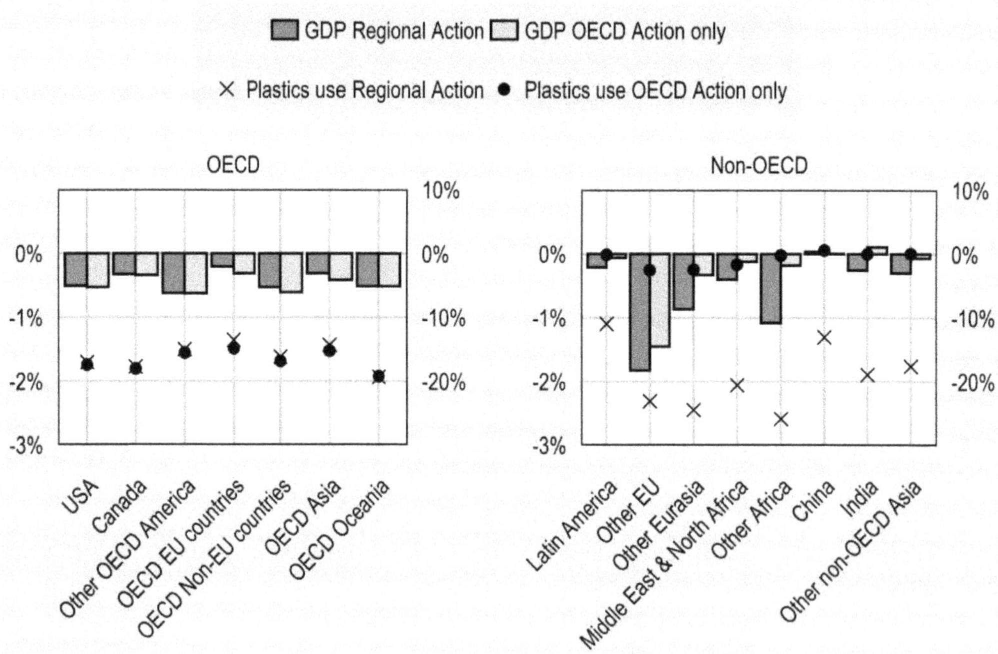

Note: For the sake of simplicity, in the OECD Action only scenario, the non-OECD EU countries do not implement the policy package.
Source: OECD ENV-Linkages model.

StatLink https://stat.link/jw4yo0

In OECD countries, the differences are very small. The impacts on GDP are a bit bigger, as some comparative advantage is lost to non-OECD countries. Production activities of plastics and plastics-using sectors shifts a bit more to non-OECD countries, driving higher costs but also somewhat larger plastics use reductions. The latter effect is very limited however.

In some non-OECD countries, most notably China, plastics use actually increases above Baseline levels, as production of plastics-intensive commodities shift there. But on balance plastics use in non-OECD countries remains at Baseline level. There is thus not a big "plastics pollution haven" effect where action in OECD countries only would be ineffective due to worsening levels elsewhere.

The effects of the OECD actions on GDP in non-OECD countries varies: in the non-OECD European Union countries a significant drop in GDP remains, despite the absence of a domestic policy package. The relatively high costs in this region are purely driven by trade effects related to the close integration with the OECD-EU economies, and not by domestic policy costs. In contrast, in Africa almost all macroeconomic costs disappear, indicating that the domestic policy effect is much more important than the trade effects.

7.4.2. Much higher investment in waste treatment is needed to curb plastic leakage

An essential part of the *Regional Action* policy package is investing in recycling capacity – including increased waste sorting and recycling – and investing in improved waste treatment – including waste collection and landfilling – to avoid mismanaged waste. The cost of these policy-induced investments, which partially drive the macroeconomic effects on GDP presented above, are calculated by multiplying waste flows with unit treatment costs; they are additional to the investments in waste management in the *Baseline* scenario, which are projected to increase from around USD 35 bn in 2019 to more than USD 100 bn in 2060.

The investment costs associated with improving recycling and reducing mismanaged waste used in this analysis are based on Soós, Whiteman and Gavgas (2020[8]), who provide harmonised estimates for different waste management solutions. The estimates include labour costs, fixed and variable operating and maintenance costs, and annualised capital costs. Table 7.1 depicts the annualised benchmark costs for each solution and how they map to the waste management categories considered in ENV-Linkages.[10]

Table 7.1. Annualised benchmark costs for waste management solutions

Waste management solution	Annual cost range (USD/tonne/year)
Mixed waste collection and transfer	40.7 - 86.4
Source separated waste collection and transfer	48.8 - 103.9
Sorting station for clean recyclables	29.9 - 86.4
Plastics recycling facility	54.8 - 98.8
Mechanical biological treatment for mixed waste	60.4 - 91.5
Incineration with energy recovery	89.8 - 149.1
Landfilling	28.5 - 33.6
Litter collection	1 000 - 2 000

Note: Operating costs include costs of personnel, energy and fuel, consumables, administration, taxes and insurance. Maintenance costs comprise of maintenance and repair, spare parts and services. Depreciation and interest payments are included in the calculations. For the Global Plastics Outlook analysis, the median estimates were used and applied globally for all treatment methods except recycling, where the high estimates are used in the policy scenarios to reflect the high ambition level of the recycling targets.
Source: Based on (UNEP and ISWA, 2015[9]), (Pfaff-Simoneit, 2013[10]) , (Soós, Whiteman and Gavgas, 2020[8]) and (WRAP, 2021[11]).

As it is difficult to distinguish plastic waste management from mixed municipal waste systems, estimates of the management costs of the entire municipal solid waste stream are used as a proxy for the unit (per tonne) costs of plastic waste management. The exceptions are plastic waste pre-processing installations that focus on plastic waste only, and sorting facilities for mixed dry recyclables that include only dry waste.

In general, investments required for one tonne of recycling, which include sorting stations for clean recycling and investments in plastics recycling facilities, are larger than the costs of incineration; landfilling is still cheaper. Litter collection is by far the most costly.

The total recycling investments required to achieve the waste treatment levels of the *Regional Action* scenario are significant in both OECD and non-OECD regions. They are highest in countries that have to handle relatively large amounts of waste (such as China), and in countries where the difference in recycling rates between the *Baseline* and the *Regional Action* scenarios is relatively large (such as the USA). Globally, cumulative investments in recycling amount to more than USD 260 billion (Figure 7.18, Panel A). While this amount is not negligible, it is of a similar order of magnitude to the projected annual global expenditures on plastic waste management by 2060 (more than USD 100 bn) in the *Baseline* scenario and it is spread over several decades. In 2060, the projected additional investments required to enhance recycling amount to 22% on average of total plastic waste management costs in OECD countries (ranging between 21 and 28% at regional level; Figure 7.18, Panel B), and 12% in non-OECD countries.

In most OECD countries, the amount of mismanaged waste is very small, and hence the additional investment required in avoiding mismanaged waste is almost negligible (for the OECD group of countries around USD 1 bn over the period 2020-2060). In non-OECD countries, additional investment (almost USD 60 bn above *Baseline* levels) is needed in the "close leakage pathways" pillar of the *Regional Action* scenario, with regions with more mismanaged waste in 2060 in the *Baseline* having higher costs (Figure 7.18). The combined investments for recycling and reducing mismanaged waste in non-OECD countries amount to USD 160 bn. One quarter of that (USD 36 bn) is needed to improve waste management systems in Africa. The combination of the current low expenditure on waste treatment and high investment needs for both recycling and avoiding mismanaged waste imply that the additional average annual investment costs in the *Regional Action* scenario amount to around 35% of total annual waste management costs in Africa.

Figure 7.18. Significant additional waste treatment investment in the *Regional Action* scenario is needed to enhance recycling and close leakage pathways

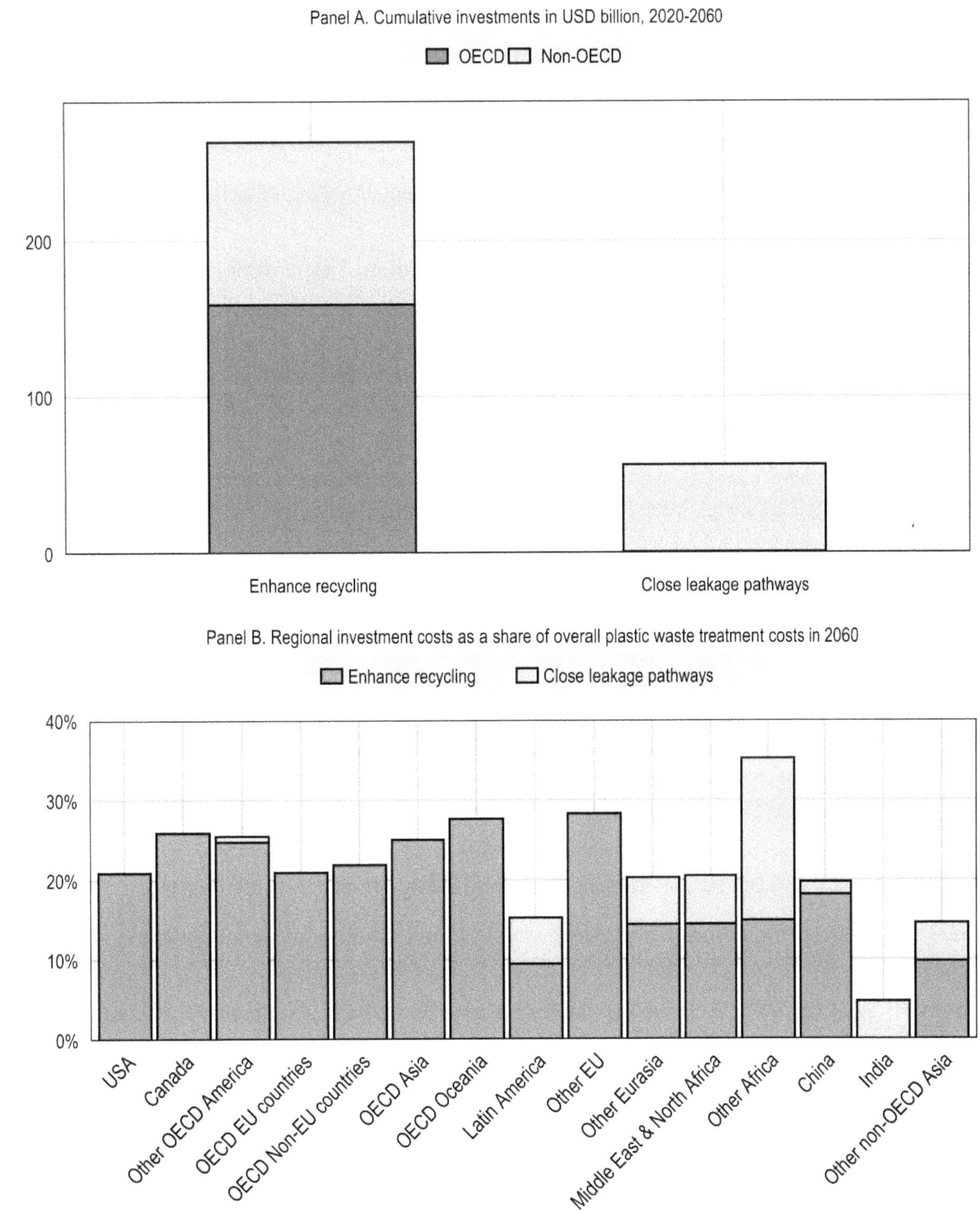

Note: Annualised investment costs reflect the annual expenditure related to the investment. In OECD countries, mismanaged waste is largely eliminated in the *Baseline* scenario and thus no additional investment is required. In India, recycling rates are already high and increasing in the *Baseline* scenario and thus recycling rates by 2060 already meet the policy scenario targets and no further recycling investment is required.
Source: OECD ENV-Linkages model.

StatLink https://stat.link/59fds4

References

Cottom, J. et al. (2022), "Spatio-temporal quantification of plastic pollution origins and transportation (SPOT)" University of Leeds, UK, https://plasticpollution.leeds.ac.uk/toolkits/spot/. [6]

European Commission (2014), "Development of Guidance on Extended Producer Responsibility (EPR)", *European Commission - DG Environment*, https://ec.europa.eu/environment/archives/waste/eu_guidance/pdf/Guidance%20on%20EPR%20-%20Final%20Report.pdf. [4]

Laubinger, F. et al. (2021), "Modulated fees for Extended Producer Responsibility schemes (EPR)", *OECD Environment Working Papers*, No. 184, OECD Publishing, Paris, https://doi.org/10.1787/2a42f54b-en. [2]

Lebreton, L. and A. Andrady (2019), "Future scenarios of global plastic waste generation and disposal", *Palgrave Communications*, Vol. 5/1, p. 6, https://doi.org/10.1057/s41599-018-0212-7. [7]

OECD (2022), *Global Plastics Outlook: Economic Drivers, Environmental Impacts and Policy Options*, OECD Publishing, Paris, https://doi.org/10.1787/de747aef-en. [1]

Pfaff-Simoneit, W. (2013), *Entwicklung eines sektoralen Ansatzes zum Aufbau von nachhaltigen Abfallwirtschaftsystemen in Entwicklungsländern vor dem Hintergrund von Klimawandel und Ressourcenverknappung [In German].*, Universität Rostock, Darmstadt/ Rostock, http://rosdok.uni-rostock.de/file/rosdok_disshab_0000000936/rosdok_derivate_0000005003/Dissertation_Pfaff-Simoneit_2013.pdf. [10]

Ryberg, M. et al. (2019), "Global environmental losses of plastics across their value chains", *Resources, Conservation and Recycling*, Vol. 151, p. 104459, https://doi.org/10.1016/j.resconrec.2019.104459. [5]

Soós, R., A. Whiteman and G. Gavgas (2020), *The cost of preventing ocean plastic pollution*, OECD Environment Directorate, Working Party for Resource Productivity and Waste. [8]

UNEP and ISWA (2015), *Global Waste Management Outlook*, UN Environment Programme, https://www.unep.org/resources/report/global-waste-management-outlook. [9]

Watkins, E. et al. (2017), "EPR in the EU Plastics Strategy and the Circular Economy: A focus on plastic packaging", *Institute European Environmental Policy*. [3]

WRAP (2021), *Financial Cost of Packaging Litter – Phase 2 – Final Report*, Prepared by Chiarina Darrah, Leyla Lugal, Paul Marsh, Kathryn Firth, Vera Lahme and Gemma Darwin. [11]

Notes

[1] For comparison, the EU tax on non-recycled plastics amounts to EUR 800 per tonne (https://ec.europa.eu/environment/topics/plastics/single-use-plastics_en), which is a little less than the USD 1000 per tonne assumed in the modelling; the exact specification of which streams exactly fall under the tax are also somewhat different, most notably the tax in the *Regional Action* scenario covers all packaging plastics, not only non-recycled plastics.

[2] The exception is China, that has a high plastics intensity in 2019, but that is projected to reduce this intensity over time; in contrast, in Other Africa and Other Eurasia the plastics intensity increases over time (see Chapter 3).

[3] The high plastics intensity at the sectoral level does not translate into a high plastics intensity at the national level, as plastics-intense sectors represent a fairly small share of total regional production.

[4] Under the assumption of a 10% increase in product lifespans, building and construction products would last an additional 3.5 years on average, while packaging and personal care product lifespans would be extended by less than a month.

[5] The time profile of global mismanaged waste in the policy scenario is not uniform over time: it gradually increases until around 2040 after which the effects of the policies become dominant, leading to declining mismanaged waste levels.

[6] The *Regional Action* policy package does not include instruments that specifically target microplastics due to lack of data on costs, such as costs necessary to reduce emissions at source and to improve the end-of-pipe capture of microplastics before they enter the environment.

[7] Importantly, the analysis here only includes the direct economic costs and abstracts from changes in damage from environmental degradation. The economic benefits from reduced leakage of plastics to the environment are not monetised.

[8] Motor vehicle repair services are included in the model in the wholesale and retail trade sector; other repair services are included in "other commercial services".

[9] The model assumes that exchange rates adjust to ensure that trade balances remain at their Baseline level. Thus, aggregate exports and imports must move together.

[10] Unfortunately, the available data do not allow a robust regional differentiation of these costs.

8 The *Global Ambition* policy scenario

Achieving the global ambition to reduce plastic leakage to zero requires a wide-ranging set of policies that tackles all drivers, including plastics use, waste management and leakage pathways. This chapter explores the *Global Ambition* policy scenario, in which a policy package is implemented to reduce plastic leakage to the environment to near zero by 2060. The package includes the same instruments as in the *Regional Action* policy scenario, but with more ambitious targets, and is implemented rapidly and globally.

Key messages

- Global implementation of ambitious circular policies to curb plastic leakage can reduce mismanaged plastic waste to almost zero by 2060 at an annual cost of less than 1% of global GDP. Early action in all countries is essential to achieve this.
- Overall implementation costs of this Global Ambition policy package will be higher in non-OECD countries than in OECD countries. This demands supportive policies to bridge any financing gap.
- Despite this ambitious circular plastics policy package, the use of plastics globally will still grow beyond 2019 levels, (827 Mt vs 460 Mt), as will plastic waste (679 Mt vs 353 Mt). However, this growth is much lower than in the *Baseline* scenario, making the proper treatment of all plastic waste more manageable. Furthermore, almost all the increase in demand for plastics can be met by recycled secondary plastics, which grow to 41% of total plastics production.
- Such an ambitious policy package entails significantly improved treatment of plastic waste to boost recycling (to around 60% of all waste) and avoid mismanaged waste. The global decline in mismanaged waste is mostly driven by improvements in non-OECD countries, which accounted for almost 90% of global mismanaged waste in 2019. This share will increase even further by 2060 unless these ambitious global policies are implemented.
- In this *Global Action* scenario, plastic leakage to the environment is projected to decrease to near zero levels by 2060, with annual leakage of plastics into the aquatic environment falling by 98% compared to the *Baseline* in 2060. However, in the interim stocks of plastics will continue to accumulate in the aquatic environment, reaching 300 Mt in 2060, which is slightly more than double the 2019 level.
- Additional measures to clean up the remaining plastic leakage to the marine environment could remove all new marine plastics pollution; while the costs of this clean up are likely to be high, they are roughly three times smaller than the costs linked to the economic and environmental damage caused by plastic pollution. Waste treatment costs per tonne of plastics are substantially lower than for cleaning up, making prevention the most rational option.

8.1. The policy package in the *Global Ambition* scenario assumes immediate global action

Reducing plastic pollution, including avoiding leakage of plastics to the environment, requires shared objectives and co-ordinated efforts at the international level. As discussed in OECD (2022[1]), many policy measures and voluntary initiatives have emerged in recent years across countries as a response to an increasing awareness of the negative environmental impacts of the plastics lifecycle. However, these efforts are poorly co-ordinated and are unable to significantly alter trends in plastics production, waste generation and leakage (OECD, 2022[1]). The recent resolution adopted by the United Nations Environment Assembly (UNEA-5) is therefore an historical step. Entitled “End plastic pollution: Towards an international legally binding instrument”, it requests that an intergovernmental negotiation committee be convened to develop an international legally binding instrument to tackle plastic pollution, including in the marine environment. This ambitious resolution has been widely welcomed by OECD members and selected partner countries (OECD, 2022[2]).

Several international initiatives and commitments helped to pave the way for the UNEA 5.2 resolution. For example, the Osaka Blue Ocean Vision (OBOV), shared by G20 leaders at the 2019 Osaka Summit, aims to "reduce *additional pollution by marine plastic litter to zero by 2050* through a comprehensive lifecycle approach" (Ministry of Foreign Affairs, Japan, 2019[3]). This includes reducing the discharge of mismanaged plastic litter by improving waste management and adopting innovative solutions, while still recognising the important role of plastics for society. In 2021, the G20 Heads of State reaffirmed their commitment to address marine plastic litter by strengthening existing instruments and developing a new global agreement or instrument (G20 Leaders, 2021[4]). Furthermore, the Sustainable Development Goals provide an important anchor for international policy action to delink economic growth and environmental degradation. Common targets and roadmaps for action on plastics have also been set at the regional level, such as in the South-East Asia region and in various regional seas conventions (ASEAN, 2021[5]; AOSIS, 2021[6]; COBSEA, 2019[7]; HELCOM, 2015[8]). As part of the European Green Deal, the European Union (EU) has set a 2030 target to reduce plastic litter at sea by 50%, and microplastic releases into the environment by 30% (European Commission, 2019[9]).

The *Global Ambition* scenario has similar ambitions – eliminating leakage of plastics to the environment as much as possible – but achieving the targets of all these initiatives and commitments is not guaranteed.[1] While the *Regional Action* scenario (Chapter 7) embodies a set of policies that build on current efforts and commitments and that take countries' different situations into account, the *Global Ambition* scenario is more ambitious, adopting a truly global approach to tackling the problem. While using the same policy toolkit, it is more stringent than the *Regional Action* scenario, assumes more rapid action and pursues similar levels of ambition for OECD and non-OECD countries alike.

The various policy instruments and their implementation in the model are grouped into the same three pillars as the *Regional Action* scenario, outlined in detail in Chapter 7 (see Section 7.1 for more details on the rationale for the policies in the different pillars and Table A B.1 in Annex B for a comparison of the stringency of the various policies between both policy scenarios):

- **Restrain plastics production and demand and enhance design for circularity:**
  - A tax on plastics packaging, increasing linearly from 0 in 2021 to reach USD 1 000/tonne by 2030 globally, then doubling to USD 2 000/t by 2060.
  - A tax on the use of all other types of plastics, reaching USD 750/tonne by 2030 globally, then doubling to USD 1 500 / t by 2060.
  - Global policy instruments to increase circularity and encourage the more durable and repairable design of plastics. These policies are designed to achieve the following global targets: (i) extending product lifespans by 15% through greater durability; (ii) decreasing the demand for durable plastics by 10-20% by 2030, driven by products' longer lifespans; (iii) achieving greater efficiency in plastics use by firms, matching the reduced household demand for durable plastics; and (iv) increasing the demand for repair services calibrated in such a way that the increased costs for repair services are as large as the avoided expenditures on durables, so that total expenditures are unaffected by the policy.
- **Enhance recycling**:
  - Recycled content targets, with all countries achieving a 40% recycled content target by 2060. The modelling assumes this is achieved through combining a tax on primary plastics with a subsidy on secondary plastics.
  - Extended Producer Responsibility (EPR) implemented for packaging, electronics, motor vehicles and clothing in all countries. See Box 7.1 in Chapter 7 for a description of EPR and the modelling assumptions for this instrument.
  - Region-specific recycling rate targets; 60% by 2030 and 80% by 2060 for EU and the OECD Pacific region; 80% recycling by 2060 for other OECD countries and the People's Republic of

China (hereafter 'China'); 60% by 2060 for the remaining countries. As with the EPR, the associated investment needs are included in the model.

- **Close leakage pathways**:
  - Investment in mixed waste collection and sanitary landfills allows all countries to eliminate the mismanagement (e.g., dumping or burning waste in open pits) of all collected waste by 2060.
  - Policies to improve litter collection see collection rates increase more rapidly with income and reach 90% for high-income countries (versus 85% in the *Baseline* scenario). In addition, collection rates for low-income countries are increased from 65% to 75%.

8.2. Plastics use and waste are largely decoupled from economic growth in the *Global Ambition* scenario

8.2.1. The combined policies almost eliminate mismanaged waste by 2060

The *Global Ambition* policy package aims at reducing global plastics use substantially by 2030, and to increase policy ambition gradually to 2060. The scenario therefore delivers a sizable reduction in plastics production and use (Figure 8.1, Panel A). As in the more limited *Regional Action* scenario, the policies aiming to restrain demand are the most effective at reducing plastics use, cutting global use by one third (in comparison, the *Regional Action* scenario reduces plastics use by less than 20%). The rapid implementation of the policies to 2030 leads to an absolute decoupling of economic growth and plastics use, so that global plastics use in 2030 (443 Mt) is less than in 2019 (460 Mt), while GDP grows by more than 40% over the same timeframe. However, after 2030 plastics use starts to grow again as most policies reach their maximum levels but economic activity continues to grow. Even in this very ambitious scenario therefore, plastics use in 2060 is at 827 Mt projected to be 80% above 2019 levels and after 2050 continues to grow at 2% per year (while GDP growth gradually declines to 2.5% per year by 2060). This shows the significant dependence of the global economy on plastics, but it also underlines that relative decoupling of plastics use from economic growth is largely feasible.

As explained in earlier chapters, plastic waste trends largely follow plastics use, albeit with a delay (Figure 8.1, Panel B). In 2060, the *Global Ambition* scenario is projected to bring plastic waste down from 1 014 Mt in the *Baseline* scenario to 679 Mt, a reduction of 33%. Although the total reduction in 2060 is very similar for plastics use and waste, their time profile is different: the deviation from the *Baseline* projection is slower for waste, and thus total plastic waste in 2030 (387 Mt) is almost 10% above 2019 levels, while global plastics use decreases slightly over the same time period. This reflects the delayed effect of policies aimed at long-lived plastics applications. The delayed effects of the stringent policies on plastics use also imply that in the longer run (after 2050), annual growth in plastic waste is, at 1.8% per year, lower than growth in plastics use.

The continued increase of plastics use and waste in the long run, despite the highly stringent policy measures, highlights the economy's significant dependence on plastics. Ambitious policies are therefore needed to avoid plastic waste from leaking to the environment. The *Global Ambition* scenario combines all three policy pillars to maximise the reduction in mismanaged waste: restraining demand to reduce the scale of waste that has to be treated; enhancing recycling to reduce the quantities of waste that have to be managed over time; and closing leakage pathways to ensure that the remaining waste is not mismanaged. Figure 8.1, Panel C shows how these three pillars combine to bring annual mismanaged waste flows down from 153 Mt in the *Baseline* scenario in 2060 to almost zero (6 Mt). The only leakage sources that remain in this scenario are those that are not captured by waste management systems – microplastics and uncollected litter – and which continue to leak into the environment.

Figure 8.1. Mismanaged waste is almost completely eliminated worldwide in the *Global Ambition* scenario

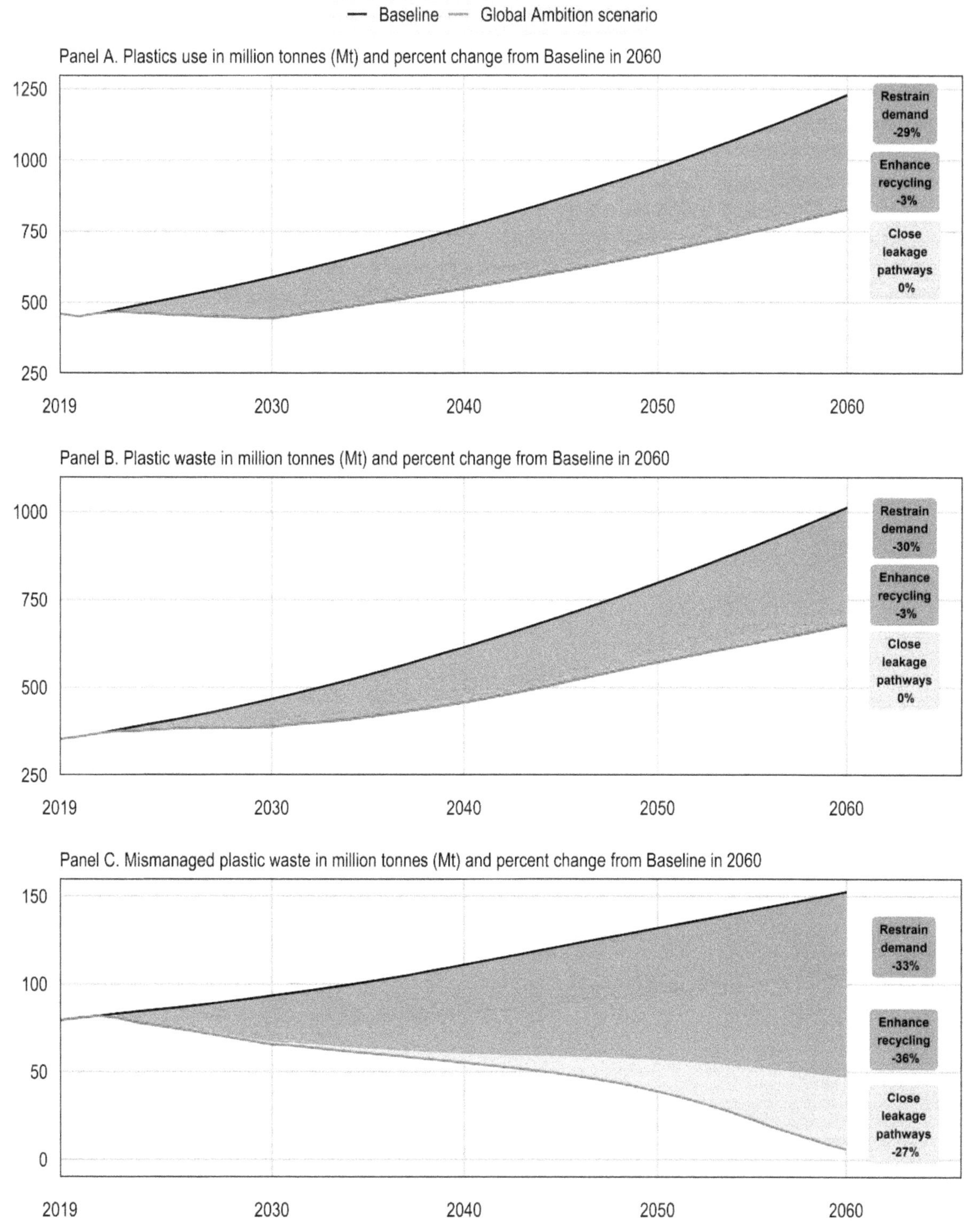

Source: OECD ENV-Linkages model.

StatLink https://stat.link/34ejc5

8.2.2. Sectors and regions vary in their reduction of plastics use

The substantial reduction in plastics use from *Baseline* levels is achieved in all regions in the *Global Ambition* scenario, but their levels of reduction vary (Figure 7.5). The global nature of the policy package ensures that low-cost opportunities to reduce plastics use are reaped everywhere and that plastics use reductions ramp up rapidly to 2030. Despite equal tax rates on plastics use being imposed globally, there are significant differences across regions in the resulting reductions of plastics use. In regions where the average plastics intensity of the economy is relatively high (cf. Chapter 3), a tax on every tonne of plastics input translates into a relatively large increase in production costs. This induces a stronger re-alignment of economic activities away from plastic-using sectors, especially in the Other Eurasia region (which includes the Russian Federation) and countries in Sub-Saharan Africa (Other Africa). Higher price increases lead to greater substitution of plastics by other materials in production, stronger shifts away from the sectors that use large amounts of plastics, and a shift towards more efficient foreign producers. While these all imply lower levels of plastics use, they also imply higher macroeconomic costs (see Section 8.4 below).

Figure 8.2. Regional reductions in plastics use to 2030 are substantial in the *Global Ambition* scenario

Percentage change in plastics use compared to the Baseline, 2060

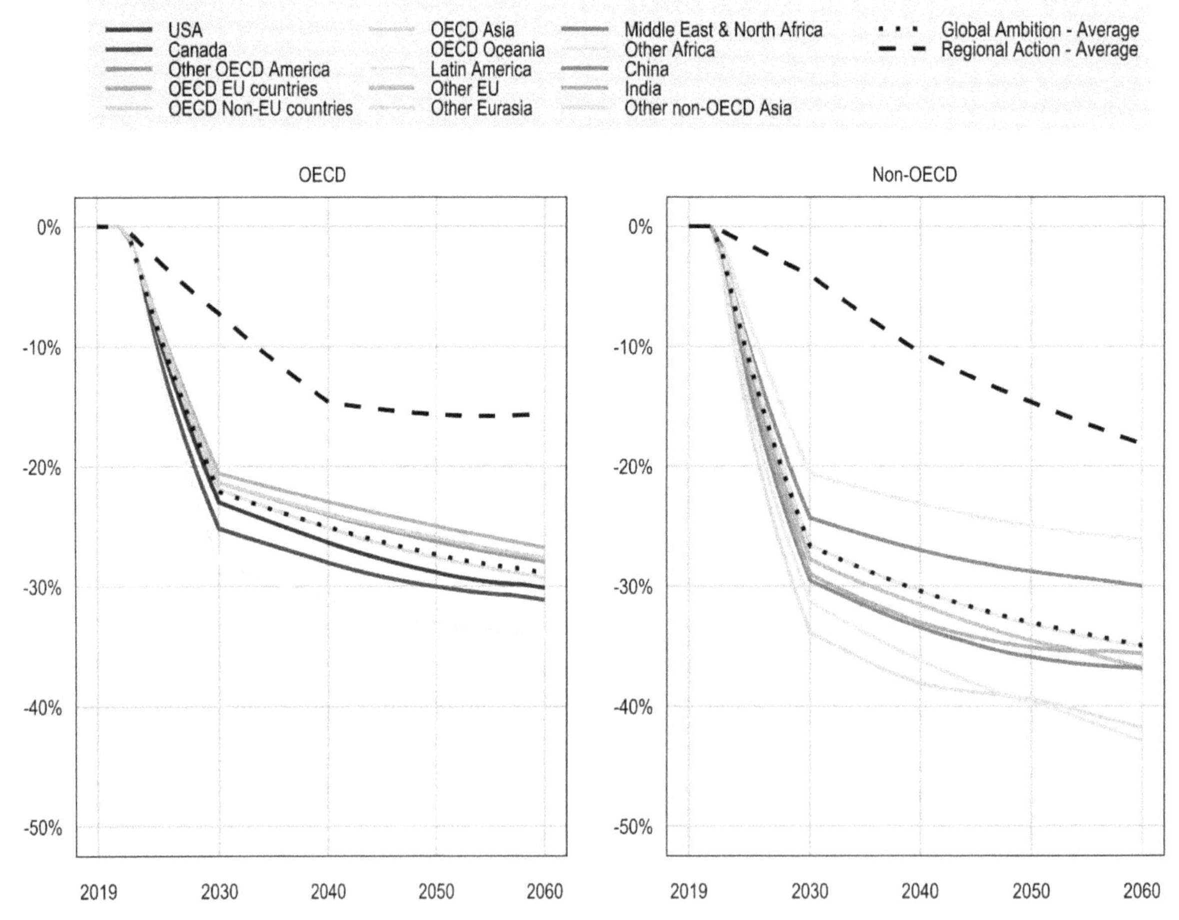

Source: OECD ENV-Linkages model.

StatLink https://stat.link/2k9oxv

The stronger reductions in plastics use in the *Global Ambition* scenario compared to the *Regional Action* scenario occurs in all sectors, though not evenly (Figure 8.3). In both scenarios and in both OECD and non-OECD regions, the strongest reductions in plastics use are in the Business services sector, due to its sheer size and the fact that it is a major user of plastics. The degree of difference in ambition levels between the *Regional Action* and *Global Ambition* scenarios varies according to the policy instrument (see Annex B). For instance, the EPR scheme is extended to non-OECD countries in the *Global Ambition* scenario, leading to substantially larger plastics use reductions in the sectors concerned, especially motor vehicles. In OECD countries, the additional reductions can largely be attributed to the higher taxes on plastics use. The use of plastics in construction is reduced significantly in both OECD and non-OECD countries, driven by both higher tax rates and stronger ecodesign policies that reduce demand for construction.

Figure 8.3. A few sectors make up the bulk of plastics use reductions in the *Global Ambition* scenario

Difference in plastics use between the Global Ambition and Baseline scenarios in million tonnes (Mt), 2060

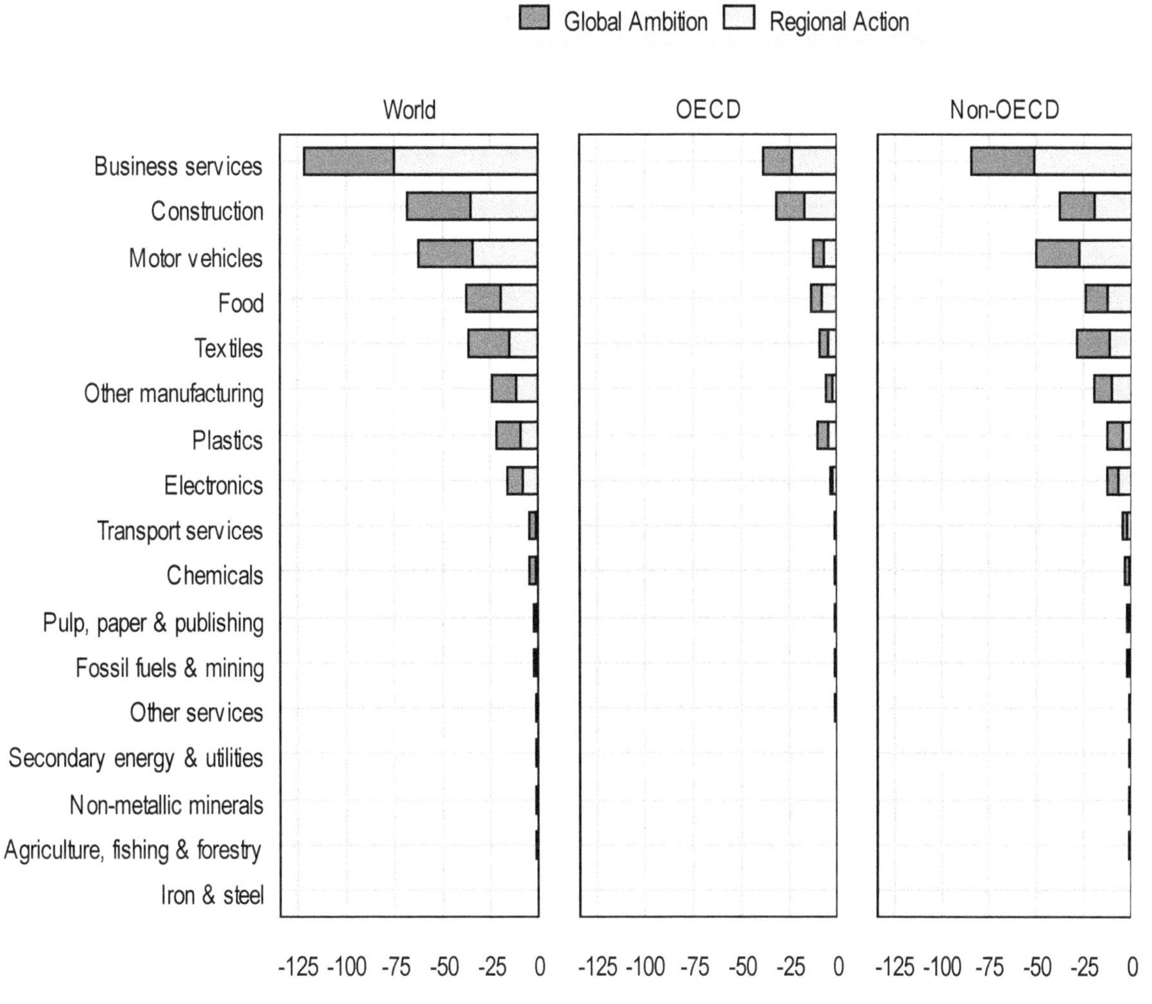

Source: OECD ENV-Linkages model.

StatLink https://stat.link/12jsgr

The policies in the *Global Ambition* scenario are just about strong enough to avoid any major increase in primary plastics use: the total increase in primary plastics production between 2019 and 2060 is projected to be 13%, all occurring after 2030 (Figure 8.4). This is the result of a combination of lower overall demand and the faster penetration of secondary plastics. The share of secondary plastics rises to 41% by 2060, substantially larger than the 12% in the *Baseline* and 29% in the *Regional Action* scenario. Compared to the *Regional Action* scenario, the increase in secondary production is much stronger in non-OECD countries in the *Global Ambition* scenario, as the recycled content targets are increased from 20% to 40%. For OECD countries, the amount of secondary plastics produced in 2060 (129 Mt) is smaller than in the *Regional Action* scenario (155 Mt), despite having the same recycled content targets (40% in both scenarios). This is explained by the lower level of total plastics produced in the more ambitious scenario: on the one hand there is less demand for plastics (311 Mt plastics use in OECD in the *Global Ambition* scenario vs. 369 Mt in the *Regional Action* scenario); and on the other, less waste is generated (253 Mt in *Global Ambition* vs 297 Mt in *Regional Action*), reducing the availability of plastic scrap from recycling (despite higher recycling rates, see Section 8.2.3).

Figure 8.4. Secondary plastics production can meet almost all demand growth in the *Global Ambition* scenario

Plastics production in million tonnes (Mt)

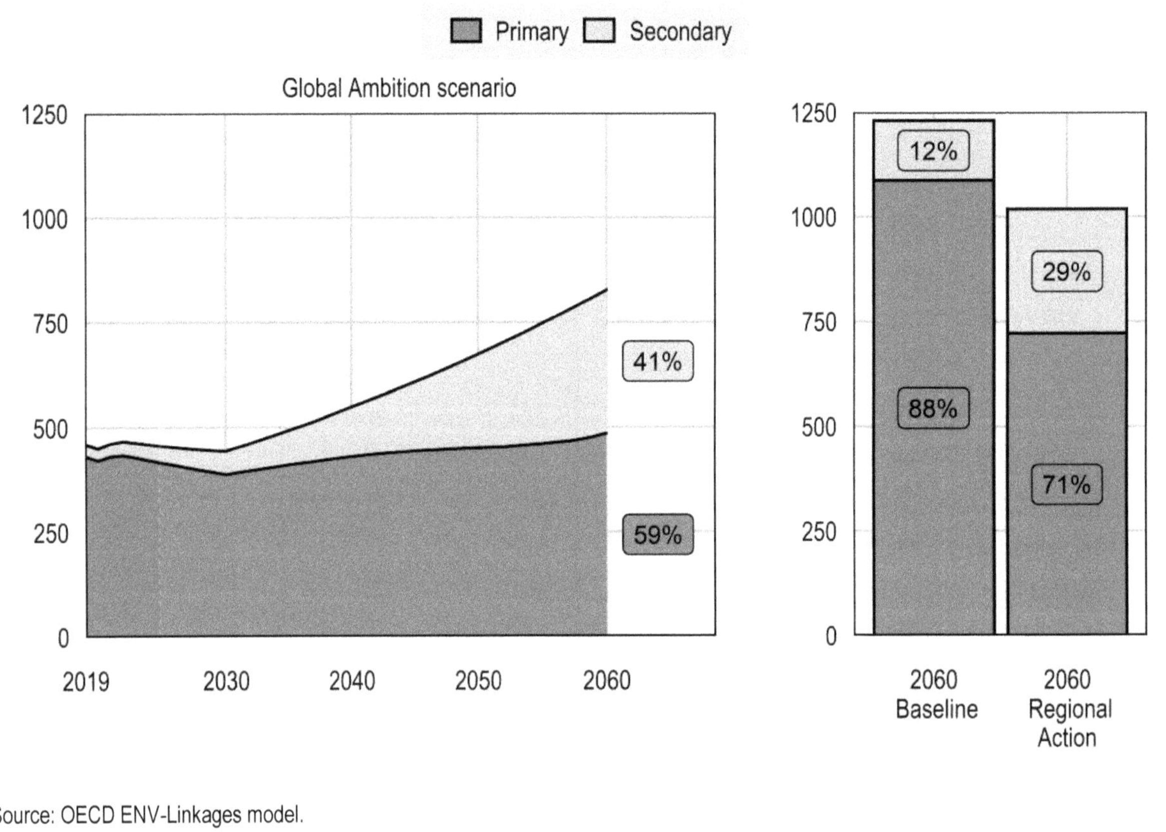

Source: OECD ENV-Linkages model.

StatLink https://stat.link/65e1li

8.2.3. The Global Ambition *policies completely transform how waste is treated*

The *Global Ambition* scenario is designed to prevent significant leakage of plastics to the environment by ensuring proper treatment of all plastic waste: all plastics are recycled where possible; when recycling is not possible they are either incinerated (and energy recovered) or landfilled in a sanitary manner. In this way, mismanaged waste is minimised and the only sources of leakage that remain are those that cannot be treated easily, such as microplastics and uncollected litter, accounting for 6 Mt globally in 2060. The result is that recycling rates more than triple globally (to 59% in 2060, from 17% in the *Baseline*), while mismanaged waste falls (Figure 7.9). As expected, the Restrain demand pillar is an effective way to reduce the scale of the plastic waste problem, while the Enhance recycling policies are key to increasing recycling rates. The Close leakage pathways policy reduces all mismanaged waste that is treated by the waste facilities to zero, leaving only uncollected (mismanaged) waste.

Figure 8.5. In the *Global Ambition* scenario recycling rates triple while mismanaged waste is almost completely eliminated

Plastic waste in million tonnes (Mt), 2060

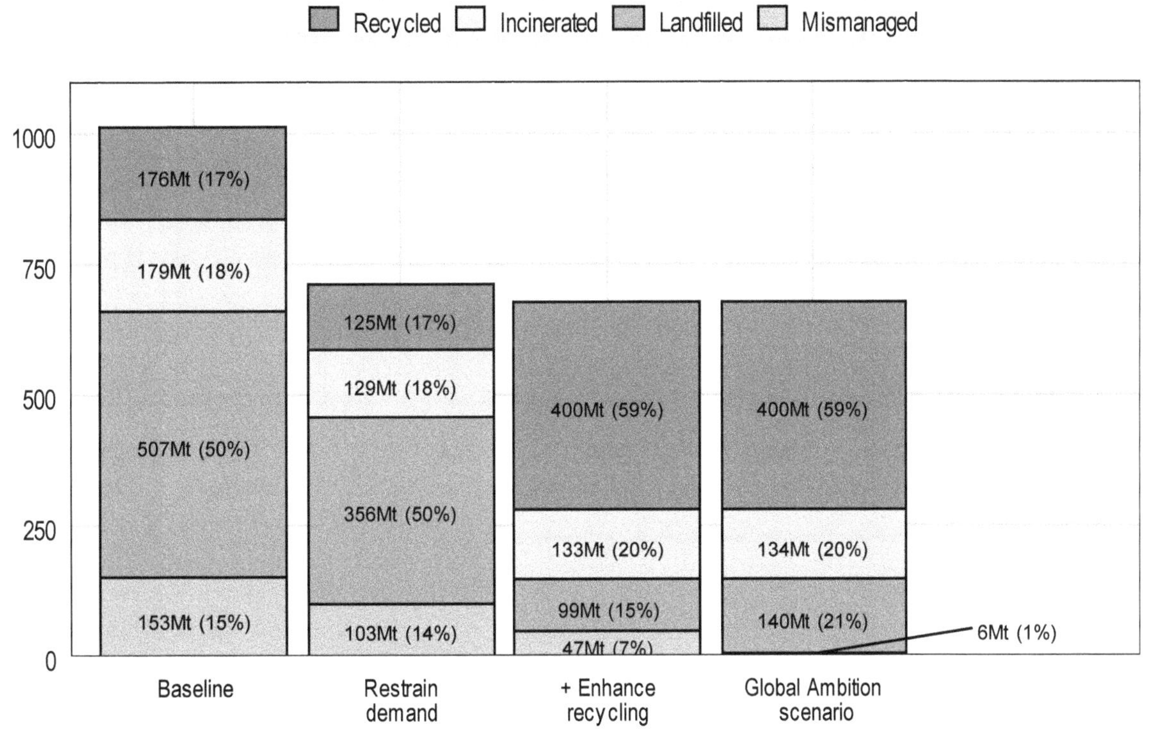

Note: The chart presents the cumulative impacts of the individual policy pillars, with the far-right column showing the entire *Global Ambition* scenario.
Source: OECD ENV-Linkages model.

StatLink https://stat.link/1psoby

The global decline in mismanaged waste is mostly driven by improvements in non-OECD countries, thanks to much more stringent policies in the *Global Ambition* scenario (). These countries accounted for almost 90% of global mismanaged waste in 2019; and this share is projected to increase even further by 2060 in the *Baseline* scenario. By 2060, non-OECD countries reduce mismanaged waste to a residual 4.1 Mt in the Global Ambition scenario, 65.8 Mt less than in 2019. OECD countries already reduce mismanaged waste to near zero in the *Regional Action* scenario; the *Global Ambition* scenario reduces their mismanaged waste by another 7.5 Mt, leaving only 2.0 Mt.

Figure 8.6. Mismanaged waste gradually declines to almost zero in the *Global Ambition* scenario

Mismanaged plastic waste in million tonnes (Mt)

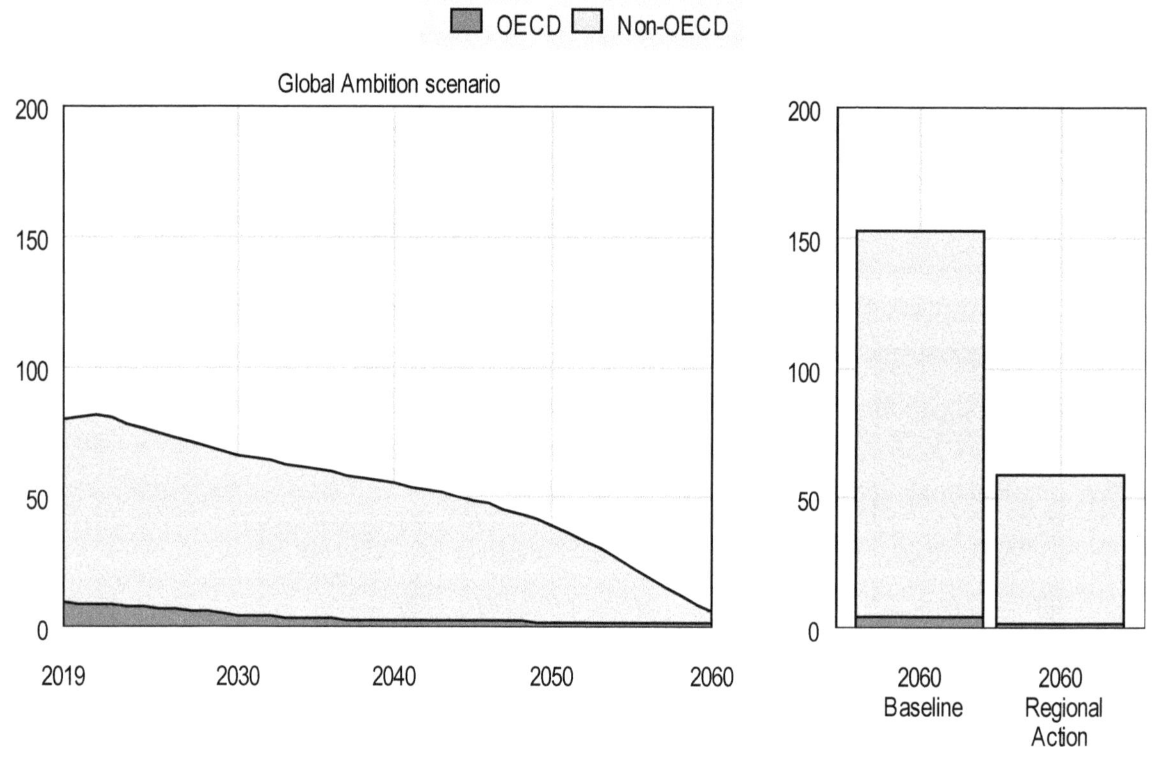

Source: OECD ENV-Linkages model.

StatLink https://stat.link/hy41xl

8.3. The environmental benefits of the *Global Ambition* scenario are substantial

8.3.1. Leakage of both macro- and microplastics is curbed

The implementation of the *Global Ambition* scenario is projected to substantially curb the leakage of plastics in the environment (Figure 8.7). By 2060, global plastic leakage to the environment is projected to decrease by 85% compared to the *Baseline* scenario, from 44.2 Mt to 6.4 Mt. This is an additional 30 percentage point decrease below the reductions projected for the *Regional Action* scenario in Chapter 7. Most of this additional decrease is driven by non-OECD countries, where the more ambitious policies implemented compared to the *Regional Action* scenario result in substantially lower losses to the environment, falling 89% below the *Baseline* levels in 2060, to 4.7 Mt (from 41.6 Mt in the *Baseline* scenario). These are well below the 2019 levels.

Figure 8.7. All pillars combined reduce plastic leakage to the environment dramatically

Plastic leakage to the environment in million tonnes (Mt)

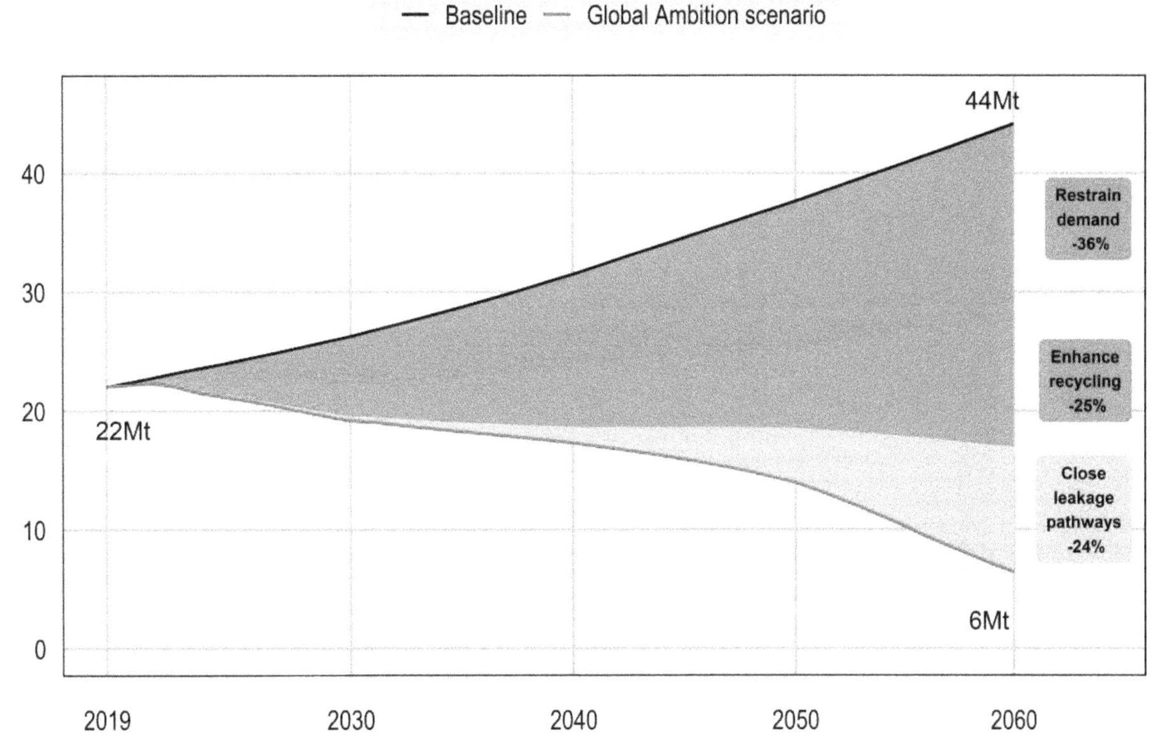

Source: OECD ENV-Linkages model, using the methodology adapted from Ryberg et al. (2019[10]) and Cottom et al. (2022[11]).

StatLink https://stat.link/r34zjn

Across regions, the reductions in macroplastic leakage from the policy package dwarf those of microplastic leakage (Figure 8.8). This difference reflects the fact that the *Global Ambition* policy package primarily focuses on macroplastics. The *Global Ambition* scenario is projected to almost eliminate leakage of macroplastics into the environment, which falls by 97% in 2060 compared to the *Baseline* scenario.

Figure 8.8. Non-OECD countries account for the largest reductions in plastic leakage to 2060 in the *Global Ambition* scenario

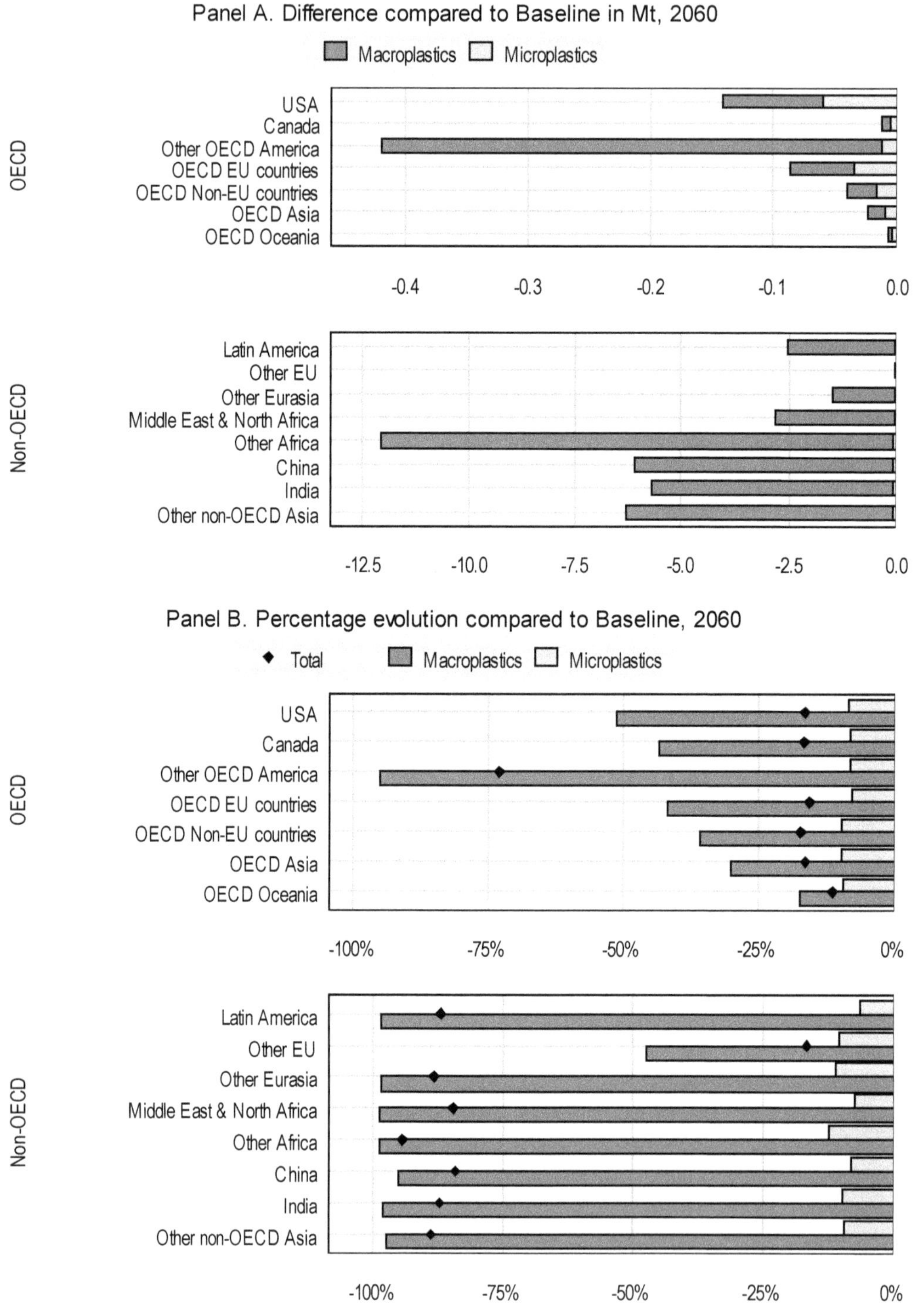

Source: OECD ENV-Linkages model, using the methodology adapted from Ryberg et al. (2019[10]) and Cottom et al. (2022[11]).

StatLink https://stat.link/9fhaw7

In the *Global Ambition* scenario, losses of microplastics into the environment fall 9% below the *Baseline* scenario in 2060 (from 5.8 Mt in the *Baseline* scenario to 5.3 Mt in the *Global Ambition* scenario). These reductions are mostly driven by lower use of plastics in the economy overall. Furthermore, the reductions are evenly distributed across regions, with the largest reductions occurring in non-OECD countries, especially Other Africa and Other Eurasia (Figure 8.8, panel B).

Primary pellets,[2] wastewater sludge and road markings account for the largest reductions in microplastic leakage (Figure 8.9). While both OECD and non-OECD regions stem losses from primary pellets, wastewater sludge is the largest source of leakage reductions in OECD countries.[3] Eroded road markings are another important source for both OECD and non-OECD countries, but are not reduced by the policy package, explained above.

The reduction in macroplastic leakage stems from the decrease in mismanaged waste, as shown in Figure 8.9. As explained in Section 8.2.3, most sources of mismanaged waste are eliminated in the *Global Ambition* scenario by 2060.

Figure 8.9. The plastic leakage reductions in the *Global Ambition* scenario stem from different sources in OECD versus non-OECD countries

Difference compared to *Baseline* in million tonnes (Mt), 2060

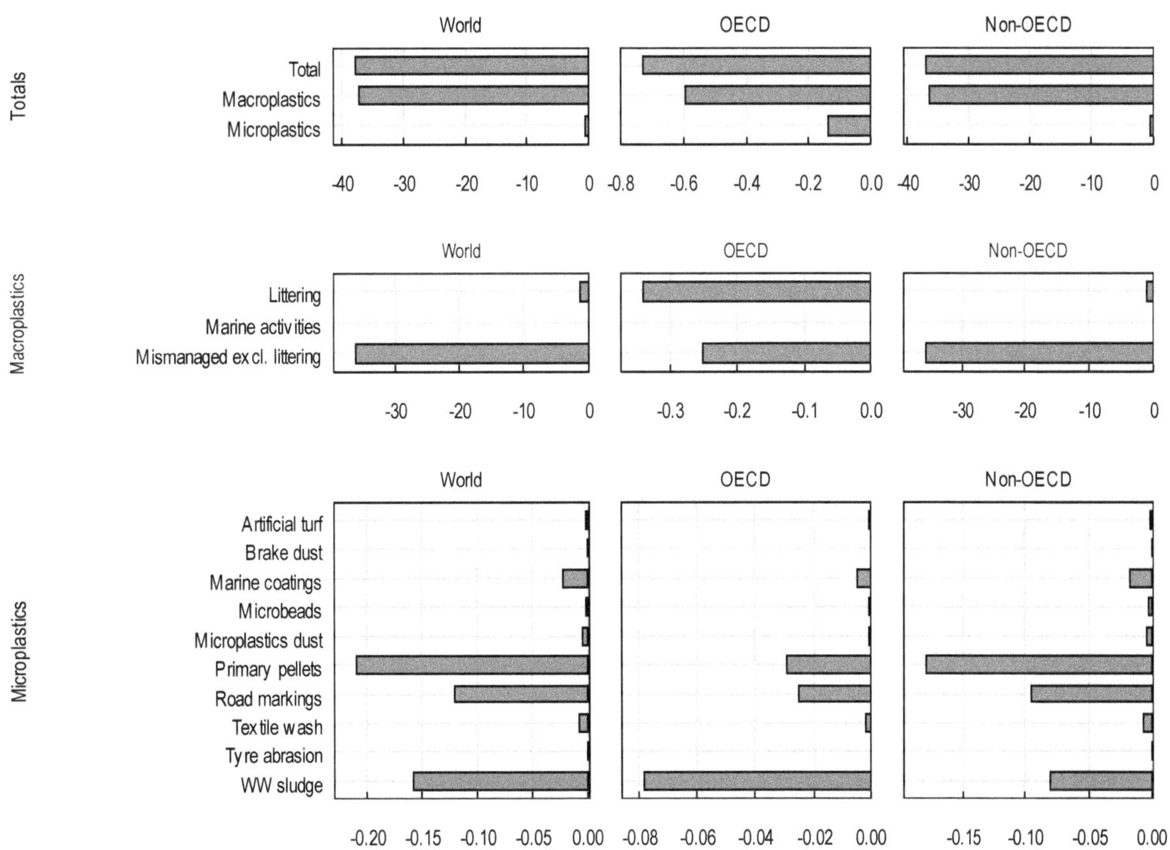

Note: scales differ for each panel. WW = wastewater.

Source: OECD ENV-Linkages model, using the methodology adapted from Ryberg et al. (2019[10]) and Cottom et al. (2022[11])

StatLink https://stat.link/q64ui2

8.3.2. Leakage to aquatic environments is almost eliminated by 2060 in the Global Ambition scenario

The *Global Ambition* scenario is projected to almost eliminate global plastic leakage to aquatic environments by 2060, with a 98% reduction from the *Baseline* (Figure 8.10), from 11.6 Mt in the *Baseline* to 0.2 Mt. By comparison, the *Regional Action* scenario only achieves a 60% reduction from the *Baseline*, with substantial leakage remaining in non-OECD countries. Thus, the stronger policy action in the *Global Ambition* scenario drives an additional 38 percentage point decrease. The uncertainty surrounding this projection, as discussed in Chapter 5, is substantial (Box 8.1).

The scale of the effects varies across regions, with non-OECD countries experiencing the largest leakage declines. All non-OECD countries achieve substantial reductions compared to 2060 *Baseline* levels, and all reduce absolute levels below those of 2019. Small amounts of plastic leakage remain in Africa and non-OECD Asia.

Box 8.1. The reductions in leakage to aquatic environments are large, regardless of uncertainties

As highlighted in Chapter 5, there are significant uncertainties surrounding the projections of plastic leakage to aquatic environment. These uncertainties affect both the *Baseline* and policy scenarios. Therefore, the results in terms of percentage reduction from baseline are more robust than assessments of the absolute reductions in million tonnes (Table 8.1).

Table 8.1. The reduction in plastic leakage to aquatic environments in the *Global Ambition* scenario is substantial across a range of model assumptions

	Global Ambition scenario compared to *Baseline* (percentage difference)			
Estimate	2030	2040	2050	2060
Central	-30%	-50%	-70%	-98%
High	-30%	-50%	-70%	-98%
Low	-31%	-50%	-69%	-98%
	Global Ambition scenario compared to *Baseline* (difference in Mt)			
Estimate	2030	2040	2050	2060
Central	-2.2	-4.2	-7.0	-11.4
High	-3.0	-6.0	-9.9	-16.5
Low	-1.2	-2.4	-3.8	-6.0

Note: Each estimate for the *Global Ambition* scenario is compared to the corresponding estimate for the *Baseline*, using the same methodology as in Chapter 5, to quantify the uncertainty ranges.
Source: OECD ENV-Linkages model, based on (Lebreton and Andrady, 2019[12]).

The effect of the policies increases over time, but will still fail to totally eliminate the accumulation of plastics leaked to aquatic environments in the coming decades. While net inflows of plastic leakage decrease to near-zero levels by 2060, more than 60% of the plastic leakage flows projected in the *Baseline* will still take place, mostly in earlier decades, adding to the stocks of plastics already in rivers and the ocean: these continue to rise from 109 Mt in 2019 to 197 Mt in 2060 (+87 Mt) for rivers and lakes and from 30 Mt to 103 Mt (+73 Mt) in the ocean, respectively, in the *Global Ambition* scenario (Figure 8.11). The combined amount of plastics accumulating in rivers and the ocean between 2019 and 2060 is thus projected to equal 300 Mt, more than the 140 Mt estimated to be already present in 2019: even with ambitious global policy measures, the stocks of plastics more than double by 2060. In conclusion, while the *Global Ambition* scenario largely solves the long-term problem, as it almost eliminates the net inflows of plastics in 2060, in the interim clean-up solutions need to be implemented to deal with the plastics that have leaked to aquatic environments.

Figure 8.10. Plastic leakage to aquatic environments will be vastly reduced across all non-OECD regions in the *Global Ambition* scenario

Plastic leakage to aquatic environments in million tonnes (Mt), 2060

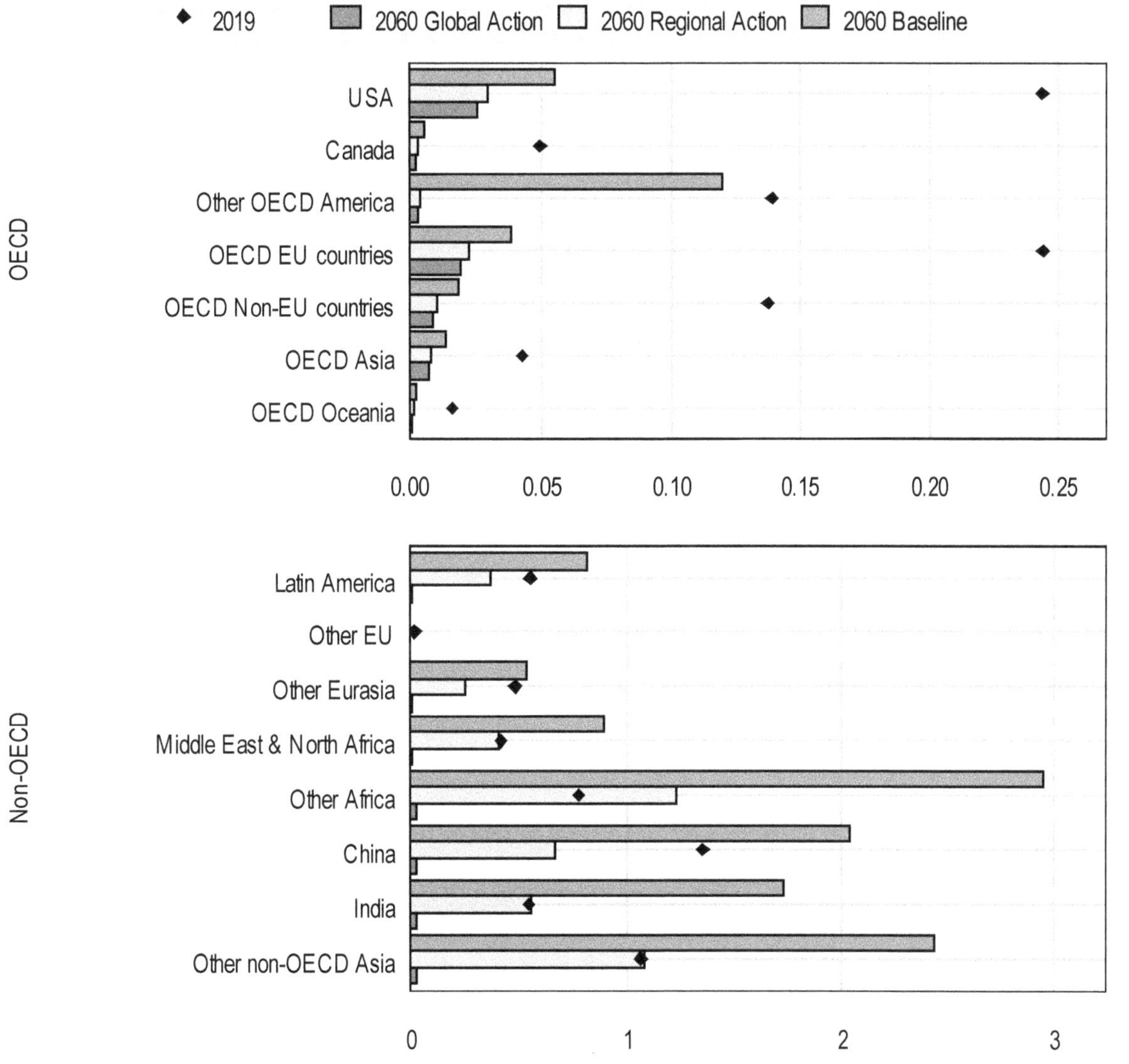

Source: OECD ENV-Linkages model, adapted from (Lebreton and Andrady, 2019[12]) methodology

StatLink https://stat.link/s46gf9

Figure 8.11. Despite ambitious global action, stocks of plastics in aquatic environments still grow substantially

Plastic leakage to aquatic environments in million tonnes (Mt) in 2019 and 2060 in the *Baseline* and *Global Ambition* scenarios

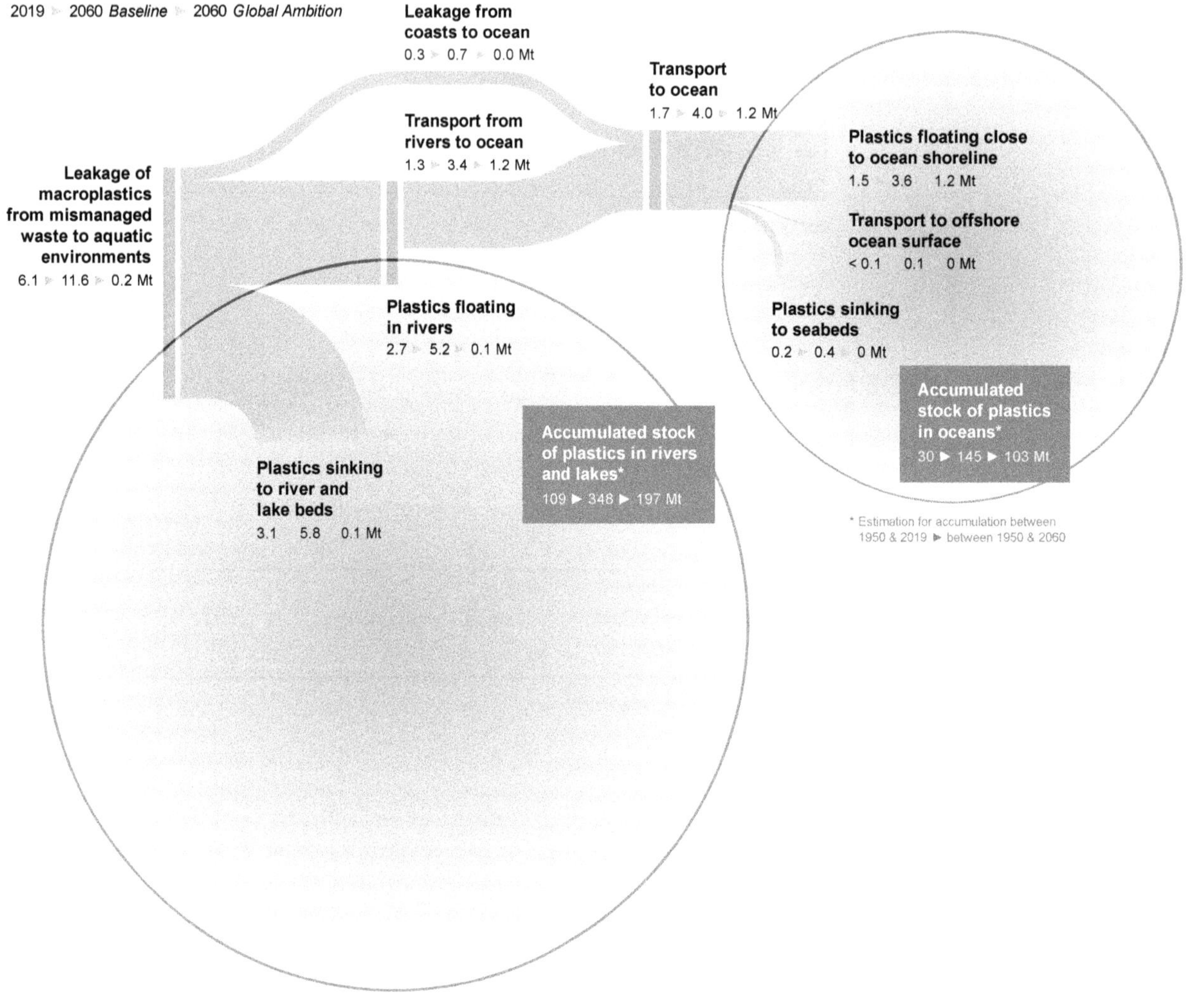

Source: OECD ENV-Linkages model, based on Lebreton and Andrady (2019[12]).

8.4. The macroeconomic impact is limited, though highest for non-OECD countries

8.4.1. The costs of global action are largely falling on non-OECD countries

The macroeconomic costs of the *Global Ambition* scenario are, as expected, higher than in the *Regional Action* scenario, but are still limited to less than 1% of *Baseline* GDP globally in 2060 (Figure 8.12). This equates to a value of around USD 3.4 trillion. While that is a large absolute number, it should be seen in the context of significant economic growth of more than 3% on average annually to 2060. The impact of the policy package on the economies of non-OECD countries is certainly not negligible and will require supportive policies to ensure the situation for vulnerable households is not exacerbated. Countries already use Official Development Assistance (ODA) to support action to address plastic leakage in developing countries, but the financial flows are a fraction of what is needed and additional sources of funding will be required (OECD, 2022[1]).

In the short run, the efficiency gains induced by the policy package, and the shifts in comparative advantage, may increase economic activity in some countries, notably China. These shifts are driven by the policies for ecodesign in the "restrain demand" pillar, which reduce plastics use in manufacturing of durable commodities, while simultaneously boosting demand for repair activities. In some regions, this boosts economic growth. Furthermore, as prices of plastics-intensive commodities do not increase equally across countries, comparative advantages start to shift, leading to gains in some regions and losses in others.

Figure 8.12. The additional costs of *Global Ambition* are concentrated in non-OECD countries

Percentage change in GDP from Baseline

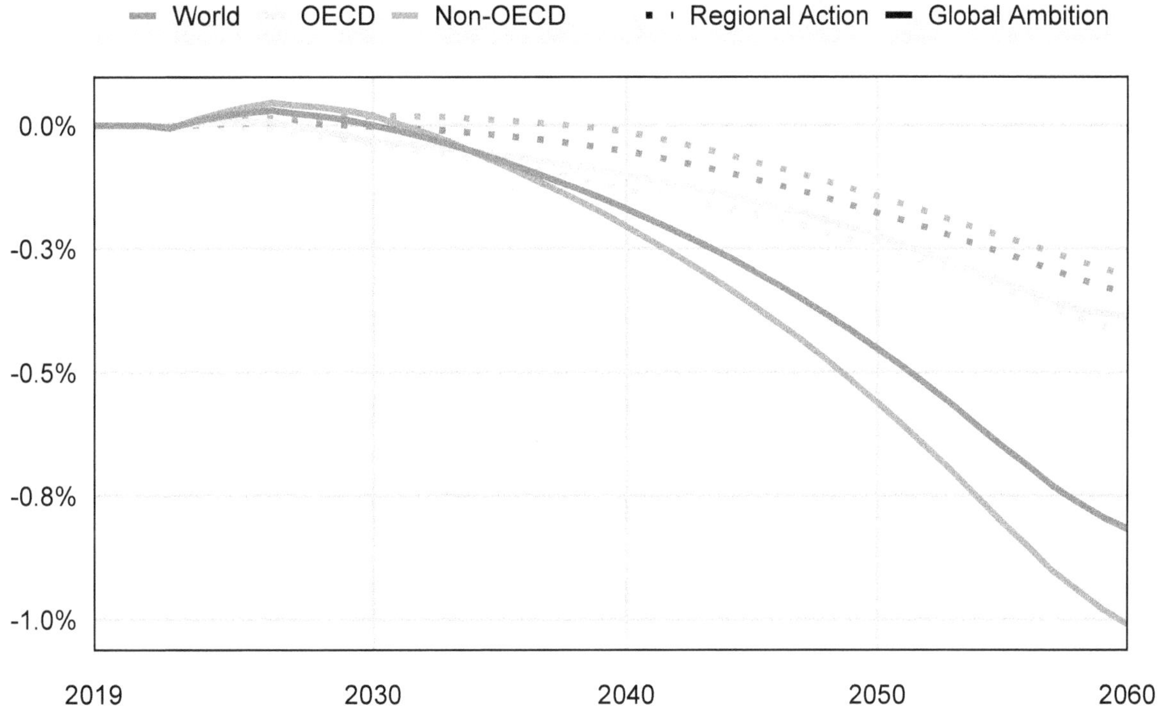

Source: OECD ENV-Linkages model.

StatLink https://stat.link/uc4ti7

The regional economic implications of the *Global Ambition* scenario are uneven: costs are very limited in China and the OECD EU countries, but higher for the non-OECD EU countries and Sub-Saharan Africa (Other Africa) (Figure 7.16.). The largest costs are projected for Sub-Saharan Africa, where GDP declines 2.8% below the *Baseline*, not least because substantial investments in improved waste management must be made to achieve the ambitious policy targets.

Given the complexity of the policy package, in which seven policy instruments all interact, along with interactions between sectors and regions, the regional costs cannot be attributed to one single cause. They are driven by a mixture of domestic policy costs from the fiscal instruments and regulations; investment in waste systems; induced effects on demand for goods and services, as relative prices shift and income levels change; and competitiveness changes between competitors in different countries and related changes in exchange rates. All relative prices change and regional and global economies find new equilibria in sectoral and regional demand and supply.

Figure 8.13. The effects on regional GDP of the *Global Ambition* scenario are strongest outside of OECD

Percentage change in GDP and plastics use from *Baseline*, 2060

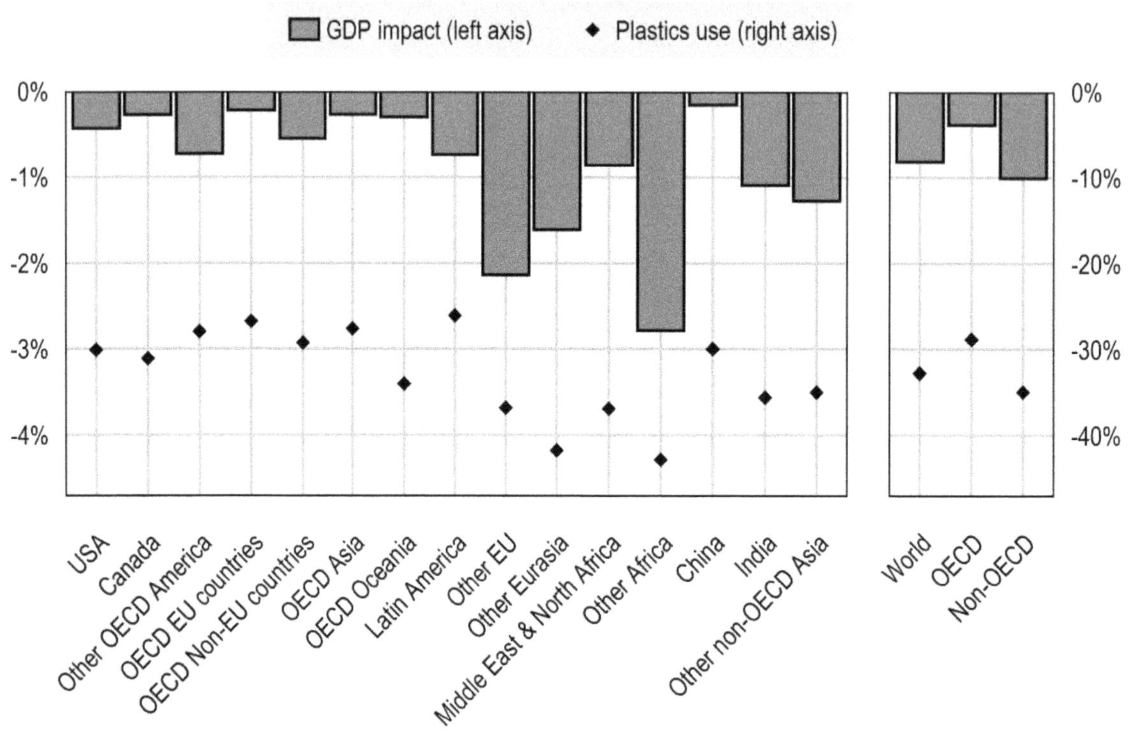

Source: OECD ENV-Linkages model.

StatLink https://stat.link/p4mkxq

8.4.2. Though expensive, cleaning up plastic leakage is worthwhile given the high costs of environmental damage it causes

The analysis in this chapter has shown that mismanaged waste streams can be reduced to nearly zero by implementing a broad and ambitious policy package (Section 8.2). Even so, substantial amounts of plastics will continue to leak into the environment up until 2060, further adding to existing stocks of plastics in the aquatic environment (Section 8.3).

These residual flows of leaked plastics, and the stock of plastics already in rivers and the ocean, can in principle be cleaned up. The environmental benefits of clean-up activities are clear, and the damage avoided could be substantial, including in monetary terms. One recent study estimates the economic impacts of marine pollution at between USD 3 300 and USD 33 000 per tonne per year, based on ecosystem damage alone (Beaumont et al., 2019[13]). Another study, reported in OECD (2021[14]), estimates that even removing less than 10% of the derelict pots and traps in major crustacean fisheries could result in USD 831 million annual savings globally (Scheld, Bilkovic and Havens, 2016[15]).[4]

Technological developments in recent years have made the option to remove plastics from the environment more attainable, even if the costs remain substantial. One study estimates current expenditures on cleaning up to be about USD 2 bn globally, based on costs of cleaning up plastics pollution that range from USD 0.01 to USD 2.51 per capita per region (Deloitte, 2019[16]). The literature on the costs of cleaning up marine plastics pollution provides a wide range of estimates, but can provide insights into the size of the challenge (Table 8.2).

Table 8.2. Estimates of clean-up costs vary widely

Clean-up scope	Clean-up cost	Country scope	Source
Beach litter	EUR 121/t	United Kingdom	(Mouat, Lopez Lazano and Bateson, 2010[17])
Beach litter	EUR 1 877/t	Netherlands and Belgium	
Derelict fishing gear	USD 25 000/t	North-West Hawaiian Islands	(Raaymakers, 2007[18])
Shoreline cleaning / Marine debris	USD 1 300/t	Korea	(Hwang and Ko, 2007[19])
Shoreline cleaning / Marine debris	Mechanical: USD 1 100 – 11 400/t Manual: USD 2 200 – 22 800/t	France	(Kalaydjian et al., 2006[20])
Shoreline cleaning / Marine debris	USD 2 339/t (Direct costs only: USD 1 766/t)	Southeast Alaska	(McIlgorm, Campbell and Rule, 2009[21])
Shoreline cleaning / Marine debris	USD 8 900/t	Aldabra Atoll (a remote small island)	(Burt et al., 2020[22])

While these clean-up costs are substantial, they represent on average around one-third of the estimated damage costs cited above. Thus, as clean-up activities will create a net benefit to society, it makes economic sense to scale them up.

More importantly, not taking policy action would lead to significantly higher leakage levels to the environment, implying much higher clean-up costs. Having to clean up the full stock of 145 Mt plastics in the aquatic environment in the *Baseline* scenario, at costs of more than USD 1 000 per tonne, would be much more costly. Considering that waste treatment costs range from less than USD 100 per tonne for landfilling to less than USD 300 per tonne for recycling (Table 7.1 in Chapter 7), they are an order of magnitude lower, prevention is clearly more economically rational than cleaning up afterwards.

To conclude, more ambitious policies that prevent plastic leakage are much more cost-effective than allowing plastics to leak to the environment, but cleaning up is still more cost-effective than allowing plastics to pollute natural environments.

References

AOSIS (2021), *Alliance of Small Island States Leaders' Declaration*. [6]

ASEAN (2021), *ASEAN Regional Action Plan for Combating Marine Debris in the ASEAN Member States (2021 – 2025)*, https://asean.org/book/asean-regional-action-plan-for-combating-marine-debris-in-the-asean-member-states-2021-2025-2/. [5]

Beaumont, N. et al. (2019), "Global ecological, social and economic impacts of marine plastic", *Marine Pollution Bulletin*, Vol. 142, pp. 189-195, https://doi.org/10.1016/j.marpolbul.2019.03.022. [13]

Burt, A. et al. (2020), "The costs of removing the unsanctioned import of marine plastic litter to small island states", *Scientific Reports*, Vol. 10/1, https://doi.org/10.1038/s41598-020-71444-6. [22]

COBSEA (2019), *Regional Action Plan on Marine Litter 2019 (RAP MAL)*, https://www.unep.org/cobsea/resources/policy-and-strategy/cobsea-regional-action-plan-marine-litter-2019-rap-mali. [7]

Cottom, J. et al. (2022), "Spatio-temporal quantification of plastic pollution origins and transportation (SPOT)" University of Leeds, UK, https://plasticpollution.leeds.ac.uk/toolkits/spot/. [11]

Deloitte (2019), *The price tag of plastic pollution. An economic assessment of river plastic*, https://www2.deloitte.com/content/dam/Deloitte/nl/Documents/strategy-analytics-and-ma/deloitte-nl-strategy-analytics-and-ma-the-price-tag-of-plastic-pollution.pdf. [16]

European Commission (2019), *The European Green Deal*, European Commission, Brussels, https://eur-lex.europa.eu/legal-content/EN/TXT/?qid=1576150542719&uri=COM%3A2019%3A640%3AFIN (accessed on 20 November 2020). [9]

G20 Leaders (2021), *G20 Rome Leaders' Declaration*, https://www.consilium.europa.eu/media/52730/g20-leaders-declaration-final.pdf (accessed on 29 April 2022). [4]

HELCOM (2015), *Marine litter action plan*, https://helcom.fi/media/publications/Regional-Action-Plan-for-Marine-Litter.pdf. [8]

Hwang, S. and J. Ko (2007), *Achievement and progress of marine litter retrieval project in near coast of Korea - based on activities of Korea Fisheries Infrastructure Promotion Association*, Presentation to Regional Workshop on Marine Litter, Rhizao, China, June 2007. North West Pacific Action Plan. [19]

Kalaydjian, R. et al. (2006), , Marine Economics Department, IFREMER, Paris, France. [20]

Lebreton, L. and A. Andrady (2019), "Future scenarios of global plastic waste generation and disposal", *Palgrave Communications*, Vol. 5/1, p. 6, https://doi.org/10.1057/s41599-018-0212-7. [12]

McIlgorm, A., H. Campbell and M. Rule (2009), *Understanding the economic benefits and costs of controlling marine debris in the APEC region (MRC 02/2007). A report to the Asia-Pacific Economic Cooperation Marine Resource Conservation Working Group*, National Marine Science Centre (University of New England and Southern Cross University), Coffs Harbour. [21]

Ministry of Foreign Affairs, Japan (2019), "G20 Osaka Leaders Declaration", *G20 2019 Japan*, https://www.mofa.go.jp/policy/economy/g20_summit/osaka19/en/documents/final_g20_osaka_leaders_declaration.html (accessed on 29 April 2022). [3]

Mouat, J., R. Lopez Lazano and H. Bateson (2010), *Economic Impacts of Marine Litter*, Kommunernes International Miljøorganisation [Local Authorities International Environmental Organisation], http://www.kimointernational.org/wp/wp-content/uploads/2017/09/KIMO_Economic-Impacts-of-Marine-Litter.pdf. [17]

OECD (2022), "Declaration on a Resilient and Healthy Environment for All", *OECD/LEGAL/0468*, https://legalinstruments.oecd.org/en/instruments/OECD-LEGAL-0468 (accessed on 11 April 2022). [2]

OECD (2022), *Global Plastics Outlook: Economic Drivers, Environmental Impacts and Policy Options*, OECD Publishing, Paris, https://doi.org/10.1787/de747aef-en. [1]

OECD (2021), "Towards G7 action to combat ghost fishing gear: A background report prepared for the 2021 G7 Presidency of the United Kingdom", *OECD Environment Policy Papers*, No. 25, OECD Publishing, Paris, https://doi.org/10.1787/a4c86e42-en. [14]

Raaymakers, S. (2007), *The Problem of Derelict Fishing Gear: Global Review and Proposals for Action Food and Agricultural Organisation*. [18]

Ryberg, M. et al. (2019), "Global environmental losses of plastics across their value chains", *Resources, Conservation and Recycling*, Vol. 151, p. 104459, https://doi.org/10.1016/j.resconrec.2019.104459. [10]

Scheld, A., D. Bilkovic and K. Havens (2016), "The Dilemma of Derelict Gear", *Scientific Reports*, Vol. 6/19671, https://doi.org/10.1038/srep19671. [15]

Notes

[1] One key difference is that the *Global Ambition* scenario targets policy implementation to 2060, whereas OBOV aims for 2050.

[2] Small blocks of polymers ready for conversion into the production of primary plastics, and that can be spilled accidentally during production, transport or storage.

[3] Wastewater treatment plants filter out plastics from sewage water and concentrate them in the resulting sludge. Since sludge is commonly used as compost on agricultural fields in many countries, some of the microplastics captured during wastewater treatment may end up in the environment. As countries become richer, they invest more in wastewater treatment. That means that while fewer microplastics from other sources are released into water, more microplastics end up in the resulting wastewater sludge. This sludge is sometimes spread on land, which means that more sludge also means more leakage.

[4] Derelict fishing gear is a major source of marine debris which has been charged with damaging sensitive habitats, creating navigational hazards, as well as reducing populations of target and non-target species.

9 Interactions between plastics and climate mitigation policies

This chapter introduces a *Climate Mitigation* scenario involving a global carbon tax and decarbonisation of the global power sector. With the fossil-based nature of plastics fundamentally linked to climate change, the aim is to better understand the interlinkages between plastics and climate mitigation policies and to provide insights into synergies and trade-offs between the two policy areas. The chapter compares the effects on greenhouse gas emissions of the *Global Ambition* scenario presented in Chapter 8 and of the *Climate Mitigation* scenario, and then looks at the emissions and economic impacts of combining the two in a joint *Global Ambition* and *Climate Mitigation* scenario.

Key messages

- The plastics lifecycle is fundamentally linked to climate change. Plastics are largely derived from fossil fuels, and plastics production and waste management both use energy and thus lead to greenhouse gas (GHG) emissions.
- In addition to significantly reducing plastic leakage (its primary objective), the *Global Ambition* scenario (presented in Chapter 8) is also projected to reduce plastics lifecycle GHG emissions in 2060 by 2.1 gigatonnes of carbon dioxide equivalent (Gt CO_2e), namely 50% below the *Baseline* scenario. This reduction is mostly due to the strong decrease in plastics use.
- The *Climate Mitigation* scenario has as its primary objective the reduction of GHG emissions. Through a global carbon tax and decarbonistion of the power sector, it is projected to reduce global GHG emissions in 2060 by around one-third below *Baseline* levels, corresponding to a level of global gross emissions of 63 Gt CO_2e. While the effects on plastics use are limited, the *Climate Mitigation* scenario slightly increases the share of secondary (recycled) plastics by increasing the price of fossil fuel inputs for primary plastics production.
- Combining plastics and climate mitigation policies fully exploits the complementarity of the two environmental policy domains. The *Global Ambition and Climate Mitigation* scenario is projected to decrease plastics lifecycle GHG emissions by 67% from *Baseline* levels in 2060 (from 4.3 Gt CO_2e to 1.4 Gt CO_2e, which is lower than 2019 emissions levels). While plastics policies mainly mitigate plastics lifecycle GHG emissions by reducing plastics use and waste generation, climate change mitigation policies further reduce GHG emissions by improving the GHG-intensity of both plastics production and waste management.
- Flanking policies are necessary to prevent any emissions trade-off between plastics policies and climate change in waste management. Waste management GHG emissions could increase if recycling replaced sanitary landfilling. If recycling replaced incineration, the impact on GHGs would depend on the use of waste-to-energy processes and the carbon intensity of the energy that this process would replace.

9.1. Climate mitigation policies complement policy action on plastics

The plastics lifecycle is fundamentally linked to climate change in many, and sometimes opposing, ways. Plastics contribute to climate change because greenhouse gases (GHGs) are emitted throughout their lifecycle – from production to their end of life (see Chapter 6). In some instances, there are clear synergies between plastics and climate mitigation policies, for example, when they lead to more efficient use of resources in the economy. In other cases, there are trade-offs, such as plastic waste management, where recycling leads to GHG emissions. Therefore, the interactions between plastics and climate mitigation policies warrants a broad approach in which policies work together to exploit synergies and overcome the trade-offs.

This chapter introduces a *Climate Mitigation* scenario to understand better the interlinkages between plastics and climate mitigation policies and to provide insights into relevant synergies and trade-offs between the two policy areas. This scenario is considered individually, and in combination with the *Global Ambition* scenario on plastics, presented in Chapter 8 (the *Global Ambition and Climate Mitigation* scenario).

The climate mitigation policies modelled in these scenarios target a decarbonisation of all sectors of the global economy. This would see global GHG emissions in 2060 around one-third lower than the levels projected in the *Baseline* scenario for 2060, corresponding to a level of global gross emissions of 63 gigatonnes of carbon dioxide equivalent (Gt CO_2e).[1] There are two main interactions between plastics and climate:

- ***Plastics production and waste management use energy.*** GHG emissions related to plastics production depend on the type of plastics produced – the emissions from producing and converting 1 tonne of primary plastics may vary from 2.7 to 6.3 t CO_2e depending on the polymer involved, as well as on the energy used to produce plastics and the electricity mix of the country where plastics are produced. This is also the case for waste recycling, which uses energy to convert plastic waste to secondary plastics.
- ***Fossil fuels are the main feedstock in plastics production***. As fossil fuels are used as feedstock in the production of primary plastics, plastics production is inevitably interlinked with fossil fuel markets. An increase in demand for fossil inputs by the plastics sector leads, all things being equal, to an increase in fossil fuel prices, which in turn affects fossil fuel combustion and GHG emissions in other sectors. Conversely, any increase in fossil fuel prices, whether induced by climate mitigation policies or not, increases the relative price of fossil-based plastics, hence decreasing their production and related GHG emissions (see Box 6.1 in Chapter 6). Changes in the demand for primary plastics also affect the demand for other types of plastics, such as secondary (recycled) and biobased plastics, with consequent changes in GHG emissions.[2]

The *Climate Mitigation* scenario analyses these interactions in detail by modelling the impact of major decarbonisation instruments: carbon pricing and the structural transformation of the power sector (Table 9.1 and Annex B).[3] In this scenario, carbon pricing curbs GHG emissions from fossil fuel combustion in the whole economy, including households and all sectors, while the structural transformation of the power sector reduces a large share global GHG emissions thanks to the deployment of low-GHG power generation technologies.[4]

Table 9.1. Description of the *Climate Mitigation* scenario

Policy instrument	Principle	Quantification
Carbon pricing	Global carbon price gradually increasing from 2020 to 2050, constant thereafter.	World average carbon price progressively rises to USD 69 /tCO_2 in 2060 (USD 155 /tCO_2 in the OECD, USD 42 /tCO_2 in non-OECD countries), compared to USD 6 /tCO_2 in the *Baseline*.
Structural transformation of the power sector	Gradual shift in power from fossil fuels to low-GHG sources in all regions between 2020 and 2050, constant share thereafter.	The share of fossil-based power generation decreases from 69% in 2019 to 15% in 2060 (versus 62% in 2060 in *Baseline*).

Note: More details on the assumptions are provided in Annex B.

When plastics and climate mitigation policies are implemented jointly (*Global Ambition and Climate Mitigation* scenario), two more interlinkages are taken into account:

- ***The sectoral demand for plastics responds to changes in plastics prices.*** Sectors that require plastic as an input also require energy and sometimes generate GHG emissions from other sources. Hence, any change in plastics prices triggers substitutions and change these sectors emissions. The plastics content of the goods produced by these sectors may also influence the amount of energy involved in using them (e.g. by influencing the weight), hence changing greenhouse gas emissions from the use-phase of such goods. In addition, the sectors providing alternatives to plastics as inputs (e.g. aluminium, glass, etc.) also demand energy and sometimes generate process GHG emissions. Consequently, any substitution towards these alternatives also has implications for overall greenhouse gas emissions.

- ***GHG emission intensity varies across waste management techniques.*** The use of plastics leads to waste, which in turn contributes to GHG emissions. Of the various end-of-life fates of plastics, incineration emits the most greenhouse gases (2.3 tCO_2e per tonne of plastics on average). Some of these emissions might be offset if energy is recovered through waste-to-energy processes, but the mitigation potential heavily depends on a country's electricity generation mix (OECD, 2022[1]). Recycling and subsequent production of secondary plastics produces on average 0.9 tCO_2e per tonne of plastics, which is less than is emitted from the primary plastics production process. On balance, the switch to secondary plastics production can help to reduce GHG emissions if a region's GHG intensity of recycling is low enough (considering a global average GHG intensity of recycling and depending per polymer, at least 1.8 tCO_2e per tonne of primary plastics replaced by secondary can be abated). Sanitary landfilling is the least GHG-intensive end-of-life fate for plastics, at 0.1 t CO_2e per tonne of plastics.

Other interlinkages between plastics and climate mitigation policies could not be taken into account in the OECD ENV-Linkages model. For example, recent research by Royer et al. (2018[2]) based on experimental data shows that plastic leakage to the environment also has an impact on GHG emissions. The annual global methane emissions due to uncontrolled plastic degradation in the environment are estimated to be roughly 2 Mt CO_2e (Shen et al., 2020[3]). Furthermore, emerging studies suggest that plastics in the environment exacerbate the impacts of climate change on wildlife and ecosystems (Ford et al., 2022[4]). In the ocean, plastics may reduce the photosynthetic efficiency of marine phytoplankton and affect ocean carbon sequestration (Shen et al., 2020[5]). In addition, the presence of microplastics may be a further stressor in highly fragile ecosystems such as the Polar Regions, where they may potentially decrease the capacity of the surface to reflect solar radiation, thus accelerating melting (Evangeliou et al., 2020[6]).

Overall, these climate scenarios are tailored to be ambitious yet not overly disruptive. The scenarios focus on the interaction mechanisms, and do not intend to contribute directly to the discussion of a transition to a "net-zero economy". Doing so would require a more comprehensive analysis of the implications for energy demand of plastics use in products in the use phase, as well as a quantification of the many disruptions to economic structures and production strategies stemming from full decarbonisation. For example, the modelling analysis would need to be able to quantify more precisely substitutions away from conventional fossil-based plastics to low-carbon alternatives, including the impacts of bioplastics on land-use change and corresponding carbon sequestration (see Chapter 6), as well as the plastics requirements specific to low-carbon transition technologies. Although some very recent work is beginning to tackle these issues regionally – such as by SYSTEMIQ (2022[7]) for Europe – there is not yet enough information for a detailed global assessment.

9.2. The *Global Ambition* scenario contributes to climate change mitigation but only limitedly

To better understand the interactions between plastics and climate mitigation policies, it is useful to first identify channels through which plastics policies can affect greenhouse gas emissions. The primary objective of the *Global Ambition* scenario is to virtually eliminate plastic leakage to the environment and; none of the policies in the scenario aim directly at reducing GHG emissions from plastics lifecycle (see Chapter 8). Nevertheless, the policies in this scenario influence GHG emissions by changing the amount and structure of plastics use and the end-of-life fates of plastics. Furthermore, plastics policies affect plastics production processes, for which fossil fuel input and energy use play an important role. Overall, the *Global Ambition* scenario reduces these emissions by 2.1 Gt CO_2e (far right bar in Figure 9.1) compared to the *Baseline* (far left bar), which corresponds to a 50% decrease in plastics lifecycle GHG emissions compared to the *Baseline* in 2060.

These GHG emission reductions result from various factors (Figure 9.1),[5] but the factors with the greatest impact are decrease in plastics use (second bar) and waste generation (third bar). This "volume" effect amounts to a reduction in global plastics lifecycle GHG emissions of around 2.3 Gt CO_2e in 2060, of which

2.1 Gt is due to the decrease in plastics use (the *Global Ambition* scenario leads to a reduction of plastics use by around 400 Mt; see Chapter 8), compounded with the shift to secondary plastics.

All other factors, including the composition of waste and changes in the GHG intensity of plastics production and waste, have an impact of one order of magnitude below the "volume" effect, and tend to increase GHG emissions. In the *Global Ambition* scenario, the share of more GHG-intensive polymers such as fibres increases, as well as the share of more GHG-intensive end-of-life fates, notably recycling. The policies in this scenario also slightly increase the GHG intensity of plastics production and end of life. These effects come from the role of plastics in fossil fuel markets: with a decrease in fossil fuel demand due to the *Global Ambition* scenario, global fossil fuel prices tend to decrease slightly, leading to lower relative prices of GHG-intensive products (e.g. fibres) compared to others. The plastics policies also result in a higher demand for fossil fuels for energy in economic activities, which include plastics production and recycling.

Figure 9.1. The *Global Ambition* scenario is projected to halve plastics lifecycle GHG emissions, mainly by reducing volumes of plastics use

Factors contributing to the change in GHG emissions from *Baseline*, in gigatonnes of carbon dioxide equivalent (Gt CO_2e), 2060

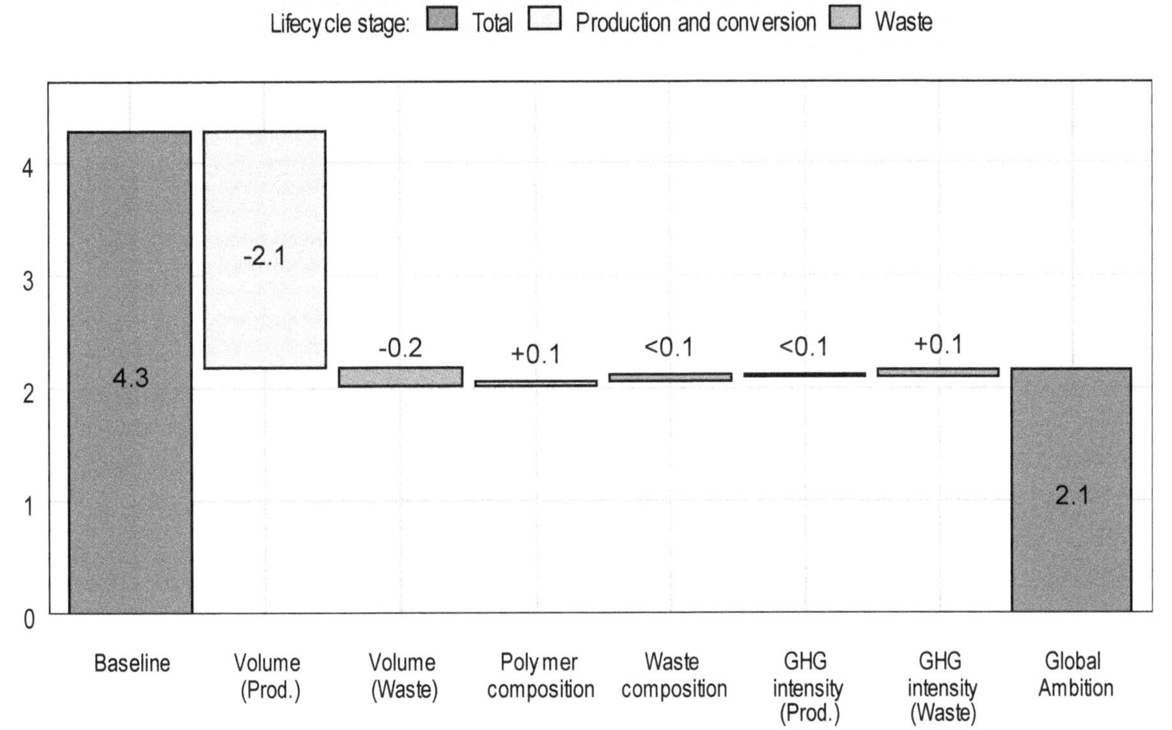

Note: This waterfall chart depicts the plastics lifecycle GHG emissions in the *Baseline* (far left bar) and *Global Ambition* (far right bar) scenarios. The other bars show the contributions of the various drivers to the change in plastics lifecycle emissions between this scenario and the *Baseline*. Production refers to the emissions generated from production of raw polymers while conversion refers to the emissions from their conversion to plastics products. Waste refers to emissions from their end of life (incinerated, recycled or landfilled plastics). The details of the driver bars are as follows (from left to right, see Annex A for details):

1. "Volume (Prod.)" shows the change in emissions from total plastics use, assuming *Baseline* emission factors and composition.
2. "Volume (Waste)" shows the change in emissions from total plastic waste generated, assuming *Baseline* emission factors and composition.
3. "Polymer composition" adds the effect of the projected change in plastics use composition.
4. "Waste composition" adds the effect of the projected change in the composition of end-of-life fates, including the shift between primary and secondary plastics and the changes in incineration (without accounting for waste-to-energy processes impacts).
5. "GHG intensity" adds the changes in emission factors (due to the changes in the production structure in ENV-Linkages), both for production and conversion ("Prod.") and waste ("Waste").

Source: OECD ENV-Linkages model.

StatLink https://stat.link/hdsk45

Of the three pillars of the *Global Ambition* (see Chapter 8), restraining demand for plastics mitigates the most greenhouse gas emissions, closely followed by enhancing recycling (Figure 9.2, Panel A). This is because the bulk of the emissions increase in the *Baseline* is due to the increase in plastics use (Chapter 6) and these pillars directly target the consumption and production of plastics products through taxes or extending product lifespans. However, part of the GHG mitigation from waste management induced by the enhancing recycling pillar is offset by the increase in recycling to replace sanitary landfilling and mismanaged waste, which are less emissions intensive.[6] Finally, closing leakage pathways has very limited impact on plastics lifecycle GHG emissions.

These results emphasise that the climate change mitigation potential of plastics policies mostly lies in decreasing plastics demand (both primary and secondary), while the structure and technology of production and waste management only play a minor role. As highlighted in *OECD Global Plastic Outlook: Economic Drivers, Environmental Impacts and Policy Options* (OECD, 2022[1]), a more precise conclusion on this issue demands a closer look at the GHG impact of potential substitutions of plastics by other products and materials, and the impact of plastics policies on other sectors of the economy.

The policies in the *Global Ambition* scenario also affect total GHG emissions (Figure 9.2, Panel B) – not just emissions from the plastics lifecycle. Changes in global GHG emissions respond to very different drivers compared to plastics-related emissions: plastics-related emissions are concentrated in a few economic sectors and do not necessarily represent a large percentage of these sectors' GHG emissions, while global GHG emissions take all sectors into account. Global GHG emissions changes result from changes in economic activity and in the average GHG-intensity of economic activity, which reflects policy-induced changes in sectoral production. If the decrease in plastics use was strongly compensated for by the use of more GHG-intensive materials, global emissions could increase. This is fortunately not the case, as changes in global GHG emissions in the *Global Ambition* scenario are projected to be –0.8 Gt CO_2e (–0.8%) below *Baseline* emissions in 2060.

This reduction in global GHG emissions is larger than the reduction in economic activity (–0.7%, as shown in Figure 9.7). This reveals small positive climate-related spillovers of the plastics policies on other sectors of the economy, which imply that plastics policies do not trigger large substitution by more GHG-intensive materials. They also do not seem to significantly increase emissions from the use of plastics products which are not included in plastics lifecycle emissions (e.g. from replacing plastics in car production with heavier materials, which increase car weight and therefore GHG emissions). This result therefore shows that plastics policies are an effective way to reduce plastics lifecycle GHG emissions.[7]

As for plastics lifecycle GHG emissions, restraining demand is the largest contributor to global GHG emission reductions. Enhancing recycling and closing leakage pathways increase global emissions, but by a much smaller order of magnitude than reducing demand. Interestingly, closing leakage pathways has a larger effect on total GHG emissions than on plastic lifecycle emissions. While the direct effects on plastics production and on the amounts of plastics recycled or incinerated are limited, the investments included in this pillar change the sector allocation of value added towards waste management and construction activities (see Chapter 8) to the detriment of other activities; these effects results in a small increase in total GHG emissions.

Figure 9.2. Restraining plastics demand contributes the most to emissions reductions

Global Ambition variation from the *Baseline* in gigatonnes of carbon dioxide equivalent (Gt CO_2e), 2060

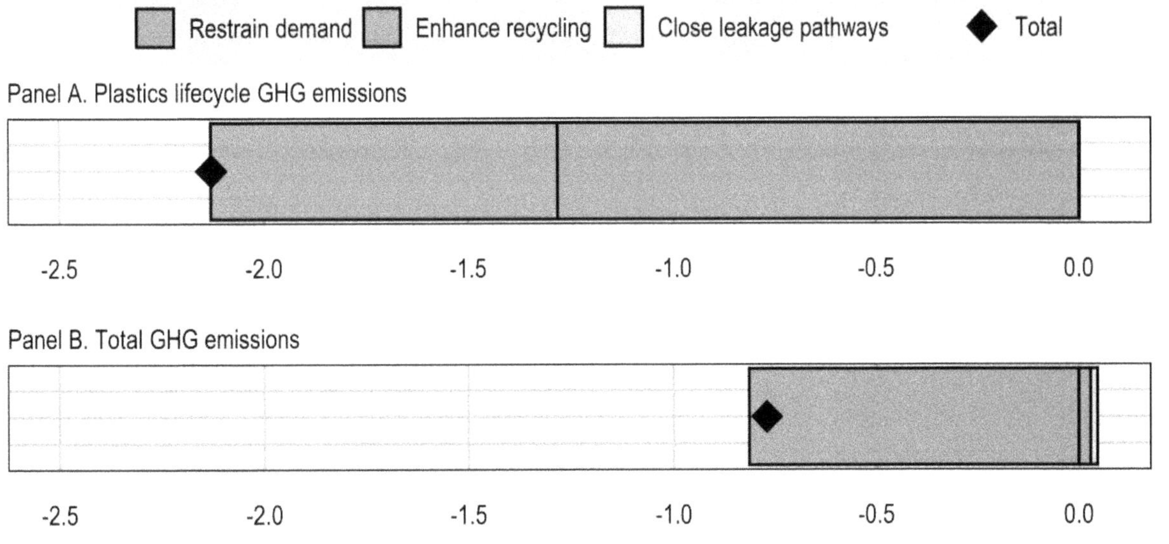

Note: Plastics lifecycle GHG emissions correspond to GHG emitted throughout plastics lifecycle, while Total GHG emissions refer to all GHG emitted globally by all sectors and agents.
Source: OECD ENV-Linkages model.

StatLink https://stat.link/phkefb

9.3. The joint *Global Ambition and Climate Mitigation* scenario decreases plastics lifecycle greenhouse gas emissions

9.3.1. Climate mitigation policies alone have little impact on plastics use

Although not specifically focused on the plastics sector, the *Climate Mitigation* scenario is projected to reduce plastics use by 34 million tonnes (Mt) by 2060, and by 24 Mt if implemented jointly with the *Global Ambition* scenario (Figure 9.3). These reductions in plastics use are small compared to the overall amount of plastics use projected to 2060, which is 1 231 Mt in the *Baseline*, and compared to the decrease in plastics use in the *Global Ambition* scenario (around 403 Mt). This is because the policies in the *Climate Mitigation* scenario do not address plastics production directly, and only influence it through carbon pricing and electricity prices, which in turn have an effect on plastics production prices and on the energy mix used to produce plastics. Compared to the USD 1 000 per tonne tax on plastics in the *Global Ambition* scenario, the world average carbon price of USD 69 per tonne of CO_2 in the *Climate Mitigation* scenario translates into only USD 241 per tonne of plastics (using the 2060 average baseline CO_2 intensity). Meanwhile, the taxes on plastics use are also complemented by other policies in the *Global Ambition* scenario.

Figure 9.3. The *Climate Mitigation* scenario alone has limited impact on global plastics use

Global plastics use (Mt), 2060

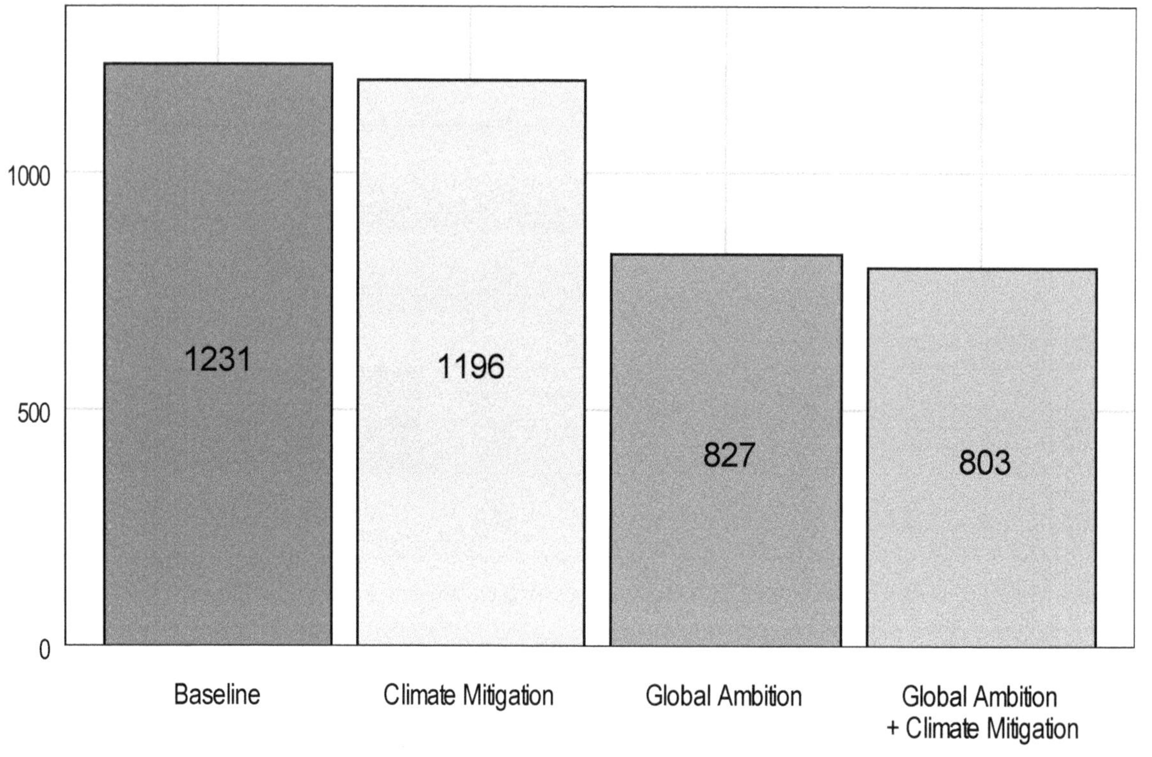

Source: OECD ENV-Linkages model.

StatLink https://stat.link/aocfuq

Despite having little effect on total global plastics use, the climate mitigation policies do influence the *structure* of plastics use, especially the balance between primary and secondary plastics (Figure 9.4). The *Climate Mitigation* scenario is projected to decrease both primary and secondary plastics production, because both production technologies demand energy. However, primary plastics production is more affected than secondary production because primary production is more energy-intensive. This results in a further increase in the share of secondary plastics in total plastics production when the climate mitigation policies are implemented alone. When climate mitigation policies are combined with plastics policies in the *Global Ambition and Climate Mitigation* scenario, the share of secondary plastics in total plastics use does not increase as much as with climate mitigation policies alone. This is because secondary plastics also have a sizable GHG emission profile.

Figure 9.4. The *Climate Mitigation* scenario reduces primary plastics more than secondary plastics

Absolute change in plastics use compared to the *Baseline* in megatonnes (Mt), 2060

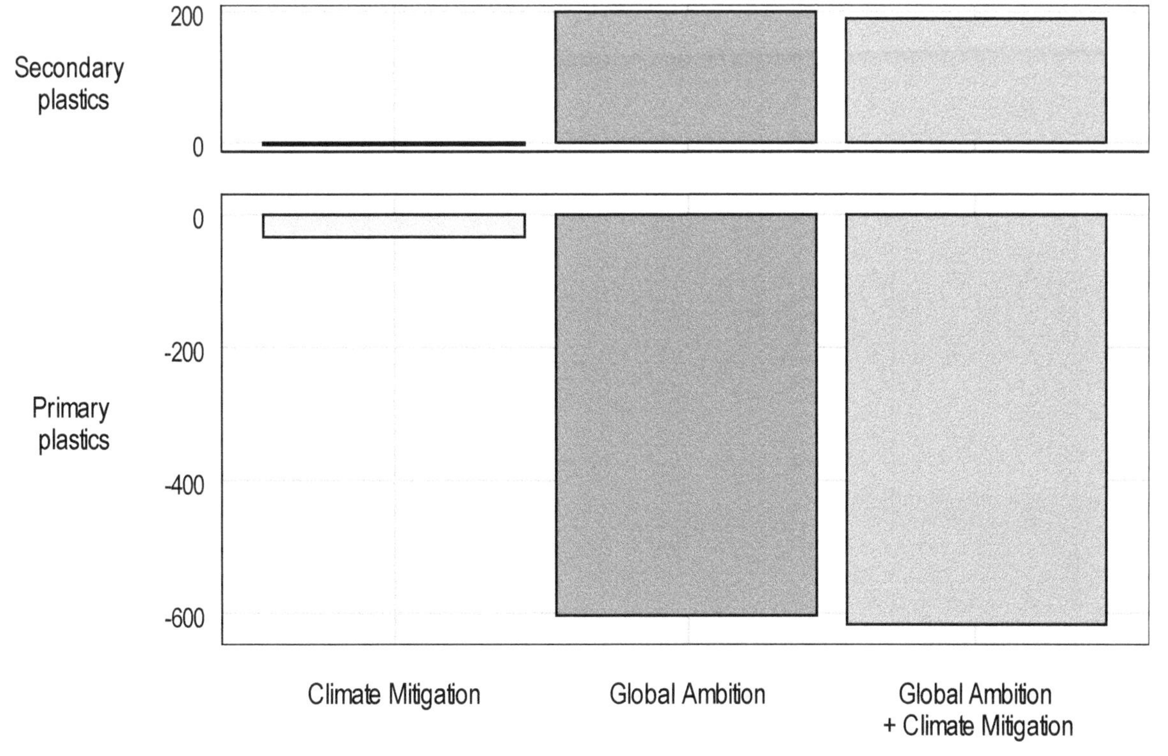

Source: OECD ENV-Linkages model.

StatLink https://stat.link/l5sevq

9.3.2. A combined policy package reduces plastics lifecycle GHG emissions significantly

The policies in the *Climate Mitigation* scenario have a significant impact on plastics lifecycle GHG emissions (Figure 9.5), decreasing them by 1.3 Gt CO_2e in 2060 compared to *Baseline* (a fall of 31%). The combined *Global Ambition and Climate Mitigation* scenario reduces plastics lifecycle GHG emissions even more – by 2.8 Gt CO_2e in 2060 (a decrease of 67%), falling to 1.4 Gt CO_2e, which is even lower than 2019 emissions levels.

Figure 9.5. The *Global Ambition and Climate Mitigation* scenario reduces plastics lifecycle GHG emissions to below 2019 levels

Greenhouse gas emissions from plastics lifecycle in gigatonnes of carbon dioxide equivalent (Gt CO_2e), 2019 and 2060

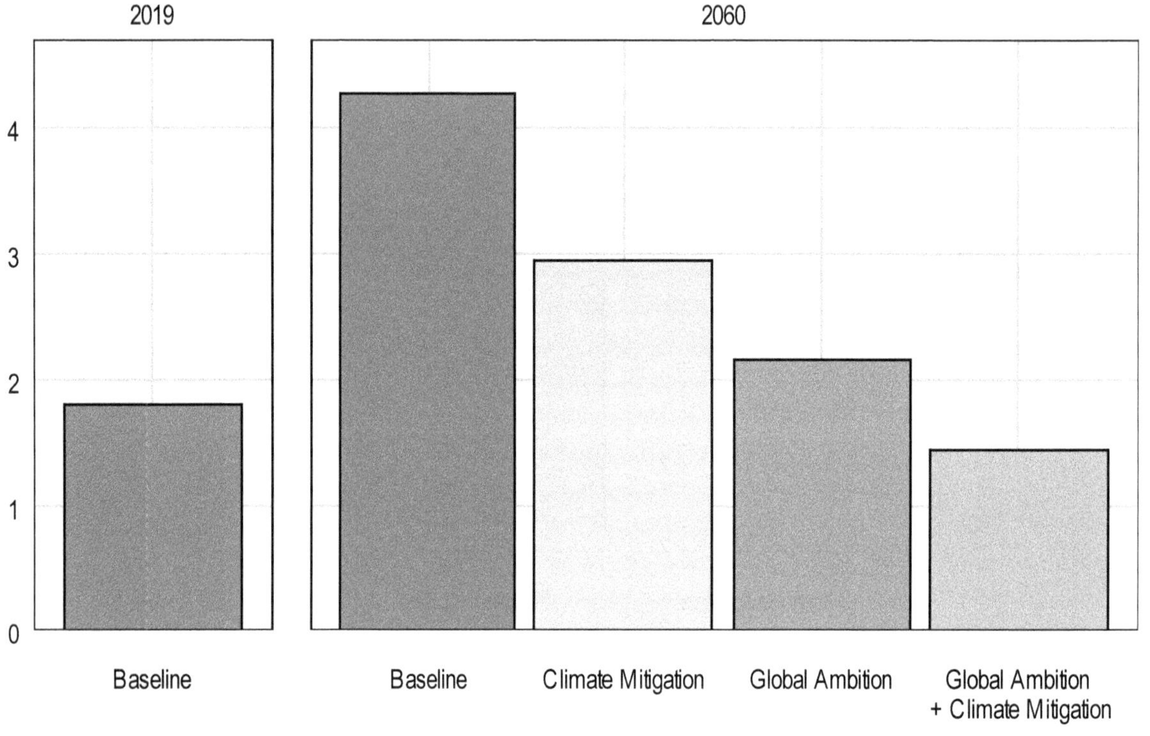

Source: OECD ENV-Linkages model.

StatLink https://stat.link/a2qd5f

The main channel through which the *Climate Mitigation* scenario affects plastics lifecycle GHG emissions is a shift of energy use in plastics-related activities (production and conversion, and to a lesser extent end of life) from more to less carbon intensive sources, such as electricity and gas. This is the case whether the *Climate Mitigation* scenario is implemented alone (Panel A in Figure 9.6) or jointly with *Global Ambition* (Panel B). This shift in energy use towards less GHG-intensive sources is driven both by carbon pricing, which reduces the share of fossil energy, and the structural transformation of the power sector, which reduces indirect GHG emissions from electricity generation. Recycling is the only disposal option that is affected by carbon pricing – because GHG emissions from incineration are mostly direct emissions and not related to energy use, and because emissions from sanitary landfilling are very low. Carbon pricing leads to a decrease in recycled plastics, but given that the recycling sector is not very GHG-intensive, the decrease is limited. This is why the end-of-life contribution to GHG mitigation is limited. Polymer and waste composition do not contribute to the mitigation effort, but this might be due to a limitation of the ENV-Linkages model, which does not differentiate GHG intensity of polymers due to the lack of information on the cost structures of different polymers, preventing any polymer-specific impact of climate mitigation policies.

Figure 9.6. The policies in the *Climate Mitigation* scenario mainly reduce the GHG intensity of plastics production

Factors contributing to the change in plastics lifecycle GHG emissions in gigatonnes of carbon dioxide equivalent (Gt CO_2e), 2060

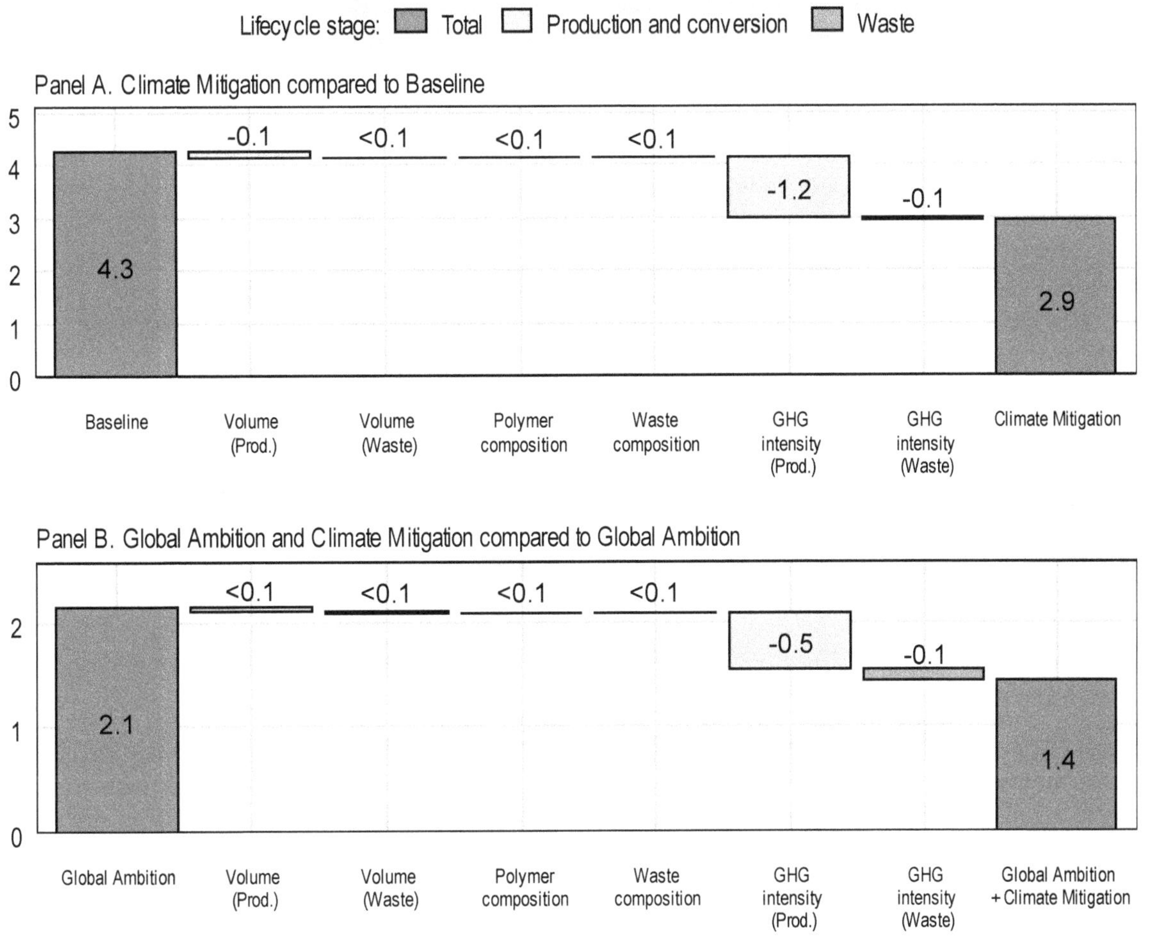

Note: This waterfall chart depicts the plastics lifecycle GHG emissions in the scenarios without climate mitigation (far left bar) and the same scenario with climate mitigation (far right bar). The other bars show the contributions of the various drivers to the change in plastics lifecycle GHG emissions between the scenarios with climate change mitigation and those without climate change mitigation. Production refers to the emissions generated from production of raw polymers, while conversion refers to the emissions from their conversion to plastics products. Waste refers to emissions from their end of life (incinerated, recycled or landfilled plastics). The details of the driver bars are as follows (from left to right, see Annex A for details):

1. "Volume (Prod.)" shows the change in emissions from total plastics use, assuming *Baseline/Global Ambition* emission factors and composition.
2. "Volume (Waste)" shows the change in emissions from total plastic waste generated, assuming *Baseline/Global Ambition* emission factors and composition.
3. "Polymer composition" adds the effect of the projected change in plastics use composition.
4. "Waste composition" adds the effect of the projected change in the composition of end-of-life fates, including the shift between primary and secondary plastics and the changes in incineration (without accounting for waste-to-energy processes impacts).
5. "GHG intensity" adds the changes in emission factors (due to the changes in the production structure in ENV-Linkages), both for production and conversion ("Prod.") and waste ("Waste").

Source: OECD ENV-Linkages model.

StatLink https://stat.link/206im4

Climate change mitigation policies and plastics policies therefore influence plastics lifecycle GHG emissions through different channels – the GHG intensity of plastics production for the former (Figure 9.6), and the decrease in plastics use for the latter (Figure 9.1). This means that the two sets of policies have synergies for maximising the mitigation of plastics lifecycle GHG emissions.

Looking beyond plastics lifecycle GHG emissions, the *Climate Mitigation* scenario reduces global GHG emissions by 31.6 Gt CO_2e in 2060, which corresponds to a 33% reduction (Figure 9.7, Panel B), which is its primary objective. The plastics policies in the *Global Ambition* scenario have limited effects on GHG emissions, with an overall reduction of 0.8 Gt CO_2e (Section 9.3), while the G*lobal Ambition and Climate Mitigation* scenario reduces global GHG emissions by 32.1 Gt CO_2e. The overall effects of the two sets of policies on global GHG emissions are greater than the sum of their parts, showing that plastics and climate mitigation policies are highly complementary. However, climate mitigation policies cannot be used as a substitute for plastics policies to reduce plastic leakage (as shown in Section 9.3.1), and plastics policies cannot replace dedicated climate mitigation action.

9.3.3. The economic effects of combining Global Ambition with Climate Mitigation highlight their complementarity

Since reducing greenhouse gas emissions is the primary objective of climate mitigation policies, they are more cost-effective than plastics policies in achieving this goal (Panel A in Figure 9.7). The cost of the policies in the *Climate Mitigation* scenario is projected to amount to a 2.2% reduction of GDP in 2060, and reduces GHG emissions by 33%. On its own, the *Global Ambition* scenario reduces GDP by 0.7%, and GHG emissions are reduced by 0.8% as an incidental effect. Thus, climate mitigation policies are a more cost efficient way to abate emissions. This is normal, because the climate mitigation policies target the whole economy, while plastics policies only target the plastics sector. However, GHG emission reductions are not the primary goal of plastics policies, and they provide other important environmental benefits, not least reducing plastic leakage to the environment (Chapters 7 and 8).

The cost of climate mitigation policies is not significantly affected by the presence of plastics policies. The GDP impact of climate mitigation policies, whether taken alone or on top of the impacts of plastics policies, is around –2.2% of GDP compared to the *Baseline* in both cases. Ultimately, at the global level, the policies in the two scenarios are complementary, because the cost of the joint plastics and climate scenario (*Global Ambition and Climate Mitigation*) is very close to the sum of the costs of the two individual scenarios. This emphasises the fact that the synergies between plastics and climate mitigation policies mostly lie in the plastics sector itself.

Figure 9.7. The GDP and emissions effects of climate and plastics policies are greatest when they are combined

Percentage variation from *Baseline*, 2060

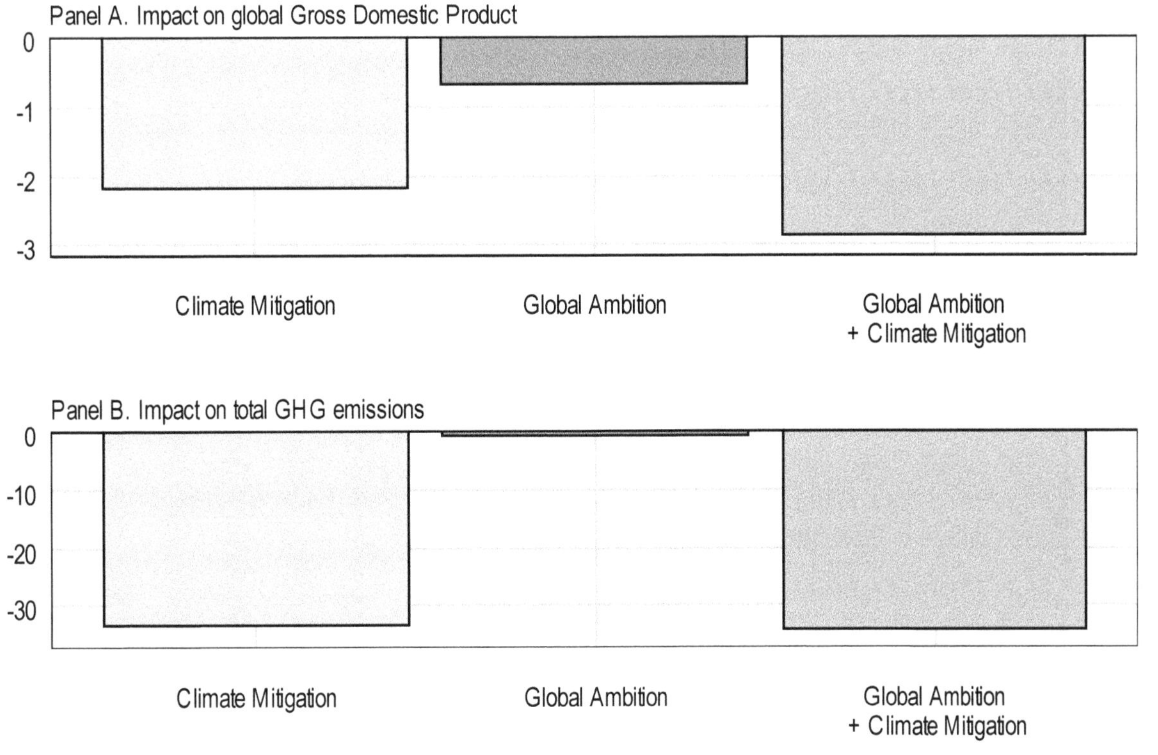

Source: OECD ENV-Linkages model.

StatLink https://stat.link/r8e4q0

References

Evangeliou, N. et al. (2020), “Atmospheric transport is a major pathway of microplastics to remote regions”, *Nature Communications*, Vol. 11/1, p. 3381, https://doi.org/10.1038/s41467-020-17201-9. [6]

Ford, H. et al. (2022), “The fundamental links between climate change and marine plastic pollution”, *Science of The Total Environment*, Vol. 806, p. 150392, https://doi.org/10.1016/j.scitotenv.2021.150392. [4]

International Energy Agency (2018), *World Energy Outlook 2018*, International Energy Agency, Paris, https://www.iea.org/reports/world-energy-outlook-2018. [8]

OECD (2022), *Global Plastics Outlook: Economic Drivers, Environmental Impacts and Policy Options*, OECD Publishing, Paris, https://doi.org/10.1787/de747aef-en. [1]

Royer, S. et al. (2018), “Production of methane and ethylene from plastic in the environment”, *PLOS ONE*, Vol. 13/8, https://doi.org/10.1371/journal.pone.0200574. [2]

Shen, M. et al. (2020), “(Micro)plastic crisis: Un-ignorable contribution to global greenhouse gas emissions and climate change”, *Journal of Cleaner Production*, Vol. 254, p. 120138, https://doi.org/10.1016/j.jclepro.2020.120138. [3]

Shen, M. et al. (2020), “Can microplastics pose a threat to ocean carbon sequestration?”, *Marine Pollution Bulletin*, Vol. 150, p. 110712, https://doi.org/10.1016/j.marpolbul.2019.110712. [5]

SYSTEMIQ (2022), *ReShaping Plastics: Pathways to a Circular, Climate Neutral Plastics System in Europe*, http://www.systemiq.earth (accessed on 27 April 2022). [7]

Notes

[1] This reduction in global GHG emissions is not sufficient to achieve the Paris Agreement goals of limiting global temperature increase to well below 2°C, and possibly 1.5°C. However, the scenario is still useful for illustrating the impact of climate change policies on plastics and the potential synergies with plastics policies.

[2] Secondary plastics use less energy in production, but the recycling process needed to create scrap material is associated with significant GHG emissions. The production of primary biobased plastics involves less direct emissions than fossil-based plastics production. However, the overall effects, taking into account potential land-use change, are ambiguous, and depend on the biomass production techniques and the amount of deforestation that could be triggered by biobased plastics production increases (as analysed in detail in Section 6.1.2 in Chapter 6).

[3] Both instruments are calibrated relying on information from the sustainable development scenarios (SDS) of the *2018 World Energy Outlook* (WEO) (International Energy Agency, 2018[8]). Overall, this scenario represents a moderate climate mitigation ambition, since it reduces GHG emissions by around a third by 2060 (see Section 9.3.3).

[4] The two instruments are modelled jointly in the OECD ENV-Linkages model. The model includes a detailed representation of the power sector with different technologies; and mitigation options for firms and households by allowing for substitution between fuels in the different firms' production function and households' utility function. The model has been updated to include the production structure and end-of-life fates of both primary and secondary plastics, and to adopt a lifecycle approach to the GHG emissions attributable to plastics (see Annex A). As a global general equilibrium model, ENV-Linkages is also able to capture the rich interlinkages between sectors and regions. As such, it is particularly fit to explore interactions between climate change mitigation policies and plastics policies. However, limitations in data availability and the model structure mean that the assessment does not include the land-use change impacts of bioplastics production, or the possible mitigation potential of waste to energy. These are minor gaps, as the *Global Ambition* scenario does not include a transition to bioplastics, and the mitigation potential of waste-to-energy electricity generation is still subject to debate.

[5] More details on the methodology to analyse the effects that lead to changes in emissions are provided in Annex A.

[6] This effect might be over- or under-estimated depending on the share of waste incinerated using waste-to-energy processes, and the electricity mix of the country where this incineration occurs.

[7] The magnitude of the emission reductions due to plastics policies would also need to be confirmed by more fine-grained analysis of substitution effects, as the modelling of these substitutions in the ENV-Linkages model is only implemented at an aggregate sector level.

Annex A. Modelling framework

This Annex presents the methodologies applied to provide the projections contained in this report and in the OECD Plastics Outlook Database. These projections include, for the 2019 -2060 period, plastics use, plastic waste generation, plastic waste management and related environmental impacts. The environmental impacts are described by theme: (i) leakage to the environment, detailing the macroplastics and microplastics fractions, (ii) leakage to aquatic environments, (iii) particulate matter emissions from tyre and brake abrasion, (v) greenhouse gas emissions from the plastics lifecycle, and (vi) lifecycle impacts related to the production and disposal of plastics.

The Annex contains the following sections:

- Overview of the ENV-Linkages modelling framework.
- Overview of the data sources used for the plastics module calibration.
- Modelling plastics use in ENV-Linkages.
- Modelling plastic waste and end-of-life fates in ENV-Linkages.
- Modelling plastic leakage to the environment (Technical University of Denmark, DTU).
- Modelling plastic leakage to terrestrial and aquatic environments (University of Leeds).
- Modelling plastic leakage to aquatic environments (Laurent Lebreton).
- Modelling particulate matter emissions to air from tyre and brake wear (Norwegian Institute for Air Research, NILU).
- Modelling greenhouse gas emissions from plastics in ENV-Linkages.
- Modelling the effects of higher penetration rates of biobased plastics (CGE Box model).
- Modelling other lifecycle health and environment impacts from plastics (Ghent University).

Overview of the modelling framework

This section explains in more detail the methodologies employed to prepare the database, which is also part of the OECD Plastics Outlook Database (OECD.stat, 2022[1]), and used for the projections. Estimates for the 2019 base year have been generated by building on output from the OECD computable general equilibrium (CGE) model (ENV-Linkages) (Chateau, Dellink and Lanzi, 2014[2]), by filling existing data gaps and by generating projections on the environmental impacts. The projections are also based on the ENV-Linkages model.

The modelling of economic flows, plastics use, plastic waste and environmental impacts involves different steps, as illustrated in Figure A A.1. Plastics use is linked to sectoral and regional economic projections, which therefore drive the evolution of plastics use over time. Volumes of plastics are then used to calculate generated waste, based on product lifespans of different applications. The waste generated is further broken down by waste treatment, i.e. recycled (collected for recycling), incinerated, landfilled, mismanaged and littered waste (see Chapter 2 for definitions), taking into account differences across regions. Finally, projections for a subset of environmental impacts are calculated: leakage of microplastics and macroplastics to the environment, leakage to aquatic environments, particulate matter linked to tyre and brake wear, greenhouse gas (GHG) emissions, the effects of higher penetration rates of biobased plastics and other lifecycle health and environment impacts.

The analysis relies on a suite of modelling tools. More specifically, projections of the economic flows, plastics, plastic waste, and greenhouse gas emissions (Steps 1-4) rely the OECD in-house modelling tools, while other environmental impacts rely on external models (Step 5). The methodology is not fully linear: some of the information provided by external models in Step 5 have been used to calibrate the ENV-Linkages models in Steps 1-4.

Figure A A.1. Methodological steps

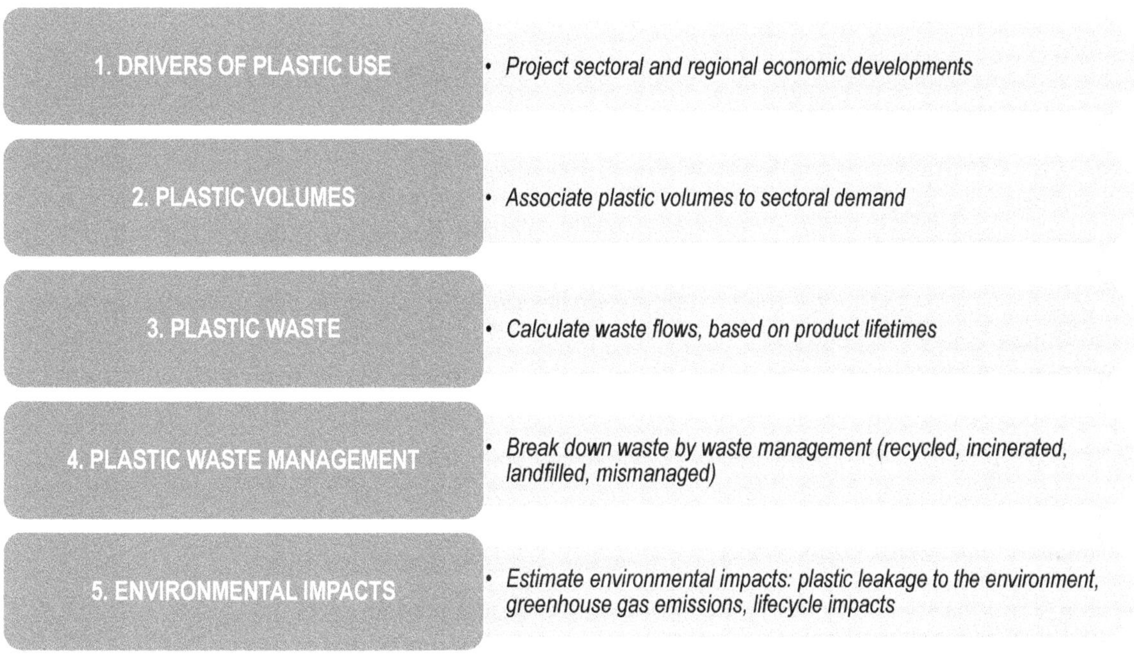

Source: Authors' own elaboration.

The OECD's in-house dynamic computable general equilibrium (CGE) model ENV-Linkages is used as the basis to estimate the economic activities that drive plastics use in 2019. ENV-Linkages is a multi-sectoral, multi-regional model that links economic activities to energy and environmental issues. A more comprehensive model description is given in Chateau, Dellink and Lanzi (2014[2]). A description of the *Baseline* scenario construction procedure is given in Chateau, Rebolledo and Dellink (2011[3]), while recent baseline results are illustrated in OECD (2019[4]).

The model is based on the Social Accounting Matrices (SAM) contained within the GTAP 10 database (Aguiar et al., 2019[5]). This database describes bilateral trade patterns, production, consumption and intermediate use of commodities and services, including capital, labour and tax revenues and use. The base year of the SAM and of the model is 2014. Therefore, to obtain estimates for 2019, the ENV-Linkages model was run to 2019 (Box A A.1 for an overview of the functioning of the model). The short-term changes to the economy from 2014 to 2019 reflect short-term economic changes from international databases: the OECD Economics Department (OECD, 2020[6]) and the International Monetary Fund (2020[7]).

Box A A.1. The ENV-Linkages model

Production in ENV Linkages is assumed to operate under cost minimisation with perfect markets and constant returns-to-scale technology. The production technology is specified as nested Constant Elasticity of Substitution (CES) production functions in a branching hierarchy. This structure is replicated for each output, while the parameterisation of the CES functions may differ across sectors. The model adopts a putty/semi-putty technology specification, where substitution possibilities among factors are assumed to be higher with new vintage capital than with old vintage capital. In the short run this ensures inertia in the economic system, with limited possibilities to substitute away from more expensive inputs, but in the longer run this implies a relatively smooth adjustment of quantities to price changes. Capital accumulation is modelled as in the traditional Solow/Swan neo classical growth model, where economic growth is assumed to stem from the combination of labour, capital accumulation and technological progress.

Household consumption demand is the result of static maximisation behaviour, which is formally implemented as an "Extended Linear Expenditure System". A representative consumer in each region – who takes prices as given – optimally allocates disposal income among the full set of consumption commodities and savings. Saving is considered as a standard good in the utility function and does not rely on forward looking behaviour by the consumer. The government in each region collects various kinds of taxes in order to finance government expenditures. Assuming fixed public savings (or deficits), the government budget is balanced through the adjustment of the income tax on consumer income. In each period, investment net-of-economic depreciation is equal to the sum of government savings, consumer savings and net capital flows from abroad.

International trade is based on a set of regional bilateral flows. The model adopts the Armington specification, assuming that domestic and imported products are not perfectly substitutable. Moreover, total imports are also imperfectly substitutable between regions of origin. Allocation of trade between partners then responds to relative prices at the equilibrium.

Market goods equilibria imply that, on the one side, the total production of any goods or services is equal to the demand addressed to domestic producers plus exports; and, on the other side, the total demand is allocated between the demands (both final and intermediary) by domestic producers and the import demand.

ENV-Linkages is fully homogeneous in prices and only relative prices matter. All prices are expressed relative to the numéraire of the price system that is arbitrarily chosen as the index of OECD manufacturing exports prices. Each region runs a current account balance, which is fixed in terms of the numéraire.

As ENV-Linkages is recursive-dynamic and does not incorporate forward-looking behaviour, price-induced changes in innovation patterns are not represented in the model. The model does, however, entail technological progress through an annual adjustment of the various productivity parameters, including e.g. autonomous energy efficiency and labour productivity improvements. Furthermore, as production with new capital has a relatively large degree of flexibility in choice of inputs, existing technologies can diffuse to other firms. Thus, within the CGE framework, firms choose the least-cost combination of inputs, given the existing state of technology. The capital vintage structure also ensures that such flexibilities are larger in the long run than in the short run.

Source: (Chateau, Dellink and Lanzi, 2014[2]).

For the development of this Outlook, ENV-Linkages has been enhanced to include data on plastics use, waste and waste treatment. In ENV-Linkages, plastics projections follow economic projections, and, more precisely, the evolution of the production and consumption of goods in different sectors and regions.

The sectoral aggregation of the model adopted in this report is given in Table A A.1, while the regional aggregation is presented in Table A A.2.

Table A A.1. Sectoral aggregation of ENV-Linkages

Agriculture, fisheries and forestry	Manufacturing
Paddy rice	Food products
Wheat and meslin	Textiles
Other grains	Wood products
Vegetables and fruits	Chemicals
Oil seeds	Basic pharmaceuticals
Sugar cane and sugar beet	Primary rubber and plastic products
Fibres plant	Secondary plastic products
Other crops	Pulp, paper and publishing products
Cattle and raw milk	Non-metallic minerals
Other animal products	Fabricated metal products
Fisheries	Electronics
Forestry	Electrical equipment
	Motor vehicles
Non-manufacturing Industries	Other transport equipment
Coal extraction	Other machinery and equipment
Crude oil extraction	Other manufacturing including recycling
Natural gas extraction	Iron and steel
Other mining	Non-ferrous metals
Petroleum and coal products	**Services**
Gas distribution	Land transport
Water collection and distribution	Air transport
Construction	Water transport
Electricity transmission and distribution	Insurance
Electricity generation (8 technologies)	Trade services
Electricity generation: Nuclear electricity; Hydro (and Geothermal); Solar; Wind; Coal-powered electricity; Gas-powered electricity; Oil-powered electricity; Other (combustible renewable, waste, etc.).	Business services n.e.s.
	Real estate activities
	Accommodation and food service activities
	Public administration and defence
	Education
	Human health and social work

Source: Authors' own elaboration.

Table A A.2. Regional aggregation of ENV-Linkages

Macro regions		ENV-Linkages countries and regions	Most important comprising countries and territories
OECD	OECD America	USA	United States of America
		Canada	Canada
		Other OECD America	Chile, Colombia, Costa Rica, Mexico
	OECD Europe	OECD EU countries	Austria, Belgium, Czech Republic, Denmark, Estonia, Finland, France, Germany Greece, Hungary, Ireland, Italy, Latvia, Lithuania, Luxembourg, Netherlands, Poland, Portugal, Slovak Republic, Slovenia, Spain, Sweden
		OECD Non-EU countries	Iceland, Israel,[1] Norway, Switzerland, Turkey, United Kingdom
	OECD Pacific	OECD Oceania	Australia, New Zealand
		OECD Asia	Japan, Korea
Non-OECD	Other America	Latin America	Non-OECD Latin American and Caribbean countries
	Eurasia	Other EU	Bulgaria, Croatia, Cyprus,[2] Malta, Romania
		Other Eurasia	Non-OECD European and Caspian countries, including Russian Federation
	Middle East and Africa	Middle East & North Africa	Algeria, Bahrain, Egypt, Iraq, Islamic Rep. of Iran, Kuwait, Lebanon, Libya, Morocco, Oman, Qatar, Saudi Arabia, Tunisia, United Arab Emirates, Syrian Arab Rep., Western Sahara, Yemen
		Other Africa	Sub-Saharan Africa
	Other Asia	China	People's Republic of China, Hong Kong (China)
		India	India
		Other non-OECD Asia	Other non-OECD Asian and Pacific countries

Source: Authors' own elaboration.

Overview of the data sources used for the plastics module calibration

Table A A.3. Data sources and methodologies

Category	Variable	Source
Production	Primary and secondary economic split	OECD ENV-Linkages model, based on GTAP10 (Aguiar et al., 2019[5]) split using Exiobase for cost structure (Stadler et al., 2018[8]), Grand View Research (2020[9]) data for total shares (in tons).
	Plastic sectors	OECD ENV-Linkages model projections, resulting from mapping of sectoral/polymer flows to economic baseline. Secondary plastics incorporates recycling loss rates from the literature (Cottom et al., 2022[10]; Chruszcz and Reeve, 2018[11]; Roosen et al., 2020[12]; VinylPlus, 2019[13]).
Use by region, application and polymer	Historical use	Global consumption from Geyer, Jambeck and Law (2017[14]) for 1950-2014. Regional split based on waste weight estimates from Kaza et al. (2018[15]) The split by polymers and applications per region is based on weight estimates from Ryberg et al. (2019[16]) in 2015, and is constant for 1950-2014.
	Use	For the calibration year (2015), primary plastics use by polymer and application from Ryberg et al. (2019[16]) has been associated to different sectors and regions in the OECD ENV-Linkages model. Secondary plastics use stems from waste generation (derived in the model), recycling rates (see below) and recycling loss rates from the literature (Cottom et al., 2022[10]; Chruszcz and Reeve, 2018[11]; Roosen et al., 2020[12]; VinylPlus, 2019[13]). For future years, OECD ENV-Linkages model projections result from the mapping of sectoral/polymer flows to economic baseline.
Waste by region, application and polymer	Historical waste	OECD ENV-Linkages model, based on historical consumption (for 1950-2015), and product lifespans from Geyer, Jambeck and Law (2017[14]).
	Waste	OECD ENV-Linkages model projections, based on product lifespans from Geyer, Jambeck and Law (2017[14]).
Waste management end-of-life fates	Recycling share	For 1980-2019: Country sources (Table A A.5), Geyer, Jambeck and Law (2017[14]), and Kaza et al. (2018[15]). Rates for non-MSW assumed to match MSW.
	Incineration share	For 1980 -2019: Geyer, Jambeck and Law (2017[14]) and Kaza et al. (2018[15]) Rates for non-MSW assumed to match MSW.
	Sanitary landfilling	Cross country regression (residual) based on What a Waste 2.0 (Kaza et al., 2018[15]) (*) Rates for non-MSW assumed to match MSW, when excluding littering.
	Littering share	(Jambeck et al., 2015[17]) for share in MSW and zero for non-MSW.
	Mismanaged share	Cross-country regression based on Kaza et al. (2018[15]) (*) Rates for non-MSW assumed to match MSW, when excluding littering.
Environmental impacts	Total leakage of macroplastics and microplastics to the environment by category	Based on plastic consumption, waste and waste management projections from OECD ENV-Linkages model, adapted from Ryberg et al. (2019[18]) methodology. The central estimate for macroplastic leakage from mismanaged waste (the largest source of leakage) is equal to the average between the estimate provided with the methodology of Ryberg et al. (2019[18]) and the estimate provided by Leeds University (Cottom et al., 2022[10]).
	Plastic leakage and accumulation in aquatic environments	Based on waste management projections from OECD ENV-Linkages model, and the leakage estimates described above, adapted from the Lebreton and Andrady (2019[19]) methodology.
	Plastic leakage to air from terrestrial transport	Based on transport projections from OECD ENV-Linkages model, adapted from Evangeliou et al., (2020[20]) methodology.
	GHG emissions for plastic lifecycle	Based on plastic consumption, waste and waste management projections from OECD ENV-Linkages model, based on Zheng and Suh (2019[21]).

Note: (*) The cross-country regressions based on the What a waste 2.0 database (Kaza et al., 2018[15]) include:

a) $waste\_pc_i = \alpha + \beta * ln(gdp\_pc_i) + r_i$

b) $inc_i/(inc_i + dis_i) = \alpha + \beta * ln(gdp\_pc_i) + r_i$

c) $mis_i/dis_i = \alpha + \beta * ln(gdp\_pc_i) + oecd_i$

where waste_pc = MSW per capita, mis = mismanaged waste, inc = incinerated waste, dis = mismanaged + landfilled, gdp_pc = GDP per capita, oecd = dummy for OECD economies, r = regional dummies for 15 regions of ENV-Linkages, i = country.

Source: Authors' own elaboration.

Modelling plastics use in ENV-Linkages

Volumes

The ENV-Linkages model has been extended to include plastics volumes, for both primary and secondary (recycled) plastics use. The plastics use data is presented in million metric tonnes (Mt) and plastics use is split by region, polymer and application.

Volumes of primary plastics for 2015 rely on data from Ryberg at al. (2019[18]), that updates and expands on the seminal work by Geyer, Jambeck and Law (2017[14]). Since the estimates provided by Ryberg et al. (2019[18]) were either by region and application or by application and polymers, an assumption of homogeneity of polymers by application was taken to estimate the primary plastics use by region, polymer and application.

Secondary plastics volumes for 2015 were estimated following a methodology deriving secondary plastics through waste collected for recycling and recycling losses. Loss rates including sorting losses and reprocessing losses were estimated using a methodology developed by the University of Leeds based on a review of the literature (see next section on Losses from sorting and reprocessing).

The estimates for 2019 are based on the 2015 year, using the link between plastics volumes in Mt and plastic inputs to sectors in USD, as described below. In addition, these are complemented with plastics use for the past between 1950 and 2014, for two reasons. The first reason is to be able to accurately compute waste flows in the future, since plastic lifespans can span up to decades. The second reason is to form the basis for the computation of environmental impacts, as for instance plastic leaked in the ocean accumulates over time.

The 1950-2014 historical plastics use is calculated following a step-wise approach. First, global plastics use is taken from the Geyer, Jambeck and Law (2017[22]) study. The regional split of plastics use is then based on weight-based estimates of waste, from a cross country regression of municipal solid waste on GDP per capita using What a Waste 2.0 (Kaza et al., 2018[15]), multiplied by the regional consumption shares in 2015. Finally, for each region, the split by polymer and application is assumed to be constant prior to 2014, based on the estimates from Ryberg et al. (2019[18]). This methodology is constrained by data availability (and thus necessarily imperfect) but provides estimates of plastics use by region, polymer and application.

Losses from sorting and reprocessing – University of Leeds

Plastic waste that has been collected for recycling almost always includes some non-plastic materials and articles. Moreover, collected plastic waste typically includes a multitude of plastics with varying chemical and physical composition. The degree to which these items, objects and fragments are useful to a plastics reprocessor depends on wide range of factors that influence the value of the material. In general, high income countries implement recyclate collection schemes (programmes) that are designed to yield high material mass through an accessible and simplified system that is easy for people to understand. Conversely, in low- and middle-income countries, plastic waste collection for recycling is carried out by informal workers (IRS) who selectively collect (cherry pick) items and objects that are most valuable, focusing on quality and concentration rather than high yield. Even with diligent, selective collection, plastic articles contain a multitude of intentionally and non-intentionally appended, entrapped, adhered and entrained materials and objects that must be removed from the dominant plastic before it can be most often comminuted and remelted under pressure in an extruder. A list of characteristics of waste plastics and their influence on the value of materials and hence their recyclability is reported by Cottom et al. (2022[10]) and shown in (Table A A.4).

Table A A.4. Characteristics of waste plastics and their influence on sorting reprocessability

Characteristic	Example	Effect on value
Plastic type	Usually denoted by the polymer that makes up the majority of the mass (e.g. polypropylene or polyvinyl chloride)	• Must be technically recyclable which usually excludes non-melting plastics (thermosets) with the exception of polyurethane foam that can be recycled into an agglomerate using adhesive • Must be abundant enough to support the business case for recovering from a material mixture. For instance it is extremely rare for post-consumer polystyrene or PVC packaging to be reprocessed in high income countries due to their low abundance in the municipal waste stream
Object shape	Bottles are largely cylindrical, trays for meat are often rectangular with an opening along one or two faces	• Non-conforming –dominant objects may not be easily separable (sortable) by mechanical methods which may be calibrated to particular target shapes
Dimension	Packaging containers are often three dimensional whereas wrapping is comparatively two dimensional	• Sorting equipment may select two dimensional plastic items alongside other two dimensional objects such as writing or news paper
Material thickness	Commonly occurring plastic objects can range in thickness from a few microns to tens of millimetres	• Material that is too thin may not be easily sortable from materials that are thicker as the sorting machinery will
Object or fragment size	Plastic objects and fragments range in size from larger items such as panels in vehicles or water reservoirs to very small items such as toothpicks or drink closure gaskets	• Larger objects are sometimes challenging to store, comminute or compress. They are also less common and storage, transport and sorting systems may not be calibrated to handling them • Smaller objects are sometimes less likely to be targeted for reprocessing because a large quantity of small items is required to achieve a mass that is commercially viable to store, transport and reprocess. Smaller items may also be challenging to sort or may escape from sorting, storage and transport systems.
Flexibility	Films (foils) are more flexible than rigid containers for instance	• Flexible foils are challenging to separate using machinery which often relies on classification using air jets which are calibrated for rigid items and which are less accurate for selecting flexible plastics of different sizes.
Co-occurrence as part of an assembly	The dominant, or 'target' plastic type may occur with other plastic or non-plastic items, objects or material as an assembly or composite material (sometimes referred to as multi-materials).	• If components or items are not easily separable, then the whole object may be rejected: o It is technically challenging to separate polyethylene from food and drink cartons to a high enough quality for commercially viable reprocessing o Plastic packaging waste reprocessors are experienced at removing labels and closure assemblies from drinks bottles
Residues from previous use	Food or beverage residues are common in packaging plastics. In particular, flexible plastics have a high surface area and high static attraction which sometimes results in high surface contamination with residues	• Though expected by reprocessors in food packaging, food residues require cots and effort (e.g. surfactant and hot water) to remove and damage the business case for reprocessors. • Some critical contaminants can spread through a load causing rejection or very high decontamination costs.
Residues from handling, sorting and comingling	Single stream collection results in co-occurrence of materials with plastic. Material recovered from dumpsites or landfills is likely to have a high degree of surface contamination and may also include items and objects that have become adhered to or entrained with the plastic item.	• These types of residue may be of unknown composition. The risk that these substance or materials might be passed on to the secondary pro duct may preclude their use as such lowering their potential value.

Source: Based on Cottom et al. (2022[10]).

Robust and generalisable loss rates during sorting and reprocessing for plastic waste that has been collected for recycling are not commonly reported. Hestin, Faninger and Milios (2015[23]) proffered 18% and 30% for sorting and reprocessing respectively, based on surveys of European reprocessors. However, the nature of the survey was not reported and it is possible that plastic and non-plastic material and objects may have been reported alongside plastic losses. The ENV-Linkages model is only concerned with plastic so data for non-plastic were excluded from this component of the model.

A theoretical model based on material value was developed by the University of Leeds for plastic waste collected for recycling in high-income countries and low- and middle-income countries. Acknowledging that collection and sorting systems vary enormously worldwide, these two generalised groups were chosen because high income countries largely operate, either single stream collection of dry recyclate or co-collection of mixed plastic waste alongside metal packaging. Conversely in low-income and middle-income countries, collection of plastic waste for recycling is largely carried out by the informal recycling sector whose participants selectively collect materials and have much lower loss rates.

To estimate recycling losses, for packaging waste collected for recycling in high income countries, a dataset that reports a weighted average for all collection scheme types across the United Kingdom was used (Chruszcz and Reeve, 2018[24]). For LDPE, an approximation was made based on data reported by Lau et al. (2020[25]) (P_2O model). The reason for this is that LDPE is predominantly used as a as a flexible foil in packaging. Although LDPE is commonly collected for recycling, if it is from a post-consumer household source, it is almost never reprocessed in high income countries due to the challenges associated with surface contamination and selectivity detailed in Table A A.5. On the other hand, post-consumer LDPE from commercial sources is commonly recycled in high-income countries as it is easily collectable and separately and can be extruded dry, often without undergoing substantial cleaning. The result is a low loss rate. The assumptions from Lau et al. (2020[25]) were used to determine the proportion of material that was from commercial/institutional sources compared to household sources.

A probability of plastic waste items being selected at the sorting stage based on material, value was applied to each of the packaging and plastic types as detailed in Table A A.6 and Table A A.7. These probabilities were estimated using cost data summarised by SystemiQ and the Pew Charitable Trust (2020[26]), recyclability imperatives detailed by Recoup (2019[27]) and data on material actually recycled reported by Antonopoulos, Faraca and Tonini (2021[28]) and Plastics Recyclers Europe (2020[29]). In general HDPE, PET and LDPE were considered to have a 100% chance of being selected for reprocessing at the MRF and PVC and PS were considered to have 0% chance of being selected for reprocessing at the MRF. Although the evidence for PVC is more clear-cut, Antonopoulos, Faraca and Tonini (2021[28]) reported some post-consumer PS selection taking place in Europe. However these quantities are reported by Plastics Recyclers Europe (2020[29]) to be small and unusual, there is a likelihood that they do not refer to post-consumer material. The probability was set to zero for packaging but an overall probability of 98.5% was set to allow for some small occurrences of non-packaging material.

The loss rates at the reprocessor were approximated using data on plastic content reported by Roosen et al. (2020[30]); non-plastic content reported was excluded and the relative masses normalised.

High-income countries were assumed to have formal collection and the plastic packaging reported there was subject to loss rates at both sorting and reprocessing. Low and middle-income countries were assumed to have informal collection and the loss rates were therefore assumed to occur only at the reprocessing stage as informal actors selectively collect.

The assumptions for non-packaging applications were based largely on estimates from the project expert team, as there are no published data to support them. Consumer and institutional products were assumed to be the same as packaging except for PVC for which evidence from VinylPlus (2019[31]) indicates some recycling takes place. For the textiles (fibres), an estimate of 20% from financial modelling by Thompson et al. (2012[32]) was used in the absence of any other robust data. Readers should note that this loss rate is approximated on the basis that post-consumer textiles that been recycled into shoddy fibres and/or flocking (stuffing) rather than items that have been 'reused' and are out of scope of this study.

Table A A.5. Assumptions used to determine loss rates for plastic packaging waste that has been collected for recycling

Plastic item[1]	Plastic type by dominant polymer[1]	Weighted composition[1]	High-income countries			Low- & middle-income countries		
			Probability of being rejected before reprocessing[2]	Loss rate at reprocessor adjusted for wastage[3]	Net losses after sorting & reprocessing[4]	Probability of being rejected before reprocessing[2]	Loss rate at reprocessor adjusted for wastage[3]	Net losses after sorting & reprocessing[4]
Film LA recycling sacks	LDPE	2.9	100	0.00	2.90	25	1.00	0.75
FILM Other film	LDPE	11.2	100	0.00	11.20	25	1.00	2.88
FILM Carrier bags	LDPE	1.5	100	0.00	1.50	25	1.00	0.39
B PET NATURAL	PET	26.4	0	13.45	3.55	0	13.45	3.55
B PET JAZZ	PET	3.1	0	13.45	0.42	0	13.45	0.42
B HDPE Milk Bottles	HDPE	13.2	0	15.93	2.10	0	15.93	2.10
B HDPE All non-milk bottles	HDPE	7.7	0	15.93	1.23	0	15.93	1.23
B PVC ALL	PVC	0	100	0.00	0.00	100	0.00	0.00
B PP ALL	PP	0.4	50	21.31	0.24	0	21.31	0.09
Pack PET NATURAL	PET	10.3	0	14.63	1.51	0	14.63	1.51
Pack PET JAZZ	PET	0.5	0	14.63	0.07	0	14.63	0.07
Pack HDPE NATURAL	HDPE	0.1	100	0.00	0.10	0	14.63	0.01
Pack HDPE JAZZ	HDPE	0.6	100	0.00	0.60	0	14.63	0.09
Pack PVC ALL	PVC	0.1	100	0.00	0.10	100	0	0.10
Pack PP NATURAL	PP	4.4	100	0.00	4.40	0	2.08	0.09
Pack PP JAZZ	PP	5.3	100	0.00	5.30	0	2.08	0.11
Pack PS ALL	PS	1.5	100	0.00	1.50	100	0	1.50
Pack EPS ALL	EPS	0.4	100	0.00	0.40	100	0	0.40
Black PET	PET	1.9	100	0.00	1.90	100	0	1.90
Black PP	PP	0.6	100	0.00	0.60	100	0	0.60
Black Other	Mixture	1.1	100	0.00	1.10	100	0	1.10
Other	Mixture	0.2	100	0.00	0.20	100	0	0.20
Unidentified	Mixture	1.9	100	0.00	1.90	100	0	1.90
Plastic non-packaging	Mixture	4.4	100	0.00	4.40	100	0	4.40

1. (Chruszcz and Reeve, 2018[24]).
2. Assumptions based on polymer value SYSTEMIQ & The Pew Charitable Trust (2020[26]), recyclability reported by Recoup (2019[27]), and material reported to have been recycled by Antonopoulos, Faraca and Tonini (2021[28]) and Plastics Recyclers Europe (2020[29]).
3. (Roosen et al., 2020[30]). 4. Calculated.

Table A A.6. Average loss rates by plastic type and application for high income countries and low- middle income countries (MSW)

Plastic type by dominant polymer	Consumer & Institutional			Electrical/Electronic			Packaging[1]			Textile sector - clothing			Textile sector - others			Total (t y⁻¹)
	Mass (t y⁻¹)	Loss rate HIC (%)	Loss rate LMIC (%)	Mass (t y⁻¹)	Loss rate HIC (%)	Loss rate LMIC (%)	Mass (t y⁻¹)	Loss rate HIC (%)	Loss rate LMIC (%)	Mass (t y⁻¹)	Loss rate HIC (%)	Loss rate LMIC (%)	Mass (t y⁻¹)	Loss rate HIC (%)	Loss rate LMIC (%)	
Fibres										0.17	20.0[4]	20.0[4]	0.10	20.0[4]	10.0	0.27
HDPE										0.2	20.0[4]	20.0[4]	0.1	20.0[4]	10.0	0.3
LDPE, LLDPE	1.9	18.7	15.9	0.2	95.0	40.0	11.8	18.7[2]	15.9[2]							13.9
Other	1.4	79.0	80.5	0.2	100.0	50.0	6.9	79.0	80.5							8.5
PET	0.0	98.0	98.0	0.0	100.0	50.0	0.0	98.0	98.0							0.1
PP							9.6	17.6	17.6							9.6
PS	2.8	98.5	8.3	0.6	95.0	40.0	6.8	98.5	8.3							10.2
PUR	0.4	100.0	100.0	0.1	100.0	100.0	0.5	100.0	100.0							0.9
PVC	0.2	40.0[3]	10.0[3]	0.1	100.0[3]	100.0[3]	0.0	100.0[3]	100.0[3]							0.2

Source: Cottom et al. (2022[10]).

Table A A.7. Average loss rates by plastic type and application for high income countries and low- middle income countries (Non-MSW)

Plastic type by dominant polymer	Building and Construction			Industrial/Machinery			Other			Transportation - Other			Total (t y⁻¹)
	Mass (t y⁻¹)	Loss rate HIC (%)	Loss rate LMIC (%)	Mass (t y⁻¹)	Loss rate HIC (%)	Loss rate LMIC (%)	Mass (t y⁻¹)	Loss rate HIC (%)	Loss rate LMIC (%)	Mass (t y⁻¹)	Loss rate HIC (%)	Loss rate LMIC (%)	
Fibres							0.1	100.0	100.0	0.0	100.0	100.0	0.1
HDPE	1.0	20.0	5.0	0.1	20.0	5.0	1.1	20.0	5.0	0.6	98.0	90.0	2.9
LDPE, LLDPE	0.1	2.0	2.0	0.1	2.0	2.0	0.7	2.0	2.0	0.1	98.0	90.0	1.0
Other	0.0	100.0	100.0				0.2	100.0	100.0	0.1	100.0	100.0	0.4
PP	0.2	20.0	5.0	0.1	20.0	5.0				1.2	100.0	100.0	1.5
PS	0.1	100.0	100.0				0.1	100.0	100.0				0.2
PUR	0.1	40.0	10.0	0.0	40.0	10.0	0.4	40.0	10.0	0.2	100.0	100.0	0.6
PVC	0.6	18.7[3]	18.7[3]				0.4	18.7[3]	18.7[3]	0.1	100.0[3]	100.0[3]	1.1

1. Calculated from Chruszcz and Reeve (2018[24]) and Roosen et al. (2020[30]).
2. Calculated from Lau et al. (2020[25]).
3. Approximated from data reported by VinylPlus (2019).
4. Thompson Willis and Morley (2012[32]).

Source: Estimated by project team, if not stated in the notes.

For simplicity, OE6, O22, USA, and CAN were considered to have formal collection and all other regions were considered to have predominantly informal collection for recycling. The exception was People's Republic of China (hereafter 'China') which has been undergoing a partial transition from informal to formal collection for recycling. Due to the lack of robust data on the informal recycling sector, this component of the model assumed a 70 : 30 ratio for informal: formal collection for recycling. Table A A.8 puts forward the outcome of the technical calculations. The loss rates of PS and other have been lowered to 72.3%, the second highest level of losses between polymers, to represent that these polymers are sometimes recycled, but only in small quantities. Furthermore, to reflect that a large share of recycling of PET is rather a downcycling transformation of PET into fibres, the modelling assumes 35% of recycled PET is transformed into fibres.

Table A A.8. Average loss rates by plastic type and OECD region for MSW and non-MSW combined

Region	HDPE	LDPE, LLDPE	Other	PP	PS	PUR	PVC	Fibres	PET	Mean
USA	23.7	71.4	99.8	96.1	100	58.1	47.8	35	17.6	51.8
Canada	23.6	71.5	99.8	96.2	100	58.1	48.3	34.9	17.6	51.9
Other OECD America	16.7	70.8	95.2	18.1	100	30.8	52.9	42.2	17.6	31.3
OECD EU countries	22.6	69.9	99.8	93.8	100	54	38.2	41.7	17.6	49.7
OECD Non-EU countries	22.2	70.9	99.8	95.1	100	54	42.2	41.1	17.6	50.2
OECD Oceania	19.1	76.4	98.7	23.2	100	46.9	53.7	19.1	17.6	33.3
OECD Asia	21.2	72	99.8	94.9	100	51.8	39.9	33.3	17.6	49.6
Latin America	16.6	71.6	95.2	16.7	100	30.1	59.8	41.4	17.6	31.1
Other EU	21.1	74	97.3	30.2	100	51	51.9	35.2	17.6	35.8
Other Eurasia	21.1	74.3	97.2	29.4	100	50.8	56.5	34.4	17.6	35.9
Middle East & North Africa	17.7	73.3	95.9	20.2	100	37.2	52.6	33.2	17.6	32.4
Other Africa	16.5	71.9	95.5	15.9	100	29.3	61.1	44.4	17.6	31
China	18.5	73.9	97	41.4	100	40.7	63.3	31.8	17.6	37.7
India	17.2	76	96.1	16.1	100	35.2	69.2	20.2	17.6	31.9
Other non-OECD Asia	19.2	75	96.6	23.1	100	45.7	67	27.3	17.6	33.7
Mean	**20.3**	**72.3**	**98.1**	**59.8**	**100.0**	**47.2**	**48.9**	**34.1**	**17.6**	**42.1**

Source: Estimated by project team.

Economic flows

The ENV-Linkages model has been modified to include primary and secondary plastics production. While in the original database that the model relies on - the GTAP 10 database (Aguiar et al., 2019[5]) - primary and secondary plastic production are aggregated in the same sector (Rubber and plastic products; rpp), this study enhanced the representation of plastic to allow the distinction of a technology producing primary plastic and an alternative technology producing secondary plastics.

Similar to coal power plants and gas power plants both providing the same good (electricity), these two technologies produce a similar plastic good, with an elasticity of substitution of two. The production of plastic goods was thus split with two data sources. First, the total shares in production for primary and secondary plastics was taken from the volumes in tonnes described above (Ryberg et al. (2019[18]) for primary and own estimates for secondary plastics). Table A A.9 describes the calculated share for the secondary plastic production technology. Furthermore, the Exiobase 3 database (Stadler et al., 2018[8]) was used to adapt the cost structures. The main difference stem from the material inputs: the primary technology uses fossil fuels, while the secondary technology uses inputs from the chemical sector.

Table A A.9. Share of the secondary production technology

	Region	Share of secondary technology in 2015 (in tonnes)
OECD America	USA	3.9%
	Canada	4.8%
	Other OECD America	8.3%
OECD Europe	OECD EU countries	9.5%
	OECD Non-EU countries	6.1%
OECD Asia	OECD Pacific	5.6%
	OECD Oceania	2.8%
Other America	Latin America	9.6%
Eurasia	Other EU	5.2%
	Other Eurasia	3.6%
Middle East and Africa	Middle East & North Africa	3.6%
	Other Africa	5.9%
Other Asia	China	10.1%
	India	7.0%
	Other non-OECD Asia	5.0%

Source: Own calculations, based on Ryberg et al. (2019[18]) for primary and GVR (2020[9]) for secondary plastics.

Link between volumes and economic flows

To model plastics use in ENV-Linkages, data on plastics volumes by application and polymer have been linked to the detailed sectoral production structure of the model and the GTAP database that underlies the model. This is done for 14 polymer categories (Table A A.10).

Table A A.10. The large range of polymers allows for a multitude of plastics applications

Polymer	Abbreviation	Examples of use
Polypropylene	PP	Food packaging, automotive parts
Low-density polyethylene	LDPE	Reusable bags, food packaging film
High-density polyethylene	HDPE	Toys, shampoo bottles, pipes
Polyvinylchloride	PVC	Window frames, floor covering, pipes, cable insulation
Polystyrene	PS	Food packaging, insulation, electronic equipment
Polyethylene terephthalate	PET	Beverage bottles
Polyurethane	PUR	Insulation, mattresses
ABS, elastomers, biobased plastics, PBT, PC, PMMA, PTFE, ...	Other	Tyres, packaging, electronics, automotive, ...
Fibres made of different polymers	Fibres	Textile applications but also in many other sectors

Note: ABS stands for Acrylonitrile butadiene styrene, PBT for Polybutylene terephthalate, PC for Polycarbonates, PMMA for Poly (methyl methacrylate) (also known as plexiglas) and PFTE for Polytetrafluoroethylene.

Two main sources of data (volumes and economic flows described above) were used and put in coherence: (i) plastics production and consumption by economic sector by GTAP10 adapted with a primary and secondary production technology in monetary values, and (ii) regional flows of a range of plastic polymers and application-specific flows of plastics in tonnes. Table A A.11 summarises the mapping of the economic sectors and plastics applications. The initial values for this mapping are calibrated using data from (Ryberg et al., 2019[18]), combining polymer distribution by application at the global level with distribution of total plastics use by region and application. The polymer distribution was taken from the global averages and applied for each region taking into account the specific economic structures of the various regions.

Based on the initial picture in 2014, primary plastics use is projected following the flows of "plastics products" into the various corresponding demand sectors, from initial values, following the methodology developed for the OECD's Global Material Resources Outlook (OECD, 2019[4]). In particular, the model incorporates a series of plastics chains from initial production to final demand, either partially or in full depending on the particular structure of each regional economy. The basis for the chain includes flows from "oil" or "biomass" to "chemicals", that are then used for the production of "plastic products" which serve as intermediate goods or for sectors such as food product/appliances/motor vehicles/construction, before reaching final demand. The underlying assumption is that the coefficient (tonne/USD per polymer, per application, per region) that links monetary flows to physical flows (in tonnes), is kept constant. Plastics production then follows these demands, based on trade flows and plastics use.

There are three steps to project plastics use and the split of primary and secondary plastics to fulfil demand in baseline projections. First, total demand for plastics use is estimated following the evolution of the demand for the plastic commodity (produced by both the primary and secondary technologies). Second, as collected and sorted materials (further referred to as plastic scrap) are – after correcting for loss rates (see Annex section on Losses from sorting and reprocessing) - generally fully used to produce secondary plastics, the tonnes of secondary plastics follow the growth of the secondary sector in the ENV-Linkages projections. Third, the volumes of primary are calculated as a residual between the two. This is fully consistent as the demand for the plastic commodity relies on the growth of the primary and secondary technology, such that total demand for plastics is met.

Table A A.11. Mapping of plastics use by application to economic sectors

Input sectors	Applications	Output sectors	Polymers*
Plastic products	Building & Construction	Construction	ABS, ASA, SAN; Bioplastics; HDPE; LDPE, LLDPE; PP; PS; PUR; PVC; Other
	Consumer & Institutional products	Accommodation and food service activities; Air transport; Education; Health; Insurance; Lumber; Non-metallic minerals; Business services; Other manufacturing; Public services; Land transport; Pulp, paper and publishing; Real estate; Textile; Water transport	ABS, ASA, SAN; Bioplastics; HDPE; LDPE, LLDPE; PP; PS; PUR; PVC; Other
	Electrical/Electronic	Electrical equipment; electronics	ABS, ASA, SAN; Bioplastics; HDPE; LDPE, LLDPE; PP; PS; PUR; PVC; Other
	Industrial/Machinery	Fabricated metal products; iron and steel; nonferrous metal; Machinery and equipment	HDPE; LDPE, LLDPE; PP; PUR
	Packaging	Food products; Chemical products	Bioplastics; HDPE; LDPE, LLDPE; PET; PP; PS; PUR; PVC; Other
	Personal care products	Chemical products	HDPE; PET
	Transportation - other	Motor vehicles; Public services; Other transport equipment	ABS, ASA, SAN; Bioplastics; Fibres; HDPE; LDPE, LLDPE; PP; PUR; PVC; Other
	Other	Other sectors	Other
Chemicals	Marine coatings	Other manufacturing, other transport equipment	Marine coatings
	Road markings	Construction	Road markings
	Textile sector - clothing	Textiles	Bioplastics; fibres
	Textile sector - other	Textiles	Fibres
	Transportation - tyres	Plastic products	Elastomers (tyres)

* See Table A A.10 for abbreviations and examples of use for those polymers.
Source: OECD ENV-Linkages model.

Modelling plastic waste and end-of-life fates in ENV-Linkages

Plastic waste is calculated linking plastics use to the lifespan distribution of different products. Specifically, it is calculated as a function of plastics use (in volumes), following Geyer, Jambeck and Law (2017[22]), using a methodology based on lifespan distributions,[1] under the assumption of global homogeneity.[2]

Plastic waste of different applications are grouped into three main categories: Municipal Solid Waste (MSW), Other and Markings & Microbeads. MSW includes packaging, consumer & institutional products, electrical/electronic and textiles. 'Other' incorporates waste that is not included in MSW, therefore mostly reflecting waste from industrial applications (including building and construction, industrial and machinery applications, transportation applications). Markings & Microbeads include marine coatings, road markings and personal care products.

End-of-Life Fates

Plastic waste is divided into different waste management streams (end-of-life fates) by applying end-of-life shares that vary across countries, polymers and waste categories. MSW and Other plastic waste categories can be (i) recycled, (ii) incinerated or (iii) discarded. The latter is further disaggregated into waste that is disposed of in sanitary landfills, mismanaged waste and, in the case of MSW, littering.[3] Littering is presented as included with mismanaged waste. It is is set as a constant share of municipal solid waste following the assumption in Jambeck et al. (2015[17]). Markings & Microbeads form a very small stream (by mass) that is assumed not to be managed and to leak directly to the environment.

The sources of end-of-life fate shares for the base year, 2019, vary across regions. Recycling (defined here as material that has been collected for recycling) shares for plastics are exogenously fixed based on a range of sources, primarily country sources (Table A A.12). Notably, for the EU the recycling rate reported by Plastics Europe (2020[33]) was adjusted to ensure that polymer specific recycling rates are within the range of the EU plastics packaging recycling rates. For China, the official recycling rate in 2017 was used (Ministry of Commerce, 2019[34]). Recycling rates for other non-OECD regions were based on estimates of MSW recycling rates from What a Waste 2.0 (Kaza et al., 2018[15]) and consultations with experts. For the Middle East & North Africa, Other Africa, Other Eurasia and Latin America regions, projections were adjusted to account for informal recycling that is not reported but typically recovers high value streams such as HDPE and PET bottles.

The recycling shares are further split across polymers by multiplying the recycling shares for plastics by factors that reflect the recyclability and value of individual polymers based on expert consultations and ensuring that the estimated recycled volumes do not exceed the recycling capacities subject to data availability. Overall, PET and HDPE are assumed to have the highest recycling rates, followed by LDPE, PP and PVC (for construction). PUR, fibres, elastomers, bioplastics, marine coatings and road markings are not recycled, while only a very small proportion of PS, ABS, ASA, SAN and other polymers can be recycled.

Table A A.12. Data sources for plastic recycling rates in base year

Region	Recycling Rate Source and Assumptions
USA	United States Envrionmental Protection Agency (EPA) (2020[35]; 2020[36])
Canada	Environment and Climate Change Canada (2019[37]) *
Other OECD America	Based on SEMARNAT (2020[38]) and FCH (2021[39])
OECD EU countries Other EU	Polymer-specific recycling rates have been determined based on expert opinion and applied to the volumes of polymers collected for recycling by ENV-Linkages.**
OECD Non-EU countries	Based on EU adjusted by the proportion of region's MSW recycling rate to EU MSW recycling rate from What a Waste 2.0 (Kaza et al., 2018[15])
OECD Asia	Plastic Waste Management Institute (2019[40]) and expert judgement to account for recycling rates in Korea
OECD Oceania	Australian Government (2020[41]) ***
Latin America	Based on Other OECD America adjusted to account for a larger informal sector
Other Eurasia	What a Waste 2.0 (Kaza et al., 2018[15])
Middle East & North Africa	What a Waste 2.0 (Kaza et al., 2018[15])
Other Africa	What a Waste 2.0 (Kaza et al., 2018[15])
China	China Recycling Industry Development Report (2013-2018) by the Ministry of Commerce (2019[34])
India	Central Pollution Control Board (2019[42]) and UNIDO (2020[43])
Other non-OECD Asia	What a Waste 2.0 (Kaza et al., 2018[15])

* An updated report is available: (Statistics Canada, 2022[44]).
** For the EU, the calculated recycling rate for total plastics has been benchmarked with the numbers presented by Plastics Europe (2020[33]). In ENV-Linkages, the total amount of plastics collected for recycling is slightly higher (the numerator of the recycling rate),while the amount of plastics taken into account for the calculation is substantially higher (the denominator: total plastics includes fibres and other rarely recycled plastics). So the total recycling rate of plastics in ENV-Linkages is lower than Plastics Europe (2020[33]).
*** An updated report is available: Government of Australia (2021[45]).

To account for unreported informal recycling (which leads to understating plastic recycling rates) or overly optimistic reported recycling rates, all reported recycling rates were sense-tested, adapted and validated leveraging on consultations with experts and modelling carried out by Ed Cook, Josh Cottom and Costas Velis from the University of Leeds.

The use of incineration as a waste treatment type is country-specific and related to historic elements and local population densities. The share of plastic waste that is incinerated is strongly correlated with the share of total solid waste that is incinerated. Therefore, the incineration shares are set so that the ratio of the incineration share to the non-recycled share is equal to the corresponding ratio for total MSW from the What a waste 2.0 database (Kaza et al., 2018[15]). Moreover, the same incineration shares apply for non-MSW plastic waste, namely the 'Other' waste category.

Regarding discarded waste, its share is equal to the residual, under the assumption that 2% of MSW is littered at all times to account for the unaccounted potential losses to the environment (Jambeck et al., 2015[17]). The discarded share is further split into sanitary landfilled and mismanaged waste. In this analysis, mismanaged waste includes open dumping and unaccounted waste treatments for all income levels apart from lower and lower middle income countries, for which also unspecified landfilling, waterway treatment and other categories are included based on country level data for MSW (Kaza et al., 2018[15]) and building on assumptions for the previous version of the database in (Jambeck et al., 2015[17]). In general, mismanaged plastic waste as a share of total plastic waste is expected to decrease with income level. Following this assumption and using MSW data from (Kaza et al., 2018[15]) , the share of mismanaged plastic waste was estimated by regressing the ratio of mismanaged waste to discarded waste on GDP per capita, accounting for regulatory differences between OECD and non-OECD countries using an OECD dummy. Specifically, the following regression was estimated for 156 countries for which complete data was available:

$$MIS_i/(MIS_i + LAN_i) = \alpha + \beta * ln(gdp\_pc_i) + OECD_i$$

where MIS_i = mismanaged waste/MSW, LAN_i = Landfilled waste/MSW, gdp_pc_i = GDP per capita and $OECD_i$ = dummy for OECD countries, i = country. Finally, the share for landfilled waste is equal to the residual.

Historical data for recycling, incineration and discarded shares of plastic waste are taken from Geyer, Jambeck and Law (2017[22]) for the period 1980-1990 for four regions – United States, EU, China and Rest of the World. Following, using granular data for MSW recycling and incineration rates from Kaza et al. (2018[15]), the historical shares for 1990 were mapped to the 15 regions within ENV-Linkages, and were linearly interpolated for the period 1990-2018 in line with the methodology previously applied in Geyer, Jambeck and Law (2017[22]). Historical data for mismanaged and landfilling following the same methodology as in the base year.

Modelling international trade in plastic waste

The model has been extended to include inter-regional trade in plastic waste per application and polymer type. Volumes of plastic waste exports and imports are calculated based on data from UN Comtrade (United Nations Statistics Division, 2020[46]) following two steps. First, total exports of plastic waste per country and polymer are estimated using the share of plastics exports (Comtrade) to plastic waste (output of ENV-Linkages). Second, exports are split into partner countries and polymers using the country and polymer weights in 2019 for projections, and historical data for the years before. Bilateral exports and imports weights per country (row weights) were calculated based on the bilateral data on exports and imports values for the period 2010-2019 (most recent and complete year) and for the four subcategories of plastic waste reported in the UN Comtrade database. The later were mapped to the polymer types included in ENV-Linkages (Table A A.13). To ensure that global trade balances, bilateral plastic waste imports per reporter-partner pair correspond to the bilateral export of the corresponding partner-reporter pair. Note that trade flows between countries that are grouped in a single region in the modelling framework are subsumed in the intra-regional accounting and thus excluded from inter-regional trade flows. Consequently, total trade flows in the model are around one-third lower than trade flows based on national data.

The end-of-life fates of plastic waste traded flows differ from the domestically treated waste to reflect the fact a high proportion of traded plastic waste tends to be recyclable. In particular, 50% of traded plastic waste is expected to be recycled, with the remaining being distributed across the other waste streams following the same proportions of end-of-life fates as domestically treated waste excluding littering.

Table A A.13. UN Comtrade plastic waste series mapping to polymers in ENV-Linkages

UN Comtrade code	Series Description	Polymers types in ENV-Linkages
3915	Waste, parings and scrap, of plastics	
391510	of polymers of ethylene	HDPE,LDPE, LLDPE, PET, PP,PUR, Elastomers (tyres)
391530	of polymers of styrene	PS
391530	of polymers of vinyl chloride	PVC
391590	of other	Fibres, Marine coatings, Road marking coatings, ABS, ASA, SAN, Other

Source: United Nations Statistics Division (2020[46]) and OECD ENV-Linkages.

Modelling plastic leakage to the environment (Technical University of Denmark, DTU)

Estimations on the leakage of plastics are based on an interaction of the ENV-Linkages Model with other dedicated models. Each of the dedicated models builds on earlier work that has passed peer review with respect to estimations for current plastics leakage. The sources for leakage to the environment are varied. Consequently, the modelling techniques to make projections on these flows differ. This section explains the methodology and parameters employed by Teddy Serrano, Alexis Laurent, and Morten Ryberg from the section for Quantitative Sustainability Assessment at the Technical University of Denmark (DTU) to make projections on leakage of macro and micro plastics into the environment.

Leakage of macroplastics

For losses of macroplastics, four main categories have been considered: mismanaged municipal solid waste, mismanaged non-municipal solid waste, littering, and losses from marine activities. Plastic waste generation is calculated by the ENV-Linkages model as explained in the previous sections. The methodology employed for projections in the four categories are as follows:

- **Mismanaged MSW** was calculated from plastic waste generation and the estimated shares of MSW which is mismanaged, i.e. disposed of in landfills located in low-income countries or in dumpsites. Mismanaged MSW was retrieved from the ENV-Linkages model.
- **Mismanaged non-MSW** was also retrieved from the ENV-Linkages model. Due to a lack of data on the fate of mismanaged non-MSW, the share of mismanaged non-MSW lost to the environment is assumed to be equal to the share of mismanaged MSW lost to the environment (32%).
- Losses occurring via **littering** were calculated as the fraction of MSW in two steps. First, in line with Jambeck et al. (2015[17]) and studies carried out for the United Kingdom and Belgium (OVAM, 2018[47]; Resource Futures, 2019[48]), it was assumed that 2% of MSW is littered. Second, a substantial fraction of this littered waste happens in an urban environment and is cleaned up before it makes it to the environment. It is assumed that between 15% and 40% of littered waste is not captured by street sweeping, storm drain catchments and pump stations (Jambeck et al., 2015[17]). The estimated share of litter lost to the environment in each region was established according to the income level (as GNI/cap, US dollars), with lower shares for the high-income countries, as illustrated in (Table A A.14).
- **Losses from marine activities** (fishing gear and non-netting waste) were calculated based on production data on fishing gear in Europe (PRODCOM, 2016) (Eunomia, 2018[49]; Eurostat, n.d.[50]) upscaled to the rest of the world based on the projected growth of fishing activity to 2060 (from ENV-Linkages model), the assumption that 28% of plastic waste in the fishing and aquaculture sector comes from netting (Viool et al., 2018[51]), and the assumption that 15% of fishing gear material is lost every year during use (Viool et al., 2018[51]).

Table A A.14. Share of litter lost the environment considered based on income levels of the regions

Category	Low and lower-middle income	Upper-middle income	High income
Income level as GNI/cap [USD]	< 4 045	4 045-12 535	> 12 535
Share of litter lost to the environment	35%	25%	15%

Note: The World Bank country classifications by income level: 2020-2021 were used to allocate regions into low and lower-middle income, upper-middle income, or high income categories.
Source: World Bank (2020[52]).

Leakage of microplastics

For losses of microplastics, ten categories have been considered: microbeads, primary pellets, textile wash, tyre abrasion, road markings, brake dust, artificial turf, marine coatings, microplastics dust and wastewater sludge. This section presents the methodology employed to calculate projections of microplastics from the sources considered. For microplastics assumed to be collected by municipal wastewater networks, their fate is discussed at the end of this section.

The category "**microbeads**" includes losses of microplastics intentionally added to rinse-off personal care and cosmetic products, detergents, and maintenance products and discharged into municipal wastewaters during use. Projections for microbead consumption in personal care and cosmetics products (PCCPs) are derived from the output of the ENV-Linkages model. Based on data from ECHA (2020[53]), microbeads in detergents and maintenance products are twice the quantity of microbeads used in PCCPs. Because current policy trends show a progressive phase-out in the use of microbeads in rinse-off PCCPs (representing ca. 75% of total microbeads employed in PCCPs) (ECHA, 2020[53]), emissions of rinse-off microbeads were assumed to decrease from 2020 onwards. Based on the classification by Anagnosti et al (2021[54]), it was assumed that regions where bans have already been implemented would stop generating rinse-off microbeads losses by 2025; by 2030 for regions that proposed a ban; by 2035 for regions that reached an agreement on phase-out, and by 2040 for other regions. All microbeads are assumed to end up in the sewage system the year they are consumed.

The category "**primary pellets**" includes losses of primary plastic pellets occurring during production, transportation, and handling. Eunomia (2018[49]) estimated losses of plastic pellets occurring in 2015 in the EU, as originating from pellet production from raw materials, intermediary handling processes, processing and conversion, off-site waste management, and transportation and shipping. Assuming that leakage is proportional to the quantity of plastics produced, losses for the EU were scaled up to the entire world based on the European production share of plastics in 2015 (Plastics Europe, 2017[55]), and then allocated to geographical regions based on production shares. Losses from producers, recyclers, processors and offsite waste management were assumed to enter the sewage network as part of wastewater. Losses from Intermediary facilities and Shipping were assumed to be directly lost to the environment.

The category "**textile wash**" includes losses of synthetic microfibres lost during the washing of textile and apparel products. Projections are computed based on the total volume (tonnes) of plastics used in the category 'Wearing apparel' in a given year, and the assumption that during the lifespan of a textile product 0.4% of material is lost during washing. The share of material lost during the lifespan of a textile and apparel product was calculated based on an assessment of existing studies accounting for the share of synthetic material lost due to washings over several wash cycles (De Falco et al., 2019[56]; Pirc et al., 2016[57]). It was assumed that all microfibres released during washing enter the sewage system.

Three sources of microplastics emissions from road transport were taken into account:

- The category "**tyre abrasion**" includes losses of elastomers originating from the abrasion of tyre treads of cars, trucks, and motorcycles. Emission projections are derived from traffic data on the yearly activity in vehicle-km for passenger cars and in tonne-km for trucks from 2016 to 2060 in each region (retrieved from ENV-Linkages model). Wear rates (i.e. average mass of tyre tread lost per vehicle-km, by vehicle type) employed are those reported from Eunomia (2018[49]) and illustrated in (Table A A.15). For trucks, an average freight tonnage of 16t/vehicle was estimated, based on data from Eurostat (2018[58]). It was assumed that 45% of tyre treads is of elastomer content (Sommer et al., 2018[59]), and that the fate of the particles is as follows: 45% are retained in the asphalt pavement or remain close to the road, 45% is transported by road runoff and 10% is airborne, in line with available estimates of the fate of these particles following emission (OECD, 2021[60]). The share of particles lost into the environment is dependent on the rural/urban population share of each region from 2016 to 2060 (as also used in the ENV-Growth and therefore

ENV-Linkages model). In rural regions, road runoff and airborne emissions are considered as lost to the environment, whereas the particles trapped in the asphalt/road sides are not. In urban regions, airborne emissions are considered as lost to the environment, particles trapped in the asphalt/road sides are not, and particles as part of road runoff are assumed to go to a sewer system and treated as in wastewater the region where the loss occurs.

- The category "**road markings**" includes losses from markings applied to road surfaces. Plastics use projections for road markings are generated by the ENV-Linkages model, and the fate of road marking particles has been assumed to be similar to that of tyre abrasion particles due to a lack of data.
- The category "**brake wear**" includes losses of synthetic polymers originating from the wear of brake pads and other components. From the average composition of brake pads described by Hallal et al. (2013[61]), the polymer content of brake pads was assumed to be 23%. Similarly to the methodology used for tyre abrasion, loss estimations were based on annual traffic data from 2016 to 2060 and abrasion rates based on calculations by Eunomia (2018[49]) and illustrated in (Table A A.16).The fate of brake dust microplastics was assumed to be similar to that of tyre abrasion particles.

Table A A.15. Tyre wear rates used

Values in grams per vehicle-kilometre (g/vkm)

Vehicle type	Passenger cars	Trucks
Upper	0.05	0.6
Lower	0.25	1
Average	0.1	0.8

Source: ETRMA values, as reported in (Eunomia, 2018[49]).

Table A A.16. Brake pads wear rates used

Values in grams per vehicle-kilometre (g/vkm)

Vehicle type	Passenger cars	Trucks
Upper	0.011	0.047
Lower	0.02	0.084
Average	0.016	0.066

Source: (Eunomia, 2018[49]).

The category "**artificial turf**" includes losses of plastics from the infill of sport turfs. Estimates in the literature find losses of 300-730 kg / year per field in Denmark and 550 kh/year in Sweden (Løkkegaard, Malmgren-Hansen and Nilsson, 2018[62]; Swedish EPA, 2019[63]). According to ECHA (2020[53]), the number of artificial sport pitches will reach 39 000 by 2020 and average infill use is between 40 and 120 tonnes of material. Assuming that annual infill consumption is 1-4% of the total volume (ECHA, 2020[53]; Eunomia, 2018[49]), average yearly infill is 101 400 tonnes. Estimates for Europe were upscaled to other regions based on artificial turf market size figures (from (ResearchNester, 2021[64])) and GDP growth projections to 2060 (from the ENV-Linkages model). Based on the composition of rubber granulate used as infill, it was assumed that 96% of all infill is microplastics.[4] In terms of losses and environmental fate, it was assumed that:

- 10% of rubber granulate particles are lost to the surrounding soil (and therefore considered as lost to the environment).

- 10% are discharged with water. Based on the rural share of the population in each region provided by the ENV-Linkages model from 2016 to 2060, it was assumed those 10% are considered as directly lost to the environment in rural areas. In urban areas, they are considered to enter the wastewater network. For those reaching a treatment system (primary, secondary, tertiary), all particles are assumed to be removed and therefore end up in sewage sludge, since turf crumbles' significant size allows them to be usually well removed in treatment plants (Løkkegaard, Malmgren-Hansen and Nilsson, 2018[62]).

The category "**marine coatings**" includes losses of paint and coatings worn off from ships and marine structures. It is expected that 10% of plastics employed in the production of marine coatings is lost over the lifespan of the product, directly into the environment (Boucher and Friot, 2017[65]).

The category "**microplastics dust**" is used to refer to unintentional losses of microplastics occurring during the use phase of a number of products. Specifically, in the model five sources were taken into account: microplastics in household textile dust, the wear off of paint from interior surfaces, the wear off of paint from exterior surfaces, losses from construction and demolition activities, and shoe sole abrasion. These categories do not embody an exhaustive list of all microplastics losses not reported in other sections, but only those for which sufficient literature has been found to include them in this model.

For each source, with the exception of household textile dust, projections are based on reported losses at the scale of a country or the European Union, which have been scaled down to calculate per capita emissions or per USD of GDP at constant PPP created, and finally scaled up to calculate the emissions for the entire world for each year between 2016 and 2060, using data provided by the ENV-Linkages model. For interior and exterior paints, as well as exterior construction and demolition sources of dust, GDP was used as a scaling proxy under the assumption that the use of these materials is correlated to wealth.

For shoe sole abrasion, population data was considered a more relevant proxy. Because a person can only wear one pair of shoes at a time, the wear of shoes is assumed to be dependent on the activity of the person and not on wealth. In lack of better data, trends in the use of shoes are assumed to follow population trends. The model does not take into account future changes in the number of people using shoes nor future developments in shoe sole material composition.

The losses estimations of household textile dust are based on a recent study, according to which airborne-emitted synthetic fibres from textile and apparel products could represent a third of those lost to water during washings (De Falco et al., 2020[66]). Therefore, the emissions of textile fibres previously calculated during textile wash were used to calculate the losses of household textile dust.

A summary of the sources used to calculate those losses can be found in Table A A.17. It was assumed that 15% of household textile dust (Kawecki and Nowack, 2020[67]) and 100% of microplastics from interior paints ends up in wastewater. For other sources, particles emitted in urban areas were also assumed to enter wastewater systems, whereas they were considered lost to the environment for rural areas.

Table A A.17. Losses sources of microplastics dust and losses values for the year 2060

Microplastics dust sources	Reference (Country or region)	Scaling method
Household textile dust	ENV-Linkages model's textile projections	-
Interior paints	(Eunomia, 2018[49])(EU)	GDP (USD, PPP)
Exterior paints	(Eunomia, 2018[49]) (EU)	
Exterior construction and demolition	(Kawecki and Nowack, 2020[67]) (Switzerland)	
Shoe sole abrasion	(Lassen et al., 2016[68]) (Denmark)	Population

The category "**wastewater sludge**" includes losses of microplastics occurring via the application of wastewater sludge to land, as detailed in the next section.

The wastewater pathway and losses via sludge application to land

A large share of the emitted microplastics end up in wastewater or stormwater runoff (OECD, 2021[60]). Hence, an overview of relevant end-of-pipe treatment systems is needed in order to estimate the quantities of microplastics that reach the environment. The model considers a number of possible fates for microplastics, in line with Ryberg et al. (2019[18]) and as illustrated in Figure A A.2. Ultimately, microplastics can either be retained by wastewater treatment or be lost to the environment.

Figure A A.2. Fate of microplastics in wastewaters

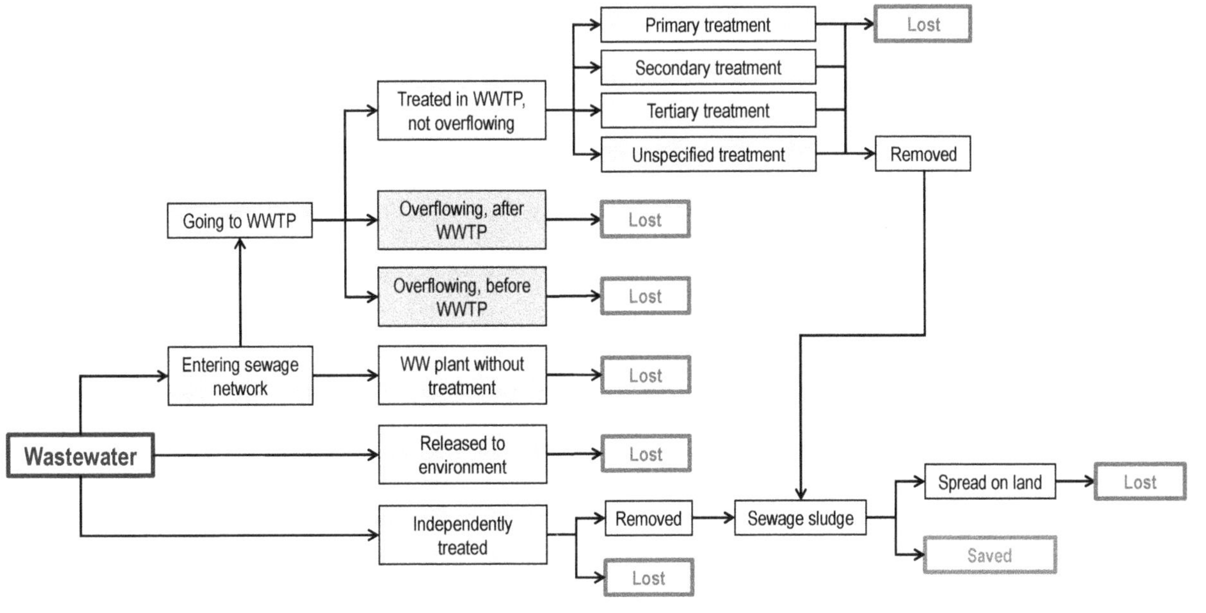

Source: Methodology adapted from (Ryberg et al., 2019[18]).

The share of microplastics emissions ending up in different pathways varies according to state of wastewater infrastructure coverage in different countries. Allocation shares for each fate were estimated on a regional level. For each region, most allocation shares leading to treatments (represented by yellow boxes in Figure A A.2) were calculated using allocation shares averages of the countries composing the region, weighted by the population of each country. An assessment of data for 187 countries showed high variability in data availability and quality across countries. For most OECD countries, as well as Brazil, Colombia and South Africa, the latest available data from (OECD.stat, 2017[69]) was used and considered representative for wastewater treatment in 2016. For China and India, allocation shares were based on Kalbar, Muñoz and Birkved (2017[70]).

For other countries, it has been decided to rely on data from the WHO/UNICEF Joint Monitoring Programme for Water Supply, Sanitation and Hygiene (JMP, 2020[71]). This data is used for monitoring development in SDG 6.3.1 "Proportion of safely treated domestic wastewater flows (%)". In the dataset, the following classification is used:

- Safely managed: use of improved facilities, which are not shared with other households and where excreta are safely disposed in situ or transported and treated off-site.
- Basic: use of improved facilities, which are not shared with other households.
- Limited: use of improved facilities shared between two or more households.
- Unimproved: use of pit latrines without a slab or platform, hanging latrines or bucket latrines.

- Open defecation: disposal of human faeces in fields, forests, bushes, open bodies of water, beaches and other open spaces or with solid waste (JMP 2020).

The "safely managed" share of the wastewater was assumed to at least undergo primary treatment. The remaining share of the wastewater is modelled as being directly released to the environment. Although this is a conservative assumption, it was not possible to retrieve more detailed data on the treatment levels for certain regions.

Based on information from the literature, a microplastics removal rate was assigned to different levels of wastewater treatment (primary, secondary, and tertiary, as illustrated in Table A A.18) and employed to calculate the fate of microplastics passing through wastewater treatment, following the approach by Ryberg et al. (2019[18]). The removal rate of unspecified and independent wastewater treatment was assumed equal to the removal rate for primary treatment. Regional data on loss of wastewater due to overflow (represented by blue boxes in Figure A A.2) is generally lacking and the loss share was therefore modelled using the same loss shares for all regions. It is estimated that 0.6% and 2.4% of the wastewater is lost due to overflow of the sewer system and of the waste water treatment plant (WWTP), respectively (Magnusson et al., 2016[72]; Ryberg et al., 2019[18]).

Table A A.18. Microplastics removal rate for different levels of wastewater treatment

Treatment technology	Microbeads	Fibres	Other microplastics
Primary treatment	86%	87%	69%
Secondary treatment	92%	92%	96%
Tertiary treatment	99%	96%	99%

Source: Calculations from (Michielssen et al., 2016[73]).

Because the share of wastewater treated is likely to evolve between 2019 and 2060, multiple linear regressions (MLRs) were carried out to estimate the development in the share of wastewater going to a treatment plant and the treatment technology in place (i.e. primary, secondary or tertiary). The microplastics removal rates within a country were also derived based on MLRs. The MLR models use values for 2019, GDP per capita [USD PPP] and the region on which the country is located as input parameters. The MLRs were weighted with the population of each country. Due to a lack of data, the development in wastewater losses due to overflow of the sewers or WWTPs, the share of wastewater undergoing independent treatment, or the share of sewage sludge applied to land were modelled as being constant between 2016 and 2060.

Wastewater sludge is the waste by-product of wastewater treatment containing the water pollutants removed from the influent. Sludge reuse for agricultural applications is encouraged in several countries, mainly due to the high nutrient content and its beneficial effects on crops, as well as to reduce the need for landfilling or incineration. However, recent evidence suggests that this practice leads to the transfer of a share of the microplastics retained during wastewater treatment to agricultural land (Nizzetto, Futter and Langaas, 2016[74]).

Losses into the environment via agricultural land were calculated based on the share of sludge generated in a given year that is applied on agricultural land. Due to data scarcity on the fate of microplastics during sludge treatment, it was assumed that there is no further removal of microplastics before sludge is applied to land (Ryberg et al. 2019). For Canada, China and the United States, the share of sludge applied to agricultural land follows the fractions reported by Rolsky et al. (2020[75]) (i.e. 43%, 45% and 55% for Canada, China and the United States, respectively). Due to a lack of data, the share of wastewater sludge applied on agricultural fields in all other countries was assumed to be equal to the European average (i.e. 46%) (Eurostat, 2020[76]).

Modelling plastic leakage to terrestrial and aquatic environments (University of Leeds)

This section explains the methodology and parameters employed by the experts from the University of Leeds to make projections on the fate of plastics after it becomes waste.

Waste management and leakage to environment

The end-of life fate, including plastic waste emissions to the environment from the waste management system were quantified for the Baseline 2019 scenario using the Spatiotemporal Quantification of Plastic Pollution Origins and Transportation (SPOT) model (Cottom et al., 2022[10]). The SPOT model predominantly estimates material flow at Level 2 and 3 administrative boundary resolution, and therefore it had to be adapted to provide outputs at national (Level 0) which were aggregated to OECD regional level. Material flow analysis (Brunner and Rechberger, 2016[77]) was the general methodological approach underpinning the distribution of plastic waste generation estimates provided by the ENV-Linkages model and used to describe its flow through the waste system as illustrated in the conceptual diagram (Figure A A.3). This hybrid model is described hereafter as the 'ENV-Linkages-SPOT plugin'.

Figure A A.3. ENV-Linkages-SPOT plugin model structure

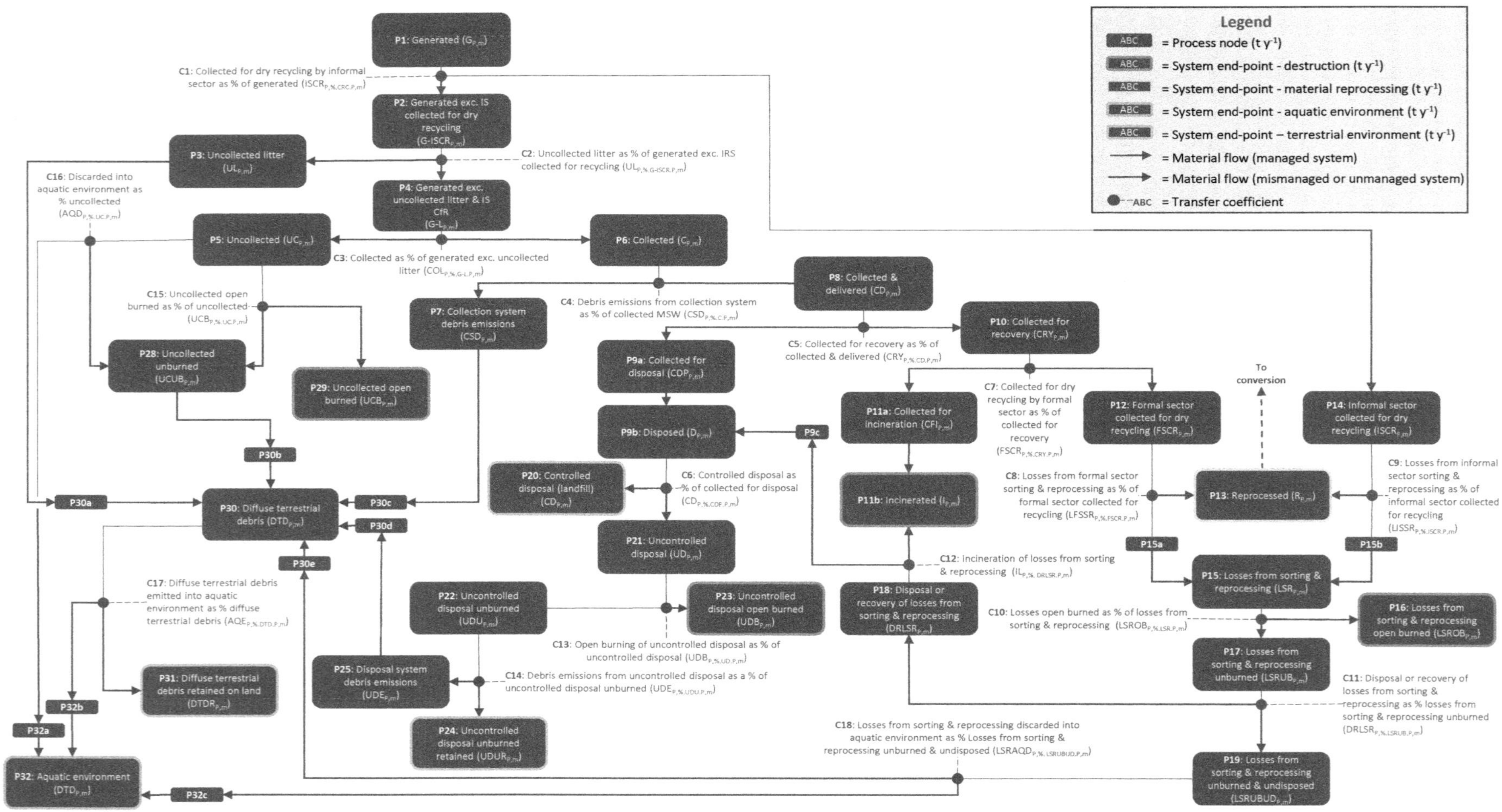

Source: Cottom et al. (2022[10]).

Model structure and basic assumptions

Data were processed using the SPOT model in three stages: 1) Municipal waste generation, composition and management data from 2007 to 2021 from four sources, Waste Wise Cities Tool (WaCT) (UN Habitat, n.d.[78]); Wasteaware Cities Benchmark Indicators (WABI) (Wilson et al., 2012[79]); United Nations Statistical Division (UNSD) (UNSD, 2021[80]); and What a Waste 2.0 (WAW2) (Kaza et al., 2018[15]), were cleaned and normalised according to a common denominator, resulting in approximately 500 data records; 2) Random forest machine learning used predictive variables to model data for the remaining 85 088 global municipalities that had no data; 3) Probabilistic material flow analysis used the interpolated data to allocate the flow of waste from the point of generation through managed, mismanaged and unmanaged process nodes.

The ENV linkages-SPOT plugin uses the aggregated country level (Level 0) mass of rigid and flexible plastic waste estimated by the SPOT model, to determine transfer coefficients used to allocate material between process nodes. However, the SPOT does not present all data in the format required for the ENV-Linkages-SPOT plugin to function, so adjustments are made.

Incineration data were not specifically reported in this version of the SPOT model due to the lack of spatial granularity in the source data, which resulted in their aggregation with other types of recovery. Therefore, data obtained from Kaza et al. (2018[15]) were used in the ENV-Linkages-SPOT plugin alongside further research which was used to verify or amend some data points as detailed in Table A A.19.

Table A A.19. Validation of incineration data

Country	Mass of MSW incinerated (t y^{-1})	Proportion of MSW incinerated (%)	Verification / addition	Source
Liechtenstein	8 268	25.4	add	Liechtenstein Institute for Strategic Development (2020[81])
Azerbaijan	400 000	9.6	add	Islamic Development Bank (2020[82])
Vietnam	1 602 764	5.4	add	Tun et al. (2020[83])
Thailand	1 389 627	5.0	Verified	Tun et al. (2020[83])
Ethiopia	350 000	2.5	add	Cleere et al. (2020[84]) and Muuben et al. (2019[85])
Lao PDR	32 637	2.0	add	Tun et al. (2020[83])
India	1 916 250	0.7	add	Central Pollution Control Board (2021[86])
Myanmar	21 900	0.2	add	JFE Engineering Corporation (2017[87])

Source: Kaza et al. (2018[15]).

The proportion of waste collected for recycling by the informal recycling sector was estimated using a model adapted from one first presented by Lau et al. (2020[25]) (P_2O). Additional data reported by (Cottom et al., 2022[10]) for average productivity per waste picker, number of waste pickers per head of urban population, proportion of waste collected that is plastic (Table A A.20) and an assumption that workers operate for 235 days on average accounting for sickness, vacation and other downtime.

Table A A.20. Data used to model the activities of the informal recycling sector

Income group (World Bank)	Proportion of urban population that is an informal waste worker (%)	Productivity per waste picker (kg d^{-1})	Proportion of waste collected by informal recycling sector that is plastic (%)
High income	0.01	37.0	5
Upper middle-income	0.26	37.0	28
Lower middle income	0.19	37.0	35
Low income	0.14	37.0	35

Source: Cottom et al. (2022[10]).

Dumping mismanaged waste in water

Data to support the deliberate dumping of waste into water by waste generators are scarce. This section presents a rapid review of census data that indicate the mass deposited directly into water by householders in the absence of a waste collection services (Table A A.21). Acknowledging the uncertainty in the data, high variability and the fact that the data do not necessarily represent the global population, a conservative approach was adopted and approximated by using the mean of the country level median proportion treated in this way (4.8% of uncollected waste).

Table A A.21. Deliberate dumping into water

Country	Proportion of population engaged in behaviour (median % of uncollected waste)	Source
Malawi	1.0	(National Statistical Office, 2020[88])
Guatemala	1.8	(Guatemala, Instituto Nacional de Estadística, 2018[89])
Indonesia	7.6	(Sub Direktorat Statistik Lingkungan Hidup, 2014[90])
Fiji	0.5	(Fiji Bureau of Statistics, 2018[91])
Brazil	0.4	(Instituto Brasileiro de Geografia e Estatística, 2010[92])
Bolivia	15.6	(Instituto Nacional de Estadistica, 2012[93])
Samoa	0.4	(Samoa Bureau of statistics, 2019[94])
Ethiopia	10.9	(Population Census Commission, 2007[95])

Plastic debris emissions to the environment

Waste transfer from the terrestrial to aquatic environment was estimated using transfer ratios suggested by Lau et al. (2020[25]) and detailed in Table A A.22.The GWPv4 (2015) (United Nations, 2019[96]) UNAdj population density map (CIESIN, 2018[97]) was used to estimate the proportion of rural and urban inhabitants using definition from was estimated using Dijkstra and Poelman (2014[98]) that a grid cell has >300 population and >5 000 inhabitants in contiguous cells. The urban and rural attribution was mapped onto the HydroSHEDS 30 arc river and coastline dataset. Population data for countries above 60°N latitude were approximated using ratios for nearest similar countries which were below 60°N.

Waste transfer from the terrestrial to aquatic environment was estimated using transfer ratios suggested by Lau et al. (2020[25]) and detailed in Table A A.22. The GWPv4 (2015) (United Nations, 2019[96]) UNAdj population density map (CIESIN, 2018[97]) was used to estimate the proportion of rural and urban inhabitants using definition from was estimated using Dijkstra and Poelman (2014[98]); that a grid cell has >300 population and >5 000 inhabitants in contiguous cells. The urban and rural attribution was mapped onto the HydroSHEDS 30 arc river and coastline dataset. Population data for countries above 60°N latitude were approximated using ratios for nearest similar countries which were below 60°N.

Table A A.22. Plastic waste transfer rate from terrestrial to aquatic environment

Flexibility	Distance population to aquatic environment	Proportion plastic waste in terrestrial environment that transfers to the aquatic environment (% wt.)
Rigid	<1 km	10
	>1 km	3
Flexible	<1 km	35
	>1 km	8

Source: Lau et al. (2020[25]).

Projected mismanaged waste data to 2060

Transfer coefficients from the 2019 baseline in ENV-Linkages-SPOT plugin were used to distribute mismanaged waste emissions to the environment for future years, driven by the mass of mismanaged waste projected by the ENV-Linkages model. Table A A.23and Table A A.24 show these multipliers by region for mismanaged waste and Table A A.25 and Table A A.26 show the multipliers used to distribute waste that has not accumulated in dumpsites through each of the societal and waste management nodes through which it may transfer.

Table A A.23. Transfer coefficients used to distribute mismanaged plastic waste from MSW to four main components of the ENV-Linkages-SPOT plugin

Percentage of. mismanaged waste per year in million tonnes (Mt)

Region	Dumpsite (uncontrolled)	Open burning	Terrestrial environment	Aquatic environment
Canada	60%	26%	10%	4%
China	39%	45%	10%	6%
Other EU	26%	54%	13%	7%
India	57%	30%	8%	5%
Latin America	51%	36%	8%	5%
Middle East and North Africa	60%	31%	7%	3%
OECD EU countries	50%	31%	14%	5%
Other Africa	38%	31%	21%	10%
Other OECD America	42%	43%	9%	6%
OECD Oceania	60%	27%	10%	3%
Other non-OECD Asia	49%	33%	12%	6%
OECD Non-EU countries	41%	43%	11%	5%
OECD Pacific	26%	36%	29%	9%
Other Eurasia	57%	33%	7%	4%
USA	56%	28%	11%	5%
World	49%	35%	11%	6%

Source: ENV-Linkages-SPOT plugin.

Table A A.24. Transfer coefficients used to distribute mismanaged plastic waste from Non-MSW to four main components of the ENV-Linkages-SPOT plugin

Percentage of mismanaged waste per year in million tonnes (Mt)

Region	Dumpsite (uncontrolled)	Open burning	Terrestrial environment	Aquatic environment
Canada	60%	26%	12%	3%
China	39%	45%	12%	4%
Other EU	26%	54%	15%	5%
India	57%	30%	9%	3%
Latin America	52%	37%	9%	3%
Middle East and North Africa	60%	31%	7%	2%
OECD EU countries	50%	31%	15%	4%
Other Africa	39%	31%	25%	6%
Other OECD America	42%	44%	10%	4%
OECD Oceania	60%	27%	10%	3%
Other non-OECD Asia	49%	33%	14%	4%
OECD non-EU countries	41%	43%	12%	4%
OECD Pacific	26%	36%	32%	6%
Other Eurasia	57%	33%	8%	2%
USA	56%	28%	13%	3%
World	50%	35%	12%	3%

Source: ENV-Linkages-SPOT plugin.

Table A A.25. Transfer coefficients used to attribute mismanaged plastic waste from MSW excluding waste in dumpsites to components of the ENV-Linkages-SPOT plugin

Percentage of mismanaged waste excluding dumpsites per year in million tonnes (Mt)

Region	Uncollected litter	Uncollected dumped on land	Uncollected dumped into aquatic environment	Collection system debris	Disposal system debris	Uncollected open burned	Uncontrolled disposal open burned	Losses from sorting & reprocessing open burned	Losses from sorting & reprocessing mismanaged on land
Canada	18%	25%	18%	5%	2%	27%	35%	1%	3%
China	3%	17%	3%	2%	1%	55%	15%	3%	4%
Other EU	3%	18%	3%	1%	0%	63%	8%	1%	3%
India	2%	18%	2%	1%	1%	36%	31%	3%	5%
Latin America	2%	16%	2%	1%	1%	47%	25%	2%	3%
Middle East and North Africa	2%	16%	2%	2%	2%	38%	35%	2%	3%
OECD EU countries	15%	27%	15%	7%	1%	37%	24%	2%	3%
Other Africa	1%	34%	1%	1%	1%	31%	15%	4%	8%
Other OECD America	2%	15%	2%	2%	1%	55%	17%	2%	4%
OECD Oceania	14%	24%	14%	5%	2%	31%	36%	1%	2%
Other non-OECD Asia	2%	23%	2%	1%	1%	39%	23%	3%	5%
OECD non-EU countries	4%	18%	4%	2%	1%	54%	17%	2%	3%
OECD Pacific	25%	39%	25%	11%	0%	39%	8%	2%	4%
Other Eurasia	2%	16%	2%	1%	1%	42%	32%	2%	3%
USA	15%	25%	15%	7%	1%	31%	30%	2%	3%
World	3%	21%	3%	2%	1%	43%	22%	3%	4%

Source: ENV-Linkages-SPOT plugin.

Table A A.26. Transfer coefficients used to attribute mismanaged plastic waste from Non-MSW excluding waste in dumpsites to components of the ENV-Linkages-SPOT plugin

Percentage of mismanaged waste excluding dumpsites per year in million tonnes (Mt)

Region	Uncollected litter	Uncollected dumped on land	Uncollected dumped into aquatic environment	Collection system debris	Disposal system debris	Uncollected open burned	Uncontrolled disposal open burned	Losses from sorting & reprocessing open burned	Losses from sorting & reprocessing mismanaged on land
Canada	18%	25%	18%	5%	2%	27%	35%	1%	3%
China	3%	17%	3%	2%	1%	55%	15%	3%	4%
Other EU	3%	18%	3%	1%	0%	63%	8%	1%	3%
India	2%	18%	2%	1%	1%	36%	31%	3%	5%
Latin America	2%	16%	2%	1%	1%	47%	25%	2%	3%
Middle East and North Africa	2%	16%	2%	2%	2%	38%	35%	2%	3%
OECD EU countries	15%	27%	15%	7%	1%	37%	24%	2%	3%
Other Africa	1%	34%	1%	1%	1%	31%	15%	4%	8%
Other OECD America	2%	15%	2%	2%	1%	55%	17%	2%	4%
OECD Oceania	14%	24%	14%	5%	2%	31%	36%	1%	2%
Other non-OECD Asia	2%	23%	2%	1%	1%	39%	23%	3%	5%
OECD non-EU countries	4%	18%	4%	2%	1%	54%	17%	2%	3%
OECD Pacific	25%	39%	25%	11%	0%	39%	8%	2%	4%
Other Eurasia	2%	16%	2%	1%	1%	42%	32%	2%	3%
USA	15%	25%	15%	7%	1%	31%	30%	2%	3%
World	3%	21%	3%	2%	1%	43%	22%	3%	4%

Source: ENV-Linkages-SPOT plugin.

Modelling plastic leakage to aquatic environments (Laurent Lebreton)

This section explains the methodology and parameters employed by Laurent Lebreton to make projections on the fate of waste plastics after they enter the environment. More specifically, the model calculates the amount of leaked plastics ending up in aquatic environments and assesses their mobility as well as degradation in rivers and oceans.

With a wide variety of polymer types, object shapes and sizes, and the dynamic nature of aquatic environments, quantifying sources and the fate of plastics in rivers, lakes, and the ocean is not trivial. Some studies have recently attempted to quantify the amount of mismanaged plastic waste generated by countries worldwide, which likely reach an aquatic environment (Borrelle et al., 2020[99]) and subsequently the ocean (Meijer et al., 2021[100]). These studies utilise spatial models describing the generation of mismanaged plastic waste in relation to topography and other environmental parameters. This section raised country-scale emission results to the modelled global regions represented in the ENV-Linkages model. The transport of emitted plastics was estimated considering geographical variations. Then the fate of plastics for the different regions was modelled as a function of polymer types predicted by projections of waste generation from various sectors of the economy. Finally, the mass of plastics accumulated in different aquatic environments for each region is reported.

To calculate inputs of plastics by region into aquatic environments, results from a previous study by Borrelle et al. (2020[99]) which estimated leakage of mismanaged plastic waste into rivers, lakes, and the ocean at a global scale were used. The model supporting the results of this study includes global high-resolution distribution of plastic waste generation derived from population density, gross domestic product (GDP) per capita, and country scale municipal waste statistics (Lebreton and Andrady, 2019[19]). The model then computes the probability for mismanaged plastic waste to reach an aquatic environment (rivers, lakes, and oceans) as a function of distance and terrain slope direction. By integrating over land, the study reports the national probability of emissions of plastics into aquatic environments, which is independent of the total amount of waste generated but may differ around the world as a function of population location and topography of countries (adapted from Borrelle et al. (2020[99])). In this study, the probability of emissions by region was computed by weighing country scale emission probability by population size and formulating a regional average including confidence intervals (Figure A A.4). The likelihood of plastic waste emissions varies by region. OECD Oceania (Australia and New Zealand) and OECD Pacific (Japan and Korea) have the highest chance of leakage into aquatic environments, reflecting inputs from island nations with predominantly coastal populations.

Figure A A.4. Probability of mismanaged and littered plastic waste emissions into aquatic environments

Weighted probability of emissions by OECD ENV-Linkages model regions

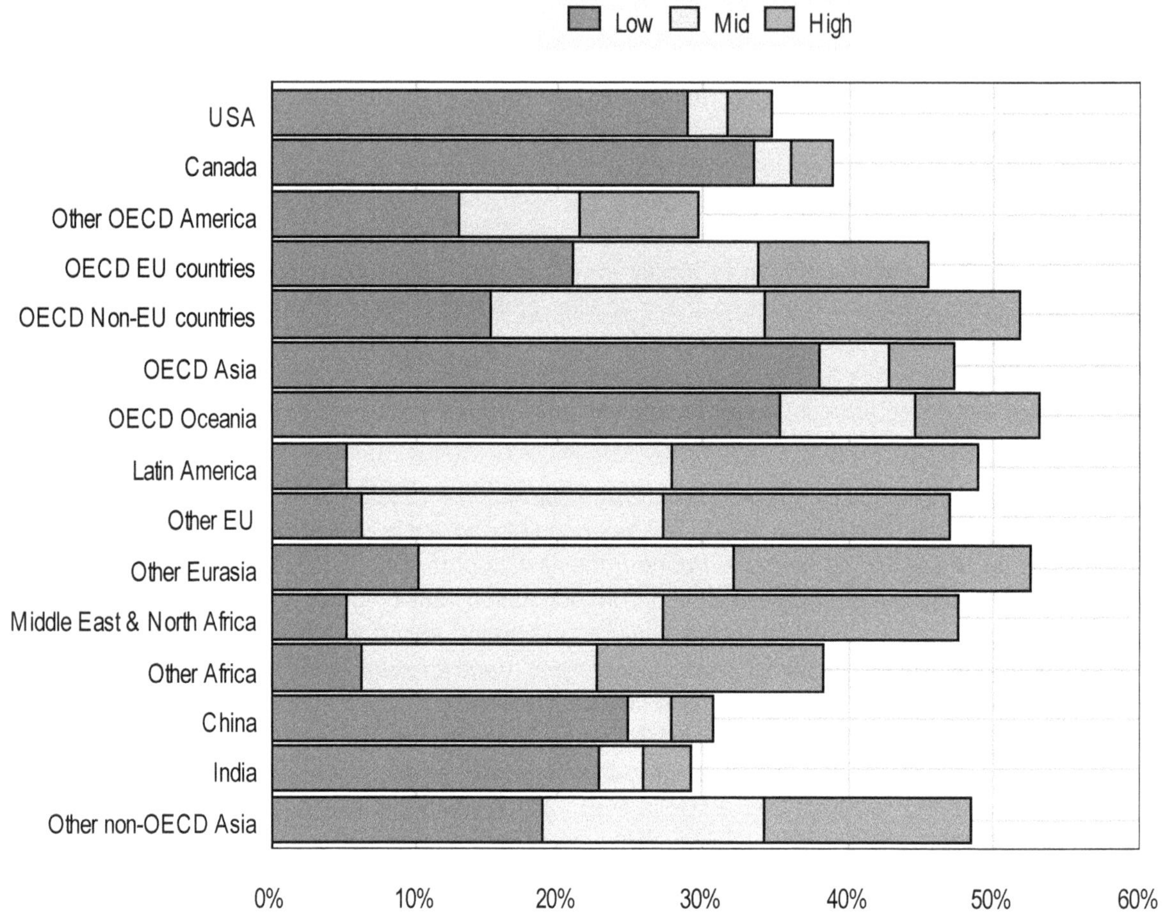

Note: The probability was calculated as the average of the country-scale fraction of emissions weighted by the population size of countries.
Source: Calculations based on Borrelle et al. (2020[99]).

StatLink https://stat.link/51gc96

In freshwater, floating plastics may be transported downstream and sinking plastics (plastics with a larger density than freshwater, e.g. PET, PVC or PS) will inevitably reach bottom sediments. Floating plastics may also be retained in freshwater environments in vegetation bordering the river, sediments in the river banks, artificial barriers (e.g. dams), or lakes. Some floating plastics may also be colonised by organisms and sink due to loss of buoyancy. A recent study estimating direct global inputs of plastics into the ocean via waterways reported that only 1% to 2% of mismanaged plastics generated annually have a chance to reach the sea globally within a year (Meijer et al., 2021[100]). The study utilised the same probability framework derived from location and quantities of mismanaged waste generation to the nearest river network. Still, it computed additional transport probabilities to river mouth from distance to the river mouth, river discharge, and river network order.

Table A A.27. Fraction of mismanaged plastic waste entering aquatic environment and fraction reaching the ocean environment

Macro region	Region	Fraction of mismanaged and littered waste entering aquatic environments	Fraction of aquatic plastics reaching the ocean
OECD America	USA	32%	3%
	Canada	36%	3%
	Other OECD America	21%	5%
OECD Europe	OECD EU countries	34%	3%
	OECD non-EU countries	34%	4%
OECD Asia	OECD Pacific	43%	11%
	OECD Oceania	44%	2%
Other America	Latin America	28%	5%
Eurasia	Other EU	27%	1%
	Other Eurasia	32%	1%
Middle East and Africa	Middle East & North Africa	27%	4%
	Other Africa	23%	4%
Other Asia	China	28%	2%
	India	26%	4%
	Other non-OECD Asia	34%	14%

Source: Fraction of mismanaged and littered plastic waste entering aquatic environments (adapted from Borrelle et al. (2020[99])) and fraction of waste in aquatic environment entering the ocean environment (adapted from Meijer et al. (2021[100])) by region.

In the ocean, plastics with a larger density than seawater will sink at the bottom, accumulating in deep-sea canyons and trenches by the action of gravity. Floating plastics, however, will be transported by the action of waves, wind and currents. The most significant fraction of these plastics, however will rapidly reencounter land and beach on a coastline. A study presenting a model of dispersion of plastics in the ocean from global coastal sources reported that within a year, around 97% of released model particles had resided near a coastline for more than two consecutive days (Lebreton and Andrady, 2019[19]), suggesting a significant fraction had likely beached in that time. Rich coastal ecosystems will also facilitate the retention of floating plastics near the coastline as, similarly to freshwater environments, organisms in the marine environment will colonise floating plastics. Objects with smaller volume to surface ratios, such as plastic films or small microplastics, will likely sink near the coastline. Fragments and objects with a sufficiently large volume to maintain their buoyancy can escape the coastal environments. Over time debris tend to accumulate offshore in subtropical latitudes. Five accumulation zones have been widely reported in the literature from field observations and numerical models. The largest one is located in the North Pacific Ocean between Hawaii and California (Lebreton et al., 2018[101]).

Environmental conditions will also dictate the fate of plastics during their journey in freshwater and marine environments. Particularly under the action of sunlight, plastics degrade by photo-oxidation. As such, it is expected that plastics near the surface in rivers, lakes, or in the ocean are more likely to degrade into smaller particles, commonly referred to as microplastics with varying definitions (usually, particles below 1-5 mm and larger than one micron). Due to the large complexity of mechanisms and under varying conditions, data on the degradation of plastics in natural environments is scarce. Still, results are starting to appear with long-term experiments on the degradation of plastics in controlled environments. Fragmentation rates expressed in the percentage of weight loss per year did not exceed 5% in a laboratory seawater microcosm for various conventional thermoplastics (Gerritse et al., 2020[102]). This is in good agreement with modelled whole-ocean plastic degradation rates expected by numerical models (i.e. 3% of total ocean plastic mass degraded per year from macro- to microplastics, (Lebreton and Andrady, 2019[19]).

For the purpose of this work, the whole-ocean plastic mass budget model presented in (Lebreton and Andrady, 2019[19]) was expanded to a simplified representation of the global aquatic environment. The model now differentiates between annual inputs in freshwater and the ocean, allowing floating plastic waste to circulate from one compartment to the other over time. The model was also enhanced by differentiating inputs by polymer types using the OECD ENV-Linkages model estimates and waste projections presented in this report. The likely fate of emitted plastics was determined depending on their density. Additionally, the degradation rates varied between polymers based on laboratory results (Gerritse et al., 2020[102]). The general model framework is presented in Figure A A.5. To differentiate between freshwater and marine environment inputs, the model uses the results from Meijer et al. (2021[100]), which provides country-scale probabilities of emissions to the ocean. These results were upscaled to the modelled region by following the same weighted method as for inputs into aquatic environments (see the previous section). Thus was estimated the fraction of waste emitted in freshwater and the fraction emitted directly into the ocean for every region and per year. Starting the model in 1951, plastics were emitted into the modelled aquatic environment from every region. Polymers with a density higher than water were assumed to sink on the riverbed, lakebed, or seabed. Floating polymers circulating at the surface could directly reach the coastal ocean surface within the first year or remained in the freshwater system, likely stranded on river and lakeshores. The model also remobilised accumulated waste in river and lakeshores, adding onto inputs from the following year. Floating polymers in the coastal ocean surface followed the same dynamics as in the model presented in Lebreton and Andrady (2019[19]), with recirculation between the shoreline and the sea surface and transfer from coastal to offshore waters. Floating plastics accumulated in river and lake shore or on the ocean surface and shoreline were considered in contact with sunlight, and a fraction of their mass was degraded yearly to a sink term representing the mass of microplastics accumulated in freshwater and marine environments. The cycle was repeated every year until 2019.

Figure A A.5. Mass balance budget model for plastic in global aquatic environments

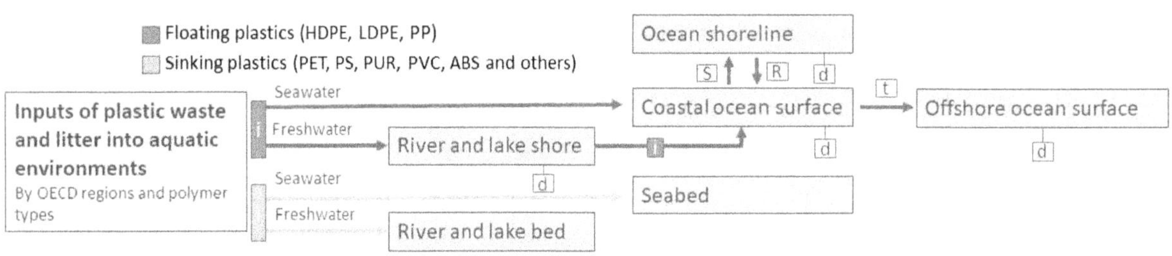

Note: Mass inputs by modelled region, characterised by polymer types, are accumulated from 1951 to 2060 into the plastic fate model. Plastics with a density higher than water sink and accumulate in riverbed, lakebed and seabed. Floating plastics (density lower than water) are transported between different aquatic compartments and are allowed to degrade into microplastics over time from contact with sunlight. The region-specific parameter 'i' is the ratio between plastics remaining in freshwater and the plastics entering the marine environment (Table A A.27). The parameters 's' and 'r' represent the fraction of stranding and release from the global shoreline. The parameter 't' is the fraction of floating plastic circulating from the coastal to the offshore ocean. (s = 97%, r = 3%, t = 33%, (Lebreton, Egger and Slat, 2019[103])). Finally, 'd' is the mass fraction degrading into microplastics annually and varies with polymer types (Table A A.28).
Source: OECD ENV-Linkages model, adapted from Lebreton and Andrady (2019[19]) methodology.

Table A A.28. Parameters for fate of plastic in aquatic environments by polymer type

Polymer type	Micro	Floats	Degradation rate in % of mass per year
HDPE	No	Yes	0.6
LDPE, LLDPE	No	Yes	0.8
PP	No	Yes	0.0
PET	No	No	4.9
PS	No	No	0.1
PUR	No	No	3
PVC	No	No	-
ABS, ASA, SAN	No	No	-
Bioplastics	No	No	-
Elastomers (tyres)	No	No	-
Fibres	No	No	-
Road marking coatings	Yes	No	-
Marine coatings	Yes	No	-
Other	No	No	-

Source: Degradation rates are sourced from laboratory experiments (Gerritse et al., 2020[102]).

This model produced time series from 1951 to 2060 of inputs and accumulation of plastic waste from global regions into rivers, lakes, and the ocean. The main concerning result is a severe worsening of pollution in all aquatic environments in the *Baseline* scenario. The model allows us to produce first-order of magnitude estimates of mass distribution in different compartments of the global aquatic environment.

This simplified model has some limitations, and care should be given in the interpretation of the results. The fate of plastics will vary significantly depending on the situation. These projections should be seen as a whole, describing the regional quantity of plastic waste expressed by orders of magnitude of mass. Some assumptions were made in the design of the model, which does not always reflect reality. For instance, polymers such as PET, PVC or PUR were considered as sinking plastics, but by design, objects made with these polymers can float for a variable period of time (e.g. empty PET bottles with cap on, PVC buoys, or extended PUR foam). On the contrary, some floating plastics such as HDPE or LDPE may also sink rapidly (e.g. biobased plastic bags) in rivers while still considered movable in the model.

By investigating inputs, transport and fates of plastics from the beginning of mass production to 2060, the generation of secondary microplastics can be estimated in the environment, allowing comparisons between the contribution of old legacy plastics versus new inputs. By looking back, the contribution of early polluters can be assessed and observed throughout a century how the problem has and will continue shifting geographically. These results help target priority regions for mitigation of pollution, focusing on the Asian and African continents.

Modelling particulate matter emissions from tyre and brake wear (NILU)

This section explains the methodology and parameters employed by Nicolaos Evangeliou from the Norwegian Institute for Air Research (NILU) to make projections on the emission of airborne road-traffic-related microplastics and their contribution to particulate pollution.

Calculation of emissions of tyre and brake wear

Tyre and brake wear particles (TWPs and BWPs) are calculated using the GAINS (Greenhouse gas – Air pollution Interactions and Synergies) model (Amann et al., 2011[104]). GAINS is an integrated assessment model where emissions of air pollutants and greenhouse gases are estimated for nearly two hundred regions globally considering key economic activities, environmental regulation policies and region-specific emission factors. For emissions of particulate matter (PM), GAINS provides PM distinguishing PM_1, $PM_{2.5}$, PM_{10}, total PM, as well as carbonaceous particles (BC, OC) that derive from combustion processes, as described in Klimont et al. (2017[105]).

Emissions of non-exhaust PM in GAINS include TWPs, BWPs, as well as road abrasion. The calculation of these emissions is based on region-specific data and estimates of distance driven (km/vehicle-type/year) and vehicle-type specific emission rates (mg/km). The types of vehicles considered include motorcycles, cars, light-duty vehicles, buses, and heavy-duty vehicles. The estimates of distance driven for 2015 are derived using data on fuel use in road transport from the International Energy Agency's Word Energy Outlook (IEA, 2011[106]), supported by national data on vehicle numbers and assumptions of per-vehicle mileage travelled. Considering vehicle-type specific emission rates and use, allows for better reflection of significant regional differences in fleet structure, e.g. large number of motorcycles in South and South-East Asia and lower car ownership numbers in parts of the developing world. GAINS emissions are estimated globally at the grid level (0.5°×0.5°) using road network data, assumptions about road-type vehicle density, and population data.

The vehicle-type specific TWP and BWP emission factors used in GAINS draw on a review of several measurement papers (Klimont et al., 2002[107]) that were recently updated (Klimont et al., 2017[105]) using primarily van der Gon et al. (2013[108]), EEA (2013[109]) and Harrison et al. (2012[110]). There are large uncertainties in emission factors including the PM size distribution. GAINS provides total suspended particulates (TSP), and then assumes that PM_{10} from TWPs represent about 10% of TSP, and $PM_{2.5}$ about 1% of total TWPs, whereas PM_{10} from BWPs is about 80% of TSP and $PM_{2.5}$ is 40–50% of total BWPs (Klimont et al., 2002[107]).

Atmospheric transport modelling

Emissions of PM_{10} calculated with the GAINS model are used as input in the FLEXPART (FLEXible PARTicle) atmospheric transport model version 10.4 (Pisso et al., 2019[111]). Atmospheric dispersion of particulate matter, including both transport and deposition of particles, were simulated for the reference year 2014. The FLEXPART model was run in forward mode from 2014. Atmospheric processes affecting particle transport in clouds (e.g. boundary layer turbulent mixing and convection processes) are parameterised in the model (Forster, Stohl and Seibert, 2007[112]). The model was driven by 3-hourly 1°×1° operational analyses from the European Centre for Medium Range Weather Forecast (ECMWF), the spatial output resolution of concentration and deposition fields was set to 0.5°×0.5° in a global domain with a daily temporal resolution. In FLEXPART the dispersion of road microplastics is modelled assuming a spherical shape of particles (Pisso et al., 2019[111]).

The simulations also accounted for below-cloud scavenging and dry deposition, assuming a particle density for TWPs of 1234 kg/m^3, which is in the middle of the densities of 945 kg/m^3 for natural rubber and 1522 kg/m^3 for synthetic rubber (Walker, 2019[113]; Federal Highway Administration Research and

Technology, 2019[114]). This density is within the reported range for microplastics (940-2 400 kg/m^3) (Unice et al., 2019[115]). For BWPs a higher density was assumed (2 000 kg/m^3) considering that BWP may also contain metals (Grigoratos and Martini, 2014[116]). Plastics are generally hydrophobic and should therefore be rather inefficient cloud condensation nuclei (CCN) (Di Mundo, Petrella and Notarnicola, 2008[117]; Ganguly and Ariya, 2019[118]). However, coatings may make the particles more hydrophilic with time in the atmosphere (Bond et al., 2013[119]). The efficiency of aerosols to serve as ice nuclei (IN) is also not well known. Based on Evangeliou et al. (2020[120]), it is more realistic to use intermediate scavenging coefficients for CCN/IN in the model.

Extrapolation of the model results until 2060

The aforementioned emissions of TWPs and BWPs were extrapolated using the road passenger data from the IEA's World Energy Outlook (IEA, 2018[121]) for 15 geographical regions with global coverage, following the regional aggregation of the ENV-Linkages model.

Year 2014 was taken as base year and the ratio to year 2014 was calculated for each year between 2015 and 2020 and for each of the 15 regions (from now on referred as "regional scaling factor"). This regional scaling factor could be negative, if the road passenger data decreased as compared to 2015, or positive, if an increase is shown.

Having obtained estimates of TWPs and BWPs, the FLEXIPART model was used to calculate their global annual transport and deposition (atmospheric dispersion) for each year between 2015 and 2060. Running FLEXIPART for so many years is computationally expensive. Furthermore, since meteorological fields necessary for FLEXPART are only available until present times (2021), it would be necessary to run a climate model until 2060 to generate the meteorological fields for FLEXPART, thus further increasing the computational time needed. To avoid these issues, it was assumed that the meteorology will remain approximately constant over the years, and that changes in the global dispersion of TWPs and BWPs will only be due to emission changes in the various regions.

With these assumptions, FLEXPART was run with the 2014 emissions for the 15 ENV-Linkages regions; thus creating 15 different model simulations, each representing the dispersion from the respective region. Then, the regional scaling factor was used to scale modelled dispersion that results from each individual regional emission for each year between 2015 and 2060. Finally, the 15 regional annually-scaled modelled dispersions were used to calculate global TWP and BWP estimates.

Modelling greenhouse gas emissions from plastics in ENV-Linkages

This section explains the methodology and parameters employed to make projections on the contribution of the lifecycle of plastics to GHG emissions, on a global level.

An emission-factor-based approach

In the GTAP database (Aguiar et al., 2019[5]), plastics production occurs in two sectors: Chemicals and Rubber and plastics products. The plastic products sectors has been split into primary and secondary plastics production. The plastics producing sectors use inputs from the electricity generation sector, fossil fuel extraction sectors and other sectors of the economy. However, since these plastics producing sectors also produce other goods, not all emissions can be attributed to plastics. Therefore, to approximate the global lifecycle emissions from plastics, an emission factor-based approach is retained, in line with the most recent estimates from the literature:

$$Emi_{g,t}^{plastics} = \sum_{p} (\lambda_{g,p,t}^{prod} + \lambda_{g,p,t}^{conv})\, C_{p,t} + \sum_{f} \lambda_{g,f,t}^{eol} W_{f,t}$$

where $Emi_{g,t}^{plastics}$ are emissions of greenhouse gas g (comprising CO_2, CH_4 and N_2O, measured in CO_2-equivalents[5]) from the plastics lifecycle at time t, $\lambda_{g,p,t}^{prod}$ and $\lambda_{g,p,t}^{conv}$ are respectively the emission factors per tonne of plastic product for production and conversion of plastic for polymer p that are applied to the level of plastics consumption $C_{p,t}$ estimated by the model. Finally, $\lambda_{g,f,t}^{eol}$ is the emission factor for a specific end-of-life fate f (incineration, sanitary landfilling and recycling only are considered, due to data availability), applied to the amount of plastic waste generated $W_{j,t}$.

The literature provides estimates of emission factors for year 2015 (Zheng and Suh, 2019[21])[6] that are used to calibrate emissions for 2015 (Figure A A.6). These emission factors comprise emissions from the whole value-chain of plastics production, and are not constant over time due to structural changes in the production process the change in GHG intensity of plastics production and conversion over time is endogenously determined in the model. A GHG-efficiency index is computed based on the global average scope 2 emissions (direct emissions plus emissions from electricity demand) of the most relevant plastics-related sectors (Chemicals, primary Rubber and plastics products, Oil extraction, Gas extraction and Petroleum and coal products). Regarding the GHG intensity of recycling, an index is built based on scope 2 emissions of the secondary plastics sector, while for incineration and landfilling, emissions factors are constant.

Figure A A.6. Greenhouse gas emission factors for plastics lifecycle in ENV-Linkages

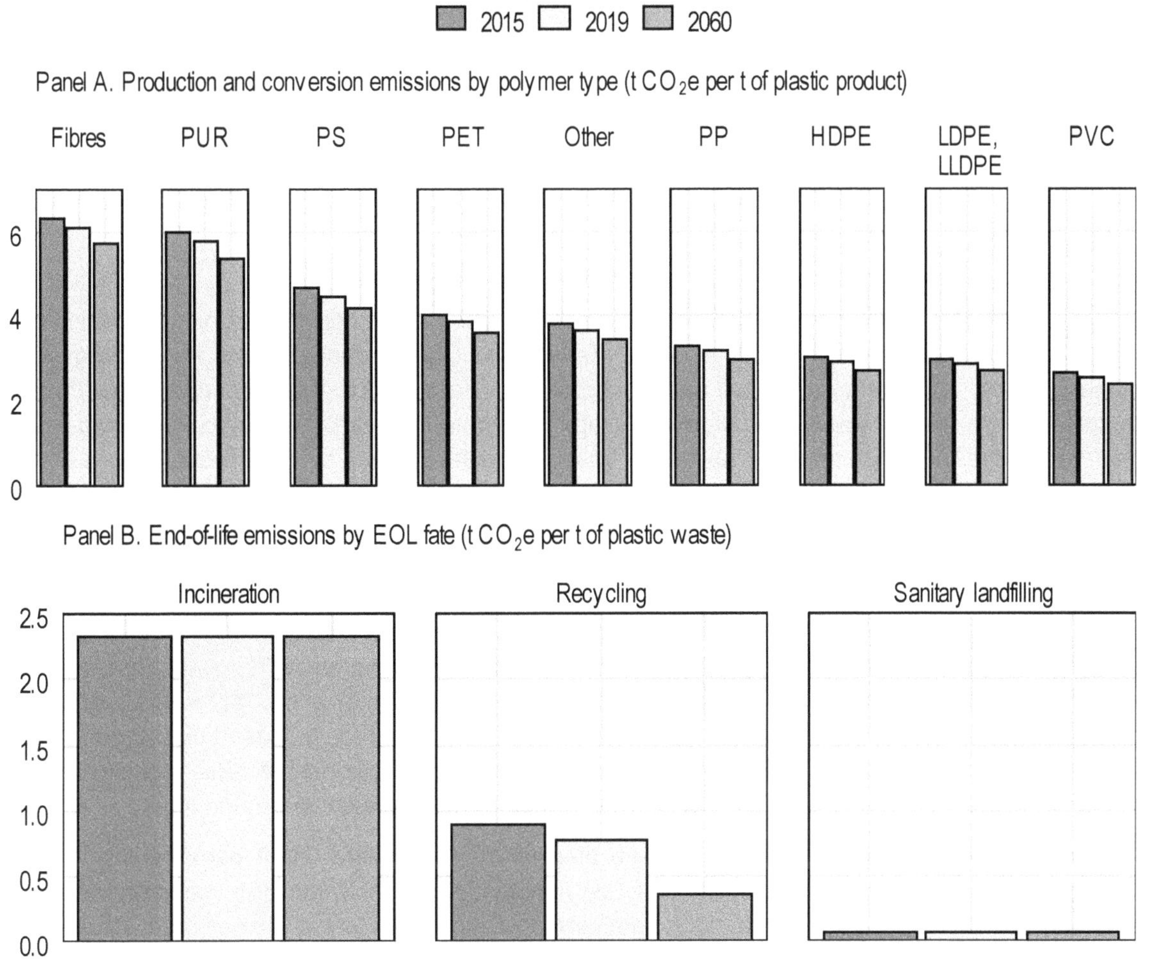

Note: Emissions from recycling and incineration are direct emissions from their respective industrial processes. Avoided emissions (emissions from electricity generation that are replaced by waste incineration and emissions from primary plastics production that are replaced by secondary plastics) are not included in the emission factors depicted here, because they are included directly in the ENV-Linkages model (changes in the input structure of the electricity generation sector and changes in the balance between primary and secondary plastics, both being driven by the change in the relative prices of products endogenously determined by the model).
Source: Adapted from Zheng and Suh (2019[21]).

StatLink https://stat.link/i7ytcn

Decomposition of changes in plastics emissions

To analyse the changes in emissions E between two situations, labelled 1 and 0 (e.g. between 2060 and 2019 in the baseline or between the policy scenario and the baseline), the following decomposition of emissions was used (e.g. for end-of-life):

$$E_1 - E_0 = \left(\sum_f W_{f,1} - \sum_f W_{f,0}\right) \sum_f \lambda_{f,0} \frac{W_{f,0}}{\sum_{ff} W_{ff,0}} + \left(\sum_f W_{f,1}\right) \sum_f \lambda_{f,0} \left(\frac{W_{f,1}}{\sum_{ff} W_{ff,1}} - \frac{W_{f,0}}{\sum_{ff} W_{ff,0}}\right) + \sum_f (\lambda_{f,1} - \lambda_{f,0}) W_{f,1}$$

where the first term can be interpreted as a "scale" effect (change in total plastic waste generated at initial emission factor and composition), the second can be interpreted as a "composition" effect (change in the relative shares of the different waste management options) and the third term as a "GHG intensity" effect (change in emission factors at final composition and scale). The same decomposition is done for production and conversion emissions, where the "scale" effect corresponds to the changes in the amount of plastic produced at initial emission factor and polymer mix, the "composition" effect corresponds to the change in the share of the different polymers in total production, and the "GHG intensity" effect corresponds to the changes in emission factors at final composition and scale.

Modelling the effects of higher penetration rates of biobased plastics (Neus Escobar and Wolfgang Britz)

The assessment was carried out with the integrated GTAP-based framework "GGEBox" (Britz and van der Mensbrugghe, 2018[122]). First, the original GTAP 10 database (Aguiar et al., 2019[5]) was aggregated into 18 larger regions, while keeping the full sectoral resolution. Second, fossil-based and biobased plastics were split from the "rubber and plastic products" (rpp) aggregate in five major producing regions – Brazil, China, the EU, the United States and Thailand –, based on relative output shares. These regions currently represent around 60% of the global biobased plastic market. Although Thailand's bioplastics market is relatively smaller, the country is expected to become a production hub of biodegradable and biobased plastics, in view of recent investment in the last years (Fielding and Aung, 2018[123]; OECD, 2013[124]). Besides wheat and sugarcane, already explicitly represented in the GTAP database, corn and cassava were disaggregated respectively from "other grains" and "fruits and vegetables", to include relevant bioplastic feedstock. Additional adjustments were made to the GTAP database to increase the cost share of agricultural raw materials in the bioplastic industry relative to the original "rpp" sector, which uses petroleum as input instead of crops. China and the United States produce biobased plastics mainly from corn (>85%) but also wheat; OECD EU utilises both corn and wheat to almost the same extent (about 50% each); Brazil employs entirely sugarcane while Thailand also uses cassava at around 40%.

Substitution between fossil-based and biobased plastics in intermediate input demand was modelled through a Constant Elasticity of Substitution (CES) function. An initial value of 5 was assumed for the substitution elasticity (subelas) to capture the relatively large market shares of drop-in products, which are expected to be maintained in the future (IEA, 2020[125]). These refer to those plastics that have identical technical characteristics to their fossil counterparts and allow for direct market substitution, such as polyethylene and polyethylene (PE) and polyethylene terephthalate (PET).

CGEBox incorporates multiple GTAP extensions to be able to estimate GHG emissions from Indirect Land Use Changes (ILUC) as well as from endowment use and agricultural production. The land transformation module simulates land conversion across major uses (cropland, pasture and managed forest) at the Agro-Ecological Zone (AEZ) level, based on differences in returns to land according to a Constant Elasticity of Transformation (CET) function. Each land use is associated with AEZ-specific carbon pools in soil, above- and below-ground biomass and litter, including foregone carbon sequestration over a 30-year period (Gibbs, Yui and Plevin, 2014[126]; Pelvin et al., 2014[127]). Moreover, CGEBox introduces the possibility of agricultural land expansion into natural land, with a land supply elasticity (landelas) of 0.05 for all regions considered. Carbon stocks in natural land uses were estimated by assuming that natural forests have twice as much carbon as managed forest (Kindermann et al., 2008[128]); grassland, savannah, and shrubland have the same carbon content as pastureland; and the remaining "other" land has 10% of the carbon in pastureland – see (Escobar and Britz, 2021[129]) for further details.

The analysis focuses on the effects of an increased market penetration of biobased plastics in Brazil, China, OECD EU, United States and Thailand, compared to the baseline in 2060.[7] This requires that biobased plastics have a cost-advantage over fossil-based ones, which is here simulated with two alternative scenarios, namely (A) introducing fiscal policies to regulate the plastics market and (B) promoting technical progress in the bioplastic industry through R&D. The two scenarios are described as follows:

- ***Mandate* scenario:** represents a government intervention simulating a mandate to increase consumption of biobased plastics at the cost of conventional ones. This is done by subsidising bioplastics consumption by firms and final consumers to replace 5% of the total plastics market (in monetary values) in each of the five regions considered by 2060. The targeted level of market penetration is consistent with projections for the EU 28 region (Schipfer et al., 2017[130]). As a result, the level of the subsidy varies across bioplastic producing regions, depending on the respective sizes of both their bio- and fossil-based plastic sectors. The greatest drop in ad-valorem taxes on demand for biobased plastics is estimated for China (-47.0%) and the smallest for Brazil (- 14.0%), with an average decrease of 41.0% globally. At the same time, consumption taxes on oil, gas, coal, petroleum and fossil-based plastics increase in each region, referring to both domestic and import demand by all agents (consumers, firms, investors and governments). The same change in ad-valorem tariffs is applied to these five products in all regions to keep total indirect tax income constant in real terms. This can be interpreted as changes in value added tax rates to ensure that public services (health, education, etc.) are maintained.
- ***Efficiency* scenario:** introduces technical progress in the bioplastic industry beyond the baseline, as a result of R&D investment and subsequent upscaling of technologies that allow for enhanced biomass use efficiencies. These in turn refer to pathways based on non-food feedstock (e.g. algae, perennial crops or waste) or cascading uses and closed-loop approaches (e.g. in integrated biorefineries). Hence, technical progress is simulated as a more efficient use of crop-based inputs for plastic production, as combined with higher factor productivity. It is assumed that demand for agricultural raw materials per unit of bioplastic produced decreases by 60% in 2060, implying a rate of 1.3% per annum. Additionally, labour and capital requirements are reduced by 30% (0.65% per annum). Similar efficiency improvements were considered in other studies for the long-term development of bioenergy and biochemical sectors both in industrialised and emerging countries (Lee, 2016[131]; van Meijl et al., 2018[132]), and at the world level (Escobar and Britz, 2021[129]). At the same time, taxes on fossil-based plastics are introduced in all regions – not only in bioplastic producing ones – to keep real GDP constant.

Both the Mandate and Efficiency scenarios yield approximately the same levels of biobased plastics production in 2060 on a global scale (ca. 60 Mt), with these accounting for around 3% of the total plastics market. Whereas the market penetration of bioplastics is exactly the same across producing regions in *Mandate* (5%), the *Efficiency* scenario delivers different levels of bioplastics consumption across the five regions. The greatest market shares are obtained for Thailand (6.3%) and Brazil (17.6%) due to improvements in the conversion efficiency of sugarcane, which becomes the most cost-effective feedstock. The market share of bioplastics in China, OECD EU and the United States is around 4% in 2060 in *Efficiency*. Outcomes from the two scenarios were then assessed against the baseline, in order to understand the economy-wide impacts of each intervention.

Scenarios with alternative parameters were considered as part of an uncertainty analysis. First, the parameter reflecting the substitutability between fossil-based and biobased plastics (*subelas*) for different applications (e.g. packaging, electronics, buildings or automotive) was varied to understand how easily industries can replace conventional plastics with biobased plastics. Second, the ease of converting natural land into agricultural and managed forestland areas (*landelas*) was varied to understand how the implementation of different conservation policies and other governance strategies can promote or prevent natural land cover loss when biomass demand increases. These two parameters were varied around the central values considered (subelas=5 and landelas=0.05) to analyse the uncertainty of results (see Table A A.29).

Table A A.29. Uncertainty parameters for the analysis of biobased plastics penetration rates

Mandate scenario		Efficiency scenario	
Subelas	Landelas	Subelas	Landelas
5	0	5	0
5	0.025	5	0.025
5	**0.05**	**5**	**0.05**
5	0.10	5	0.10
5	0.25	5	0.25
1	0.05	1	0.05
2.5	0.05	2.5	0.05
5	**0.05**	**5**	**0.05**
7.5	0.05	7.5	0.05
10	0.05	10	0.05

Note: subelas = elasticity of substitution between conventional and biobased plastics; landlelas: land supply elasticity. The central values of 5 and 0.05 were respectively taken for subelas and landelas in the assessment of both Mandate and Efficiency scenarios. The reference scenario using the central values is in bold in the table.
Source: CGE-Box model.

Projecting other health and environment impacts from the life cycle of plastics (Ghent University)

This section explains the methodology, parameters and impact categories employed by the experts of the Sustainable Systems Engineering Group of Ghent University to make projections for the health and environment impacts from plastics using a life cycle assessment (LCA) approach.

Goal and scope

The goal of the LCA is to analyse the environmental impacts of plastics on a global scale. The assessment includes the production from cradle to gate of polymers serving as feedstock for industry and the end-of-life (EoL) treatment of such plastics considering recycling, landfilling, incineration, dumping and open burning.

Seven polymer types are included in the analysis: Polyvinyl chloride (PVC), Polyurethane (PUR), Polystyrene (PS), Polypropylene (PP), Polyethylene terephthalate (PET), Low-density Polyethylene (LDPE), High-density Polyethylene (LDPE).

The functional unit is the production and end-of-life of polymers on a global scale in 2019. The system boundary includes the primary and secondary production from cradle to gate and selected waste management methods. Figure A A.7 shows a simplified scheme of the system boundary.

Figure A A.7. Considered stages of the LCA analysis for the seven polymer types

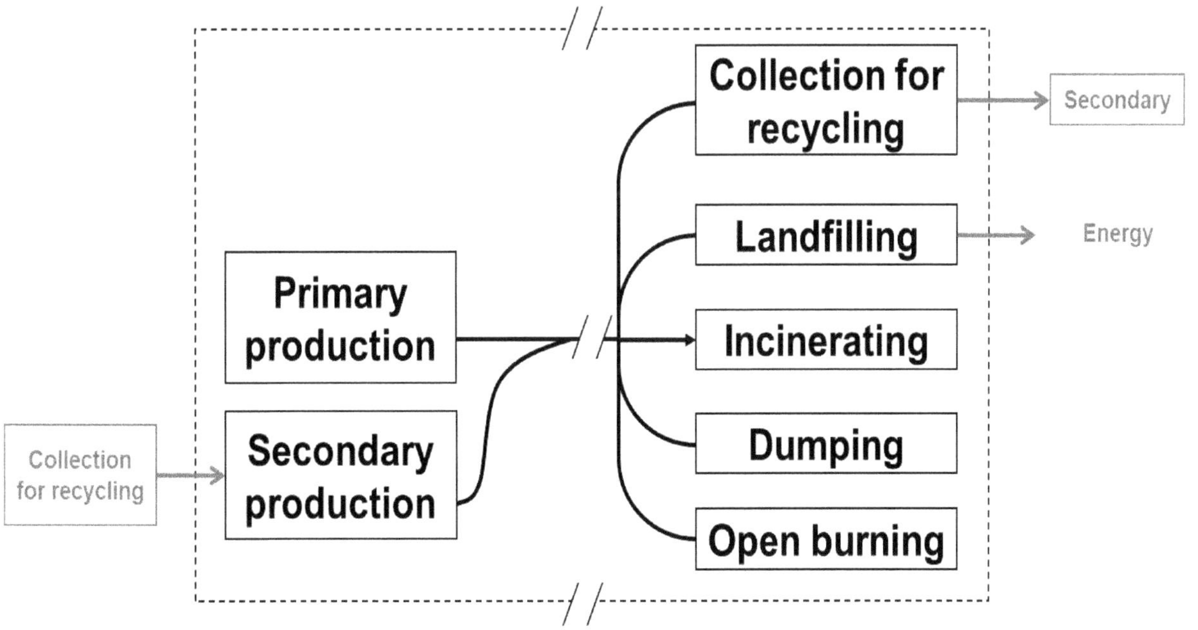

The geographical scope is global. OECD data for the global use of plastics were used as a base for the global production of plastics. Also for global waste management, OECD data were used. The assessment did not apply regional differentiation of production for the environmental impacts of plastics. Generally, global energy mixes of electricity and heat are used to calculate the environmental impacts. Some datasets related to incineration and landfilling do not have global averages; in those cases, estimates rely on Europe as a geographical reference.

The temporal scope relates to two periods: 2019 and 2060. The difference between the two periods only affects the projected volumes of plastics use and waste. The inventory information for plastics production per end-of life fate was not modified and no changes in future technology or future global energy mix were incorporated.

Some key limitations of this study: there is no consideration of the use stage of plastics, the manufacturing of plastic products and the impacts related to the production of other polymers not mentioned in this report.

Life Cycle Inventory

The compilation of inventory was made with SimaPro 9.1.1.1. Life cycle data of plastics was sourced from Ecoinvent v3.6, with the cut-off by classification model. In the cut-off by classification model, "recyclable materials are cut off from the producing product system" (Wernet et al., 2016[133]). This means for plastics that the feedstock for recycling (waste plastic) comes burden-free to the secondary producer. The secondary producer bears only the burden of the recycling and secondary material production processes; hence, no burdens from the primary production are attributed to secondary materials (Wernet et al., 2016[133]).

The foreground system boundary followed the structure of the database modelling approach. As presented in Figure A A.7, the secondary production at the beginning of life (Secondary) includes the activities after the collection of plastics until the production of the secondary polymer (e.g., regranulates). To keep consistency at the EoL, "recycling" only bears the impact of waste collection before the recycling process itself.

Data assumptions:

- **Primary production:** The technology pathway to produce a certain polymer can differ. Some of these pathways are reflected in the database and sometimes need to be manipulated before use in the assessment. For example, the production of PVC is detailed by three polymerisation technologies: suspension, emulsion and bulk polymerisation. Evidently, different technology pathways will show different environmental impacts, so an arithmetic average of the impacts from different technology pathways to produce polymers has been used for the projections.
- **Secondary production (mechanical recycling):** Data for secondary production of plastics is quite limited compared to primary production. Only data of secondary HDPE and PET via mechanical recycling is available in Ecoinvent. Hence, an arithmetic average of the environmental impact of these polymers was used for the calculation of PVC, PS, and PP. For LDPE, the same impact was assumed as for HDPE. PUR is not included as there is no reported secondary production of such material in the OECD model. The analysis starts with the collected plastic waste (burden-free) and includes the steps of separation, shredding, washing, floating, drying, cutting, and regranulation according to the Ecoinvent datasets information.
- **Secondary production (chemical recycling):** Data for thermochemical recycling was derived from (Civancik-Uslu et al., 2021[134]), considering sorted waste streams of PP and PE for naphtha production. Due to confidentiality, only aggregated environmental impact data can be presented. The downstream processes after naphtha production (i.e. cracking, polymerisation, and granulation) were based on calculations from (Civancik-Uslu et al., 2021[134]) using Ecoinvent data for primary production of PP and HDPE. On the one hand, the uncertainty for the estimation of these downstream processes is high. On the other, data for the production of naphtha via thermochemical recycling is based on high-quality measures derived from primary data collection in Belgium. Finally, data on the thermochemical recycling process was adapted using global energy production (electricity and heating) to represent global impacts.
- **End-of-life (EoL):** The EoL stage was evaluated in five groups: recycling, incineration, landfilling, dumping and open burning. For recycling, as commented in section 1.2, only impacts related to collection are attributed to this process (downstream processes are attributed to secondary material production). For the other waste management methods, polymer-specific datasets were used. For incineration, the data concerned municipal incineration with fly ash extraction and sanitary landfill.

The background data, i.e. the upstream data of energy, materials, infrastructure and auxiliaries for the provision of the above-mentioned processes, were not modified from the Ecoinvent database. In this respect, the energy mixes are related to the regions represented in the datasets

Life Cycle Impact Assessment (LCIA)

The environmental impact calculation used SimaPro 9.1.1.1. As LCIA methodology the 'ReCiPe 2016 Midpoint (H) V1.04 / World (2010) H' was used, in which 11 impact categories were selected for computation of environmental impact results: Ozone formation - Human health, Ozone formation – Terrestrial ecosystems, Terrestrial acidification, Freshwater eutrophication, Marine eutrophication, Terrestrial ecotoxicity, Freshwater ecotoxicity, Marine ecotoxicity, Human carcinogenic toxicity, Human non-carcinogenic toxicity and Land use.

Description of the LCA impact categories

Land use refers the land surface used to produce a resource or execute an activity, for example the area occupied by a mine, landfill or agricultural activity. This land is then temporarily unavailable for other uses, or for nature and ecosystems. The impacts are measured as land use (in m2).

Ozone formation or photochemical oxidation is the formation of reactive chemical compounds such as ozone by the action of sunlight on certain primary air pollutants, sometimes visible as smog. These reactive compounds may harm damage health, ecosystems, and crops. The impacts are measured as emissions of substances (VOC, CO) to air (in kg ethylene equivalents). These emissions are translated into a category indicator 'tropospheric ozone formation' using the Photochemical Ozone Creation Potential (POCP) of different gases (Jenkin and Hayman, 1999[135]; Derwent et al., 1998[136]; Derwent, Jenkin and Saunders, 1996[137]).

Euthrophication covers all potential impacts of excessively high environmental levels of macronutrients, the most important of which are nitrogen (N) and phosphorus (P). Nutrient enrichment may cause undesirable shift in species composition and elevated biomass production in ecosystems and affects sources suitable for drinking water. These emissions are translated into a category indicator 'deposition/N/P equivalents in biomass' using a stoichiometric procedure, which identifies the equivalence between N and P for both terrestrial and aquatic systems (Heijungs, 1992[138]). Marine eutrophication is measured in kg of N-eq, and freshwater eutrophication is measured in kg of P-eq.

Ecotoxicity refers to the impacts of toxic substances on species in freshwater aquatic or terrestrial ecosystems. The impacts are measured as emissions of toxic substances to air, water and soil (in kg 1.4-dichlorobenzene equivalents). These emissions are translated into a category indicator 'predicted environmental concentration/predicted no-effect concentration' using Freshwater Aquatic Ecotoxicity Potentials (FAETP) (Huijbregts, 2000[139]; Huijbregts, 1999[140]) and the USES 2.0 model developed by RIVM, describing fate, exposure and effects of toxic substances into Terrestrial Ecotoxicity Potentials (TETP) (Huijbregts, 2000[139]; Huijbregts, 1999[140]).

Human **toxicity** covers the impacts on human health of toxic substances in the environment, either by inhalation or via the food chain. Such impacts cover widely varying symptoms reaching from irritation to mortality. The impacts are measured as emissions of toxic substances to air, water and soil (in kg 1,4-dichlorobenzene equivalents). These emissions are translated into a category indicator 'acceptable daily intake/predicted daily intake' using Human Toxicity Potentials (HTP) (Huijbregts, 2000[139]; Huijbregts, 1999[140]).

Acidification is the corrosive impact that pollutants such as sulphur dioxide (SO_2) and Nitrous Oxides (NOx) have on soil, groundwater, surface waters, biological organisms, ecosystems and materials (buildings). The impacts are measured as emissions of acidifying gases to the air (in kg SO_2 equivalents). These emissions are translated into an indicator 'deposition/acidification critical load', describing the fate and deposition of acidifying substances as Acidifying Potentials (AP average Europe) of different gases (Huijbregts, 1999[140]).

References

Aguiar, A. et al. (2019), "The GTAP Data Base: Version 10", *Journal of Global Economic Analysis*, Vol. 4/1, pp. 1-27, https://doi.org/10.21642/jgea.040101af. [5]

Amann, M. et al. (2011), "Cost-effective control of air quality and greenhouse gases in Europe: Modeling and policy applications", *Environ. Model. Softw.*, Vol. 26, pp. 1489–1501. [104]

Anagnosti, L. et al. (2021), "Worldwide actions against plastic pollution from microbeads and microplastics in cosmetics focusing on European policies. Has the issue been handled effectively?", *Marine Pollution Bulletin*, Vol. 162, p. 111883, https://doi.org/10.1016/j.marpolbul.2020.111883. [54]

Antonopoulos, I., G. Faraca and D. Tonini (2021), "Recycling of post-consumer plastic packaging waste in the EU: Recovery rates, material flows, and barriers", *Waste Management*, Vol. 126, pp. 694-705, https://doi.org/10.1016/j.wasman.2021.04.002. [28]

Australian Government, D. (2020), *2018-19 Australian plastics recycling survey - national report*, https://www.awe.gov.au/environment/protection/waste/publications/australian-plastics-recycling-survey-report-2018-19 (accessed on 28 October 2021). [41]

Bond, T. et al. (2013), "Bounding the role of black carbon in the climate system: A scientific assessment", *J. Geophys. Res. Atmos.*, Vol. 118, pp. 5380–5552. [119]

Borrelle, S. et al. (2020), "Predicted growth in plastic waste exceeds efforts to mitigate plastic pollution", *Science*, Vol. 369/6510, pp. 1515-1518, https://doi.org/10.1126/science.aba3656. [99]

Boucher, F. and D. Friot (2017), *Primary Microplastics in the Oceans: A Global Evaluation of Sources*, International Union for Conservation of Nature. [65]

Britz, W. and R. Roson (2018), "G-RDEM: A GTAP-Based Recursive Dynamic CGE Model for Long-Term Baseline Generation and Analysis", *SSRN Electronic Journal*, https://doi.org/10.2139/ssrn.3167781. [142]

Britz, W. and D. van der Mensbrugghe (2018), "CGEBox: A Flexible, Modular and Extendable Framework for CGE Analysis in GAMS", *Journal of Global Economic Analysis*, Vol. 3/2, pp. 106-177, https://doi.org/10.21642/jgea.030203af. [122]

Brunner, P. and H. Rechberger (2016), *Handbook of Material Flow Analysis: For Environmental, Resource, and Waste Engineers*, CRC Press, https://doi.org/10.1201/9781315313450. [77]

Central Pollution Control Board (2021), *Report of Waste to Energy Plants in Delhi by CPCB in OA No. 640 of 2018 (Earlier O.A. No. 22 of 2013(THC)*, Sukhdev Vihar Residents Welfare Association Vs State of NCT of Delhi, https://greentribunal.gov.in/report-waste-energy-plants-delhi-cpcb-oa-no-640-2018-earlier-oa-no-22-2013thc-sukhdev-vihar. [86]

Central Pollution Control Board (CPCB) (2019), *Annual Report for the year 2018-2019 on Implementation of Plastic Waste Management Rules*, Ministry of Environment, Forest and Climate Change, Govt of India. [42]

Chateau, J., R. Dellink and E. Lanzi (2014), "An Overview of the OECD ENV-Linkages Model: Version 3", *OECD Environment Working Papers*, No. 65, OECD Publishing, Paris, https://doi.org/10.1787/5jz2qck2b2vd-en. [2]

Chateau, J., C. Rebolledo and R. Dellink (2011), "An Economic Projection to 2050: The OECD "ENV-Linkages" Model Baseline", *OECD Environment Working Papers*, No. 41, OECD Publishing, Paris, https://doi.org/10.1787/5kg0ndkjvfhf-en. [3]

Chruszcz, A. and S. Reeve (2018), "Composition of plastic waste collected via kerbside. Banbury, UK: W. a. R. A. P. (WRAP)", https://www.wrap.org.uk/sites/files/wrap/Composition%20of%20Plastic%20Waste%20Collected%20via%20Kerbside%20v2.pdf. [11]

Chruszcz, A. and S. Reeve (2018), *Composition of plastic waste: Results of a waste compositional analysis of plastics at MRFs and PRFs*, WRAP. [24]

CIESIN (2018), *Gridded population of the world, version 4 (GPWv4): population count adjusted to Match 2015 revision of UN WPP country totals, revision 11.*, Center for International Earth Science Information Network - Columbia University, https://sedac.ciesin.columbia.edu/data/set/gpw-v4-population-count-adjusted-to-2015-unwpp-country-totals-rev11. [97]

Civancik-Uslu, D. et al. (2021), "Moving from linear to circular household plastic packaging in Belgium: Prospective life cycle assessment of mechanical and thermochemical recycling", *Resources, Conservation and Recycling*, Vol. 171, p. 105633, https://doi.org/10.1016/j.resconrec.2021.105633. [134]

Cleere, R. (2020), "The New Reppie Incinerator at Koshe Landfill in Addis Ababa, Ethiopia.", *[Online data set] Environmental Justice Atlas*, https://ejatlas.org/conflict/the-new-reppie-incinerator-at-koshe-landfill-in-addis-ababa-ethiopia-leaves-the-wastepickers-without-livelihood. [84]

Cottom, J. et al. (2022), "Spatio-temporal quantification of plastic pollution origins and transportation (SPOT)" University of Leeds, UK, https://plasticpollution.leeds.ac.uk/toolkits/spot/. [10]

De Falco, F. et al. (2020), "Microfiber Release to Water, Via Laundering, and to Air, via Everyday Use: A Comparison between Polyester Clothing with Differing Textile Parameters", *Environmental Science & Technology*, doi: 10.1021/acs.est.9b06892, pp. 3288-3296, https://doi.org/10.1021/acs.est.9b06892. [66]

De Falco, F. et al. (2019), "The contribution of washing processes of synthetic clothes to microplastic pollution", *Scientific Reports*, Vol. 9, p. 6633, https://doi.org/10.1038/s41598-019-43023-x. [56]

Derwent, R., M. Jenkin and S. Saunders (1996), "Photochemical ozone creation potentials for a large number of reactive hydrocarbons under European conditions", *Atmospheric Environment*, Vol. 30/2, pp. 181-199, https://doi.org/10.1016/1352-2310(95)00303-g. [137]

Derwent, R. et al. (1998), "Photochemical ozone creation potentials for organic compounds in northwest Europe calculated with a master chemical mechanism", *Atmospheric Environment*, Vol. 32/14-15, pp. 2429-2441, https://doi.org/10.1016/s1352-2310(98)00053-3. [136]

Di Mundo, R., A. Petrella and M. Notarnicola (2008), "Surface and bulk hydrophobic cement composites by tyre rubber addition", *Constr. Build. Mater.*, Vol. 172, pp. 176–184. [117]

Dijkstra, L. and H. Poelman (2014), *A harmonised definition of cities and rural areas: the new degree of urbanisation*, https://ec.europa.eu/regional_policy/sources/docgener/work/2014_01_new_urban.pdf. [98]

ECHA (2020), *Committee for Risk Assessment (RAC) Committee for Socio-economic Analysis (SEAC). Opinion on an Annex XV dossier proposing restrictions on intentionally added microplastics*. [53]

EMEP/EEA (2013), *Air pollutant emission inventory guidebook 2013: Technical guidance to prepare national emission inventories*, https://doi.org/10.2800/92722. [109]

Environment and Climate Change Canada (2019), *Economic Study of the Canadian plastic industry, markets and waste*, Environment and Climate Change Canada. [37]

Escobar, N. and W. Britz (2021), "Metrics on the sustainability of region-specific bioplastics production, considering global land use change effects", *Resources, Conservation and Recycling*, Vol. 167, p. 105345, https://doi.org/10.1016/j.resconrec.2020.105345. [129]

Eunomia (2018), "Investigating options for reducing releases in the aquatic environment of microplastics emitted by (but not intentionally added in) products", *Report for DG Env EC*, Vol. Vol. 62, N/February, pp. 1596-1605, https://doi.org/10.1002/lsm.22016. [49]

Eurostat (2020), *Statistics | Sewage sludge production and disposal.*, https://ec.europa.eu/eurostat/databrowser/view/ENV_WW_SPD/default/table. (accessed on 28 January 2021). [76]

Eurostat (2018), *Average loads for total road freight transport, 2018 (tonnes)*, https://ec.europa.eu/eurostat/statistics-explained/index.php?title=File:Average_loads_for_total_RFT,_2018_(tonnes).png. (accessed on 21 May 2021). [58]

Eurostat (n.d.), *Sold production, exports and imports by PRODCOM list (NACE Rev. 2) - annual data*, https://ec.europa.eu/eurostat/web/prodcom/data/database. [50]

Evangeliou, N. et al. (2020), "Atmospheric transport is a major pathway of microplastics to remote regions", *Nature Communications*, Vol. 11/1, p. 3381, https://doi.org/10.1038/s41467-020-17201-9. [20]

Evangeliou, N. et al. (2020), "Atmospheric transport is a major pathway of microplastics to remote regions", *Nat Commun*, Vol. 11, p. 3381, https://doi.org/10.1038/s41467-020-17201-9. [120]

FCH (2021), "NEW PLASTICS ECONOMY", https://fch.cl/en/initiative/new-plastics-economy. [39]

Federal Highway Administration Research and Technology (2019), *User Guidelines for Waste and Byproduct Materials in Pavement Construction*. [114]

Fielding, M. and M. Aung (2018), *Bioeconomy in Thailand: a case study*, Stockholm Environment Institute, Stockholm (Sweden), https://cdn.sei.org/wp-content/uploads/2018/04/sei-wp-2018-thailand-bioeconomy.pdf. [123]

Fiji Bureau of Statistics (2018), *2017 Fiji population and housing census.*, https://www.statsfiji.gov.fj/component/advlisting/?view=download&format=raw&fileId=5970. [91]

Forster, C., A. Stohl and P. Seibert (2007), "Parameterization of convective transport in a Lagrangian particle dispersion model and its evaluation", *J. Appl. Meteorol. Climatol.*, Vol. 46, pp. 403–422. [112]

Ganguly, M. and P. Ariya (2019), "Ice Nucleation of Model Nanoplastics and Microplastics: A Novel Synthetic Protocol and the Influence of Particle Capping at Diverse Atmospheric Environments", *ACS Earth Sp. Chem*, Vol. 3, pp. 1729–1739. [118]

Gerritse, J. et al. (2020), "Fragmentation of plastic objects in a laboratory seawater microcosm", *Scientific Reports*, Vol. 10/1, p. 10945, https://doi.org/10.1038/s41598-020-67927-1. [102]

Geyer, R., J. Jambeck and K. Law (2017), "Production, use, and fate of all plastics ever made", *Science Advances*, Vol. 3/7, p. e1700782, https://doi.org/10.1126/sciadv.1700782. [14]

Geyer, R., J. Jambeck and K. Law (2017), "Production, use, and fate of all plastics ever made", *Science Advances*, Vol. 3/7, p. e1700782, https://doi.org/10.1126/sciadv.1700782. [22]

Gibbs, H., S. Yui and R. Plevin (2014), "New Estimates of Soil and Biomass Carbon Stocks for Global Economic Models", *GTAP Technical Paper*, No. 33, https://ageconsearch.umn.edu/record/283432. [126]

Government of Australia (2021), *Australian plastics flows and fates 2019-2020*, https://www.awe.gov.au/sites/default/files/documents/apff-national-report_0.pdf. [45]

Grand View Research (2020), *Recycled Plastics Market: Market Analysis.* [9]

Grigoratos, T. and G. Martini (2014), *Non-exhaust traffic related emissions. Brake and tyre wear PM*, https://doi.org/10.2790/21481. [116]

Guatemala, Instituto Nacional de Estadística (2018), *Características generales del hogar. Censo 2018: Cuadro B6.1 - Hogares por forma principal de eliminación de la basura, según departamento. [Online data set]*, https://www.censopoblacion.gt/explorador. [89]

Hallal, A. et al. (2013), "Overview of Composite Materials and their Automotive Applications", in *Advanced Composite Materials for Automotive Applications*, John Wiley & Sons, Ltd, https://doi.org/10.1002/9781118535288.ch1. [61]

Harrison, R. et al. (2012), "Estimation of the contributions of brake dust, tire wear, and resuspension to nonexhaust traffic particles derived from atmospheric measurements", *Environ. Sci. Technol.*, Vol. 46, pp. 6523–6529. [110]

Heijungs, R. (1992), "Environmental life cycle assessment of products: guide and backgrounds", Vol. Centre of Environmental Science (CML), Leiden University, Leiden, The Netherlands, https://openaccess.leidenuniv.nl/handle/1887/8061 (accessed on 20 September 2018) (accessed on 22 April 2022). [138]

Hestin, M., T. Faninger and L. Milios (2015), *Increased EU Plastics Recycling Targets: Environment, Economic and Social Impact Assessment*, https://743c8380-22c6-4457-9895-11872f2a708a.filesusr.com/ugd/0af79c_d3c616e926e24896a8b82b833332242e.pdf. [23]

Huijbregts (1999), *Priority assessment of toxic substances in LCA.Development and application of the multi-media fate, exposure and effect model USES-LCA*, IVAM environmental research, University of Amsterdam. [140]

Huijbregts, M. (2000), "Priority Assessment of Toxic Substances in the frame of LCA. Time horizon dependency of toxicity potentials calculated with the multi-media fate, exposure and effects model USES-LCA", *Institute for Biodiversity and Ecosystem Dynamics, University of Amsterdam*, http://www.leidenuniv.nl/interfac/cml/lca2/. [139]

IEA (2020), *World Energy Outlook*, OECD Publishing, Paris, https://doi.org/10.1787/557a761b-en. [125]

IEA (2018), *World Energy Outlook*, OECD Publishing, Paris, https://doi.org/10.1787/weo-2018-en. [121]

IEA (2011), *World Energy Outlook*, OECD Publishing, Paris, https://doi.org/10.1787/weo-2011-en. [106]

IMF (2020), *World Economic Outlook, October 2020: A Long and Difficult Ascent*, International Monetary Fund, Washington, D.C., https://www.imf.org/en/Publications/WEO/Issues/2020/09/30/world-economic-outlook-october-2020 (accessed on 22 January 2021). [7]

Instituto Brasileiro de Geografia e Estatística (2010), *Demographic Census: Table 1395 - Permanent private households, by household situation and existence of bathroom or toilet and number of toilets for the exclusive use of the household, according to the type of household, the form of water supply, the desti*, https://sidra.ibge.gov.br/tabela/1395. [92]

Instituto Nacional de Estadistica (2012), *Disposal of garbage in the house, according to province and municipality, 2012 census [Online data set]*, https://www.ine.gob.bo/index.php/estadisticas-sociales/vivienda-y-servicios-basicos/censos-vivienda/. [93]

IPCC (1995), *Climate Change 1995: A report of the Intergovernmental Panel on Climate Change - IPCC Second Assessment*. [141]

Islamic Development Bank (2020), *Waste to Energy: Averting environnmental damage in Azerbaijan.*, https://www.isdb.org/sites/default/files/media/documents/2020-06/Success_Lflt_Azerbaijan_EN.pdf. [82]

Jambeck, J. et al. (2015), "Plastic waste inputs from land into the ocean", *Science*, Vol. 347/6223, pp. 768-771, https://doi.org/10.1126/science.1260352. [17]

Jenkin, M. and G. Hayman (1999), "Photochemical ozone creation potentials for oxygenated volatile organic compounds: sensitivity to variations in kinetic and mechanistic parameters", *Atmospheric Environment*, Vol. 33/8, pp. 1275-1293, https://doi.org/10.1016/s1352-2310(98)00261-1. [135]

JFE Engineering Corporation (2017), *Opening Ceremony for Myanmar's First Waste to Energy Plant*, https://www.jfe-eng.co.jp/en/news/2017/20170410.html. [87]

JMP (2020), *Wash Data*, https://washdata.org/data/household#!/table?geo0=region&geo1=sdg. (accessed on 29 January 2021). [71]

Kalbar, P., I. Muñoz and M. Birkved (2017), "WW LCI v2: A second-generation life cycle inventory model for chemicals discharged to wastewater systems.", *Sci Total Environ.*, https://doi.org/10.1016/j.scitotenv.2017.10.051. [70]

Kawecki, D. and B. Nowack (2020), "A proxy-based approach to predict spatially resolved emissions of macro- and microplastic to the environment", *Science of The Total Environment*, Vol. 748, p. 141137, https://doi.org/10.1016/j.scitotenv.2020.141137. [67]

Kaza, S. et al. (2018), *What a Waste 2.0: A Global Snapshot of Solid Waste Management to 2050*, The World Bank, https://doi.org/10.1596/978-1-4648-1329-0. [15]

Kindermann, G. et al. (2008), "A global forest growing stock, biomass and carbon map based on FAO statistics", *Silva Fennica*, Vol. 42/3, https://doi.org/10.14214/sf.244. [128]

Klimont, Z. et al. (2002), "Modelling Particulate Emissions in Europe. A Framework to Estimate Reduction Potential and Control Costs", *IIASA, IR-02-076*. [107]

Klimont, Z. et al. (2017), "Global anthropogenic emissions of particulate matter including black carbon", *Atmos. Chem. Phys.*, Vol. 17, pp. 8681–8723. [105]

Lassen, C. et al. (2016), *Microplastics Occurrence, effects and sources of releases to the environment in Denmark*, Danish Environmental Protection Agency, Copenhagen. [68]

Lau, W. et al. (2020), "Evaluating scenarios toward zero plastic pollution", *Science*, Vol. 369/6510, pp. 1455-1461, https://doi.org/10.1126/science.aba9475. [25]

Lebreton, L. and A. Andrady (2019), "Future scenarios of global plastic waste generation and disposal", *Palgrave Communications*, Vol. 5/1, p. 6, https://doi.org/10.1057/s41599-018-0212-7. [19]

Lebreton, L., M. Egger and B. Slat (2019), "A global mass budget for positively buoyant macroplastic debris in the ocean", *Scientific Reports*, Vol. 9/1, p. 12922, https://doi.org/10.1038/s41598-019-49413-5. [103]

Lebreton, L. et al. (2018), "Evidence that the Great Pacific Garbage Patch is rapidly accumulating plastic", *Scientific Reports*, Vol. 8/1, https://doi.org/10.1038/s41598-018-22939-w. [101]

Lee, D. (2016), "Bio-based economies in Asia: Economic analysis of development of bio-based industry in China, India, Japan, Korea, Malaysia and Taiwan", *International Journal of Hydrogen Energy*, Vol. 41/7, pp. 4333-4346, https://doi.org/10.1016/j.ijhydene.2015.10.048. [131]

Liechtenstein Institute for Strategic Development (2020), *Circular economy strategy for Liechtenstein.*, https://www.alpine-space.org/projects/greencycle/deliverables/t2/lisd---circular-economy-strategy-for-liechtenstein-vol1-10-03-2020-1.pdf. [81]

Løkkegaard, H., B. Malmgren-Hansen and N. Nilsson (2018), *Mass balance of rubber granulate lost from artificial turf fields, focusing on discharge to the aquatic environment.* [62]

Magnusson, K. et al. (2016), *Swedish Sources and Pathways for Microplastics to the Marine Environment..* [72]

Meijer, L. et al. (2021), "More than 1000 rivers account for 80% of global riverine plastic emissions into the ocean", *Science Advances*, Vol. 7/18, https://doi.org/10.1126/sciadv.aaz5803. [100]

Michielssen, M. et al. (2016), "Fate of microplastics and other small anthropogenic litter (SAL) in wastewater treatment plants depends on unit processes employed", *Environmental Science: Water Research and Technology*, Vol. 2/6, pp. 1064-1073, https://doi.org/10.1039/c6ew00207b. [73]

Ministry of Commerce (2019), *The China Recycling Industry Development Report (2013-2018).* [34]

Mubeen, I. and A. Buekens (2019), “Chapter 14 - Energy From Waste: Future Prospects Toward Sustainable Development”, in Kumar, S., R. Kumar and A. Pandey (eds.), *Current Developments in Biotechnology and Bioengineering*, Elsevier, https://doi.org/10.1016/B978-0-444-64083-3.00014-2. [85]

National Statistical Office (2020), *2018 Malawi population and housing census: water and sanitation report Zomba*, http://www.nsomalawi.mw/images/stories/data_on_line/demography/census_2018/Thematic_Reports/Water%20and%20Sanitation%20Report.pdf. [88]

Nizzetto, L., M. Futter and S. Langaas (2016), *Are Agricultural Soils Dumps for Microplastics of Urban Origin?*, American Chemical Society, https://doi.org/10.1021/acs.est.6b04140. [74]

OECD (2021), *Policies to Reduce Microplastics Pollution in Water: Focus on Textiles and Tyres*, OECD Publishing, Paris, https://doi.org/10.1787/7ec7e5ef-en. [60]

OECD (2020), *OECD Economic Outlook, Volume 2020 Issue 2*, OECD Publishing, Paris, https://doi.org/10.1787/39a88ab1-en. [6]

OECD (2019), *Global Material Resources Outlook to 2060: Economic Drivers and Environmental Consequences*, OECD Publishing, Paris, https://doi.org/10.1787/9789264307452-en. [4]

OECD (2013), “Policies for Bioplastics in the Context of a Bioeconomy”*, OECD Science, Technology and Industry Policy Papers*, No. 10, OECD Publishing, Paris, https://doi.org/10.1787/5k3xpf9rrw6d-en. [124]

OECD.stat (2022), *OECD Plastics Outlook database*, https://www.oecd-ilibrary.org/environment/data/global-plastic-outlook_c0821f81-en. [1]

OECD.stat (2017), *Environment Database - Wastewater treatment (% population connected)*, http://stats.oecd.org/index.aspx?DatasetCode=WATER_TREAT (accessed on 29 January 2021). [69]

OVAM (2018), *Huishoudelijk afval en gelikkaardig bedrijfsafval.*, https://www.ovam.be/inventarisatie-huishoudelijke-afvalstoffen. [47]

Pelvin, R. et al. (2014), *Agro-ecological Zone Emission Factor (AEZ-EF) Model: A model of greenhouse gas emissions from land-use change for use with AEZ-based economic models*, https://ww2.arb.ca.gov/sites/default/files/classic//fuels/lcfs/lcfs_meetings/aezef-report.pdf. [127]

Pirc, U. et al. (2016), “Emissions of microplastic fibers from microfiber fleece during domestic washing”, *Environ Sci Pollut Res*, Vol. 23, pp. 22206–22211, https://doi.org/10.1007/s11356-016-7703-0. [57]

Pisso, I. et al. (2019), “The Lagrangian particle dispersion model FLEXPART version 10.4”, *Geosci. Model Dev.*, Vol. 12, pp. 4955–4997. [111]

Plastic Waste Management Institute (2019), *An Introduction to Plastic Recycling*. [40]

Plastics Europe (2020), “Plastics – the Facts 2020”. [33]

Plastics Europe (2017), *Plastics: the Facts (2017) An analysis of European plastics production, demand and waste data*, Plastics Europe. [55]

Plastics Recyclers Europe (2020), *Report on Plastics Recycling Statistics*, http://743c8380-22c6-4457-9895-11872f2a708a.filesusr.com/ugd/dda42a_2544b63cfb5847e39034fadafbac71bf.pdf. [29]

Population Census Commission (2007), *2007 Population and Housing Census of Ethiopia.*, https://microdata.worldbank.org/index.php/catalog/2747/download/39216. [95]

Recoup (2019), *Recyclability by Design*, https://www.bpf.co.uk/design/recyclability-by-design. [27]

ResearchNester (2021), *Artificial Turf: Market Insights, Demand & Growth Forecast 2027.*, https://www.researchnester.com/reports/artificial-turf-market/995. (accessed on 28 January 2021). [64]

Resource Futures (2019), *Composition analysis of litter waste in Wales.* [48]

Rolsky, C. et al. (2020), "Municipal sewage sludge as a source of microplastics in the environment.", *Curr. Opin. Environ. Sci. Heal.*. [75]

Roosen, M. et al. (2020), "Detailed Analysis of the Composition of Selected Plastic Packaging Waste Products and Its Implications for Mechanical and Thermochemical Recycling", *Environmental Science & Technology*, Vol. 54/20, pp. 13282-13293, https://doi.org/10.1021/acs.est.0c03371. [12]

Roosen, M. et al. (2020), "Detailed Analysis of the Composition of Selected Plastic Packaging Waste Products and Its Implications for Mechanical and Thermochemical Recycling", *Environmental Science & Technology*, doi: 10.1021/acs.est.0c03371, pp. 13282-13293, https://doi.org/10.1021/acs.est.0c03371. [30]

Ryberg, M. et al. (2019), "Global environmental losses of plastics across their value chains", *Resources, Conservation and Recycling.* [16]

Ryberg, M. et al. (2019), "Global environmental losses of plastics across their value chains", *Resources, Conservation and Recycling*, Vol. 151, p. 104459, https://doi.org/10.1016/j.resconrec.2019.104459. [18]

Samoa Bureau of statistics (2019), *Samoa's Experimental Solid Waste Accounts FY2013-14 to FY2015-16*, https://www.sbs.gov.ws/digi/Samoa's%20Experimental%20Solid%20Waste%20Arrounts_2013-2014%20to%202015-2016.pdf. [94]

Schipfer, F. et al. (2017), "Advanced biomaterials scenarios for the EU28 up to 2050 and their respective biomass demand", *Biomass and Bioenergy*, Vol. 96, pp. 19-27, https://doi.org/10.1016/j.biombioe.2016.11.002. [130]

SEMARNAT (2020), *Diagnostico basico para la gestion integral de los residuos.* [38]

Sommer, F. et al. (2018), "Tire Abrasion as a Major Source of Microplastics in the Environment", *Aerosol and Air Quality Research*, Vol. 18/8, pp. 2014-2028, https://doi.org/10.4209/aaqr.2018.03.0099. [59]

Stadler, K. et al. (2018), "EXIOBASE 3: Developing a Time Series of Detailed Environmentally Extended Multi-Regional Input-Output Tables", *Journal of Industrial Ecology*, Vol. 22/3, pp. 502-515, https://doi.org/10.1111/jiec.12715. [8]

Statistics Canada (2022), *Pilot physical flow account for plastic material, 2012 to 2018*, https://www150.statcan.gc.ca/n1/daily-quotidien/220323/dq220323f-eng.htm. [44]

Sub Direktorat Statistik Lingkungan Hidup (2014), *Indikator Perilaku Peduli Lingkungan Hidup (2014 Environmental Care Behavior Indicators*, https://www.bps.go.id/publication/2015/12/23/2cdc2ef08c706d6f205c69fc/indikator-perilaku-peduli-lingkungan-hidup-2014.html. [90]

Swedish EPA (2019), *Microplastics in the Environment 2019*, http://www.naturvardsverket.se/Om-Naturvardsverket/Publikationer/ISBN/6900/978-91-620-6957-5/. [63]

SystemIQ and the Pew Charitable Trust (2020), *Breaking the Plastic Wave: A Comprehensive Assessment of Pathways Towards Stopping Ocean Plastic Pollution*, https://www.systemiq.earth/breakingtheplasticwave/. [26]

Thompson, P., P. Willis and N. Morley (2012), *A review of commercial textile fibre recycling technologies*, Waste and Resources Action Programme (WRAP), UK, https://refashion.fr/eco-design/sites/default/files/fichiers/A%20review%20of%20commercial%20textile%20fibre%20recycling%20technologies.pdf. [32]

Tun, M. et al. (2020), “Renewable Waste-to-Energy in Southeast Asia: Status, Challenges, Opportunities, and Selection of Waste-to-Energy Technologies”, *Applied Science*, Vol. 10/20, p. 7312, https://doi.org/10.3390/app10207312. [83]

UN Habitat (n.d.), *Cities’ Waste Data*, https://unhabitat.org/waste-wise-cities-waste-data (accessed on 20 September 2021). [78]

Unice, K. et al. (2019), “Characterizing export of land-based microplastics to the estuary - Part I: Application of integrated geospatial microplastic transport models to assess tire and road wear particles in the Seine watershed”, *Sci. Total Environ.*, Vol. 646, pp. 1639–1649. [115]

UNIDO (2020), *Recycling of plastics in Indian perspective*, UNIDO Office, VIC, Vienna, https://www.unido.org/sites/default/files/files/2018-11/Plenary%202%20-%20Plastics%20-%20Mohanty.pdf. [43]

United Nations (2019), *World urbanization prospects: The 2018 revision.*, https://population.un.org/wup/Publications/Files/WUP2018-Report.pdf. [96]

United Nations Statistics Division (2020), *UN Comtrade*, https://comtrade.un.org (accessed on 21 September 2020). [46]

United States Envrionmental Protection Agency (EPA) (2020), “Advancing Sustainable Materials Management: 2018 Tables and Figures”, https://www.epa.gov/sites/default/files/2021-01/documents/2018_tables_and_figures_dec_2020_fnl_508.pdf. [35]

United States Envrionmental Protection Agency (EPA) (2020), *Plastics: Material-Specific Data*, https://www.epa.gov/facts-and-figures-about-materials-waste-and-recycling/plastics-material-specific-data. [36]

UNSD (2021), *UNSD Environmental Indicators: Waste In Environment Statistics*, https://unstats.un.org/unsd/envstats/qindicators.cshtml. [80]

van der Gon, H. et al. (2013), "The policy relevance of wear emissions from road transport, now and in the future--an international workshop report and consensus statement", *Air Waste Manag Assoc.*, Vol. 63/2, pp. 136-49, https://doi.org/10.1080/10962247.2012.741055. [108]

van Meijl, H. et al. (2018), "On the macro-economic impact of bioenergy and biochemicals – Introducing advanced bioeconomy sectors into an economic modelling framework with a case study for the Netherlands", *Biomass and Bioenergy*, Vol. 108, pp. 381-397, https://doi.org/10.1016/j.biombioe.2017.10.040. [132]

VinylPlus (2019), "PVC Recycling in Action", https://vinylplus.eu/uploads/images/Leaflets/Recovinyl_21x21_04-05_web.pdf. [13]

VinylPlus (2019), *PVC Recycling in Action*, https://vinylplus.eu/uploads/images/Leaflets/Recovinyl_21x21_04-05_web.pdf. [31]

Viool, V. et al. (2018), *Study to support impact assessment for options to reduce the level of ALDFG*. [51]

Walker, R. (2019), *The mass of 300 different 'dry' materials*. [113]

Wernet, G. et al. (2016), "The ecoinvent database version 3 (part I): overview and methodology", *The International Journal of Life Cycle Assessment*, Vol. 21/9, pp. 1218-1230, https://doi.org/10.1007/s11367-016-1087-8. [133]

Wilson, D. et al. (2012), "Comparative analysis of solid waste management in 20 cities", *Waste Management & Research*, doi: 10.1177/0734242X12437569, pp. 237-254, https://doi.org/10.1177/0734242X12437569. [79]

World Bank (2020), *New World Bank country classifications by income level: 2020-2021.*, https://blogs.worldbank.org/opendata/new-world-bank-country-classifications-income-level-2020-2021 (accessed on 28 January 2021). [52]

Zheng, J. and S. Suh (2019), "Strategies to reduce the global carbon footprint of plastics", *Nature Climate Change*, Vol. 9/5, pp. 374-378, https://doi.org/10.1038/s41558-019-0459-z. [21]

Notes

[1] As it is not possible to use lifespan distributions from historical years, in the first years an exogenous component of waste generated by earlier produced commodities is added.

[2] Due to lack of country/application specific lifespan data.

[3] Littering is included as a separate category to reflect the unaccounted potential losses to the environment. It is set as a constant share of municipal solid waste only following the assumption in (Jambeck et al., 2015[17]).

[4] In particular, ECHA (2020[53]) reports that the share of end-of-life tyre-derived granules would represent 78% on the infill, whereas EPDM and TPE would account for 18%, and cork 4%, by 2028. As artificial turf is only made up of the rubber part of tyres (EuRIC MTR 2020), 96% of all infill is assumed to be microplastics.

[5] The nominal emissions of CH_4 and N_2O are converted to CO_2-equivalents using the 100-year GWP from 2nd assessment report (IPCC, 1995[141]).

[6] The authors of this paper are gratefully acknowledged for providing for providing greenhouse-gas specific emission factors that are not available directly in their paper.

[7] The baseline was generated over the period 2014-2060 with the G-RDEM model in CGEBox (Britz and van der Mensbrugghe, 2018[122]; Britz and Roson, 2018[142]), based on projections of population and GDP from the OECD's ENV-Linkages model under the impacts of COVID-19. The baseline also includes projections of both biobased plastics and total plastics consumption in physical units.

Annex B. Details on the Baseline, Regional Action, Global Ambition, and Climate Mitigation scenarios

This Annex presents the details on (i) the incorporation of the effects of the COVID-19 pandemic and associated government response measures in the *Baseline* scenario, (ii) the quantification of the various policy instruments in the *Regional Action* and *Global Ambition* plastics scenarios, and (iii) the climate change mitigation scenario.

The COVID-19 update of the *Baseline* scenario

The pre-COVID socioeconomic trends that drive the *Baseline* scenario projection as laid out in OECD (2019[1]) have been updated to reflect the consequences of the COVID-19 pandemic and government response measures. As described in more detail in (Dellink et al., 2021[2]), a detailed assessment, as of April 2021, is made of the economic shocks caused by the pandemic, the lockdown measures and the government stimulus packages. The scenarios are based on the following modelling assumptions:

- Increases in regional unemployment levels in 2020 are based on the OECD Economic Outlook 108 (OECD, 2020[3]), the updates on GDP forecasts in the Interim Outlook (OECD, 2021[4]) and on the IMF Economic Outlook for the countries that are not covered by the OECD forecasts (IMF, 2020[5]). For the few countries missing in both databases, ad-hoc assumptions are made based on effects in similar countries.
- Sectoral demand shocks are implemented for 2020 following Arriola and Van Tongeren (2021[6]). For energy sectors, the shocks are based on (IEA, 2020[7]).
- Government stimulus packages are implemented as a reduction in capital and labour taxes for firms and as a reduction in income taxes for households. These packages are based on Arriola et al. (2021[6]).
- Trade shocks are implemented as an increase in the costs of international trade ("iceberg costs"), with a differentiation between services sectors and agriculture and manufacturing. This mimics the trade shocks in Arriola et al. (2021[6]).
- Reductions in regional labour productivity reflect productivity losses during lockdown (incl. effects of teleworking) and is included crudely as a uniform decline in productivity in all sectors and regions, based on Arriola et al. (2021[6]).
- Finally, regional total factor productivity shocks reflecting the combined effects of all elements not captured explicitly above are added based on the macroeconomic decline in GDP (OECD, 2020[3]). This approach ensures that the immediate effects of the pandemic on the macro economy are scaled to reach the GDP growth rates for 2020 as forecast by (OECD, 2020[3]) and by the IMF for the countries that are not covered by the OECD forecasts (IMF, 2020[5]). In addition, a rebound effect on total factor productivity is included for 2021 and 2022 for those countries where the short-term forecasts are more optimistic than can be explained by the recovery rates calibrated in the model.

All shocks are assumed to fade gradually over time after 2020, each year becoming less strong than the year before. These recovery rates are region-specific and based on the GDP forecasts until 2025 made by IMF. However, long-term economic activity levels – and the associated environmental pressures – do not necessarily return to the levels as projected in the *Baseline* excluding the COVID shocks. The main reason is that the shocks alter savings and investment behaviour and thus long-term economic growth and environmental pressure.

The Slow recovery scenario

The *Slow recovery scenario* reflects a situation in which recovery from the initial 2020 shock to the economy caused by the COVID-19 pandemic and government response measures will be roughly twice as slow as in the reference *Baseline* scenario. The shock in 2020 is identical to the COVID-19 scenario but the recovery is slower (annual recovery rates are half as high and there is no rebound effect in 2021).

Quantification of the *Regional Action* and *Global Ambition* plastics scenario

The circular plastics scenarios are designed to reduce plastic leakage to the environment, considering plastics use in the different steps of the lifetime of products. The policy package addresses three main aspects: (i) Restrain production and demand and design for circularity, (iii) Enhance recycling, and (iv) Close leakage pathways. Different policy instruments are implemented for each of these three 'pillars' (Table A B.1).

Table A B.1. Details on the implementation of the circular plastics scenarios

Pillar	Policy instrument	*Regional Action* scenario	*Global Ambition* scenario
Restrain plastics production and demand and design for circularity (hereafter Restrain demand)	Packaging plastics tax	*EU*: USD 1 000/tonne by 2030, constant thereafter *Rest of OECD*: USD 1 000/tonne by 2040, constant thereafter *Non-OECD*: USD 1 000/tonne by 2060	*Global*: USD 1 000/tonne by 2030, doubling by 2060
	Non-packaging plastics tax	*OECD*: USD 750/tonne by 2040, constant thereafter *Non-OECD*: USD 750/tonne by 2060	*Global*: USD 750/tonne by 2030, doubling by 2060
	Ecodesign for durability & repair	*Global*: 10% lifespan increase, 5-10% decrease in demand for durables, increase in demand for repair services such that ex ante total expenditures are unchanged	*Global*: 15% lifespan increase, 10-20% decrease in demand for durables, increase in demand for repair services such that ex ante total expenditures are unchanged
Enhance recycling	Recycled content target	*OECD*: 40% recycled content target *Non-OECD*: 20% recycled content target	*Global*: 40% recycled content target
	EPR for packaging, electronics, automotive and wearable apparel	*OECD + EU*: 20% points increase in recycling, tax on plastics inputs – USD 300/tonne by 2030, constant thereafter, subsidy on waste sector such that the instrument is budget neutral	*Global*: 20% points increase in recycling, tax on plastics inputs - USD 300/tonne by 2030, constant thereafter, subsidy on waste sector such that the instrument is budget neutral
	Enhance recycling through waste management	*EU, Japan & Korea*: 60% recycling rate target by 2030, 70% by 2060 *Rest of OECD, the People's Republic of China (hereafter 'China')*: 60% recycling rate target by 2060 *Rest of non-OECD*: 40% recycling rate target	*EU, Japan & Korea*: 60% recycling rate target by 2030, 80% by 2060 *Rest of OECD, China*: 80% recycling rate target by 2060 *Rest of non-OECD*: 60%

Pillar	Policy instrument	*Regional Action* scenario	*Global Ambition* scenario
		by 2060	recycling rate target by 2060
Close leakage pathways	Improved plastic waste collection	*OECD*: full reduction of mismanaged waste shares* *Non-OECD*: halving of mismanaged waste shares*	*Global*: full reduction of mismanaged waste shares*
	Improved litter collection	*High income countries* collection rates increase 5%-points; *middle income countries* income-scaled increase	*Low income countries* collection rates increase 10%-points; *high income countries* collection rates increase 5%-points; *middle income countries* income-scaled increase

* Waste streams from uncollected litter and from markings and microbeads are not included in this policy, as they are not managed as waste.

The climate change mitigation scenario

The purpose of the climate policy package is to illustrate the potential interactions between policies focused on plastics and climate policies. This climate scenario is therefore not meant to represent an actual possible decarbonisation pathway, but it is rather a stylised climate policy package. The climate policy package consists of two of the major decarbonisation instruments: a carbon pricing trajectory and a structural transformation of the power sector.

Carbon pricing trajectory

The carbon pricing trajectory is designed following the WEO SDS scenario from 2020 to 2050 and maintains a constant carbon price between 2050 and 2060. This assumption leads to a world average carbon price of USD 69 in 2060, compared to USD 6 in the *Baseline* scenario. Table A B.2 provides the regional details of the carbon pricing scenario. While, in the *Baseline*, carbon pricing is limited between USD 0 and USD 12 in 2060 for aggregate regions, the climate policy package increases them to between USD 5 and USD 160. Overall, carbon pricing is higher in OECD countries, compared to non-OECD countries.

Table A B.2. Carbon pricing in the *Baseline* and *Climate Mitigation* scenarios

USD per tonne of CO_2 in 2060

Region	*Baseline*	*Climate Mitigation*
OECD	**7**	**155**
OECD America	3	157
OECD Europe	12	151
OECD Pacific	7	160
Non-OECD	**6**	**42**
Eurasia	1	93
Middle-East and Africa	0	5
Other America	0	70
Other Asia	9	54
World	**6**	**69**

Source: OECD ENV-Linkages model, based on IEA (2018[8]).

Structural transformation of the power sector

On top of the carbon prices trajectory, the climate policy package also includes the structural transformation of the electricity generation sector. As depicted in Figure A B.1, the share of the different primary sources (coal, oil, gas, nuclear, hydro, wind, solar and other) are set according to the WEO 2018 projections between 2020 and 2050 and it assumes a constant share of the different electricity vectors between 2050 and 2060. Overall, the share of fossil-powered electricity generations decreases from 69% in 2019 to 62% in 2060 in the *Baseline*, while in the climate policy package this share decreases to 15% by 2060.

Figure A B.1. World-average electricity mix in the *Baseline* and *Climate Mitigation* scenarios

Share in power generation (%)

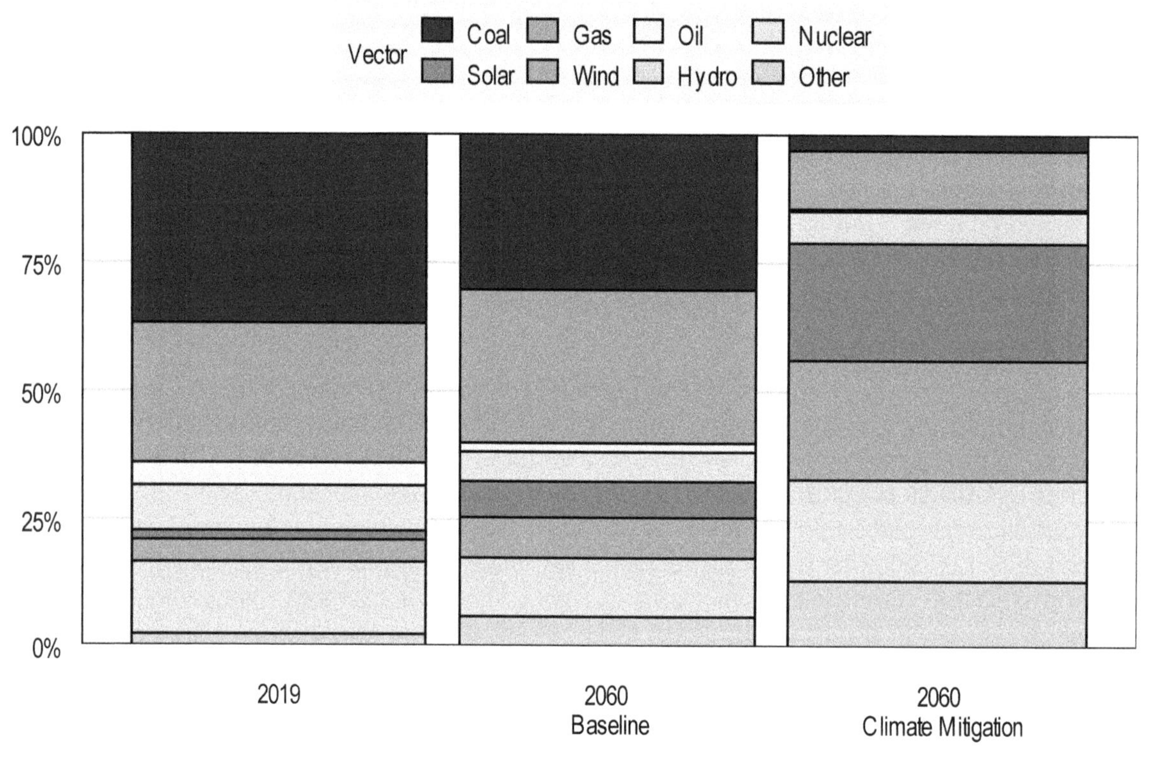

Source: ENV-Linkages model, based on IEA (2018[8]).

StatLink https://stat.link/gzutp7

References

Arriola, C., P. Kowalski and F. Van Tongeren (2021), "Assessment of the Covid-19 pandemic: insights from the METRO model", *OECD Trade Policy Papers 252*, https://doi.org/10.1787/18166873. [6]

Dellink, R. et al. (2021), "The long-term environmental implications of COVID-19", *OECD Environment Working Papers 176*, https://doi.org/10.1787/123dfd4f-en. [2]

IEA (2020), *World Energy Outlook 2020*, OECD Publishing, Paris, https://doi.org/10.1787/557a761b-en. [7]

IMF (2020), *World Economic Outlook, October 2020: A Long and Difficult Ascent*, International Monetary Fund, Washington, D.C., https://www.imf.org/en/Publications/WEO/Issues/2020/09/30/world-economic-outlook-october-2020 (accessed on 22 January 2021). [5]

International Energy Agency (2018), *World Energy Outlook 2018*, OECD Publishing, Paris, https://doi.org/10.1787/weo-2018-en. [8]

OECD (2021), *OECD Economic Outlook, Interim Report March 2021*, OECD Publishing, Paris, https://doi.org/10.1787/34bfd999-en. [4]

OECD (2020), *OECD Economic Outlook, Volume 2020 Issue 2*, OECD Publishing, Paris, https://doi.org/10.1787/39a88ab1-en. [3]

OECD (2019), *Global Material Resources Outlook to 2060: Economic Drivers and Environmental Consequences*, OECD Publishing, Paris, https://doi.org/10.1787/9789264307452-en. [1]

Glossary

Disclaimer: This glossary presents definitions for key terms employed in the report. Definitions are condensed and may not be complete. They are not to be considered official definitions, rather descriptions of terms as used for the purpose of this report.

Term	Definition used in the Global Plastics Outlook
Biobased plastics	Plastics manufactured from biomass.
Degradation	The partial or complete breakdown of a polymer as a result of e.g. UV radiation, oxygen attack, biological attack. This implies alteration of the properties, such as discolouration, surface cracking, and fragmentation.
(Waste) incineration	Incineration in a state-of-the-art industrial facility.
(Sanitary) landfilling	The final disposal of waste in or on land in a controlled way and according to state-of-the-art sanitary, environmental protection and other safety requirements.
(Plastic) leakage	Plastic leakage refers to plastics that enter terrestrial and aquatic environments.
Litter	Waste that results from littering by individuals in the environment and from fly-tipping. Littered waste is distinct from mismanaged waste, because littering behaviour not necessarily correlated to the provision of basic waste collection and disposal infrastructure. Littered waste can either be collected for further disposal or remain uncollected and leak into the environment.
Macroplastics	Recognisable plastic items, such as littered plastic bottles and packaging. In this report, the use of the term encompasses plastics above 5 mm in diameter (i.e. what is often defined as meso and macro plastics elsewhere in the literature).
Microplastics	Solid synthetic polymers smaller than 5 mm in diameter.
Mismanaged waste	Waste that is not captured by any state-of-the-art waste collection or treatment facilities. It includes waste that is burned in open pits, dumped into seas or open waters, or disposed of in unsanitary landfills and dumpsites.
Plastic	Plastic in the singular form is used as an adjective describing a noun. For example, plastic waste.
Plastic pollution	Broadly, all emissions and risks resulting from plastics production, use, waste management and leakage.
Plastics	All plastic polymers studied in the report.
Primary microplastics	Plastics that are smaller than 5 mm in diameter by design, such as cosmetic scrubbing agents and plastic pellets.
Primary or virgin plastics	Plastics manufactured from fossil-based (e.g. crude oil) or biobased (e.g. corn, sugarcane, wheat) feedstock that has never been used or processed before.
Recycling rate	Depending on the context, either the share of waste that is collected for recycling or the share of waste that is available as recycled scrap after reprocessing and after taking into account the disposal of recycling residues.
Secondary (recycled) plastics	Plastic polymers made from recycled material.
Secondary microplastics	Microplastics that are formed from the fragmentation of larger plastics, such as microplastics from tyre abrasion, synthetic microfibres shed from textile products and microplastics stemming from the degradation and fragmentation of macroplastics that have already been lost to the environment.

www.ingramcontent.com/pod-product-compliance
Ingram Content Group UK Ltd.
Pitfield, Milton Keynes, MK11 3LW, UK
UKHW051458290926
15471UKWH00008B/1287

9 789264 973640